363. 63094 PAD
ST

D1610666

Release from Prison

Release from Prison

European policy and practice

Edited by

Nicola Padfield, Dirk van Zyl Smit and Frieder Dünkel

WILLAN
PUBLISHING

Published by

Willan Publishing
Culmcott House
Mill Street, Uffculme
Cullompton, Devon
EX15 3AT, UK
Tel: +44(0)1884 840337
Fax: +44(0)1884 840251
e-mail: info@willanpublishing.co.uk
website: www.willanpublishing.co.uk

Published simultaneously in the USA and Canada by

Willan Publishing
c/o ISBS, 920 NE 58th Ave, Suite 300
Portland, Oregon 97213-3786, USA
Tel: +001(0)503 287 3093
Fax: +001(0)503 280 8832
e-mail: info@isbs.com
website: www.isbs.com

First published 2010

ISBN   978-1-84392-741-9 hardback

British Library Cataloguing-in-Publication Data

A catalogue record for this book is available from the British Library

FSC
Mixed Sources
Product group from well-managed
forests and other controlled sources

Cert no. SGS-COC-2482
www.fsc.org
© 1996 Forest Stewardship Council

Project managed by Deer Park Productions, Tavistock, Devon
Typeset by GCS, Leighton Buzzard, Bedfordshire
Printed and bound by T.J. International, Padstow, Cornwall

Contents

Part III   Converging themes

List of figures and tables

Figures

Tables

List of abbreviations

BRZ	Federal Computing Centre of Austria
CAT	Catalonia
CC	Criminal Code
Corte Cost.	Constitutional Court (Corte Costituzionale, Italy)
CPP	Code of Criminal Procedure (Italy)
CPT	Committee for the Prevention of Torture
CRP	*crédit de réduction de peine* (France)
EC/EEC	European Economic Community
ECHR	European Convention for the Protection of Human Rights and Fundamental Freedoms
ECJ	European Court of Justice
ECL	End of Custody Licence
ECPT	European Convention for the Prevention of Torture and Inhuman or Degrading Treatment or Punishment
ECtHR	European Court of Human Rights
EDL	earliest date of liberation (Scotland)
EPR	European Prison Rules
EPSA	Enforcement of Penal Sentences Act (Slovenia)
EU	European Union
FCC	Federal Constitutional Court (Bundesverfassungsgericht) (BVerfG) (Germany)
GAE	General Administration of the State (Spain)
GPS	global positioning system
GSM	global system for mobile (communications)
HDC	Home Detention Curfew
IPP	Imprisonment for Public Protection

JGG	Juvenile Justice Act 1953 (Germany)
NSSG	National Statistical Service of Greece
OFA	Office for Foreigners Affairs
PSI	Prison Service Instruction
PSO	Prison Service Order
RISI	Rules on the Implementation of the Sentence of Imprisonment (Slovenia)
ROR	risk of reconviction
RSP	*réduction de peine supplémentaire* (France)
SPACE	Council of Europe Annual Penal Statistics
SPIP	*service pénitentiaire d'insertion et de probation* (France)
StGB	Strafgesetzbuch (General Penal Code 1954) (Germany)
TEU	Treaty of Maastricht (the Treaty of the European Union)

Acknowledgements

Most of the chapters that now make up this volume were first discussed at a workshop which took place from 30 June to 2 July 2008 in Fitzwilliam College, Cambridge. We are very grateful to the British Academy for funding this workshop, to colleagues across Europe who have assisted by providing information and in many other ways, and to Willan for publishing this book so promptly and efficiently.

Notes on contributors

Matjaž Ambrož is Assistant Professor of Criminal Law, Faculty of Law, University of Ljubljana and a Researcher at the Ljubljana Institute of Criminology. He is author of numerous publications on substantive criminal law, as well as international criminal law, sentencing and the execution of penal sanctions. He has participated in several research projects on the modernization of Slovenian substantive criminal law and currently leads a research project on concepts of complicity in contemporary criminal law.

Marie-Aude Beernaert is Professor of Law at the University of Louvain, where she completed a PhD in 2002 (published in 2003) on repentant collaborators with justice (*pentiti*). She currently teaches criminal procedure, EU criminal law and the law on the execution of criminal sanctions, and has published widely on all these matters.

Kristel Beyens is Professor of Penology and Criminological Sociology at the Criminology Department at the Vrije Universiteit Brussel (Belgium). Her research focuses on sentencing, prisons and community-based sanctions. She is interested in evolutions in contemporary punishment and, in particular, in the implementation of electronic monitoring and unpaid work.

Karin Bruckmüller is University Assistant at the Department for Criminal Law and Criminology at the University of Vienna and was an Honorary Employee of the Association for Probation Service and Social Work. Her research topics are criminal sanctions, early release, alternatives to imprisonment, juvenile justice system, victims' rights and medical criminal law.

Leonidas K. Cheliotis is Lecturer and Deputy Director of the Centre for Criminal Justice at the School of Law, Queen Mary, University of London. He is the editor of *Roots, Rites and Sites of Resistance: The Banality of Good* (forthcoming) and *The Arts of Imprisonment: Control, Resistance and Empowerment* (forthcoming), and is co-editor (with Sappho Xenakis, forthcoming) of *Crime and Punishment in Contemporary Greece: International Comparative Perspectives.* He is also authoring a monograph provisionally entitled *Governing through the Looking-Glass: The Politics of Middle-Class Punitiveness under Neoliberalism.*

José Cid is Lecturer in Criminal Law and Criminology at Universitat Autònoma de Barcelona (Spain). His research on the use of judicial discretion in sentencing, the effectiveness of community penalties and the problems faced by the Spanish penitentiary system, has been published in *Punishment and Society* (2005), *The Probation Journal* (2005) and *The European Journal of Criminology* (2009). He has recently written about sentencing (*La elección del castigo. Suspensión de la pena o probation versus prisión*, 2009) and at present is conducting research into the strengths and weakness of prisoner desistance after release from prison.

Frieder Dünkel is Professor at the University of Greifswald in north-east Germany. He has published in many areas (30 books and about 400 articles), and his recent research has included a wide range of empirical studies in juvenile criminology, the imprisonment of men and women, community sanctions, alcohol and drunk driving, human rights, etc. He has been Co-editor of the journal *Neue Kriminalpolitik* since 1989 and is a member of the editorial boards of several international journals. He has been President of the Criminological Scientific Council of the Council of Europe since 2001. He has co-ordinated several Tempus-projects funded by the EU and co-ordinates Socrates exchange programmes with about 35 universities. He has been guest professor in several European universities.

Alessandra Gualazzi has a PhD in Italian and comparative criminal procedure from the University of Urbino (2006). She qualified as a lawyer in 2005 at the Bar of Ancona, where she practises in criminal law. She is a University Assistant at the Department for Criminal Procedure Law at the University of Urbino.

Veronika Hofinger is a sociologist and works as a Researcher at the Institute for the Sociology of Law and Criminology in Vienna. She is currently analysing the concept of the 'career criminal' in a historical perspective and is investigating the influence of neuroscientific knowledge in contemporary criminological discourse on repeat offenders.

Tapio Lappi-Seppälä is the Director of the National Research Institute of Legal Policy in Finland. His publications include *Long-term Changes in the Penal System* (1982), *Sentencing* (1987), *Criminal Sanctions* (2000) and *Criminology and Crime Policy* (2006), and he is the author of numerous research reports and articles in periodicals and collective works on criminal law, criminology and penal policy. He held positions in the University of Helsinki and the Ministry of Justice before moving to his present position. In 2008 he was appointed a Member of the Finnish Academy of Science.

Chiara Mancuso is a Researcher in Criminal Law and European Criminal Law at the University of Palermo. She has a PhD in comparative criminal law and qualified as a lawyer in 2005. She has been a Visiting Student at the George August Universität of Göttingen and at the University of Cambridge where she carried out her most recent research.

Martin Moerings is Professor of Penology at the University of Leiden, the Netherlands. He studied sociology at Tilburg University and law at Utrecht University. He wrote a dissertation (1977) about the social consequences of imprisonment, and he publishes in the field of criminal law, penology and criminology. His publications include *Dutch Prisons* (with Miranda Boone eds. 2007). He is a part-time judge at the Criminal Court of Arnhem, Chairman of the Prison Section of the Council for the Application of Criminal Law and Youth Protection, and an Advisory Board Member for the Minister of Justice in the Netherlands. He is a former Chairman of the Netherlands' Society of Criminology.

Thomas O'Malley is a Senior Lecturer in Law at NUI Galway, Ireland and a practising barrister, specialising in administrative law. He has published extensively in the areas of criminal law, criminal procedure and sentencing. His books include *Sources of Law* (2nd edn, 2001), *Sexual Offences: Law Policy and Punishment* (1996), *Sentencing Law and Practice* (2nd edn, 2006), *The Criminal Process* (2009) and *Principled*

Discretion: Towards a Coherent Sentencing System (forthcoming). He has served on many law reform committees and working groups and is currently a Member of the Steering Committee on the introduction of a sentencing information system in Ireland.

Nicola Padfield is a Senior Lecturer at the Law Faculty, University of Cambridge. A barrister by training, she has published widely on criminal law, sentencing and criminal justice. Her books include *The Criminal Justice Process: Text and Materials* (4th edn, 2008), *Criminal Law* (6th edn, 2008) and *Beyond the Tariff: Human Rights and the Release of Life Sentence Prisoners* (2002). She has edited other collections of essays and is editor of a monthly practitioners' newsletter, *Archbold News*. She sits as a recorder (part-time judge) in the Crown Court and is a bencher of the Middle Temple.

Ioannis Papageorgiou is a PhD student at the School of Law, University of Edinburgh. His thesis addresses the relationship between politics and prison privatization in the UK.

Ineke Pruin is a research associate at the Department of Criminology at the University of Greifswald and at the University of Heidelberg, Germany. She obtained her PhD (Dr. jur.) in 2006 ('Young Adults in the Criminal Justice System') and has been teaching criminology, juvenile criminal law and prison law at the University of Heidelberg since 2008. Her main research interests lie in juvenile justice and youth criminality, community sanctions, criminal policy and human rights in prisons.

Kim Reuflet is a judge (currently a Vice-President of the Tribunal de Grande Instance at Bobigny). She obtained her master's degrees at the University of Paris XII and at the Institut d'Études Politique de Paris. She studied at the École Nationale de la Magistrature (ENM), Bordeaux, from 1999 to 2001. Her first four years of professional life were spent as a Public Prosecutor and she then served for another four years in the Legislative Bureau of the Prison Service within the Ministry of Justice, before moving to her current position.

Sonja Snacken is Professor of Criminology, Penology and the Sociology of Law at the Vrije Universiteit, Brussels. Her research focuses on sentencing and the implementation of both imprisonment and non-custodial sanctions in Belgium and Europe. She has been involved in the drafting of Belgian legislation on the legal position of prisoners. She was elected President of the European Society of Criminology (2004–5), since 1994 has been an expert for the Committee for the Prevention of Torture (CPT) and President (since 2006) of the Council for Penological Co-operation of the Council of Europe. Recent publications include *Principles of European Prison Law and Policy: Penology and Human Rights* (with Dirk van Zyl Smit, 2009) and *Resisting Punitiveness in Europe?* (with Els Dumortier, forthcoming).

John R. Spencer is a Professor of Law at the University of Cambridge. His interests include criminal law, criminal evidence and comparative criminal procedure. In 1997 he was part of the international team of criminal lawyers that produced the EU *Corpus Juris* project and, in 2000–1, he was a consultant to Lord Justice Auld's Review of the Criminal Courts. He is a QC (*honoris causa*), an academic bencher of the Inner Temple and holds an honorary degree from the University of Poitiers.

Katja Šugman Stubbs is Professor of Criminal Law at the Faculty of Law, University of Ljubljana, Slovenia, and President of the Slovenian Association of Criminal law and Criminology. She has degrees in law and psychology and her interests are criminal procedure, evidence law, EU criminal law, and psychology and the law. Her recent research includes a proposal for a new model for Slovenian criminal procedure. She was a Visiting Fellow at Fitzwilliam College, Cambridge (2004–5) and Visiting Researcher at the Institute de Sciences Criminelles, Faculty of Law, Poitiers (2009).

Beatriz Tébar completed her PhD at the Universitat Autònoma de Barcelona on the Spanish parole system, which included research into the predictive factors of parole decision-making in Catalonia (published in 2006). She has been a Visiting Scholar at New York University and a Batista i Roca Fellow at the Institute of Criminology of the University of Cambridge. She lectured at the Universitat of Girona from 2004 to 2006 and, since 2006, has worked as a lawyer for the Catalan Public Administration. She lectures for the Criminology Degree at the Law Faculty of the Universitat Autònoma de Barcelona.

Douglas Thomson qualified as a solicitor in Scotland in 1985 and as a solicitor-advocate in 2002. He practises mainly in the field of criminal court work. Between 2001 and 2007 he was a legal member of the Parole Board for Scotland, chairing over 400 tribunals for

Scottish prisoners in prisons throughout the UK. He is currently a consultant with McArthur Stanton in Dumbarton. In addition to his court practice, he has written extensively for a number of journals on subjects relating to criminal law, legal aid, imprisonment and parole.

Dirk van Zyl Smit is Professor of Comparative and International Penal Law at the University of Nottingham. He is also Emeritus Professor of Criminology at the University of Cape Town. He has advised the governments of South Africa, Malawi, and Bosnia and Herzegovina on new prison legislation. He has acted as Expert Adviser to the Council of Europe on the European Prison Rules and on the Rules on Juvenile Offenders Subject to Sanctions and Measures, and to the UN Office for Drugs and Crime for its *Handbook on Alternatives to Imprisonment*. His publications include *Principles of European Prison Law and Policy: Penology and Human Rights* (with Sonja Snacken, 2009) and *Taking Life Imprisonment Seriously in National and International Law* (2002).

Part I

Chapter I

Introduction

Nicola Padfield, Dirk van Zyl Smit and Frieder Dünkel

The release of sentenced prisoners is of great significance, not only to the prisoners concerned but also for what it tells us about how society deals with those who have lost their liberty and are dependent on others to regain it. In practice, few prisoners are told that they will never be released from prison. All legal systems have rules, some more and some less formal, for deciding who comes out, when, and under what conditions. The application of these rules is closely watched by the prisoners themselves. However, as they are relatively powerless, it is of great importance that both the rules and wider principles that underlie them are clearly understood by criminal justice practitioners and the wider public. This book aims to contribute to such understanding by concentrating on the release of prisoners in countries of Europe, where, notwithstanding major procedural differences, there are fundamental shared values about liberty and the rule of law against which evolving systems can be critically evaluated.

I. Scope of the present research

The main focus of the book is on the rules on release from prison applicable in 13 different European Union countries. The chapters dealing with individual countries are preceded by a chapter that considers the roles of the Council of Europe and the European Union in developing law and policy that impact on the release of prisoners. A final chapter places the national accounts in a wider context and draws some overall conclusions about the processes for making decisions to release sentenced prisoners in the various countries

The importance of understanding the different approaches taken in these countries is underlined by the recent decision of the Council of Ministers of the European Union to adopt a Framework Decision for the mutual recognition of judgments in criminal matters that lead to imprisonment so that they can be enforced throughout the Union.[1] Member States are obliged to implement this Framework Decision by 5 December 2011. Soon prisoners may find themselves returned to their home jurisdictions to serve their sentences, whether or not they agree. Clearly this will give rise to many potential difficulties, not least of which will be the application of different release rules. The information on the individual countries included in this volume will be useful in unravelling these complexities.

2. Comparing early release in a wider context

The national chapters go further, and provide a clear basis for contextually-informed comparisons, not only about the rules but also about the evolutionary processes that are taking place in individual countries. Moreover, as the chapter on the pan-European dimension makes clear, policies relating to release are also being developed on a regional level. Collectively, the wider 'Europe' is having an increasing influence at the national level, but this influence too must be understood in comparative perspective, for national criminal justice systems are not equally amenable to regional policy guidance.

In many ways this collection is breaking new ground. In most countries, sentencing law has been less studied than substantive criminal law. And within the area of sentencing law, there has been more emphasis on the rules for imposing imprisonment than on those for release from prison. Even comparative studies of sentencing law have often focused more on the 'law in books' than the 'law in practice' (though for a more practical comparative analysis, see Delmas-Marty 2003). When we come to look at release and recall to prison (which can be considered 'backdoor' sentencing) both law and practice are clearly particularly important, and we recognize the importance of considering and comparing both.

We are proud to present a European perspective. Too often comparative law written in English focuses on the 'common law', English-speaking countries. But this narrow approach is blinkered. Therefore we attempt to present a wider analysis, exploring release across some very different penal systems, all of which face similar challenges, and purport to uphold similar values, even as they come under increasing pressure to be tough on crime.

[1]Council Framework Decision 2008/989/JHA of 27 November 2008 on the application of the principle of mutual recognition of judgments in criminal matters imposing custodial sentences or measures involving deprivation of liberty for the purpose of their enforcement in the European Union.

3. Law reform

It is hoped that this book will be of value to law reformers, for when we seek to reform our own systems, we can of course usefully learn from the practice elsewhere. Nevertheless, it is astonishing how many domestic policy documents or national reports fail to refer to work carried out in other jurisdictions. Currently, reform endeavours are often driven by concern about large prison populations. This arises from both a humanitarian and resource perspective, as the traditional, security-oriented prison does not seem to be effective in reducing re-offending, and it is very expensive. By adding to the literature on release we can contribute to the important debate on how prisoners should be better prepared for release in order to improve their chances of re-integration into mainstream society.

When considering reform in this area, it is important to remind ourselves that release reinstates the basic liberty of the sentenced prisoner. It should be implemented fairly and as expeditiously as possible. That imprisonment should be used as a last resort and then only to the minimum extent possible, is a well-established principle of European prison policy and, increasingly, of European prison law (van Zyl Smit and Snacken 2009). What should release be about? Is discretionary or automatic release 'better', both from a theoretical and a practical point of view? By bringing together analyses of different approaches in different countries and highlighting the current reforms in different jurisdictions, we hope we can contribute to discussion both at national and European levels.

4. Theoretical approach

A book of this kind raises complex theoretical issues. Comparisons are fraught with difficulty. Similar legal terms may have meanings that vary from one jurisdiction to another, a problem highlighted by the linguistic difficulties inherent in translation. Moreover, as Fairchild and Dammer (2006: 9) say:

> The fact is that a nation's way of administering justice often reflects deep-seated cultural, religious, economic, political, and historical realities. Learning about the reasons for these different practices can give us insights into the values, traditions, and cultures of other systems.

In order to avoid premature closure we have not sought to categorise the countries. We simply list them alphabetically, as any classification would neither advance our project nor aid our analysis. An alternative would have been to follow the approach adopted by Cavadino and Dignan (2006) in their book *Penal Systems: A Comparative Approach.*

Cavadino and Dignan would look at our list and distinguish England and Wales as 'neo-liberal', Germany, the Netherlands, Italy and France as 'conservative corporatist', and Finland as 'social democratic corporatist'. Such classifications would have limited explanatory value for our purposes, certainly within a Europe where, politically, fluidity leads to unexpected turns in penal policy. Moreover, as Nelken (2009) has pointed out, local legal cultures and other factors may be more influential than types of political economy. In times of recession, governments are likely to be more pragmatic, to seek to save money and, in some jurisdictions, to hope that solutions lie in privatization.

Sensitivity to these complexities is clearly important, but it holds the danger of a slide into relativism where all comparison becomes impossible. We recognize that for successful comparative research a sound basis is needed. What point of departure is adopted will depend on the methods used and their appropriateness to subject matter that one wishes to research (Roberts 2002).

In this instance, a partial solution was found by focusing on a specific theme, in our case early release, and on statistical information about it, which appears to provide a basis for comparison. However, statistics, even on such a specific subject as early release from prison, are gathered differently across different jurisdictions. This makes comparison difficult, although not impossible, if it is subject to adequate qualifications. In order to provide the necessary contextual qualifications, we decided not to seek to present these materials in a uniform way. By highlighting the inconsistent ways that data might be presented nationally, the statistical categories and the methods of collecting statistics became a potential subject for comparison, too.

In all, we have tried to avoid ambiguity, but to recognize ambiguity when faced with it. This is an area in which linguistic and statistical comparisons are fraught with dangers, and this book seeks to highlight the difficulties in making meaningful comparisons. In so doing we are building on the important work of others, most notably of Tubex and Tournier (2003) and Tournier (2004) who, in a questionnaire-based study and a critical overview respectively, identified similar difficulties but, nevertheless, pointed out what could be learnt by comparing the process of releasing of prisoners in different jurisdictions.

5. Framework for the national chapters

The majority of the book is written by subject specialists on the rules applicable to release from prisons in their own jurisdiction and on the practical operation of those rules. We asked our colleagues to write from a national perspective. We have sought to present the law and practice of early release through the eyes of specialists in the various countries involved, and not to iron out important differences prematurely.

The brief to the authors was that they should seek to shape their individual country reports in the following way:

- Summary.
- History. Is this an area of change? Include a review of empirical and other published research.
- Legal criteria. What guarantees exist that the prisoner will be released? Aims and objectives of release systems. Is early release mandatory or discretionary?
- Categories. Determinate and indeterminate sentences; short term/long term? Are there special rules for foreign prisoners?
- Statistical data (on coming out and coming in). Comment on their limitations.
- Types of decision-making: judicial and executive. Description of decision-makers; indirect and direct influences on release decisions.
- Recall procedures.
- Practical challenges. Explore budgetary issues; management of prisoners before and after release.
- Theoretical and other conclusions, including possible future changes.
- Bibliography.

Readers will see that contributors have adapted this proposed shape in their own way. We have not attempted to re-write the chapters submitted, except to try and clarify, and to impose some internal consistency.

Unlike Tubex and Tournier, we did not ask the authors of national chapters to complete a questionnaire but instead asked them to present their own analyses of release. This makes direct comparisons harder but we hope that this method has revealed many of the more subtle distinctions at play. We will return to these issues in the final chapter.

6. Limitations and general conclusions

The book does not purport to be a comprehensive overview of release in Europe, as we do not have national reports on every European country; even the countries of the European Union are not all included. While concentrating on selected countries for illustrative purposes can be justified, perhaps more focus on the countries that have joined the EU more recently would have been helpful. At our initial meeting we did have a useful contribution from Romania – where conditional release is common, but with just one condition, not to re-offend – but

Romania is currently striving to adopt a new Criminal Code and an up-to-date chapter proved impossible within our timeframe.

In the final chapter, however, we have sought to add information from other European countries, collected as part of a comparative study in the Department of Criminology at the University of Greifswald (Dünkel 2009) and to provide, in tabular form, a basis for wider comparisons. We also seek there to identify more systematically the many factors beyond the formal legal criteria, that influence the decision to release, and to deal with some pressing normative issues.

If funding permits, we hope to continue our comparative work on the release of prisoners and to broaden the range of countries involved. Inasmuch as we have an agenda, it is to contribute in this way to the recognition of the rights of all prisoners and to their re-integration or social rehabilitation, while at the same time pursuing an overall reductionist strategy.

In future we propose to examine in more depth the reality of supervision on conditional release, particularly for long-term prisoners and those serving life and other indeterminate sentences. We will also pay closer attention to the changing political context, where some countries are exploring the use of a mix of public and private providers to deliver community supervision.

References

Cavadino, M. and Dignan, J. (2006) *Penal Systems: A Comparative Approach*. London: Sage.

Delmas-Marty, M. (ed.) (2003) *L'Harmonisation des sanctions penales en Europe (1)*. Paris: Societe de Legislation Comparée.

Dünkel, F. (2010) 'Kommentierung § 57 StGB', in U. Kindhäuser, U. Neumann and H.-U. Paeffgen (eds) *Nomos Kommentar zum Strafgesetzbuch, Vol. 1* (3rd edn). Baden-Baden: Nomos Verlag.

Fairchild, E. and Dammer, R. (2006) *Comparative Criminal Justice Systems* (3rd edn). California, Belmont: Wadsworth.

Nelken, D. (2009) 'Comparative criminal justice: Beyond ethnocentrism and relativism', *European Journal of Criminology*, 6: 291–312.

Roberts, P. (2002) 'On Method: the Ascent of Comparative Criminal Justice', *Oxford Journal of Legal Studies*, 22: 539–561.

Tournier, P. (2004) 'Recommendation rec (2003) 22 of 24 September 2003 – pleading the case for conditional release.' Paper presented at the *ad hoc* Conference of Directors of Prison Administration and Probation Services, Rome, 25–27 November (Council of Europe, cdap\rome 2004\cdap (2004) 01 – e).

Tubex H. and Tournier P. (2003) *Study of Conditional Release (Parole) in the Member States, Analysis of Replies to the General Questionnaire* (Council for Penological Co-operation, PC-CP (2000) 24 Rev 4 (restricted)).

Van Zyl Smit, D. and Snacken, S. (2009) *Principles of European Prison Law and Policy: Penology and Human Rights*. Oxford: Oxford University Press.

Chapter 2

The European dimension to the release of sentenced prisoners

Dirk van Zyl Smit and John R. Spencer

Summary

This chapter outlines the rules of European law and policy that impact on the release of sentenced prisoners. The first section focuses on the institutions of the Council of Europe that have set standards for early release. These include various recommendations of the Committee of Ministers of the Council of Europe and reports of the Committee for the Prevention of Torture which encourage early release and recommend ways in which it can be implemented fairly and effectively. Judgments of the European Court of Human Rights that lay down binding rules for early release, particularly in the case of life imprisonment and preventive detention, are also considered closely, as are the Council of Europe Conventions that relate to the transfer of prisoners and thus potentially to their early release.

The second section sketches the growing role of the European Union in the sphere of criminal law and, more specifically, in the enforcement of sentences. Particular attention is paid to new Framework Decisions that will facilitate prisoner transfers within the European Union, which may take place without the consent of the prisoners concerned and may also impact significantly on how long such prisoners serve in practice before being released.

The final section of the chapter analyses the recent decisions of the European Court of Human Rights that could be applied to both Council of Europe and European Union rules that relate to early release. It concludes that early release, particularly when it follows after a prisoner has been transferred, raises difficult issues of equity.

A wider understanding of the human rights implications of early-release procedures is essential to avoid inequitable outcomes in these cases.

I. Introduction

Nobody who takes an interest in criminal law, criminal procedure or sentencing can fail to be aware of the influence on these subjects of Europe in the form of 'Strasbourg': the Council of Europe, the European Convention for the Protection of Human Rights and Fundamental Freedoms (ECHR), the European Court of Human Rights (ECtHR) and the Committee for the Prevention of Torture (CPT) established by the European Convention on the Prevention of Torture and Inhuman or Degrading Treatment or Punishment.[1] What is usually less well known among criminal lawyers, let alone others with a specialist interest in the release of prisoners, is that the 'other Europe', 'Brussels', has an influence as well – and one that is increasingly important.

There are two aspects to the European dimension of the release of sentenced prisoners. Firstly, there is the general concern at the European level about the right of all prisoners to be released at the appropriate time, which in the case of most, if not all, will be before the completion of the full sentences imposed upon them. Secondly, there is the specific issue of prisoners, sentenced to imprisonment in one European country, who may request or be required to serve their sentences in another country. The questions that arise in the case of such prisoners relate to when and under what conditions they are to be released.

In this chapter we sketch, first, the impact that 'Strasbourg' has had on the early release of sentenced prisoners in general and on the transfer of prisoners prior to their release. In the second section we turn to the growing role of 'Brussels', of the EU, in the latter area in particular. In a third and final section we consider the influence that European law and policy is likely to have in the future on the release of all prisoners, and, in particular, whether the dual process that is currently under way is likely to have a significant impact on the early release of prisoners in the countries of Europe that fall under the aegis of both Strasbourg and Brussels. We conclude that general European

[1] *European Convention for the Prevention of Torture and Inhuman or Degrading Treatment or Punishment* (ECPT) (26 November 1987 CETS 126).

principles relating to release raise important questions about how the release of transferred prisoners should best be implemented.

2. The influence of 'Strasbourg': early release as a human right?

'Strasbourg' institutions have had a great deal to say about the release of prisoners. Much of what has been said most directly about release has taken the form of Recommendations of the Committee of Ministers of the Council of Europe. The CPT, too, has adopted positions that impact on the release of prisoners. Most importantly, the ECtHR has applied the ECHR to the release of prisoners generally. This has included some, although not all, instances of early release. In the process of considering aspects of release the ECtHR has paid considerable attention to what it calls 'the Council of Europe Instruments', under which it includes not only formally-binding treaties but also the Recommendations of the Committee of Ministers (*Dickson* v. *United Kingdom* 4 December 2007 at 28; *Kafkaris* v. *Cyprus* 12 February 2008 at 70). The Court also refers with increasing regularity to the findings as well the more general standards of the CPT.[2] The result is that these various 'soft law' recommendations and standards are indirectly given considerable legal effect at the European level.

The Council of Europe has also initiated three Conventions[3] – the European Convention on the Supervision of Conditionally Sentenced or Conditionally Released Offenders,[4] the European Convention on the International Validity of Criminal Judgements,[5] and the Convention on the Transfer of Sentenced Persons[6] – which have some potential impact on when and how prisoners who are moved from

[2]The extent of the recognition of the CPT by the ECtHR is highlighted by the fact that in 185 cases, decided between the beginning of 2006 and the end of 2008, the ECtHR referred to the reports of the CPT (Snacken and Van Zyl Smit, 2009).
[3]A fourth Convention, the European Convention on the Punishment of Road Traffic Offences (CETS 052), also provides for transnational recognition of offences, which may impact indirectly on imprisonment of offenders and therefore on release, but has been left out of consideration here.
[4]*Convention on the Supervision of Conditionally Sentenced or Conditionally Released Offenders* (30 November 1964 CETS 051).
[5]*European Convention on the International Validity of Criminal Judgements* (28 May 1970 CETS 057).
[6]*Convention on the Transfer of Sentenced Persons* (21 March 1983 CETS 112).

one European country to another are released. These conventions too have been interpreted by the ECtHR in the light of the ECHR.

2.1 Recommendations of the Committee of Ministers of the Council of Europe

At the level of Recommendations of the Committee of Ministers of the Council of Europe there is a clear commitment to the use of early release of prisoners as an instrument of penal policy. Thus, the Recommendation concerning Prison Overcrowding and Prison Population Inflation[7] articulates the policy that imprisonment should be used only as a last resort and for the minimum period necessary. Overcrowding in prison is condemned, and early release, particularly release on parole, is recommended as an effective way of combating it (*ibid.* s. 23).

This approach is developed further by the Recommendation concerning Conditional Release (Parole).[8] The preamble to the Recommendation points to the inherent desirability of limiting the use of imprisonment and makes the positive case that conditional release is 'an effective and constructive means of preventing reoffending and promoting resettlement'. For the purpose of the Recommendation, conditional release is defined narrowly as referring only to release on individualized conditions. Individualized conditions are explicitly regarded as community measures (s. 1). The Recommendation concerning Conditional Release explicitly excludes amnesties and pardons (s. 1), although, as with other forms of early release, general conditions may be set for them too. The narrow definition is unfortunate, as there may be instances where early release on general conditions may be all that is necessary.

For current purposes, perhaps the most significant aspect of the Recommendation concerning Conditional Release is the procedural guidance that it offers for the granting and revocation of such release. The Recommendation recognizes both a mandatory and a discretionary system for granting early conditional release. The former is less problematic because it requires no exercise of discretion and

---

[7]Recommendation R(99)22 of the Committee of Ministers to Member States concerning *Prison Overcrowding and Prison Population Inflation* adopted by the Committee of Ministers on 30 September 1999 at the 681st meeting of the Ministers' Deputies.

[8]Recommendation (2003)22 of the Committee of Ministers to Member States on *Conditional Release (Parole)* adopted by the Committee of Ministers on 24 September 2003 at the 853rd meeting of the Ministers' Deputies.

is, of course, as the Recommendation points out (s. 7), cheaper to implement. It requires only that the period that prisoners must serve before being considered for release should be set by law. Discretionary release is more complex: it requires that a minimum period should be set by law after which prisoners become eligible for release (s. 16) and that the relevant authorities should take steps to ensure that a decision on release can be taken as soon as the prisoner has served the minimum period (s. 17). The criteria that prisoners need to fulfil in order to be conditionally released should be clear, explicit and realistic (s. 18).

Whatever method of granting conditional release is adopted, the actual conditions that are set should be clear and meet the substantive standards set by the European Rules on Community Sanctions and Measures.[9] This is particularly important if there is an alleged failure to comply with the conditions and the question of revocation of the conditional release fails to be considered.

Revocation procedures should not be invoked for minor infringements (s. 30). Where such procedures are instituted, the possibility of a warning, stricter conditions or temporary revocation should be considered (s. 30; see also s. 85 of the European Rules on Community Sanctions and Measures).

In procedures relating to the granting or revocation of conditional release there should be a range of procedural safeguards:

a. convicted persons should have the right to be heard in person and to be assisted according to the law;
b. the decision-making authority should give careful consideration to any elements, including statements, presented by convicted persons in support of their case;
c. convicted persons should have adequate access to their file;
d. decisions should state the underlying reasons and be notified in writing (s. 32).

In addition, 'convicted persons should be able to make a complaint to a higher independent and impartial decision-making authority established by law against the substance of the decision as well as against non-respect of the procedural guarantees' (s. 33).

[9]Recommendation R(92)16 of the Committee of Ministers to Member States on the *European Rules on Community Sanctions and Measures* adopted by the Committee of Ministers on 19 October 1992 at the 482nd meeting of the Ministers' Deputies.

Other recommendations of the Committee of Ministers of the Council of Europe reinforce those on overcrowding and conditional release. The preamble to the influential 2006 European Prison Rules[10] reiterates that imprisonment should be used only as a last resort, and s. 107 of these Rules also makes provision for conditional release. The Recommendation on the Management by Prison Administrations of Life Sentence and other Long-term Prisoners[11] points out that these prisoners too should be prepared and considered for conditional release (s. 33). It specifically makes the requirements of the Recommendation on Conditional Release applicable to them (s. 34; Snacken 2006a).

2.2 The CPT

Further strong support for the policy that measures should be taken against overcrowding and to ensure the use of conditional release is provided by the CPT. The CPT has long recognized that overcrowding in prisons is a direct cause of torture and inhuman or degrading treatment or punishment, which it is mandated to prevent.[12] In recent years it has interpreted its brief more widely and argued that the adoption of policies that limit prison numbers is the most effective way of preventing abuses.[13] As one of the ways in which prison numbers are kept in check is by a systematic policy of early release, this has the support of the CPT too. The CPT has been particularly prominent in arguing that all prisoners, including those sentenced to life imprisonment, should have access to programmes that prepare them for conditional release and that they should be considered for such release.[14] This policy position, which is also apparent in the 2003 Recommendation on the Management by Prison Administrations of Life Sentence and other Long-term Prisoners,[15] is

[10]Recommendation Rec(2006)2 of the Committee of Ministers to Member States on the *European Prison Rules* (EPR) adopted by the Committee of Ministers on 11 January 2006 at the 952nd meeting of the Ministers' Deputies.

[11]Recommendation Rec(2003)23 of the Committee of Ministers to Member States on the *Management by Prison Administrations of Life Sentence and other Long-term Prisoners* adopted by the Committee of Ministers on 9 October 2003 at the 855th meeting of the Ministers' Deputies.

[12]CPT *7th General Report* [CPT/Inf (97)10] ss. 12–15.

[13]CPT *11th General Report* [CPT/Inf (2001)16] s. 28.

[14]CPT *Hungary Visit* 2007 [CPT/Inf (2007) 24] s. 33.

[15]Recommendation Rec(2003)23 of the Committee of Ministers to Member States on the *Management by Prison Administrations of Life Sentence and other*

in clear opposition to the sentence of life imprisonment without any prospect of early release, which is still carried out in a number of European countries.

2.3 The ECHR

There can be no doubt that the ECHR, as the primary human rights convention of the Council of Europe, has had a major impact on the infusion of human rights principles into the development of criminal law and procedure throughout Europe (Trechsel 2005; Emmerson *et al.* 2007). However, the focus of this chapter is on one aspect of the criminal justice process – namely, the release of sentenced prisoners from prison. In this regard the ECHR has not been equally influential in all areas.

To understand the role that the ECHR has played hitherto with respect to imprisonment one must return to the relationship between release and the key provisions of the Convention. Imprisonment infringes directly on the right to liberty of the individual who has been imprisoned. In the first instance, therefore, one must ask what protections the ECHR offers against its infringement. Article 5.1 of the ECHR guarantees the right to liberty of every individual. The same Article, however, also allows individuals to be deprived of their liberty in a number of cases. First among these is 'the lawful detention of a person after conviction by a competent court'. Such detention is subject to procedural safeguards: the person who has been deprived of his liberty is 'entitled to take proceedings by which the lawfulness of his detention shall be decided speedily by a court and his release ordered if the detention is not lawful'. The key question that European human rights law derived from the ECHR therefore asks about release, where someone has lawfully been sentenced to imprisonment following conviction, is whether his continued detention is lawful. In some instances this question can be answered without much further ado. If the person has served the full term of his sentence, further detention is unlawful. Technical issues may arise in determining what the full term of the sentence is, or even in deciding what 'release' is, but they do not challenge the clear principle of a right to renewed liberty when a term of imprisonment has been completed, which is recognized in all European national legal systems as well.

Long-term Prisoners adopted by the Committee of Ministers on 9 October 2003 at the 855th meeting of the Ministers' Deputies.

Much more difficult questions arise when release before the end of a full term is considered. Could continued imprisonment infringe some other right? For certain individuals imprisonment, lawfully imposed, may cease to be lawful if its continued implementation would mean that it would inevitably amount to a form of inhuman or degrading treatment in contravention of Art. 3 of the ECHR. This would happen if a prisoner became so ill that he could not be treated humanely in prison. In the case of *Mouisel* v. *France* (14 November 2002) the ECtHR held that the continued detention of a sentenced prisoner who was seriously ill and whose medical needs could not be dealt with adequately in prison amounted to inhuman and degrading treatment in contravention of Art. 3. Continuation of the imprisonment was therefore unlawful. The ECtHR did not prescribe how the release of ill prisoners should be effected but noted with approval that there were new remedies that had been made available to the judge responsible for the execution of sentences, enabling prisoners whose health has deteriorated significantly to apply to be released at short notice. These remedies were additional to the existing possibility of applying for a pardon on medical grounds, which the French President alone was empowered to grant. The Court found that 'these judicial procedures may provide sufficient guarantees to ensure the protection of prisoners' health and well-being, which States must reconcile with the legitimate requirements of a custodial sentence' (*ibid*. s. 36). However, they had not yet come into force at the time the applicant had needed to be released.

Outside cases where prisoners are demonstrably seriously ill, the ECtHR has been very reluctant to interpret the ECHR as mandating any form of intervention that would require release when a court acting in terms of national law has imposed a fixed term of imprisonment. Thus, for example, in *Papon* v. *France* (7 June 2001) the Court made it clear that the advanced age of the offender alone did not compel his release. In the opinion of the Court the status of life sentences and other indeterminate sentences may be different, for it may raise complex issues about the term that has actually been imposed, as we shall see below.

Where the initial sentence is for a fixed period, the Court has persistently set its face against intervening in complaints about the process governing conditional release. The argument it deploys is brutally simple. In *Hudec* v. *Slovakia* (24 October 2006), for example, the Court dealt with a case where the applicant's sentence was for a fixed term of three years and he served exactly this term. The applicant objected to various shortcomings in the consideration of his early release. The Court explained that the detention was justified at the outset by the original conviction and subsequent appeal proceedings. The Court reiterated that the Convention did not 'confer, as such, the right to release on licence or require that parole decisions be taken by or be subject to review by a court' (*ibid.* s. 5). This meant that Art. 5.4 could not be invoked. The Court also ruled that, in cases where someone has been sentenced to a fixed term, early release proceedings do not involve a criminal charge. Accordingly Art. 6, which specifies fair trial rights for criminal matters, was not applicable (*Jankauskas* v. *Lithuania* (16 December 2003); *Dybeku* v. *Albania* (18 December 2007)).

The same approach has been adopted even where someone has been conditionally released and subsequently recalled to prison to serve the remainder of their sentence. In *Ganusauskas* v. *Lithuania* (7 September 1999) the applicant complained to the ECtHR that after release he had been recalled to the prison by proceedings that were neither 'lawful' nor 'in accordance with a procedure prescribed by law', as required by Art. 5.1 of the ECHR, and that he had not been able to challenge his recall on the basis of Art. 5.4. The ECtHR gave both arguments short shrift, rejecting them on the basis that the original lawful sentence governed the redetention for as long as the sentence was valid.

In the more recent case of *Gebura* v. *Poland* (6 March 2007) the ECtHR did hold that, where someone had been granted conditional release and there had subsequently been a delay in actually releasing him, his detention ceased to be lawful and that Art. 5.1 had been contravened. In this instance the question of the application of Art. 5.4 did not arise. However, in a somewhat Delphic further dictum, the ECtHR commented that the finding in respect of Art. 5.1 was not affected 'by the possibility of a revocation of conditional release in cases where a person has failed to comply with the relevant conditions or committed a new offence, provided that there is a sufficient connection between his conviction and a recall to prison' (*ibid.* s. 32). This test for determining whether revocation should be considered is derived from *Stafford* v. *United Kingdom* (28 May 2002), the leading case on conditional release from mandatory life imprisonment. *Gebura's* case is of considerable interest, as it seems to require a clear procedure for determining whether the criteria for revocation are met. *Stafford's* case is clear authority for the proposition that, in the case of life sentences for which a minimum term has been set, such a procedure must meet the standards set by Art. 5.4 (see the discussion below). However, it is not clear whether in *Gębura* the ECtHR meant to go this far in respect of a fixed-term sentence.[16]

2.3.1 Life imprisonment

The ECtHR has been much more actively involved in applying procedural safeguards where it regards sentences as being indeterminate and therefore requiring decisions other than the initial sentence to be made in relation to release. An important strand in the jurisprudence in this regard has been the shaping by the ECtHR of English release procedures relating to life imprisonment. For a long time English law has recognized a clear distinction between the 'tariff' or minimum period, which has to be served before release, and the balance of the sentence, which requires a decision on whether the offender still poses a danger to society. Initially, the intervention of the ECtHR was limited to discretionary life sentences where this distinction was most clearly drawn. In *Weeks* v. *United Kingdom* (2 March 1987) the Court held that the decision to release an offender after the minimum period had been served had to be taken by an independent court, or at least by an independent court-like body,[17] for it required a renewed determination of the lawfulness of the detention to meet the requirements of Art. 5.4 of the ECHR. In *Thynne, Wilson and Gunnell* v. *United Kingdom* (25 October 1990) the same argument was applied and extended also to a decision to re-imprison prisoners sentenced to life imprisonment who had been released, but who had subsequently been deemed to have breached the conditions of their release. In *Hirst* v. *United Kingdom* (24 July 2001) it was held that reconsideration of whether a prisoner was still dangerous had to take place at reasonable intervals, and two years was too long an interval for this.

[16]In early 2009 in the case of *Black (R (on the application of Black)* v. *Secretary of State for Justice* [2009] UKHL 1) the House of Lords in the United Kingdom decided by a majority that *Gębura* should not be read as saying that the ECtHR would now be prepared to evaluate in terms of Article 5.4 the procedural basis for revoking and, by extension, for granting conditional release.

[17]In *Weeks* v. *United Kingdom* (2 March 1987) and subsequently in *Hirst* v. *United Kingdom* (24 July 2001) the ECtHR found as a matter of fact that the English Parole Board had the independent features of a court. However, in February 2008 it was held by the Court of Appeal in England that the Parole Board was not sufficiently independent to be regarded as a court for the purposes of Article 5.4 of the ECHR, because of the manner of the appointment of its members and executive intervention in its functioning: see *R (Brooke and Ter-Ogannisyan)* v. *Parole Board and others* [2008] EWCA Civ 29.

More recently, the same arguments were extended, first to juveniles sentenced to life imprisonment (*Hussain* v. *United Kingdom* 21 February 1996; *Singh* v. *United Kingdom* 21 February 1996; *T* v. *United Kingdom* 16 December 1999), and then to all persons serving life sentences, including those in whose cases the imposition of the sentences had been mandatory. In what is now the leading case on this subject, *Stafford* v. *United Kingdom* (28 May 2002)[18] the applicant had been released conditionally from a mandatory sentence of life imprisonment imposed following a conviction for murder. He had subsequently returned to the community but had then been sentenced to a further term of imprisonment for an unrelated non-violent offence. The question that arose was whether he could be kept in prison by the authorities after having served the second sentence on the basis that he was now being held for having breached the conditions of his licence, imposed when he was released from his initial life sentence. However, it was held substantively that a conviction of fraud, a non-violent offence, did not justify the further detention of the applicant on the murder charge. On the procedure, the ECtHR ruled that in this case, too, the further decision amounted to a new basis for detention and had to be taken by a court in order to meet the requirements of Arts. 5.1 and 5.4 of the ECHR. The decision could not be made by the executive but had to be taken by a court-like body in order to meet the requirements of Art. 5.4.

Another interesting aspect of the *Stafford* case was the refusal by the ECtHR to accept that the executive should make this decision because it was better able to reflect public opinion on the granting of an early release. In this respect the Court endorsed the forceful ironic comment of an English judge: 'it is not apparent how public confidence in the system of criminal justice could legitimately require the continued incarceration of a prisoner who had served the term required for punishment for the offence and was no longer a risk to the public'.[19] The effect of the decision has been that, in England and Wales, in all cases involving life imprisonment, not only decisions on setting the initial period that has to be served, but also decisions on

---

[18]This decision directly overruled the earlier decision in *Wynne* v. *United Kingdom* (18 July 1994), where the ECtHR had initially held that mandatory sentences of life imprisonment for murder were not divided into two components in the same way as discretionary life sentences.

[19]*Stafford* v. *United Kingdom* [GC] 28 May 2002 s. 80 with reference to the judgment of Lord Justice Simon Brown in *R (Anderson and Taylor) v Secretary of State for the Home Department* [2001] EWCA Civ 1698.

determining whether someone has to be released once that minimum period has been reached, or redetained if they have been released, have to be taken by a court.[20] Moreover, at the stage of considering release or redetention, only the risk of the offender to society is at issue, as the minimum period is deemed to have met the other purposes of a sentence of imprisonment.

The question that remains is whether the same approach to release decisions will be adopted in other European countries where the distinction between the two stages of the life sentence is not as clear. Thus far the Court has upheld the imposition of life sentences in general terms (*Sawoniuk* v. *United Kingdom* 29 May 2001) and left the release procedures largely to the countries concerned. In *Kafkaris* v. *Cyprus* (12 February 2008), however, it ruled that a life sentence had to be *de facto* and *de jure* reducible to avoid it being an inhumane or degrading form of punishment that could offend against Art. 3 of the ECHR. In coming to this conclusion the Court quoted extensively and with apparent approval from the Recommendations of the Committee of Ministers of the Council of Europe that reflect the view that prisoners serving long sentences, including life imprisonment, should at least be considered for conditional release.[21] The Court also referred to the more general European Prison Rules that specify that 'the regime for sentenced prisoners shall be designed to enable them to lead a responsible and crime-free life' and that, as 'imprisonment is by the deprivation of liberty a punishment in itself', 'the regime for sentenced prisoners shall not aggravate the suffering inherent in imprisonment'.[22]

The ruling in *Kafkaris* raises interesting further issues about release and the manner in which it should be implemented. The Court held that a sentence from which release was a possibility did not offend Art. 3[23] or Art. 5.1 by failing to spell out the eventual release procedures. However, it was prevented, by the failure of the applicant to raise

[20]*R (Anderson and Taylor)* v. *Secretary of State for the Home Department* [2002] UKHL 46.

[21]At ss. 70–72 the ECtHR referred to the Recommendation concerning prison overcrowding and prison population inflation, and the Recommendation on conditional release, as well as the Resolution on the treatment of long-term prisoners. (Resolution(76)2 on the *Treatment of Long-term Prisoners* adopted by the Committee of Ministers on 17 February 1976 at the 254th meeting of the Ministers' Deputies.)

[22]EPR 108.

[23]The dissenting opinion of Judges Tulkens, Cabral Barreto, Fura-Sandström and Spielmann, which held that Article 3 had been infringed in the absence

the issue at the appropriate time, from dealing with the question of whether, given that some form of release procedure is required, this procedure would have to meet the standards of Art. 5.4. The logic, however, seems inescapable. If the Convention makes due process essential for the sentence to be compatible with it, the due process provisions should meet the requirements set by the Convention.[24]

2.3.2 Preventive detention

Where prisoners are held in prison for longer than normal, under an arrangement which makes it clear that the second part of their detention is purely for preventive purposes, the ECtHR has been prepared to recognize the same procedural protections that it has developed in the case of prisoners serving life sentences. It has set high procedural standards for judicial review in instances where it has determined that the continued detention or redetention of prisoners would amount to a renewed loss of liberty because the latter decision was taken administratively with different factors in mind from those that had led to the initial decision to imprison. An early example of where judicial oversight of release was found to be lacking is *Van Droogenbroeck* v. *Belgium* (24 June 1982), where a prisoner sentenced to imprisonment for two years for theft was, because of his recidivism, also placed at the disposal of the state for a further ten years during which the Minister of Justice could decide on his release. This arrangement was held not to meet the requirements of Art. 5.4 of the ECHR for review of detention by an independent court. Later decisions of the ECtHR on cases where the facts have been broadly similar have adopted the same approach (*E* v. *Norway* 29 August 1990; *Silva Rocha* v. *Portugal* 15 November 1996; *Aerts* v. *Belgium* 30 July 1998).

2.4 The Council of Europe-based conventions

The Council of Europe has pioneered the use of conventions which may impact on the release of prisoners sentenced for crimes

of a clear release procedure, was critical of the majority for not making more use of the standards to which it had itself referred.

[24]In *Léger* v. *France* (30 March 2009) a majority of the Grand Chamber declined, because of the death of the applicant before a final ruling could be given, to clarify the position in this regard. In an unusual dissenting opinion on a procedural ruling, Judge Spielmann with whom Judges Bratza, Gyulumyan and Jebens agreed, argued that the case raised major human rights concerns and should therefore nevertheless have been considered.

committed outside their home countries. Most influential has been the 1983 Convention on the Transfer of Sentenced Persons (21 March 1983 CETS 112). This is a Strasbourg-based Convention that is also open to non-European countries. The Convention on the Transfer of Sentenced Persons has been ratified by 64 contracting parties, including all Member States of the Council of Europe. Its stated objective is to 'further the ends of justice and social rehabilitation' by transferring sentenced prisoners, who are nationals[25] of the state to which will they will be transferred, to serve their sentences in their own countries. Its introduction formed part of a wider tendency apparent at the time to encourage such transfers for humanitarian reasons (Plachta 1993: 206; Kress and Sluiter 2002: 1766; van Zyl Smit 2005: 364).

The Convention on the Transfer of Sentenced Persons was preceded by the 1970 European Convention on the International Validity of Criminal Judgments. It too enabled one state to enforce the judgments of another state. However, this latter Convention was seen as creating too complex and inflexible a framework for the recognition of judgments. It is still in force, but it has been ratified by only 20 states. These do not include France, Germany, Russia or the UK. Its overall impact on the release of prisoners in Europe has been negligible. It is not considered further in this chapter, as the Convention on the Transfer of Sentenced Persons was put forward precisely because it was recognized that a simpler form of effecting the international transfer of prisoners was required. However, as Plachta (1993: 209) has pointed out, the two conventions are not identical and recourse may still be had to European Convention on the International Validity of Criminal Judgments, in instances when states are parties and when, for example, the prisoner is already in his home country after escaping from a prison in the sentencing state.

The increased transfer of prisoners as a result of the near-universal adoption within Europe of the Convention on the Transfer of Sentenced Persons has also meant that national authorities have increasingly to pay attention to how they implement sentences of imprisonment imposed by courts outside their jurisdiction. In general, international agreements, such as the Convention on the Transfer of Sentenced Persons, require not only formal co-operation between prison authorities but also some thought about the acceptability of both prison standards and release processes applied in Member

[25]The requirement that a prisoner who is to be transferred must a 'national' of the administering State is set by Art. 3 of the Convention.

States. This relates both to the term of imprisonment and to the conditions of imprisonment. In some countries it is still possible to sentence prisoners to a particular type of prison, a 'penitentiary' for example, which has a harsher regime than an 'ordinary' prison.

The Convention allows states to adopt two strategies to deal with this: 'conversion' of the sentence into a sentence of the state to which the prisoner is transferred – that is, the 'administering state' (Art. 9.1.b); and 'adoption' of the sentence by such a state, which simply continues to enforce it (Art. 9.1.a). States may elect to exclude one of these strategies. Where they have left themselves a choice, states must inform the sentencing state of which option they plan to exercise, so that the sentencing state can decide on whether it would be prepared to allow the transfer. In both instances the Convention restricts what the administering state can do when taking over the sentence. Where a sentence is converted by the administering state, Art. 11 applies. It provides:

1 In the case of conversion of sentence, the procedures provided for by the law of the administering State apply. When converting the sentence, the competent authority:

   a. shall be bound by the findings as to the facts insofar as they appear explicitly or implicitly from the judgment imposed in the sentencing State;
   b. may not convert a sanction involving deprivation of liberty to a pecuniary sanction;
   c. shall deduct the full period of deprivation of liberty served by the sentenced person; and
   d. shall not aggravate the penal position of the sentenced person, and shall not be bound by any minimum which the law of the administering State may provide for the offence or offences committed.

2 If the conversion procedure takes place after the transfer of the sentenced person, the administering State shall keep that person in custody or otherwise ensure his presence in the administering State pending the outcome of that procedure.

When an administering state adopts the sentence imposed by the sentencing state and proceeds to enforce it, the scope for changing the original sentence is much more limited, as Art. 10 provides:

1 In the case of continued enforcement, the administering State shall be bound by the legal nature and duration of the sentence as determined by the sentencing State.

2 If, however, this sentence is by its nature or duration incompatible with the law of the administering State, or its law so requires, that State may, by a court or administrative order, adapt the sanction to the punishment or measure prescribed by its own law for a similar offence. As to its nature, the punishment or measure shall, as far as possible, correspond with that imposed by the sentence to be enforced. It shall not aggravate, by its nature or duration, the sanction imposed in the sentencing State, nor exceed the maximum prescribed by the law of the administering State.

Whether a state follows the course of continued enforcement or of conversion, it may still grant a pardon, amnesty or commutation of the sentence in accordance with its constitution or other laws (Art. 12). However, the sentencing state alone has the right to decide on any application for review of the judgment (Art. 13). For the Convention to function effectively there must be mutual trust between the two states concerned. This may be difficult to engender in cases where a conviction results in very different public reactions in the two states.

A recent example is the case of a Frenchwoman, Florence Cassez, who was convicted of kidnapping in Mexico and sentenced to imprisonment for 96 years, a sentence that on appeal was reduced to 60 years. The conviction and sentence caused an outcry in France and the Presidents of the two countries agreed to attempt to resolve the issue by having Cassez moved to France in terms of the Convention on the Transfer of Sentenced Persons, which has been ratified by both states. However, press reports indicate that this is a very unpopular suggestion in Mexico, where the conviction and sentence enjoy wide public approval. The Mexican Human Rights Commission has even gone as far as to suggest that Mexico withdraw entirely from the Convention as France could not be trusted not to release Cassez early by using its powers of pardon, amnesty or commutation to appease French public opinion that doubts the soundness of the underlying conviction (Associated Press 2009).

The complex interplay between the right of the administering state to pardon and the prohibition on it reviewing the initial conviction may lead to further public controversy in this area. Such controversy has arisen in the case of Michael Shields, an Englishman who was convicted of attempted murder committed in Bulgaria in 2005 and returned to England to serve his sentence. When Shields' attempts to have his Bulgarian conviction reviewed failed, he approached the government of the UK and requested a free pardon.

The Secretary of State for Justice initially argued that he was unable to recommend the Queen to grant a pardon, as to do so would amount to a review of the conviction. However, in *R* v. *On the Application of Michael Shields* v. *Secretary of State for Justice* the Queen's Bench Division of the High Court ruled that, under Art. 12, the Secretary of State did have the power to consider a pardon. The Court was careful to hold that it could not say whether or how this power to pardon should be exercized. However, it did explain that, in principle:

> the grant of a free pardon would appear to require a conclusion that, taking the Bulgarian courts' judgment for what it is and without calling in question its correctness on the material which those courts considered, fresh evidence which the Bulgarian courts did not consider, taken with the material which they did consider and their judgment upon it, justifies a conclusion that Michael Shields is morally and technically innocent (*ibid.* s. 34).

This is a high hurdle, as it appears that most of the allegedly exculpatory evidence was placed before the Bulgarian courts at various stages of the proceedings. On 2 July 2009 the Secretary of State announced that he had adopted the test suggested by the Court and come to a 'provisional' decision not to grant a pardon. This statement was met by a further public outcry, which paid scant attention to the niceties of the legal rules involved and demanded Shields' immediate pardon and release (BBC News 2009).[26]

A positive requirement from the point of view of a prisoner who is to be transferred is that in terms of the Convention on the Transfer of Sentenced Persons the prisoner's consent is required before a transfer can be effected. However, even a prisoner who consents may be significantly worse off if he is poorly advised about the consequences of electing to be transferred. This happened in the case of *R* v. *Secretary of State for the Home Department, ex parte Read* where the offender, Read, had been sentenced in Spain to 12

[26]Michael Shields was, however, pardoned on 9 September 2009 on the basis of 'new evidence'. See http://news.bbc.co.uk/1/hi/england/merseyside/8245760.stm

years' imprisonment for forging currency, the minimum term for that offence in that country. When being sentenced Read had been told that the Court would recommend to the Spanish government that the sentence be reduced to six years but that had not taken place by the time Read applied to be transferred to England. In England the maximum sentence for the same offence was 10 years. If sentenced in England, Read would probably have received only about four years. However, the government of the UK, when ratifying the Convention on the Transfer of Sentenced Persons, had agreed only to continue the enforcement of sentences imposed by the sentencing state. As an administering state it had explicitly excluded the prospect of converting the sentence in terms of its own law. The House of Lords interpreted this aspect of the Convention strictly. It ruled that, where the court in a sentencing state imposed a sentence in excess of the maximum sentence prescribed by an English statute for a corresponding offence, the English Home Secretary adapting the sentence under Art. 10 of the Convention had the power to reduce the sentence to the English maximum but no further. This was the case even where the foreign court had imposed the minimum sentence and indicated that the prisoner should serve less than the minimum. The key to the reasoning of the House of Lords was that it treated the words 'similar offence' in Art. 10 as referring to a legally similar offence and not to the particular facts of the case, which could be considered only if the more flexible provisions of conversion procedure laid down in Art. 11 had been followed. This judgment, while technically correct, is harsh in its outcome, as the House of Lords itself recognized. Read would have been much better off had he waited in Spain to have his sentence reduced to six years before requesting a transfer to his home country.

The requirement of consent has been watered down significantly by the Additional Protocol to the Convention on the Transfer of Sentenced Persons.[27] Not only may persons who flee the sentencing state be tried in the administering state without their consent (Art. 2) but Art. 3 of the Additional Protocol also provides:

Upon being requested by the sentencing State, the administering State may ... agree to the transfer of a sentenced person without the consent of that person, where the sentence passed on the

---

[27]*Additional Protocol to the Convention on the Transfer of Sentenced Persons* (18 December 1997 CETS 167).

latter, or an administrative decision consequential to that sentence, includes an expulsion or deportation order or any other measure as the result of which that person will no longer be allowed to remain in the territory of the sentencing State once he or she is released from prison.

Where a prisoner has no choice about being transferred, the risk is greater that he may be disadvantaged by the administering state implementing a sentence in a way that does not allow release at as early a stage as would have been the case in the sentencing state (see *Szabó v. Sweden* and the other decisions of the ECtHR discussed in section 4 below).

While the 1983 Convention on the Transfer of Sentenced Persons has raised some difficulties, it has been relatively successful in the sense that it has been widely adopted and used for prisoners. The same cannot be said for the Convention designed to deal with community sentences and, most importantly for current purposes, with prisoners who, after being released conditionally, could serve a period under supervision in a country other than that in which they were sentenced but where they are ordinarily reside. The European Convention on the Supervision of Conditionally Sentenced or Conditionally Released Offenders, which the Council of Europe opened to its members for signature as far back as 1964, came into force only in 1975 when the minimum of three ratifications had been made. Currently, it has still been ratified by only 20 Member States. Moreover, nine of these states have entered reservations to substantial parts of it. Although state parties undertake to supervize such offenders, the Convention allows many grounds for refusing to do so (Art. 7). The practical effect of these various factors has been that this Convention is used very rarely.

2.5 Preliminary conclusion

There can be no doubt that at the policy level the Council of Europe is committed to encouraging the release of all prisoners, both in order to facilitate their reintegration into society and to prevent overcrowding and other abuses that the excessive use of imprisonment inevitably entails. At the policy level, this commitment to release extends to the most serious cases: all prisoners sentenced to life imprisonment should also be considered for release and prepared for it, although of course the possibility remains that they will not be released. This policy commitment should inform various legal developments at the

Council of Europe level. One of these is the creation of conventions to facilitate persons serving their sentences in their countries of origin. However, the impact of these conventions on early release is ambiguous: in some cases they may even lead to an extension of the *de facto* period that a transferred prisoner may serve.

The interpretations by the ECtHR of the ECHR and of the Convention on the Transfer of Prisoners, while recognizing the policy commitment to conditional and other forms of early release, have not paid as much attention to early release as they might have done. In the final section we put forward arguments about how this deficit could be remedied. Before doing so, we consider the initiatives of the EU that impact on early release as, for many states the influence of 'Europe' on release policy will come from this quarter too.

3. The influence of 'Brussels': the growth of EU criminal law and its impact on release

The fact that 'Brussels' has an impact in this area is a surprise to some, because the Europe of 'Brussels' was first and foremost an organization to promote trade, commerce and economic growth. It began life as the European Coal and Steel Community in 1952, out of which grew the European Atomic Energy Community and, much more significantly, the European Economic Community, alias the EEC, alias the EC.[28] Within the broad framework of economic development the main concern of 'Brussels' was and is the promotion of what are usually called the 'four freedoms': free movement of goods, free movement of persons, free movement of services and free movement of capital (Barnard 2007). So why and how did 'Brussels' become involved in criminal justice matters? And what is the basis of its competence to do so?

The main reason why 'Brussels' began to take an interest in criminal justice was the unhappy fact that the 'four freedoms' unintentionally generated a fifth one: the free movement of criminals and crime. Freedom of movement for honest citizens meant that dishonest ones could move around more easily as well, and those who had committed crimes in their own countries could now, with greater ease than heretofore, remove themselves across a border to avoid being caught and punished. A related problem was that organized crime,

[28]The EEC lost its middle 'E' and became the EC as part of the rearrangements made by the Maastricht Treaty in 1992.

like legitimate businesses, could now more easily operate across frontiers. These two related problems created pressure within Europe to simplify the rules on mutual legal assistance and extradition. But there were also other reasons why Brussels began to take an interest in criminal justice. One was the need to create the means of protecting the Community budget. The Community had finances which, like national finances, needed to be protected from those who seek to pillage or improperly divert them; and whereas the national finances of the Member States are protected by the criminal laws and criminal justice systems of the states concerned, for the finances of the Community there was originally no equivalent. Inevitably, this lacuna caused 'Brussels' to press for the creation of new crimes, and the machinery to ensure that those who commit them are caught and punished.[29] And a third factor was the existence of common problems, like terrorism and environmental pollution, which required the intervention of the criminal law, and for which a common approach between the Member States was clearly necessary.

These pressures were already becoming evident by the mid-1970s, when the French President, M. Giscard d'Estaing, put before three successive European Councils a project for the creation of what he called a 'European criminal justice area' (Weyembergh and de Kerchove 2004: 14). At the time, this ambitious scheme came to nothing. In those days, the treaties that were the constitutional basis for the 'Brussels' enterprise did not provide for any competence in criminal justice matters, and there was no will at that point to amend them to create one. The EEC (like the EC later) could make law for its Member States in the form of Regulations, which had direct effect, and Directives, which did not, but which required the Member States to give effect to them by amending their own laws. But the purposes for which it could use either of these instruments were limited, and making and enforcing Europe-wide rules about criminal law or criminal procedure or sentencing were not among them.[30]

---

[29]A seminar on this problem was sponsored by the Directorate General for Financial Control in November 1989 (see Commission (1993)).

[30]Or so it was thought at the time. In C-176/03 *Commission* v. *Council* the European Court of Justice ruled, to the surprise of some lawyers, that where the EC is competent to regulate a matter by issuing a Directive, the Directive may properly require the Member States to implement it by the use of its criminal law.

For the 15 years that followed the French initiative, various makeshift methods were adopted to try to deal with the problems which it had been designed to resolve. One was informal co-operation on criminal justice matters between the ministers and civil servants of the various Member States. The most famous of these was the 'Trevi Group' – a working group set up to counter terrorism (Bunyan 1993). Another and more formal method was for different groups of Member States to get together outside the framework of the EC and enter into binding obligations. First and foremost of these was the 1985 Schengen Treaty, under the terms of which a group of (initially) five Member States abolished frontier controls and, as part of the new arrangement, agreed a wide range of co-operative measures against crime.

One early measure that had direct relevance to the release of prisoners was the ratification in 1987 by all the Member States of the EEC of the Agreement on the Application among Member States of the European Communities of the Council of Europe Convention on the Transfer of Sentenced Persons. The Agreement had the advantage of bringing into the framework of the Convention on the Transfer of Sentenced Persons all the members of the EEC, as, at the time, they had not all ratified the Convention. Moreover, they agreed *inter se* that the requirement of the Convention that prisoners who were to be transferred had to be nationals of the administering state should be interpreted widely: each Member State undertook to 'regard as its own nationals the nationals of another Member State whose transfer is deemed to be appropriate and in the interest of the persons concerned, taking into account their habitual and lawful residence in its territory' (Art. 2).

The Agreement on the Application among Member States of the European Communities of the Council of Europe Convention on the Transfer of Sentenced Persons was a treaty between the Member States rather than an instrument of the Community itself. Then in 1992 came the Treaty of Maastricht (alias the Treaty of European Union, or TEU). This created a new legal structure, the European Union, placed alongside the EC, and it was given responsibility for two new areas of co-operation between the Member States: foreign affairs, and 'justice and home affairs'. From this point onwards, EU lawyers talked about the 'pillar structure' of the Union. The 'First Pillar' was the EC, which still handled the range of economic matters previously within the purview of the EEC; the 'Second Pillar' was the area of foreign affairs; and the 'Third Pillar', co-operation in a range of areas of government most of which, in the UK, fall within the ambit of the Home Office and the Ministry of Justice. These areas include what Title VI of the TEU called 'police and judicial co-operation'.

Title VI of the TEU began with a rhetorical flourish, stating that the objective of the EU in this area is 'to provide citizens with a high level of safety within an area of freedom, security and justice'.[31] To this end, Art. 34 of the TEU provided that Council of Ministers, acting unanimously on the initiative of any Member State or of the Commission, 'may promulgate a range of different legal instruments'. Of these, the most potent are 'Framework Decisions' for 'the approximation of the laws and regulations of the Member States'.[32] These Framework Decisions were the Third Pillar equivalent of directives issued under the First Pillar. As a matter of EU law they are binding on all Member States, which are bound to give effect to them. As a matter of national law, however, they do not have direct effect, and operate only when the Member State has changed its internal laws to comply with them. Framework Decisions did not feature on the original list of Third Pillar instruments in the Maastricht Treaty, and were added five years later by the Treaty of Amsterdam in 1997.

The addition of Framework Decisions to the list of Third Pillar instruments was most important, because they gave 'Brussels', for the first time, a wide power to make rules that are explicitly designed to impinge on the criminal justice systems of the Member States. Before 1997, the most that any 'Third Pillar' instrument could do was, in effect, to recommend a course of action, rather than require it. The strongest type of instrument available was a Convention: which, once it had been drawn up, bound a Member State only if it then chose to ratify it. The result, of course, was that the legal changes they sought to promote took a very long time to come into force. Framework Decisions, by contrast, bind all Member States automatically. At any rate, that was the position in theory, because the TEU, though declaring

[31]As amended by the Treaty of Amsterdam in 1997.
[32]Article 3(2): 'The Council shall take measures and promote cooperation, using the appropriate form and procedures as set out in this Title, contributing to the pursuit of the objectives of the Union. To that end, acting unanimously on the initiative of the Member State or of the Commission, the Council may: ... (b) adopt Framework Decisions for the purpose of approximation of the laws and regulations of the Member States. Framework Decisions shall be binding upon the Member States as to the result to be achieved but shall leave to the national authorities the choice of form and methods. They shall not entail direct effect'.

that they are binding, failed to provide an enforcement mechanism for use against a Member State that neglected to carry out its obligation, comparable with the one that existed under the First Pillar to cope with failures by Member States to implement directives.[33] And so when it adopted a Framework Decision the Council said, in effect, 'You must obey this, although we cannot make you'. This odd and unsatisfactory state of affairs was one of the matters which the Treaty of Lisbon was designed to address (Klip 2009, ch 3). At the time the previous paragraphs were written, the implementation of this Treaty appeared to be blocked for ever because Ireland had failed to ratify it, but as all readers are presumably aware, this situation has changed during the autumn of 2009 and in December – just as this book was in the final stages of production – it came into force. The Lisbon Treaty puts the powers of the EU to legislate in the area of criminal justice on a new and stronger footing. First, the previous 'pillar structure' is abolished, and what were formerly Framework Decisions will in future be Directives. Secondly, the Council is able to adopt them by a qualified majority vote in situations where it is not unanimous.[34] And thirdly, Member States that fail to implement them will, in future, be subject to an enforcement procedure.

At the time of writing, the Framework Decisions that have been adopted numbered, 30, of which no fewer than eight were adopted during 2008, in what might be crudely called a bout of 'binge law-making'. The range of topics that they cover is a wide one. An important group concern 'mutual recognition': instruments that require each Member State to recognize and enforce the judgments and orders made in criminal proceedings by the courts of other Member States. Of this group, the first and best known is the Framework Decision on the European Arrest Warrant.[35] The purpose of another group is to require all Member States to criminalize behaviour which was previously criminal in only some of them, or perhaps none at all – or if it was criminal, was thought to carry insufficiently

[33]Article 35 TEU created a procedure under which Member States may refer questions relating to Third Pillar instruments to the European Court of Justice (ECJ) at Luxembourg; but the jurisdiction operated only in respect of Member States that agreed to accept it – which the UK, among certain other Member States, did not.

[34]This new arrangement was opposed by, *inter alia*, the UK, which extracted a series of labyrinthine exceptions (Peers 2007/8).

[35]Council Framework Decision (2002/584/JHA) of 13 June 2002 on the European arrest warrant and the surrender procedures between Member States – implemented in the UK by Part I of the Extradition Act 2003.

deterrent penalties in certain Member States. Examples include the Framework Decision, issued in 2000 as part of the preparations for the introduction of the common currency, requiring Member States to make it a criminal offence to counterfeit the euro,[36] and the Framework Decision in 2002 requiring those Member States that had not already done so to criminalize acts preparatory to terrorism.[37] A more recent (and very striking) example is the Framework Decision of November 2008 requiring Member States to criminalize racism, xenophobia and holocaust denial.[38] In a different vein altogether, a Framework Decision from 2001 attempts to lay down minimum rights for victims.[39] But so far, no instruments have been adopted with a view to improving the position of defendants. In 2006 a move to adopt a Framework Decision guaranteeing certain minimum rights for defendants foundered – on the strength, it seems, of opposition organized by the UK.[40]

How far does EU law, in the shape of Framework Decisions and other weaker Third Pillar instruments, affect the laws of the Member States in relation to sentencing in general – and, in particular, the law on early release, which is the subject of this book?[41]

A number of instruments do indeed attempt to influence the Member States in respect of the penalty to be imposed. Before the Amsterdam Treaty and the arrival of the Framework Decision, the weaker forms of instruments that were then used to extend

[36]Council Framework Decision 2000/383/JHA on increasing protection by criminal penalties and other sanctions against counterfeiting in connection with the introduction of the euro.

[37]Council Framework Decision 2002/475/JHA of 13 June 2002 on combating terrorism.

[38]Council Framework Decision 2008/913/JHA of 28 November 2008 on combating certain forms and expressions of racism and xenophobia by means of criminal law.

[39]Council Framework Decision 2001/220/JHA on the standing of victims in criminal proceedings.

[40]See House of Lords European Union Committee, 2nd Report of Session 2006–2007, *Breaking the Deadlock: What Future for EU Procedural Rights?* (HL Paper 20, para 50); and *European Criminal Bar Association Newsletter* (Issue 12, July 2007, Editorial) 'New Constitution by Governments Forced to Scrap Procedural Rights Proposal'. (By the time this book went to press the UK's policy of opposition had been reversed, and in December 2009 a series of Directives designed to bolster the position of defendants were being planned.)

[41]For an excellent and detailed account, see Klip (2009, Chapter 6).

the range of criminalization within the EU tended to leave the issue of sentencing distinctly vague – typically requiring Member States to provide penalties that would be 'effective, proportionate and dissuasive', and letting each Member State decide what these would be (Weyembergh and De Kerchove 2004: s. 81). However, Framework Decisions requiring behaviour to be criminalized tend to be more prescriptive. They commonly prescribe a 'maximum minimum penalty': each Member State must ensure that the offence in question carries a maximum penalty of at least a given period of imprisonment (Weyembergh and De Kerchove 2004: s. 81). Thus, for example, Art. 3.2 of the new Framework Decision on racism and xenophobia requires certain forms of this behaviour to be punishable 'by criminal penalties of a maximum of at least between one and three years of imprisonment'. Framework Decisions sometimes also specify that the sentencing regime should allow for certain types of aggravating or mitigating factors. The Framework Decision of 2002 on human trafficking,[42] for example, states that if any of a list of four aggravating factors is present, the offence must carry a maximum sentence of not less that eight years' imprisonment. And Art. 6 of the Framework Decision of 2002 on terrorism provides that Member States may, if they so wish, provide for lower penalties where the defendant 'renounces terrorist activity' or provides assistance to the authorities. No Framework Decision or other EU instrument has yet attempted to lay down a mandatory penalty of the sort that has become increasingly popular in the UK in recent years; and, as not all Member States share the UK's current enthusiasm for them, an instrument requiring mandatory penalties seems politically unlikely. But if the political will were present, there is no obvious legal obstacle.[43]

Similarly, no EU instruments have yet presumed to lay down rules for the Member States about the way in which sentences must be executed. But, once again, it is conceivable, if not likely, that at some future point this might be done. One or two instruments have already been adopted which bear upon the rules about the execution of sentences indirectly. One of these is the Framework Decision on the Standing of Victims in Criminal Proceedings, Art. 4.3 of which provides that:

[42]Council Framework Decision 2002/629/JHA of 19 July 2002 on combating trafficking in human beings.
[43]In principle, the European Court of Justice could declare such an instrument to be illegal for various reasons, one of which would be 'disproportionality'.

Member States shall take the necessary measures to ensure that, at least in cases where there might be danger to the victims, when the person prosecuted or sentenced for an offence is released, a decision may be taken to notify the victim if necessary.

Another is the Framework Decision on the European Arrest Warrant. When this was created, some Member States that are opposed in principle to the notion of imprisonment for life were uneasy about handing over suspects or convicted persons to other Member States where such a sentence might be imposed, or perhaps already had been. With this in mind, Art. 5.2 provides that:

If the offence on the basis of which the European arrest warrant has been issued is punishable by custodial life sentence of life-time detention order, the execution of the said arrest warrant may be subject to the condition that the issuing Member State has provisions in its legal system for the review of the penalty or measure imposed, on request or at the latest after 20 years, or for the application of measures of clemency to which the person is entitled to apply for under the law or practice of the issuing Member State, aiming at non-execution of such penalty or measure.

Another EU measure that bears directly upon the issue of early release is the recent Framework Decision on the mutual recognition and enforcement of prison sentences.[44] This provides, in essence, a mechanism under which a Member State that sentences the national of another Member State to imprisonment may send the prisoner home to serve his sentence – whether or not he wants to go. The transfer of prisoners to serve their sentences raises the awkward question of whose country's rules should then apply to determine when, if ever, they should be released before the end of the full term of imprisonment that has been imposed on them. Article 17[45]

[44]Council Framework Decision 2008/989/JHA of 27 November 2008 on the application of the principle of mutual recognition to judgments in criminal matters imposing custodial sentences or measures involving deprivation of liberty for the purpose of their enforcement in the European Union. Under Article 29, Member States are obliged to implement this Framework Decision by 5 December 2011.
[45]The full text of Art. 17 reads as follows:
'(1) The enforcement of a sentence shall be governed by the law of the executing State. The authorities of the executing State alone shall, subject

attempts to regulate this by providing that, in principle, the rules of the executing state shall apply; but that Member States, when enacting implementing legislation, may 'provide that any decision on early or conditional release may take account of those provisions of national law, indicated by the [sending] State, under which the person is entitled to early or conditional release at a specified point in time'; and that, if the sending state wants to make absolutely sure that the prisoner does not get out of jail more quickly as a result of the transfer, it can ask the executing state to warn it of an impending early release, so that it can then cancel the transfer and bring the prisoner back again.

Significantly, this Framework Decision does not deal with the other side of problem: the prisoner who, as a result of the transfer, will end up spending significantly longer in prison than he would have served if the transfer had not taken place – a situation which could arise, and cause significant unfairness, in the case where (say) State A normally releases prisoners at 'half time' and its courts calculate their sentences with an eye to this, whereas State B makes them serve every last minute and its judges, knowing this, impose sentences that are nominally much shorter than are imposed by their judicial colleagues in State A.

In other words, the tendency of this Framework Decision is distinctly authoritarian; and the same is true of much of the rest of the Third Pillar legislation. Broadly speaking, the impetus behind most of it has been either the desire to see the criminal law more effectively enforced, or else the desire to see its reach extended to new areas in which it has previously not been used. Viewed from this angle, the 'area of freedom, security and justice' that is proclaimed in Title VI

to paragraphs 2 and 3, be competent to decide on the procedures for enforcement and to determine all the measures relating thereto, including the grounds for early or conditional release. (2) The competent authority of the executing State shall deduct the full period of deprivation of liberty already served in connection with the sentence in respect of which the judgment was issued from the total duration of the deprivation of liberty to be served. (3) The competent authority of the executing State shall, upon request, inform the competent authority of the issuing State of the applicable provisions on possible early or conditional release. The issuing State may agree to the application of such provisions or it may withdraw the certificate. (4) Member States may provide that any decision on early or conditional release may take account of those provisions of national law, indicated by the issuing State, under which the person is entitled to early or conditional release at a specified point in time.'

of the TEU looks rather like an area in which the public authorities have freedom to ensure national security by bringing offenders to justice (Swart 2001: 7).

At the same time as the Council adopted the Framework Decision on mutual recognition of prison sentences it adopted another Framework Decision on mutual recognition in relation to 'judgments and probation decisions with a view to the supervision of probation measures and alternative sanctions'.[46] This covers not only the mutual recognition and enforcement of probation orders, but also decisions granting prisoners 'conditional release' before the expiry of the sentence; and so, like the Framework Decision on the transfer of prisoners, it raises the spectre of tricky 'conflicts of law' issues as to which country's rules then apply to govern the recall of a convicted person for failing to respect the conditions of his licence or parole.

The Framework Decision seeks to regulate these issues as follows. The basic scheme is that, in future, each Member State will be obliged to take over the enforcement of an 'alternative sanction' imposed on someone resident within its borders, if requested by the Member State that imposed it. To this general obligation is a long list of exceptions, set out in Arts. 11 and 14.3. From the point at which the executing state has accepted the transfer, the law governing the execution of the 'alternative sanction' is the law of the executing state (Art. 13). However, by Art. 9, where

> the nature or duration of the relevant probation measure or alternative sanction, or the duration of the probation period, are incompatible with the law of the executing State, the competent authority of that State may adapt them in line with the nature and duration of probation measures and alternative sanctions ... which apply under the law of the executing State, to equivalent offences.

According to Art. 9.3 the 'adapted measure' must not be 'more severe or longer' than the measure originally imposed in the issuing state. When it 'adapts' a foreign measure in this way, the executing state must inform the issuing state, which then has the right to cancel the transfer (Art. 9) – as it also has in certain other circumstances which are set out in Art. 7.2.

[46]Council Framework Decision 2008/947/JHA of 27 November 2008.

4. Early release in policy and law

Having explored the recent flood of EU Framework Decisions we return to 'Strasbourg' and to recent decisions of the ECtHR in particular in order to try to identify whether that Court is developing a principled (enough) approach with which to gauge the effect of these new measures. The development of the law should be seen against the background of the European ideal for the policy governing the release of all persons sentenced to imprisonment. This ideal, as developed in particular in the various recommendations of the Council of Europe outlined in section 2, can be summarized as a statement of principle. Imprisonment interferes with the fundamental human rights of any person subjected to it. It should therefore be used only as a measure of last resort and therefore it should be used as sparingly as possible. This relates not only to its imposition but also to release, which means that prisoners should be released at the earliest point at which it is justifiable to do so. Such release should be done in a way which best assists the social rehabilitation and reintegration of ex-prisoners into the community. These objectives are best achieved through a system of conditional early release. Whatever procedure for deciding on release is followed, it should meet the requirements of fairness and due process.

Up to now this principled approach is reflected only partly in the jurisprudence of the ECtHR as human rights guaranteed to European prisoners. On the one hand, the Court has accepted that imprisonment limits fundamental human rights and that its implementation should be guided by the ideals of the social rehabilitation of offenders and the importance of their eventual reintegration into society. On the other hand, as explained in section 2 above, it has failed to develop an overall vision of how the release should be approached. Thus, in the extreme case of life imprisonment it has recognized that every prisoner must have a realistic chance of reintegration into the community but it has not spelt out fully what this means in procedural terms. In the case of fixed-term sentences it has refused to intervene, even where countries have set up procedures for early release that would give effect to targeted strategies for the effective reintegration of offenders into the community.

A minority of judges in the ECtHR have noted the shortcomings of European release systems in this regard. Thus, in *Kafkaris* v. *Cyprus* (12 February 2008) a number of dissenting opinions required that there be clear procedures for the consideration of early release, for a prisoner serving a life sentence in this instance.[47] This same argument was developed in more general terms by Judge Costa in a dissenting opinion in *Léger* v. *France* (11 April 2006). He commented that, where a state established a conditional release system that gave a prisoner a right to be considered for parole, it was not appropriate for the Court to hold that the decisions taken in terms of it were unreviewable. He was reluctant to do so, not only because there were already instruments laying down procedures and criteria for granting or refusing conditional release (the fact that no right to conditional release existed meant only that it would not be granted automatically to anyone who requested it, and not that it could be refused arbitrarily), but also because the right to liberty was so important. Judge Costa added that:

> if the purpose of national legislation on parole was to increase the role of the courts in dealing with applications for release, it would be ludicrous for the European Court of Human Rights to fly in the face of this trend by refusing to review the relevance, adequacy and lack of arbitrariness of the grounds on which the appropriate courts' decisions were based (*ibid.* s. 9).

Another line of argument would be to recognize more fully that imprisonment represents a continual infringement of the prisoners' right to liberty, which cannot be justified if there are good grounds for releasing them. What is required is an assessment of the continued proportionality of sentences. On occasion, the ECtHR has engaged in such a balancing exercise when assessing the appropriateness of (the imposition of) sentences, where the existence of the offence of which a person was convicted infringes his rights to privacy (Art. 8) or free speech (Art. 10). Thus, the Court has held that in extreme circumstances conduct may legitimately be criminalized even if it takes place in the private sphere (sado-masochism among consenting adults: *Laskey, Jaggard and Brown* v. *United Kingdom* (19 February 1997); or when exercising the freedom of speech [statements that are grossly libellous]: *Skałka* v. *Poland* (27 May 2003)). However, the penalties for such offences must be moderated by the recognition that any state intervention that curtails the exercise of these rights must

---

[47]See the joint partly-dissenting opinion of Judges Tulkens, Cabral Barreto, Fura-Sandström and Spielmann and the separate partly-dissenting opinion of Judge Borrego Borrego. The separate concurring opinion of Judge Bratza also argues in favour of such procedures but he relied on Article 5.4 rather than Article 3 as his dissenting colleagues had done.

be proportionate. In the latter case, even a sentence of eight months' imprisonment was thus found to be disproportionately severe. The wider principle of proportionality that should be applied in such cases has been clearly articulated by the Court: 'States are required to minimize, as far as possible, the interference with these rights, by trying to find alternative solutions and by generally seeking to achieve their aims in the least onerous way as regards human rights' (*Hatton and others* v. *United Kingdom* 2 October 2001, (GC) 8 July 2003).

These examples illustrate that the ECtHR can and does use proportionality-based arguments to justify reduced sentences where the ECHR makes it clear that specific rights it guarantees may be limited in appropriate circumstances.[48] Snacken (2006b; see also Van Zyl Smit and Snacken 2009) has criticized the Court for not offering the same protection to the right of liberty, which is guaranteed in absolute terms by Art. 5 of the Convention. The right to individual liberty has long been recognized as one of the most fundamental rights embodied in the ECHR. Although Art. 5 does allow the deprivation of liberty in narrowly circumscribed cases, it does not allow further limitations or reservations by national authorities; there is no margin of appreciation. The deprivation of liberty is inherently a severe restriction of the normal life of a citizen, and inevitably hampers the full enjoyment of other rights and freedoms, such as private and family life, association and expression. Research has described the many detrimental effects of deprivation of liberty for detainees and their families. These effects increase with the length of the detention but can be ameliorated by a targeted programme of conditional release. If the same reasoning were to be applied to the right to liberty protected by Art. 5 of the ECHR as to the cases under Arts. 8 or 10, this would mean that both the imposition of sentences and the use of early release should be designed to ensure that the deprivation of the liberty of the offender is kept to the minimum. Schemes for early release should be set up and interpreted by the courts with this in mind.

[48]The ECtHR has indicated that it may intervene if the sentence were so heavy that it would be an inhuman form of punishment or if it needs to be weighed against another Convention right (van Zyl Smit and Ashworth 2004). In the United Kingdom the House of Lords too has confirmed that mandatory prison sentences could collide with Art. 3 of the ECHR if they were completely disproportionate to the gravity of the facts (*R* v. *Drew* [2003] UKHL 25).

Some of the weaknesses of the current approach of the ECtHR are apparent in the analyses of the Court of cases involving a prisoner transferred, in terms of the Convention on the Transfer of Sentenced Persons and the Protocol to it, against his will to serve a sentence in a country to which he as a national is likely to be deported. In *Szabó* v. *Sweden* (27 June 2006) a prisoner who had been sentenced to 10 years' imprisonment in Sweden was transferred against his will to serve his sentence in Hungary. A Hungarian court confirmed the 10-year sentence. In Sweden, however, he would probably have been released after having served two thirds of the sentence while in Hungary he would have to serve four fifths. In practical terms this meant that following the applicant's transfer to Hungary he was likely to serve eight years of his ten-year prison sentence, whereas he could have expected to serve six years and eight months of that sentence in Sweden.

In response to the prisoner's complaint about the additional period that he would have to serve, the ECtHR reiterated what it saw as the positive aspect of prisoner transfers:

> To lay down a strict requirement that the sentence served in the administering country should not exceed the sentence that would have to be served in the sentencing country would also thwart the current trend towards strengthening international cooperation in the administration of justice, a trend which is reflected in the Transfer Convention and is in principle in the interests of the persons concerned (*ibid.* s. 1; see also *Drozd and Janousek* v. *France and Spain* 26 June 1992 s. 110).

The ECtHR in *Szabó* warned, however, that it did not 'exclude the possibility that a flagrantly longer *de facto* term of imprisonment in the administering State could give rise to an issue under Article 5, and hence engage the responsibility of the sentencing State under that Article'. However, the Court made it clear that it did not require that systems of early release had to be identical and did not regard the likelihood that a prisoner would have to serve an extra 20 per cent before being released as sufficiently arbitrary to infringe Art. 5 of the ECHR (see also *Veermäe* v. *Finland* 15 March 2005; *Csoszánszki* v. *Sweden* 27 June 2002).

Part of the response of the ECtHR in *Szabó*'s case is compatible with the principles underlying the European ideal about release underpinned by an attempt to reintegrate an offender into society as successfully as possible. As a rule it is probably usually true, as the earlier European Commission for Human Rights has recognized (*Wakefield* v. *United Kingdom* 1 October 1990; *Hacisüleymanoğlu* v. *Italy* 20 October 1994), that the reintegration of prisoners is assisted by their serving their sentences nearer their homes and where they are likely to be released. To this extent a transfer may be in the interest of the prisoner concerned, and the Court is right to praise the overall effect of provisions for the international transfer of prisoners.

In contrast, it is hard to argue that for a transferred prisoner to be detained longer before release is in the best interests of the prisoner concerned. Certainly Szabó did not perceive it be the case that his interests were being best served by making him serve a further 14 months. Nor presumably did the Swedish Court, which may have sentenced him on the assumption that he would be released after having served six years and eight months rather than eight years.

In Szabó's case the ECtHR retreated behind its oft-stated view that, once a fixed-term sentence had been imposed, arrangements for the execution of the sentence are not subject to the requirements of Arts. 5 and 6 of the ECHR as long as the causal connection between the sentence and the time served remained intact until the full term was complete. It found specifically that there was 'a sufficient causal connection between the conviction [in Sweden] and the deprivation of liberty in Hungary'. However, the Court's recognition that a 'flagrantly longer *de facto* term' could give rise to an issue under Art. 5 undermines its logic in this regard. Many would regard an additional loss of liberty of 14 months as 'flagrantly longer'. In reality it is extremely difficult to give meaning to this test. In our view, the ECtHR would have been better off approaching the matter differently. The Swedish sentence assumed that effective loss of liberty for six years and eight months could have been sufficient to meet all its sentencing objectives. The extra 14 months of detention of Szabó was therefore an unjustified additional infringement of his liberty. Had the ECtHR regarded ensuring that deprivation of liberty should be allowed only when clearly justified as the key principle that informed its interpretation of Art. 5, as Snacken suggests it should, it would have come to a different conclusion about whether the effect of the transfer had been to infringe the complainant's human rights. Such an outcome depends, however, on the Court regarding the routine consideration of conditional release as a normal, indeed necessary, part of the progress of a sentenced offender and not something added in the arbitrary gift of the authority responsible for executing the sentence.

This conclusion is of particular importance in the light of the attempts to facilitate the transfer of prisoners in the EU. As is so often the case, the motives of those setting up the new mechanisms cannot be reduced to a single principle. In a recent article on the transfer of sentenced persons in Europe, De Wree *et al.* (2009) point out that facilitating the reintegration of prisoners has been one factor in the initiatives emanating from both Strasbourg and Brussels. However, as they indicate correctly, while the early Council of Europe instruments in particular were designed to meet humanitarian concerns for offenders who were held in countries other than their own and were thus less likely to be successfully 'socially rehabilitated', the focus had increasingly shifted to the interests of the sentencing states. These states often want troublesome foreign offenders to be returned to their home countries, not because the offenders' interests would be better served by being returned, but because the sentencing states want to be rid of them to reduce the burden they place on overstretched resources for the implementation of sentences. Ideally prisoner transfer within Europe could serve both objectives, but often it does not. This is particularly true where prisoners are transferred against their will from one state to another. As we have seen, involuntary transfers were first facilitated by the Council of Europe Protocol to the Convention on the Transfer of Sentenced Persons, but the recent Framework Decisions of the EU have accelerated this process.

In order to ensure that this process is not abused, the principled approach to release that we have attempted to outline as emerging at the pan-European policy level should be applied to judge the acceptability of all transfers and, in particular, those that are involuntary. In order to do so, it is essential that the principles underlying an enlightened release policy be given more legal weight. It will be up to the ECtHR in the first instance to do so, as it may be called upon to intervene also in cases of offenders transferred as a result of the application of the Framework Decisions of the EU. In the future, however, the European Court of Justice, which increasingly is being called upon to interpret the many binding instruments emerging from Brussels in the light of human rights norms, including both the Charter of Fundamental Rights and the ECHR, will also have to apply itself to this question.[49] The challenge for both courts will be to develop more

[49]The Treaty of Lisbon, which came into force in December 2009, elevates the status of both of these two human rights instruments, making them a part of the body of binding law that is, under Lisbon, called 'Union Law', and not – as previously – just instruments that are taken into account when Community Law or Third Pillar Law is being interpreted.

fully the wider understanding of release implicit in these European human rights instruments so that they can be applied to prisoner transfers within Europe and ultimately also to the national systems that will continue to govern the majority of releases.

References

Associated Press (2009) 'Agency: Mexico should exit inmate-transfer treaty' (29 March) (available online at http://www.etaiwannews.com/etn/news_content.php?id=906641&lang=eng_news&cate_img=1037.jpg&cate_rss=General). (Accessed 16 December 2009).

Barnard, C.S. (2007) *The Substantive Law of the EU: The Four Freedoms* (2nd edn). Oxford: Oxford University Press.

BBC News (2009) 'Pardon appeal for Shields refused' (2 July) (available online at http://news.bbc.co.uk/1/hi/england/merseyside/8126083.stm).

Bunyan, T. (1993) *Statewatching the New Europe: A Handbook on the European State*. London: Statewatch.

Commission of the European Communities (1993) *Seminar on the Legal Protection of the Community: Progress and Prospects since the Brussels Seminar of 1989*. Dublin: Oak Tree Press.

De Wree, E., Vander Beken, T. and Vermeulen, G. (2009) 'The transfer of sentenced persons in Europe: much ado about reintegration', *Punishment and Society*, 11: 111–28.

Emmerson, B., Ashworth, A. and Macdonald, A. (2007) *Human Rights and Criminal Justice* (2nd edn). London: Sweet & Maxwell.

Klip, A. (2009) *European Criminal Law*. Antwerp, Oxford and Portland, OR: Intersentia.

Kress, C. and Sluiter, G. (2002) 'Imprisonment', in A. Cassese, P. Gaeta and J.R.W.D. Jones (eds) *The Rome Statute of the International Criminal Court. Vol. 2*. Oxford: Oxford University Press.

Peers, S. (2007/8) 'In a world of their own? Justice and home affairs and opt-outs and the Treaty of Lisbon', *Cambridge Yearbook of European Legal Studies*, 10: 383–412.

Plachta, M. (1993) *Transfer of Prisoners under International Instruments and Domestic Legislation*. Freiburg im Breisgau: Max Planck Institut für ausländisches und internationales Strafrecht.

Snacken, S. (2006a) 'Recommendation (2003) 23 on the management by prison administrations of life sentence and other long-term prisoners', *Penological Information Bulletin*, 25/26: 8–17.

Snacken, S. (2006b) 'A reductionist penal policy and European human rights standards', *European Journal on Criminal Policy and Research*, 12: 143–64.

Snacken, S. and Van Zyl Smit, D. (2009) 'Rechten van gedetineerden benaderd vanuit recente Europese ontwikkelingen', in T. Daems, P. Pletincx,

L. Robert, V. Scheirs, A. van de Wiel and K. Verpoest (eds) *Achter tralies in België*. Gent: Academia Press.

Swart, A.H.J. (2001) *Een ware Europese rechtsruimte*. Deventer: Gouda Quint.

Trechsel, S. (2005) *Human Rights in Criminal Proceedings*. Oxford: Oxford University Press.

van Zyl Smit, D. (2005) 'International imprisonment', *International and Comparative Law Quarterly*, 54: 357–86.

van Zyl Smit, D. and Ashworth, A. (2004) 'Disproportionate sentences as human rights violations', *Modern Law Review*, 67: 541–60.

van Zyl Smit, D. and Snacken, S. (2009) *Principles of European Prison Law and Policy: Penology and Human Rights*. Oxford: Oxford University Press.

Weyembergh, A. and de Kerchove, G. (2004) *L'harmonisation des législations, condition de l'espace pénal européen et révélateur de ses tensions*. Brussels: IEE.

Tables of cases

European Court of Human Rights and European Commission of Human Rights

Aerts *v.* Belgium 30 July 1998 (25357/94) (2000) 29 EHRR 50

Csoszánszki *v.* Sweden 27 June 2002 (22318/02)

Dickson *v.* United Kingdom [GC] 4 December 2007 (44362/04) (2008) 46 EHRR 41

Drozd and Janousek *v.* France and Spain 26 June 1992 (12747/87)

Dybeku *v.* Albania 18 December 2007 (41153/06)

E *v.* Norway 29 August 1990 (11701/85) (1994) 17 EHRR 30

Ganusauskas *v.* Lithuania 7 September 1999 (47922/99)

Gębura *v.* Poland 6 June 2007 (63131/00)

Hacisüleymanoğlu *v.* Italy [EComHR] 20 October 1994 (23241/94)

Hatton and others *v.* United Kingdom 2 October 2001 (36022/97) (2002) 34 EHRR 1

Hatton and others *v.* United Kingdom [GC] 8 July 2003 (36022/97) (2003) 37 EHRR 28

Hirst *v.* United Kingdom 24 July 2001 (40787/98)

Hudec *v.* Slovakia 24 October 2006 (4123/02)

Hussain *v.* United Kingdom 21928/93 21 February 1996 (1996) 22 EHRR 1

Jankauskas *v.* Lithuania 16 December 2003 (59304/00)

Kafkaris *v.* Cyprus [GC] 12 February 2008 (21906/04)

Laskey, Jaggard and Brown *v.* United Kingdom 19 February 1997 (21627/93; 21826/93; 21974/93) (1997) 24 EHRR 39

Léger *v.* France 11 April 2006 (19324/02)

Léger *v.* France [GC] 30 March 2009 (19324/02)

Mouisel *v.* France 14 November 2002 (67263/01) (2004) 38 EHRR 34

Papon *v.* France 7 June 2001 (64666/01)
Sawoniuk *v.* United Kingdom 29 May 2001 (63716/00)
Silva Rocha *v.* Portugal 15 November 1996 (18165/91)
Singh *v.* United Kingdom 21 February 1996 (23389/94)
Skałka *v.* Poland 27 May 2003 (43425/98) (2004) 38 EHRR 1
Stafford *v.* United Kingdom [GC] 28 May 2002 (46295/99) (2002) 35 EHRR 32
Szabó *v.* Sweden 27 June 2006 (28578/03)
T *v.* United Kingdom [GC] 16 December 1999 (24724/94) (2000) 30 EHRR 121
Thynne, Wilson and Gunnell *v.* United Kingdom 25 October 1990 (11787/85; 12009/86; 11978/86) (1991) 13 EHRR 666
Van Droogenbroeck *v.* Belgium 24 June 1982 (7906/77) (1982) 4 EHRR 443
Veermäe *v.* Finland 15 March 2005 (38704/03)
Wakefield *v.* United Kingdom [EComHR] 1 October 1990 (15817/89)
Weeks *v.* United Kingdom 2 March 1987 (9787/82) (1988) 10 EHRR 293
Wynne *v.* United Kingdom 18 July 1994 (15484/89) (1995) 19 EHRR 333

European Court of Justice

C-176/03 Commission *v.* Council [2005] ECR 1-7879

United Kingdom

R (Anderson and Taylor) *v.* Secretary of State for the Home Department [2001] EWCA Civ; [2002] UKHL 46
R (on the application of Black) *v.* Secretary of State for Justice [2009] UKHL 1
R (Brooke and Ter-Ogannisyan) *v.* Parole Board and others [2008] EWCA Civ 29
R *v.* Drew [2003] UKHL 25
R *v.* Secretary of State for the Home Department, *ex parte* Read [1988] 3 WLR 948.
R *v.* on the application of Michael Shields *v.* Secretary of State for Justice [2008] EWHC 3102 (Admin); [2009] 3 WLR 765.

Part 2

Country perspectives

Chapter 3

Austria

Karin Bruckmüller and Veronika Hofinger

Summary

The Austrian Criminal Code provides in principle an early – conditional – release from a custodial sentence under three preconditions: the prisoner has served a minimum period of the sentence (half of the term, but not less than three months for adults or one month for juveniles and young adults); the conditional release has at least the same special preventative effect on the offender as serving the remainder of the prison term; and the termination of the period of supervision from one to three years. The decision is made by a senate of the regional court where the prisoner is under arrest. There is an additional provision for foreign prisoners who agree to leave the country, as well as special rules for conditional release from indeterminate preventative detention.

Although Austria has quite a long history of legal instruments for conditional release, the legal provisions and, especially, release practice were very restrictive until a reform of the Criminal Code brought a significant increase in the use of early release instruments. In 2008, therefore, a steep rise in early release numbers was observed. If all the mechanisms for conditional release, pardon and the suspension of initially-unsuspended sentences are grouped together, a long-term trend towards more early release decisions becomes apparent. Together with a reduction in pre-trial detention and a decrease in admissions in general, this led to a reduction of the prison population in 2008. However, recent data from 2009 show an increase in the prison population, which might be threatening the long-term effect of the reform.

I. History

The history of conditional release in Austria began in the eighteenth century with a decree of the Royal Court (*Hofresolution*) in 1712 which promised prisoners that they might be pardoned and released from prison early if they were open to reform and rehabilitation (Miklau 2005: 8). It was only at the beginning of the twentieth century, in 1920, however, that the first Austrian law regarding early conditional release was passed. This law was amended in 1960 when the type of decision-making authority changed from being a mixture of judicial (*Vollzugsgericht*) and administrative (*Vollzugskommission*) to being solely judicial (Miklau 2005: 9). In the course of this amendment the provisions concerning conditional release were tightened. For example, prisoners who had been sentenced to life imprisonment were to be released only if it could be 'fully guaranteed'[1] that they would not commit further crimes after release. The law that was amended in 1960 was the first legal provision to include 'general prevention' as a precondition for conditional release. General prevention in this context means that a factor to be considered is that the early release of a prisoner should not undermine the legal system in general (Miklau 2005: 10).

In the new Austrian Criminal Code[2] of 1975 this criterion of 'general prevention' remained untouched. The possibility for early release was extended to prisoners who had served half their prison term – but only under very restricted conditions (Miklau 2005: 10). It was in the 1987 Amendment of the Criminal Code (*Strafrechtsänderungsgesetz*) that the possibilities for conditional release were extended. Conditional release after half the time served was facilitated, but release after two thirds should be the norm, not the exception. The term 'general prevention' still appeared in the law but it was only to be considered

---

[1]Amendment of the Criminal Code 1960 (BGBl. 152 s. 12(3)); see also (http://ris.bka.gv.at/Dokumente/BgblPdf/1960_152_0/1960_152_0.pdf
[2]Austrian Criminal Code (*Strafgesetzbuch – öStGB*) 1975 (BGBl. 60/1974), currently as amended by BGBl. 112/2007.

under special conditions (Miklau 2005: 10). Despite this broadening in the application of conditional release, relatively little use was made of it in practice (Bittmann 2008: 247).

After another reform in 2002, which, *inter alia*, broadened the possibilities for extending the period of supervision, a further Amendment to the Criminal Code came into force in early 2008. This was the so-called *Haftentlastungspaket* – a bundle of measures relating to release. As is described below, these amendments strongly encourage the use of conditional release and make the preconditions for granting it less restrictive. As the statistical data in section 4 below show, these new provisions have brought about a significant increase in the use of conditional release from prison.

2. Legal criteria

2.1 Legal reorganization of conditional release in force since the beginning of 2008

The declared aim of the *Haftentlastungspaket* was not only to reduce the strain on the prison system but also 'to improve security by cutting the time spent in prison' (Grafl *et al.* 2004: 61). Compared with the legal situation before 1 January 2008, this reorganization increases the scope for conditional release *(bedingte Entlassung)* from prison, in particular by redefining the criteria for release and by partly overruling considerations of a general preventive nature. The reform also enhances the role of the probation services. This increase in the scope for conditional release, which is increasingly linked to accompanying measures, is designed above all to attain two goals: on the one hand, it is supposed to reduce the likelihood of recidivisim; on the other, it is trying to take into account the population's security needs.[3] An important side-effect of the reform is – as mentioned before – a reduction of the strain on the prison system (Grafl *et al.* 2004: 61; Gratz 2006: 222).

---

[3]See http://www.bmj.gv.at/gesetzesentwuerfe/index.php?nav=13&id=103 for a commentary on the Amendment. This report also mentions that, in the light of a comparative analysis involving a number of European countries, increasing the scope for early release is to be recommended. On the balance between early release and security, see also Fuchs (2005: 153).

2.2 General background: prison sentences according to Austria's penal law

The Austrian Criminal Code (referred to hence as *öStGB*) provides for the pronouncement of unconditional custodial sentences which, in the normal course, must be served in prison. It also provides for partly-suspended custodial sentences, which mean that the offender will serve in immediate custody only the part of the term that is stipulated when sentence is passed, whereas the remainder of the term is 'suspended' for a period during which the offender is subject to supervision. In practical terms, this means that part of the sentence is not executed for the time being. In addition, the *öStGB* provides for fully-suspended custodial sentences, which result in the offender being placed under supervision for a period.

If a custodial sentence is recorded as either partly- or wholly-suspended, together with a statement of the duration of the period of supervision, the suspended sentence is not executed, provided the offender is not reconvicted within the probation period. Reconviction may result in the suspension of the execution of the punishment being revoked, or in an extension of the period of supervision. The mere fact that an offender violates a court directive (*Weisung*; see section 2.5.1 below) may (but does not normally) lead to the execution of the initially suspended sentence. Conditional release from serving an unconditional custodial sentence or from serving the unconditional part of a partly suspended custodial sentence is therefore possible.

2.3 Conditional release from a custodial sentence

According to s. 46 of the *öStGB*, a conditional release depends on three preconditions: serving a minimum period of the term; an assessment of the risk of recidivism; and the determination of the length of the period of supervision. In cases of early release from prison a distinction needs to be made between release from serving a fixed-term custodial sentence and from serving a life sentence.[4]

2.3.1 Conditional release from a fixed-term custodial sentence

Minimum term served Conditional release is possible once the convicted offender has served:

---

[4]A temporal custodial term lasts at least one day and, at most, 20 years; a sentence of life imprisonment is imposed 'for life' (see *öStGB* s. 18). However, the offender may be considered for release after 15 years (see below).

- half the term of the unconditional custodial sentence handed down to him; or
- half the unconditional part of a partly-suspended custodial sentence,[5]

provided this does not amount to less than three months. The minimum duration of three months of the term served will be reduced to one month if the custodial sentence has been passed for a crime committed by a juvenile[6] (Juvenile Justice Act (*öJbb*) s. 17) or for a crime that has been committed before the offender completed his twenty-first year (*öStGB* s. 46(3)).

If an offender serves several custodial terms or remainders of terms consecutively, the overall duration of these custodial terms needs to be taken into account in appraising the possibility of conditional release. After 15 years at the latest a decision has to be reached with reference to such a release.

2.3.2 Prognosis of the risk of recidivism

Significance of considerations of special prevention Early release from prison has to take place once it may reasonably be assumed that the offender will not be less constrained from committing further offences by conditional release than by serving the remainder of his sentence. Early release from prison takes precedence if it may reasonably be assumed to have at least the same special preventive effect on the offender as serving the remainder of his prison term, and if no special preventive effect is attributed to him serving the remainder of the term. By implication, this means that his serving the remainder of the term cannot be expected to hold out the prospect of a special preventive effect that is greater than that of conditional release. In assessing the risk of recidivism, one needs to take into account the change in the circumstances compared with those under which the crime was committed, for which the offender has served part of his sentence. Likewise, the beneficial effects of a directive and/or supervision (see section 2.5 below) that the offender may be placed under when he is conditionally discharged need to be considered (*öStGB* ss. 46(1) and (4)), as well as the extent to which these may compensate for negative factors that may still be present (*öStGB* s. 46(4)).

[5]Or the part of a fixed-term custodial sentence determined by a pardon.
[6]A person aged between 14 and 18 years (until their eighteenth birthday).

If, during his prison term, the offender has already taken part in an addiction-recovery programme or has undergone psychotherapeutic or medical treatment that he is prepared voluntarily to continue after release, conditional release has to be considered an option. This applies even in cases with a prognosis which is not wholly positive. The criterion is if the probability of committing further punishable offences within a prolonged period of supervision can be reduced significantly by a programme, therapy or treatment (*öStGB* s. 46(4)).

Taking general prevention into account A convicted offender who has served half the custodial sentence, but not yet two thirds, is eligible for conditional release according to s. 46(2) of *öStGB* only[7] if this is not considered inadvisable for reasons of 'general prevention'. If it is deemed necessary with regard to the seriousness of the crime, early release may have to be ruled out in exceptional cases to prevent punishable offences being committed by others ('negative general prevention'). This does not apply if the offence has been committed by a juvenile. In such cases considerations of general prevention are never applicable (*öJGG* s. 17).

2.3.3 Imposition of a period of supervision

Conditional release from serving a custodial sentence necessarily entails the imposition of a period of supervision. Section 48 of *öStGB* contains a number of provisions relating to the supervision period.

Length of period of supervision In principle, conditional release from a custodial sentence entails a period of supervision lasting between a minimum of one year and a maximum of three years. If a prisoner voluntarily begins an addiction-recovery programme or psychotherapeutic or medical treatment in prison and its continuation is considered necessary to justify an early release, the length of the term of supervision will be fixed between a minimum of one year and a maximum of five years. If the remainder of the term that has been conditionally suspended amounts to more than three years, the period of supervision will last five years.

Expiry of the period of supervision The period of supervision begins when the decision in favour of an early release comes into force. The time served in remand detention or any other deprivation of liberty by order of the authorities does not count as part of the period of

---

[7]Also in cases where the above preconditions apply.

supervision. As a rule, the period of supervision expires on the date originally specified. Only in the case of a juvenile offender can the term of supervision be terminated earlier; after one year, if new facts support the prognosis that the delinquent will commit no further punishable offences (*öJGG* s. 18).

2.4 Conditional release from serving a life sentence

In the case of the execution of a life sentence the offender is eligible for conditional release only after serving at least 15 years and if the prognosis is justified that he will commit no more punishable offences. The law requires a considerably more stringent prognosis in such cases. The imposition of a period of supervision is also mandatory in these cases (*öStG* s. 46(6)). Such supervision is required for ten years after release.

2.5 Directives and supervision

If necessary or advisable for reasons of special prevention, the court has to give directives (*Weisungen*) to the offender when he is released conditionally or place him under the supervision and guidance of a probation officer (*Bewährungshilfe*) (*öStGB* s.50(1)). The time limit for such directives or supervision is determined by the court but must not exceed the term of supervision.

2.5.1 Directives

Directives are orders or restrictions that are deemed suitable to prevent the offender from committing further punishable offences, such as a ban on drinking alcohol. What is inadmissible is the unreasonable curtailment of personal rights and unreasonable interference with a person's lifestyle. Participation in an addiction-recovery programme or in a psychotherapeutic or medical course of treatment may be prescribed only with the consent of the offender. Surgical operations may not be prescribed at all.

2.5.2 Supervision

The offender invariably has to be placed under probation if he is released conditionally from serving:

- a custodial sentence of more than five years (for at least the first year after his release); or
- a life sentence. In this case, he is to be supported and supervised by a probation officer for at least the first three years after his release.

In principle the offender has to be subjected to a period of supervision if he is released conditionally:

- before he has served two thirds of his sentence; or
- from serving a custodial sentence for an offence committed before the completion of his twenty-first year.

If it may reasonably be assumed that the offender will not commit any more offences even without being placed under the supervision of a probation officer – due to his personality, development or the kind of punishable offences that have led to the conviction – he need not be subjected to such supervision.

2.6 Revocation of conditional release

Conditional release may be revoked according to *öStGB* s. 53 if the offender:

- is convicted again during the term of conditinal release;
- recklessly disregards directives despite formal warnings; or
- persistently fails to keep in contact with his probation officer,

if revocation of the conditional release seems advisable in view of the circumstances to prevent the offender from committing further punishable offences. If the conditional release is not revoked, the period of supervision can be extended to a maximum of five years (in the case of a conditional discharge, from a life sentence to a maximum of 15 years).

2.7 Decision on a conditional discharge

According to ss. 152 and 152a of the Prison Act (*öStVG*) decisions on conditional discharges are made by the senate of a regional court located in the administrative district where the prison in which the offender is serving his sentence is located. Such decisions may be taken at the request of the offender, the head of the prison and the public prosecutor. In addition to the offender's files, the application will usually include depositions by the offender, the head of the prison, the public prosecutor and, if needed, by expert witnesses. The decision may be implemented without delay or within the next three months if time is needed to organize it, or if it is advisable first to prepare the offender for life in freedom (see also Bittmann, 2008: 248).

2.8 Special forms of early release (temporary suspension of execution of the sentence due to the offender being prohibited from remaining in the country)

Owing to the way asylum seekers are processed in Austria, to legislation pertaining to this group of individuals and to penal court judicature, there has been a significant increase in the number of convicted foreign prisoners in Austrian prisons (Kollmann 2008: 157). In order to reduce this strain on the system (for details, see Gratz 2006: 223) and at the same time to harmonize the intentions of the legislation pertaining to aliens with the objectives of the penal system, a new paragraph has been added to the Code of Imprisonment. In the initial stages, this provision was the subject of a good deal of controversy as the question was raised whether or not the procedures it advocated discriminated unfairly against Austrian prisoners.

In the case of foreign prisoners, s. 133a of *öStVG* stipulates the suspension of the further execution of their sentences when they have served half their term (but at least three months) and if:

- there is a legally valid prohibition on their staying in the country;
- they declare themselves willing to leave the country without undue delay and if it may be reasonably assumed that they will act accordingly; and
- there are no other legal or factual obstacles to the prohibition and the departure being implemented.

If the offender is sentenced to more than three years of custody, a temporary suspension is possible only when two thirds of the term have been served. A suspension of the sentence is not admissible if the foreign prisoner has been convicted of:

- a sex offence;
- an offence against life and limb carrying a sentence of more than three years in custody; or
- some other offence carrying a sentence of more than five years in custody.

Elements of general or special prevention do not apply here; all that is relevant is whether or not the formal preconditions are met.

The head of the prison is mandated to inform the foreign prisoner of the possibility of this type of conditional release. The head of the prison is also obliged to inform the alien's relevant police authority about the procedure and to ask it for its legal opinion whether there are any factual or legal obstacles that would block the convict's departure. The decision on whether an application for a conditional suspension of the prison sentence on account of a prohibition on the convict's staying in the country may go ahead falls within the remit of the court of execution, which is the Regional Court of Criminal Justice in whose administrative area the prison sentence would be served.

In the case of a positive decision, the head of the prison is mandated to supervise the departure as far as the border of the convict whose sentence has been conditionally suspended.[8] He is also obliged to notify the alien's police authority of the convict's departure (*öStVG* s. 133a(3)–(5)).

If an alien remains in Austria in contravention of their duty to leave the country, or if they return to Austria before the prohibition on their re-entering the country has expired, they are to be arrested forthwith and to be made to serve the remainder of their prison sentence. In practice this has given rise to problems in cases where a conditionally-released offender is required to re-enter Austria to appear in a trial before a court of appeal. A solution to this problem would be an offer of 'free passage'.

According to s. 133a of *öStVG*, this type of procedure is applicable only at a subsidiary level – that is, it is limited to cases where there are no interstate agreements regarding the transference of law enforcement and where extradition or conditional release according to the Criminal Code (*öStGB* s. 46, see above) are inapplicable (Kollmann 2008: 159; see also Birklbauer 2008: 717).

2.9 Early release from preventative measures

The Austrian criminal law also provides for preventive measures that do not focus on the culpability of the offender but on the danger that he or she poses to the public. The Criminal Code (s. 21 ff.) established three categories of offenders who may possibly be subjected to preventive detention: the dangerously disturbed, addicts in need of drug detoxification, and dangerous recidivists. These preventative measures remain in effect as long as they are deemed necessary. Therefore, the judge does not specify a temporal limit for

---

[8]According to the letter of the provision, the decision as to the offender's release is a discretionary one, yet in view of the remainder of the provision there is in fact no scope for discretion (Birklbauer, 2008: 716).

the measure in the sentence. However, the situation will be reviewed regularly as to whether the convict is eligible for release, and the maximum periods of detention are two years for criminals in need of drug detoxification and ten years for dangerous recidivists. After the expiry of the period in question, detainees have to be released. For the detention of dangerously-disturbed offenders there is no upper limit.

The law provides in s. 47 the *öStGB* for a conditional early release from a preventative measure. Conditional release is to be granted if – in light of the detainee's development during his custodial sentence, his state of health, his previous record and his chances of earning a livelihood by honest means – it may safely be assumed that the danger to society, which the preventative measure was designed to counteract, has ceased to exist.

The period of supervision after a release from an institution for dangerously-disturbed criminals and for dangerous recidivists as a rule lasts ten years (the exception being cases where the maximum sentence for the crime committed is ten years, in which case the period of supervision is five years). After release from an institution for criminals in need of drug detoxification, the period of supervision may vary from one to five years. If deemed necessary, there is also the possibility of imposing probation or a regime of court directives.

3. Research

Austrian research on early release focuses mainly on regional differences in the use of release mechanisms. Pilgram (2005), for example, compared the practice of conditional release from prison during 2001–4 for more than 27,000 prisoners, and he found considerable regional differences. While in a Western court district one prisoner out of three was conditionally released, in another district only one out of 20 prisoners was released conditionally. But these differences can be accounted for in regional variations in the offender population, especially concerning the length of their prison term. Pilgram therefore compared only prisoners within the same category of length of sentence, and found that regional differences still remain, albeit on a smaller scale. The probability of a prisoner serving a sentence of from three to six months, for example, being released conditionally was four times higher in Western Austria than in parts of Lower Austria. Similar differences can be found in other categories of length of sentence. Pilgram calculated that 600 prison places could be saved if the whole country followed the more generous practice of early conditional release employed in Western Austria (2005: 84–7).

Some of these regional variations may result from the different use of partly-suspended sentences. Until the beginning of 2008 prisoners could not be conditionally released from a partly-suspended prison term. The fewer conditional releases in Vienna may, to some extent, be attributed to the fact that these partly-suspended prison sentences are widely used in the capital city. Another factor is the existence of regional differences in the use of amnesties or pardons by the Federal President. The stricter the practice of conditional release, which in terms of s. 46 of *öStGB* must granted by a court, the more prisoners are pardoned (for example, at Christmas by the President). In sum, regional differences decrease if amnesties and pardons are taken into account but still remain to a remarkable extent, showing the court district of Vienna to be more restrictive than the Western district Innsbruck.

In a recent research project at the University of Linz, conducted by Hirtenlehner and Birklbauer (2008), the relationship between mode of release and reconviction rate was examined by comparing two similar prisons with divergent release practices: does a more liberal or a more restrictive mode of release lead to different levels of recidivism? Although the inmates of the two prisons ('Garsten' and 'Karlau') did not differ in demographic and legal characteristics, the regional courts' release practices were divergent. The main result of the study is that, in spite of divergent release practices, the reconviction rates do not differ significantly. The authors thus hypothesize that there might exist not only an 'exchangeability of sanctions' with regard to their preventive effects but also an 'exchangeability of modes of release' (Hirtenlehner and Birklbauer 2008: 29, 30).

4. Statistical data

Since 2001 a database provided by the Federal Computing Centre of Austria (BRZ) includes all electronic prisoner files under the administration of the Ministry of Justice. These so-called 'IVV-data' are available for key dates as well as for admission and release. The data contain sociodemographic information on prisoners, offences and sentences, as well as on regional aspects. The statistics are not linked to police, court, probation or reconviction statistics. The following descriptions are based on IVV data and on the Austrian reconviction statistics.[9]

4.1. Release from prison

In 2008, 11,910 prisoners were released from Austrian prisons under the administration of the Ministry of Justice. Around 550 people were released twice or even more often during the same year. Thus the following numbers refer to 12,468 releases from Austrian prisons during 2008.

Figure 3.1 shows the different modes of release considering all releases from prison (including pre-trial detention). About one third of all sentenced prisoners serve their prison term until the last day of the sentence; pre-trial detainees are released by court decision. Early release mechanisms include conditional release after half or two thirds of the term served, as well as pardons and amnesties. Two main kinds of suspended execution of a sentence can be distinguished. Firstly, a prison sentence may be suspended because the offender

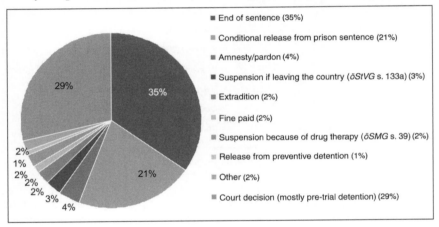

Figure 3.1 Releases from prisons under the administration of the Ministry of Justice, 2008
Note: Percentages may not add up to 100 per cent due to rounding

[9]Because of insufficient statistics for other forms of detention, such as administrative penal servitude (*Verwaltungsstrafhaft*), police arrest (*Polizeihaft*), the administrative detention of irregular migrants (*Fremdenpolizeiliche Haft*) and detention pending deportation (*Schubhaft*), it is currently not possible to provide information on releases from police detention centres (*Polizeianhaltezentren*) – that is, prisons under the administration of the Ministry of the Interior.

agrees to take part in a drug therapy programme (in terms of s. 39 of the Drugs Act [öSMG]). Secondly, there is a new special provision of early release for foreigners who agree to leave the country and return to their home country. In terms of s. 133a of öStVG, their sentence is suspended as long as they do not return to Austria.[10]

Figure 3.2 shows the numbers for sentenced prisoners only.[11] In 2008, half of all prisoners served their prison term until the end of the sentence; 30 per cent were released conditionally after half or two thirds of the prison term; and a further 6 per cent were pardoned by the President or benefited from amnesties. The new provision for suspending a prison sentence if a foreigner agrees to leave Austria was used in 4 per cent of all releases (9 per cent of all releases of foreigners).

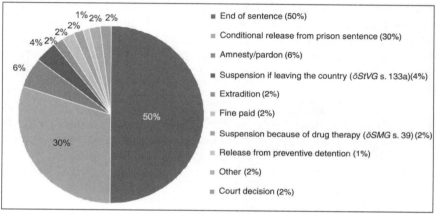

Figure 3.2 Release of sentenced prisoners, 2008.
Note: Percentages may not add up to 100 per cent due to rounding.

A different picture is obtained when only prisoners sentenced to more than three months are taken into account. Figure 3.3 shows release mechanisms for sentences of over three months (excluding mentally-ill people who are in preventive detention in terms of s. 21/1 öStGB), because three months is the minimum time for adult prisoners to serve before early release is possible. In 2008, more people were conditionally released from a prison sentence (43 per cent) than served their sentence until the last day (36 per cent).

[10]For further information on this legal provision, see section 2.8.
[11]Mentally-ill prisoners who are not sentenced but are held in preventive detention (not accountable for the offence according to s. 11 öStGB) are included in the graph.

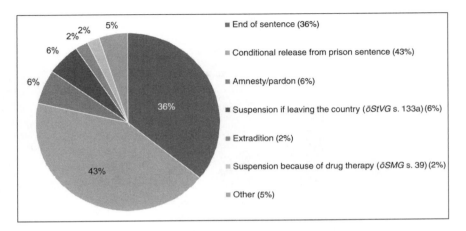

Figure 3.3 Releases from sentences of more than three months, 2008.

4.2 Effects of the reform

As outlined in section 2 above, the reform that came into force at the beginning of 2008 reorganized release mechanisms in Austria through the application of the so-called *Haftentlastungspaket*. This reform was intended to facilitate early release to relieve the pressure on overcrowded prisons. As shown in Figure 3.4, the new instruments achieved the aim of promoting early release: prisoners were conditionally released more often in 2008 than in 2007. The new provision for foreigners to be released earlier if they agree to leave the country was used in 6 per cent of all releases (12 per cent of all releases of foreigners) from sentences over three months.[12]

If all mechanisms for conditional release, pardon and suspension of initially-unsuspended sentences are grouped together, a long-term trend towards more early release decisions becomes apparent (see Figure 3.5).

The mean prison population on a given day depends on the number of incoming prisoners as well as on the length of the sentences and the *'de facto* time' spent in prison. A comparison of the prison population on key dates (1 September, 2001 to 2008) shows

[12]A regional comparison shows large local differences in the use of this new provision: 43 per cent of all foreigners released from the Vienna Court District Prison (sentenced to more than three months) are released in terms of s. 133a of *öStVG*, whereas in Western court districts only 1–5 per cent of all released foreigners benefit from this legal provision.

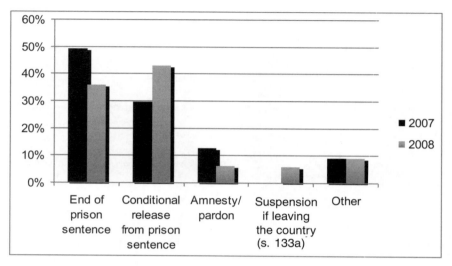

Figure 3.4 Releases from Austrian prisons, 2007–08 (for sentences over three months only)
Note: Percentages may not add up to 100% per cent due to rounding

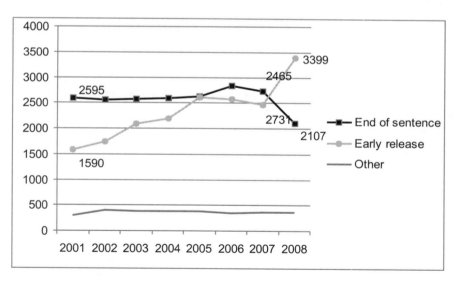

Figure 3.5 Releases from prison, 2001–08 (sentences longer than three months)

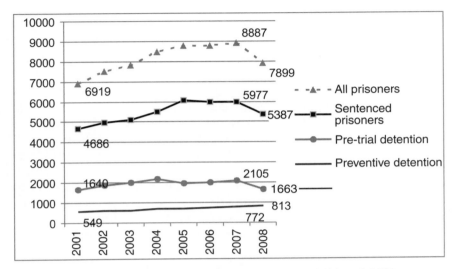

Figure 3.6 Evolution of prison population between 2001 and 2008

a remarkable decrease in the mean prison population from 2007 to 2008: from 8,887 to 7,899 prisoners (see Figure 3.6). (However, the number of prisoners is still much higher than it was at the beginning of the twenty-first century.) This decrease is caused by a reduction of sentenced prisoners (10 per cent fewer in 2008 compared with 2007) as well as a reduction of individuals held in pre-trial detention (about 20 per cent fewer).[13] On the other hand, the number of people held in preventive detention has increased steadily. The latest information from 2009 shows an increase in the prison population once more (a total of 8,270 prisoners on 1 March 2009). It is therefore too early to tell whether the reform (*Haftentlastungspaket*) will have an enduring effect on the decrease of Austria's prison population.

The reform of the Criminal Code also encouraged the intensified use of probation services for released prisoners. Although valid data on the evolution of conditional releases with or without probation are missing in the IVV, a considerable increase of the probation services' caseload from 2007 to 2008 can be ascertained.

[13]A substantial reform of the Criminal Procedure Law that also came into force at the beginning of 2008 may have influenced the use of pre-trial detention: the competence and responsibility for pre-trial detention shifted from investigating judges (*Untersuchungsrichter*) to (reportedly overloaded) Public Prosecutors.

4.3 Release and reconviction

Austrian reconviction statistics allow for the calculation of reconviction rates after different modes of release from prison. Data are presented for prisoners who were released in 2003: were they reconvicted by the end of 2007? Figure 3.7 shows that 56 per cent of all offenders released from prison in 2003 were reconvicted at least once during the observation period. Offenders who had to serve their prison sentence until the last day had the highest risk of being reconvicted, at 67 per cent. Of those who were conditionally released earlier (in terms of s. 46 of *öStGB*), 54 per cent were reconvicted by the end of 2007. Only 39 per cent of offenders who were released earlier because of amnesty or pardon, or whose initially-unsuspended prison sentences were converted into suspended sentences (by pardon or after the completion of a drug addict programme), were reconvicted.

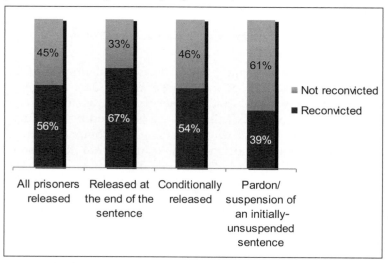

Figure 3.7 Reconviction rates after different modes of release, 2003–07
Note: Percentages may not add up to 100 per cent due to rounding.

5. Conclusions

In the past, Austria's release practice was much more restrictive than in other European countries. The vast majority of prisoners had to serve their prison term until the last day of their sentence and were released without supervision or the support of the probation services.

This situation was markedly improved through the *Haftentlastungspaket*, which came into force in 2008. Under the slogan *'Mehr Sicherheit durch weniger Haft'* ('Increase security by cutting prison terms'), the restrictions imposed by the Criminal Code on conditional release were reduced. The minimum time that offenders had to serve to become eligible for early release was cut, and considerations of general prevention were downgraded. In order to ensure that the public's security interests were being met and to guarantee the best possible rehabilitation of the released offenders, accompanying measures, such as supervision by a probation officer, were made partly mandatory. Collaboration with the probation services is supposed to start at the earliest possible date in order to ensure a smooth transition from imprisonment to freedom. However, the comprehensive obligation to provide probation services on a large scale has created financial pressures that present a still-unresolved problem.

As the reform is also supposed to have the side-effect of reducing the strain on the prison system, it does not stop at widening the scope of early release but has also added the temporary suspension of the execution of the sentence due to the offender being prohibited from remaining in the country.

The reform package has actually brought about a significant increase in the use of conditional release from prison. In 2008 a steep rise in early release numbers was observed. Together with a reduction of pre-trial detention and a decrease of admissions in general, this led to a reduction of the prison population in 2008. However, recent data from 2009 show an increase in the prison population, which might be threatening the long-term effect of the reform. If the number of prisoners keeps on rising, new political instruments will be needed to counteract this undesirable development.

References

Birklbauer, A. (2008) 'Die Neuregelung der bedingten Entlassung. Ein versuchter Kompromiss zwischen Resozialisierung, Sicherheit und Vollzugsentlassung', *Österreichische Juristenzeitung*, 710–17.

Bittmann, K.-P. (2008) 'Bedingte Entlassung aus einer Freiheitsstrafe nach § 46 StGB idF des Strafrechtsänderungsgesetzes 2008', *Richterzeitung*, 247–8.

Fuchs, H. (2005) 'Vollzug und Entlassung im Gesamtsystem strafrechtlicher Sanktionierung', *Juristische Blätter*, 153–8.

Grafl, C., Gratz, W., Höpfel, F., Hovorka, C., Pilgram, A., Scholl, V. and Soyer, R. (2004) 'Kriminalpolitische Initiative, Mehr Sicherheit durch weniger Haft!', *Journal für Rechtspolitik*, 61–6.

Gratz, W. (2006) 'Zur Situation und Einschätzung des Justizvollzuges in Österreich', *Richterzeitung*, 222–5.

Hirtenlehner, H. and Birklbauer, A. (2008) 'Rückfallsprävention durch Entlassungspolitik? Ein natürliches Experiment', *Neue Kriminalpolitik*, 1: 25–32.

Kollmann, L. (2008) 'Erfahrungsbericht zur Bedingten Entlassung neu und § 133a StVG', *Juridicum*, 156–9.

Miklau, R. (2005) 'Rechtsgrundlagen im Wandel der Zeit', in Bundesministerium für Justiz (ed.) *Moderner Strafvollzug: Sicherheit und Resozialisierung. Schriftenreihe Band 122*. Vienna/Graz: Neuer Wissenschaftlicher Verlag.

Pilgram, A. (2005) 'Die Praxis der (bedingten) Strafentlassung im regionalen Vergleich: Befunde auf neuer statistischer Grundlage', in Bundesministerium für Justiz (ed.) *Moderner Strafvollzug: Sicherheit und Resozialisierung. Schriftenreihe Band 122*. Vienna/Graz: Neuer Wissenschaftlicher Verlag.

Table 3.1 Annexe: length of prison term and release mechanism

The following table shows the figures for releases of sentenced prisoners (including prisoners held in preventive detention according to ss. 21 and 22 of öStGB – mentally ill or drug addicted) in different categories of length of prison term and for 2008.

Duration of sentence (according to verdict)	End of sentence	Conditional release from prison sentence	Amnesty/ pardon	Extra-dition	Fine paid	Suspension because of drug therapy	Suspension because of leaving the country (öStVG s. 133a)	Release from preventive detention	Court decision	Other	Total
Up to 1 month	865	1	2	4	108	5			72	11	1,068
%	81.0	0.1	0.2	0.4	10.1	0.5			6.7	1.0	100
1–3 months	1,356	67	127	2	59	2			34	21	1,668
%	81.3	4.0	7.6	0.1	3.5	0.1			2.0	1.3	100
3–6 months	657	547	150	4	30	8	10		13	16	1,435
%	45.8	38.1	10.5	0.3	2.1	0.6	0.7		0.9	1.1	100
6 months–1 year	469	676	78	6	2	13	51		9	24	1,328
%	35.3	50.9	5.9	0.5	0.2	1.0	3.8		0.7	1.8	100
1–3 years	725	891	113	50	2	101	241		8	47	2,178
%	33.3	40.9	5.2	2.3	0.1	4.6	11.1		0.4	2.2	100
3–5 years	163	254	14	33		11	38		15	30	556
%	29.3	45.7	2.5	5.9		2.0	6.7		2.7	5.4	100
5–10 years	62	124		32		2			13	7	242
%	25.6	51.2		13.2		0.8			5.4	2.9	100
10–20 years	15	27		5					3	1	51
%	29.4	52.9		9.8					5.9	2.0	100
> 20 years	2	2							0	1	5
%	40.0	40.0							0.0	20.0	100
Life-long sentence	0	6							1	1	8
%	0.0	75.0							12.5	12.5	100
Preventive detention (öStGB ss. 21 and 22)	14	7	0	1				93	9	11	135
%	10.4	5.2	0.0	0.7				68.9	6.7	8.1	100
Total	4,328	2,602	484	137	201	142	340	93	177	170	8,674
%	49.9	30.0	5.6	1.6	2.3	1.6	3.9	1.1	2.0	2.0	100

Chapter 4

Belgium

Sonja Snacken, Kristel Beyens and Marie-Aude Beernaert

Summary

The current system of early release in Belgium can best be summarized schematically (see Table 4.1).

Table 4.1 Early release in Belgium, 2009

Sentence	Mode of early release	Decision-maker
All sentences	Individual pardon	King
All sentences	Collective pardon	King
Sentences of up to three years	Provisional release	Minister of Justice/ Prison Administration
Sentences of more than three years	Conditional release	Sentence Implementation Court
Placement at the government's disposal	Conditional release	Minister of Justice

Note: This scheme is based on penal practice in 2009, which differs from the most recent legislation of 2006 and 2007 that, as is explained in the text, is not yet fully implemented.

1. Current legal criteria for the early release of sentenced prisoners[1]

1.1 Forms of early release and definitions

Release from prison can take many forms, ranging from a day's leave for a few hours, to systematic prison leave of 3 × 36 hours per trimester, to semi-detention or electronic monitoring which allows the prisoner even more freedom, to diverse forms of early release where the prisoner returns to society for good unless the measure is revoked for failure to comply with the conditions imposed or because of recidivism. While temporary forms of release are increasingly seen in Belgium as important transitional measures in order to prepare for early release, this chapter deals predominantly with the latter forms of early release.

Following Recommendation (2003)22 on Conditional Release of the Council of Europe, we define early release as all forms of the release of sentenced prisoners before they have served their full sentence, while the terms 'conditional release' or 'parole' are reserved for forms of early release which are or can be accompanied by individualized post-release conditions imposed on the prisoner, other than not to commit new crimes.

There are two major conditional release systems in Belgium, depending on the duration of the imprisonment to which the prisoner has been sentenced: prisoners sentenced to a maximum of three years' imprisonment (who represent the vast majority of prisoners in Belgium) are eligible to provisional release (*liberation provisoire/ voorlopige invrijheidstelling*), whereas prisoners sentenced to more than three years' imprisonment can benefit from conditional release or parole (*liberation conditionnelle/voorwaardelijke invrijheidstelling*).

In addition to their prison sentence, some individuals may also have been 'placed at the government's disposal' for a period of time varying from five to twenty years, according to the nature of the case. This is an additional penalty that may (or, in some cases, must) be imposed on recidivists and/or sex offenders according to the provisions of the Social Protection Act 1964, as amended by the Acts of 1990, 1998 and 2007. It becomes operative only when the principal sentence of imprisonment has been served and may then be

[1]This chapter deals with the early release of sentenced prisoners only, and not with release procedures for mentally-ill offenders under an indeterminate measure of 'internment', nor with the conditional early release possibilities for remand prisoners.

implemented either by way of an additional period of the deprivation of liberty or by way of a conditional release.

Finally, sentenced prisoners may see their sentence reduced through pardon by the King, which may also result in early release with conditions.

All four measures (provisional release for prisoners sentenced to up to three years' imprisonment, release on parole for prisoners sentenced to more than three years' imprisonment, conditional release for persons placed at the government's disposal and pardon by the King) are submitted to specific criteria (see sections 1.2–1.5) and decided following specific procedures (see section 2). Recall procedures are also different (see section 3).

1.2   Provisional release of prisoners sentenced to up to three years' imprisonment

According to Ministerial Circular 1771 of 17 January 2005,[2] the criteria applied to determine whether prisoners will be granted provisional release vary depending on the duration of the prison sentence concerned.

Prisoners sentenced to a maximum of one year's imprisonment benefit from a mandatory release system, since there is only a time condition to fulfil and no risk assessment is involved. These prisoners benefit from provisional release:

- immediately[3] if they are sentenced to a maximum of six months' imprisonment;
- after one month's detention if they are sentenced to a maximum of seven months' imprisonment;
- after two months' detention if they are sentenced to a maximum of eight months' imprisonment; or
- after three months' detention if they are sentenced to a maximum of one year's imprisonment.

Prisoners sentenced to more than one year but a maximum of three years' imprisonment, on the other hand, may benefit from provisional

[2]Provisional release has never been regulated by any statutory provision but is an administrative measure that has been set out in a number of ministerial instructions. The latest one, which is applicable at present, is Ministerial Circular 1771 of 17 January 2005.
[3]They therefore do not serve even one single day of their sentence in prison.

release after having served a third of their sentence.[4] This system, however, may be described as a discretionary one, for the benefit of the measure is here subordinated to the additional prerequisite of the absence of counter-indications. These counter-indications relate to whether it is possible for the prisoners to provide for their material needs, to the possible serious risk they represent for others' integrity or – but only for those sentenced for the sexual abuse of minors – to the risk that they may harass their victim(s). In these cases, individual conditions or guidance can be imposed, if deemed necessary by the Prison Administration.

1.3   Conditional release of prisoners sentenced to more than three years' imprisonment[5]

According to Arts. 25, 47 and 48 of the 2006 Act on the External Legal Position of the Sentenced Prisoner and the Rights of the Victims, three major conditions need to be fulfilled for a prisoner to be released on parole.

Firstly, a minimum period of detention must be served before a person may apply for parole. Sentenced prisoners who are not 'legal recidivists' may be granted release on parole after having served a third of their prison sentence or, in case of life imprisonment, ten years of that sentence. 'Legal recidivists', on the other hand, must serve at least two thirds of their prison sentence (with a maximum of 14 years), or 16 years for life imprisonment, before being eligible for release on parole.[6] Secondly, the prisoner has to present a 'reintegration plan' which shows his willingness to reintegrate into the community and establishes the efforts he has already made in this regard. Thirdly, there must be no counter-indications. Four different counter-

[4]Even if they were condemned as recidivists (i.e. the threshold of two thirds applicable in cases of conditional release does not apply; see section 1.3).
[5]The official term is 'prisoners whose remaining sentence to be implemented exceeds three years'. This three-year period can therefore be the result of a combination of several shorter sentences.
[6]'Legal recidivism' is defined according to Arts. 54–56 of the Criminal Code as recidivism by the commission of a felony (that is, an offence punishable with a sentence of five years' imprisonment or more: *crime/misdaad*), after an earlier sentence for a felony or for a misdemeanour (that is, an offence punishable with sentences of from seven days' up to five years' or in certain cases up to ten years' imprisonment: *délit/wanbedrijf*), after an earlier sentence for a felony.

indications are mentioned in the 2006 Act: the absence of possibilities of the prisoner's reintegration; the risk he will commit new, serious offences; the risk he will harass the victims; or, more generally, the prisoner's attitude towards the victim(s) of the offence(s) for which he has been sentenced.

The 2006 Act clearly states that the prisoner who fulfils all the conditions shall be released, thus emphasizing conditional release as a subjective right (Snacken 2004: 56–7; Pieters 2001: 429; 2010). However, the second and third conditions imposed are so wide-ranging and require so much interpretation that one could describe the system as being a discretionary one.

1.4 Conditional release of persons placed at the government's disposal

According to Art. 25(a) of the Social Protection Act 1964, the decision to further deprive persons placed at the government's disposal of their liberty may be taken either when, at the expiry of the principal sentence of imprisonment, their return to society seems to be impossible or when their behaviour in freedom poses a threat to society. If these conditions are not met, the offender should, on the contrary, be conditionally released, but considering the wide measure of discretion involved in deciding about such conditions one should, here again, speak rather about a discretionary release system.

1.5 Pardon by the King

The King has supreme authority to pardon. Pardon applies to final sentences in which a penalty was imposed; preventive measures and civil decisions are excluded. There are no other conditions or procedures to be followed by the King. A pardon may be requested by any person, and the consent of the convicted person or the Public Prosecutor is not required.

A pardon results in the total or partial remission of the penalty, or its replacement by a less severe penalty. A penalty of imprisonment can thus result in early release from prison. A pardon can be individual or collective. Collective pardons used to be granted on the occasion of national events (for example, royal weddings or birthdays). A pardon can be granted conditionally, which means that the decision to pardon can depend on certain conditions being met by the sentenced offender (Beernaert 2007a: 62–7).

2. Types of decision-making

2.1 Provisional release of prisoners sentenced to up to three years' imprisonment

Provisional release is normally decided by the local Prison Governor, except for those inmates sentenced to more than one year's imprisonment for the sexual abuse of minors. In these cases the decision is taken by the Minister of Justice. Prison governors assess for the presence of counter-indications for prisoners serving imprisonment of between one and three years, and for the need for additional individual guidance or conditions.

There is no hearing for the sentenced person and/or the victim, and nor is the prisoner entitled to make a complaint to a higher decision-making authority.[7] A decision to refuse provisional release should, however, state the reasons on which it was based.

2.2 Conditional release of prisoners sentenced to more than three years' imprisonment

Since February 2007, conditional release is decided upon by 'Sentence Implementation Courts' (*Tribunal d'application des peines/ Strafuitvoeringsrechtbank*), the successors to the former 'Parole Commissions' (see section 4). These courts take a reasoned decision after having heard the Public Prosecutor, the Prison Governor and the prisoner. The prisoner may be assisted by a lawyer and has access to his file before the hearing. The courts will also hear the victims when they request this. This hearing, however, considers only the conditions that should be imposed in the victim's interest.

If release on parole is not granted, a date will be fixed by the Sentence Implementation Court to reconsider the case after a maximum of six months (if the sentences served do not exceed five

---

[7]Civil jurisdictions refuse to consider such cases since the prisoners do not have a subjective right to benefit from provisional release (Civ. Bruxelles [réf.], 25 June 1999, *Journal des Tribunaux*, 2000, p. 204). As for the Council of State (*Conseil d'Etat/Raad van State*), the Supreme Administrative Court declares inadmissible all complaints directed against decisions by which the Minister of Justice (or a prison governor) directly contributes to implementing judgments delivered by the judiciary. This criterion is applied since the case De Smedt (no. 116.899), decided in general assembly by the Council of State on 11 March 2003.

years) or one year (if they do exceed five years). An appeal may, besides, be lodged against the Court's decisions before the Court of Cassation, but only on points of law. The transfer of authority from the Minister of Justice first to multidisciplinary 'Parole Commissions' and then to multidisciplinary 'Sentence Implementation Courts' is supposed to enhance the independence and expertise of the decision-making (see section 4).

2.3 Conditional release of persons placed at the government's disposal

On the expiration of the principal penalty, it is up to the Minister of Justice to decide how the additional penalty of being placed at the government's disposal shall be implemented (Art. 25 of the Social Protection Act 1964).

No hearing of the sentenced person is provided for, but he is entitled to make a complaint to a judicial authority against the decision to keep him detained. This decision may be challenged, in the first instance, before the Council Chamber (*chambre du conseil/raadkamer*) and, on appeal, before the Indictments Chamber (*Chambre des mises en accusation/kamer van inbeschuldigingstelling*) (Arts. 25(b) and 26(a) of the Social Protection Act as amended by the 1990 Act).[8] These challenges, however, are limited to the sole question of whether the Minister's decision was in compliance with the law and do not permit the reassessment of the appropriateness of the refusal to grant conditional release.

If the person remains detained on the sole basis of his placement at the government's disposal, he is entitled to ask the Minister of Justice each year to reconsider a conditional release. The prisoner has the same opportunity each time to challenge the decision, first, before the Council Chamber and, on appeal, before the Indictment Chamber (Art. 25(c) of the Social Protection Act).

According to the 2007 Act, the decision-making power in this matter should pass from the Minister of Justice to the Sentence Implementation Courts, but the implementation of that Act has been postponed to January 2012 due to the overburdening of the new Sentence Implementation Courts.

---

[8]The 1990 Act was mainly aimed at complying with the judgment of the European Court of Human Rights in the case of *Van Droogenbroeck* v. *Belgium* (1982) 4 EHRR 443.

2.4 Pardon by the King

As pardon is a prerogative of the King, there is no compulsory procedure to be followed. The King enjoys civil and penal immunity, but his decisions are taken under the responsibility of the Minister of Justice. Advice is usually required from the Public Prosecutor who prosecuted the case, as well as from the Prison Governor, if the convicted person is already being detained.

3. Recall procedures

3.1 Provisional release of prisoners sentenced to up to three years' imprisonment

Except for those sentenced to a maximum of six months' imprisonment, provisional release may be revoked (as long as the execution of the sentence is not time-barred) by the same decision-making authority which granted the measure (Governor of the prison concerned or Minister of Justice) under two distinct circumstances. When the person concerned:

- is sentenced for a new offence committed after the provisional release; or
- fails to observe the imposed conditions.

No specific procedural safeguards are to be respected before the decision to revoke is taken, nor can this decision be challenged before a higher decision-making authority.

3.2 Conditional release of prisoners sentenced to more than three years' imprisonment

Conditional release may be revoked by the Sentence Implementation Court, upon request by the Public Prosecutor, in several circumstances. When the person concerned:

- is sentenced for a new offence committed after his release on parole;
- seriously jeopardizes the physical or psychic integrity of others;
- fails to comply with the imposed conditions; or

- does not respond to appointments with the 'justice assistant' (previously 'probation officer': *assistant de justice/justitieassistent*)[9] or does not inform him or her of any change of address.

In all these cases, however, the Court may also decide to make the previously-imposed conditions stricter instead of revoking the release on parole. Its reasoned decision is taken after having heard the Public Prosecutor, the person concerned (who may be assisted by a lawyer and receives access to his file before the hearing) and even the victim insofar as the request is based on non-compliance with conditions specifically imposed in their interests. An appeal may be lodged against the Court's decisions before the Court of Cassation but, once again, only on points of law.

3.3 Conditional release of persons placed at the government's disposal

A decision to revoke the conditional release of a person placed at the government's disposal may be taken by the Minister of Justice for as long as this additional penalty is in force, whenever the Minister considers that the person's behaviour in freedom poses a threat to society. No specific procedural safeguards are to be respected before the revocation decision is taken, but this decision may, once again, be challenged, in the first instance, before the Council Chamber and, on appeal, before the Indictments Chamber.

4. History

Conditional release and provisional release are the most important forms of the early release of sentenced prisoners and have undergone important changes over the last years. We will therefore only briefly deal with pardon by the King.

[9]In 1999 probation officers officially became 'justice assistants'. This name change was the result of a general reorganization of the probation agencies and the establishment of 'Houses of Justice' in each jurisdiction. This reorganization has to be understood within a broader political attempt to regain legitimacy by taking the para-judicial agencies out of the often alienating court buildings and bringing them closer to the public. After having been part of the Directorate General of the Judicial Order and then the Directorate General of the Prison and Probation Administration, they became a separate Directorate General of the Houses of Justice within the Ministry of Justice on 1 January 2007 in order to enhance their professional status and organizational legitimacy.

4.1 Pardon by the king

Pardons were an important tool of Belgian penal policy until the mid-1990s. Examples include the former automatic pardon of death sentences commuted into life sentences (until the abolition of the death penalty by an Act of 1996), the provisional release of short-term prisoners 'in view of pardon' (see section 4.3) and the use of collective pardons to relieve prison overcrowding between 1980 and 1993 (see section 5, Table 4.2). This changed, however, with the accession in 1993 of Albert II. Despite continuing overcrowding, no collective pardons have been granted since his accession as he considered this to be a misuse of his prerogative, and the number of individual pardons has also dwindled (Snacken 2001).

4.2 Conditional release or parole

The parole system was introduced by an Act of 1888 and was thoroughly reformed by legislation in 1998 and 2006.

4.2.1 1888–1998

Under the Act of 1888, parole was granted by the Minister of Justice following an administrative procedure. First, the initiative was taken by the Minister, the Prison Governor or the 'Administrative Commission' (a supervisory body of the prison made up of external visitors). An initial selection was then performed by a 'conference of the prison staff' (the local Prison Board: governor, chief guard, psychiatrist and/or psychologist, social worker, religious representative). Advice was provided by the Administrative Commission and the Public Prosecutor who prosecuted the case. Finally, all this information was collected and summarized by the Central Prison Administration, which formulated advice to the Minister, who then took the final decision. Prisoners were eligible for parole after serving at least a third of their sentence (two thirds for recidivists) and a minimum of three months (six for recidivists); life-sentence prisoners were eligible after serving at least ten years (14 years for recidivists). Additional criteria were originally the 'reform' of the prisoner, as seen from his 'moral evolution', and his behaviour in prison (1888 Act; Royal Decree 1921). This was changed into so-called 'negative selection' in 1981 (Ministerial Circular 20 May 1981): a prisoner was entitled to parole unless specific counter-indications existed (for example, the prisoner's personality, his lack of responsibility or the availability of means of support). The parolee was subjected to supervision for a period which was at least equal to the remaining term of imprisonment, but with a minimum of two years for misdemeanours (*délits/wanbedrijven*), five years for felonies (*crimes/misdaden*) and ten years for life sentences, in which general and specific conditions were imposed. This means that, depending on the moment of release, the period of supervision could exceed the term of the sentence imposed.

This system had long been criticized, especially with regard to the lack of judicial guarantees for the prisoner, resulting in long periods of uncertainty concerning the eventual date of release, and the changing – increasingly restrictive – policies of each Minister of Justice (especially concerning violent, drug and sexual offences) (Tubex and Snacken 1999). Academics argued in favour of a transfer of the authority to decide on early release in all its forms from the Minister to an independent judicial body (Eliaerts and Rozie 1978; Eliaerts 1980), but a first attempt to introduce Sentence Implementation Courts in 1985 (Legros 1985) failed to gather political support. Small procedural changes were introduced in 1991, leading to the obligation for the 'conference of prison staff' to hear the prisoner and the possibility for his legal counsel to be heard by the Administrative Commission. The proportion of releases on parole represented a maximum of 18.4 per cent of releases of sentenced prisoners in 1990, but this steadily dwindled afterwards (see section 5, Table 4.2).

These criticisms were taken up in the 'White Paper on Penal and Prison Policy' produced by Minister of Justice, S. De Clerck, in June 1996. This White Paper criticized, among many other things, the lack of procedural transparency and of effective follow-up in conditional release cases and the lack of treatment of certain categories of prisoners, such as sex and drug offenders. Over the last 30 years, many initiatives had been taken by the Prison Administration and the Minister of Justice to open up the prisons to the outside world and to foster diverse forms of transitions from detention to liberty, such as systematic prison leave, semi-detention and early release. However, these privileges increased strongly the discretionary power of the Prison Administration and led to criticisms that the Executive Power was taking over competences that constitutionally belonged to the judiciary. Professor Lieven Dupont, a highly regarded academic from the University of Leuven, was commissioned to draft a new Prison Act that would reinforce the internal (relating to all aspects of life inside prison) and external (relating to all forms of interruption of detention and early release) legal position of prisoners and that would introduce Sentence Implementation Courts to deal with the latter (for a discussion of this distinction, see section 4.2.3).

However, in August 1996, the infamous Dutroux case, involving the alleged abduction, rape and murder of several children and young girls while the suspect was under parole, shocked society in Belgium and abroad. Expressions of popular solidarity with the victims erupted, resulting in a petition with 2.7 million signatures (from a population of 10 million) asking for the abolition of conditional release for very serious crimes, and a 'White March' through Brussels in October 1996 with 300,000 participants, both organized by victim-support movements. The aspects in the White Paper relating to the treatment of sex offenders and the problems of conditional release were therefore given immediate priority (Snacken 2007a).

A political agreement among all democratic parties, including the opposition parties (the 'Octopus agreement'), established the main principles of reforms needed to tackle these failures and to recover public trust in the criminal justice system: the reinforcement of the legal position of victims; the reinforcement of follow-up and control over parolees; and the transfer of the authority to decide on, to control and to recall conditional releases to independent multidisciplinary Sentence Implementation Courts. The transfer from the Minister of Justice to the courts was meant to reinforce the independence of the decision-making, while the choice of a multidisciplinary court was seen as a necessary condition for improving the quality of the decision-making, which required a combination of legal reasoning and expertise in social reintegration and the effects of the deprivation of liberty. However, this latter required a change to the Constitution,[10] which necessitate a parliamentary procedure spread over two legislatures. In the meantime, a transitional system was introduced by the Acts of 5 and 18 March 1998.

4.2.2 1998–2007

The Acts of 5 and 18 March 1998 reinforced not only the legal position of victims but also of prisoners in the parole procedure, and the authority to decide on conditional release was transferred from the Minister of Justice to 'Parole Commissions'. These were

[10]All courts in Belgium are composed of professional judges who are trained lawyers appointed for life, with the exception of the Court of Assizes, where lay jurors judge the most serious crimes together with professional judges (art. 150 of the Constitution), and the labour courts and the commercial courts, which also include lay judges (art. 157 of the Constitution). The creation of new multidisciplinary courts for the implementation of sentences therefore required an amendment to art. 157 of the Constitution.

multidisciplinary commissions, including an expert in social reintegration and an expert in prison matters, and headed by an acting judge. A public prosecutor was appointed to each of the six 'Parole Commissions'.

Despite demands from opposition parties to increase the proportion of time to be served by all prisoners before being eligible for parole, the existing proportions of one third of the sentence (two thirds for legal recidivists) and ten years for lifers (14 years for legal recidivists) were maintained. Each eligible prisoner was now entitled to have his case examined and to be informed of the result. If the local Prison Board advised negatively, the procedure was halted. Only after three negative decisions by the Prison Board could the prisoner file action directly with the Parole Commission. Each prisoner heard by the Commission was entitled to legal representation.

The issue of victims' rights and interests had become politically highly sensitive since 1996, following massive public empathy and support for the young victims and their families in the Dutroux case. A temporary procedure was introduced by the end of 1996 in order to inform the victims of serious crimes of the offender's eligibility and possibility for conditional release, and to consult them on possible conditions to be attached to eventual release (Tubex and Snacken 1999). During parliamentary discussions on the draft legislation on parole, the right-wing extremist Vlaams Blok Party demanded that victim organizations of parents who lost their children through crime, such as the organizations Marc and Corinne, and Parents of a Murdered Child, should be heard concerning the acceptability of maintaining the possibility of conditional release for serious offenders and the proportion of the sentence to be served. Contrary to that party's expectations, the four victim organizations produced an impressively-nuanced joint paper, expressing their immense grief and trauma but recognizing that retribution should not be the sole purpose of punishment, and accepting that the victim's interests should be balanced with the interests of the offender and of society at large. They accepted the possibility of conditional release, even for the most serious offences, on the condition that the period of detention would be used constructively in order to tackle the reasons for the crimes committed so as to enhance victims' safety in the long term. As long as this was not the case, release after a third of the sentence was considered too early, and they demanded that this proportion be increased to two thirds. They also demanded that victims who so wished should be informed about the possibility of the offender's early release and so could provide their views on the matter.

The political result was an attempt to keep the balance between the interests of victims, the offender and society – a compromise between reintegration and incapacitation (Snacken 2001; 2007a). The proportion of the sentence (a third or two thirds) to be served was maintained for all offenders, but the criteria for granting and revoking parole were made stricter and related to the prisoner's personality, his possibilities for reintegration (which he must himself actively prepare; Art. 2(2) of the 5 March 1998 Act), his behaviour in prison, his risk of recidivism and his attitude towards his victim(s) (Art. 2(3)). Sex offenders could be released on parole only following a report by a team of experts and if they agreed, upon release, to enter treatment in a specialized centre. Moreover, authority for the judge to impose the special preventive detention of 'placement at the disposal at the government' for ten years (20 years for legal recidivists) was introduced for sex offenders. A massive increase in the staffing levels of the psychosocial services of local prisons was effected in order to perform the necessary diagnoses and prognoses of the risks of recidivism (120 psychologists for 32 prisons), and some of the psychosocial services staff were trained to perform specific risk assessments for sex offenders (see, however, section 6.1).

The provisional procedure for informing victims, which had been introduced after the Dutroux case, was further developed in the new legislation. Victims of serious violent or sexual crimes now had to be informed about the offender's eligibility for parole and the start of the parole procedure. Other victims could ask to be informed if the offender was sentenced to at least one year of imprisonment. The victims could ask to be heard by the Parole Commission, but only on the question of whether specific parole conditions could be ordered in their interests, not on the decision to release the prisoner. The request by the victims' associations for the Parole Commission to include an expert member on victim issues was not adopted by Parliament (Snacken 2001; 2007a).

The Parole Commissions came into effect on 1 March 1999.

4.2.3 Since 2007

From 1999 to 2000, an 'external legal position' for prisoners and Sentence Implementation Courts were elaborated by a commission of practitioners and academics (the Holsters Commission, named after its President). This continued the work done by the Dupont Commission (named after its President), establishing an internal legal position for prisoners which led to the Prison Act 2005. While a distinction can formally be made between the 'internal' legal position of prisoners (relating to all aspects of life inside prison) and the 'external' legal position (relating to all forms of interruption of detention and early release), both areas interact with each other and should be congruent and consistent in their aims. The official aims of the implementation of a prison sentence having been defined in the Prison Act 2005 as harm reduction, reintegration, rehabilitation and reparation, both the internal prison regime and the different forms of temporary or early release should be attuned to these goals (Snacken 2004).

The development of contacts with the outside world, of education, prison labour and vocational training within the internal prison regime can help the prisoner to prepare successfully for his reintegration after release, while the introduction of day leave, systematic prison leave, semi-detention and electronic monitoring by the Prison Administration has transformed a sentence of imprisonment from the full-time deprivation of liberty in the strictest sense to different 'degrees of freedom' (Tulkens 1988; van Zyl Smit and Snacken 2009), which are also meant to sustain a successful transition from prison to liberty.[11]

This led over the years to divergent opinions on which decisions should be left to the Prison Administration and which should be transferred to the Sentence Implementation Courts. Contrary to earlier proposals which argued in favour of a transfer of all decisions involving some kind of release from prison to an independent court (Eliaerts and Rozie 1978; Dupont 1998), the Holsters Commission, eventually followed by Parliament, argued that day leave and systematic prison leave should be regarded as normal elements of a prison regime, which do not legally interrupt the prison term and should therefore be left to the Prison Administration, while other forms (such as semi-detention or electronic monitoring) fundamentally change the nature of imprisonment and should be decided by an independent authority.

Both aspects, of course, remain intertwined: the prisoner's successful completion of a series of prison leaves is an important element for the Sentence Implementation Courts in assessing the risks involved in releasing a prisoner. Because such leave may have been refused by the Prison Administration for a variety of reasons, ranging from internal conflicts with the prisoner to political sensitivity

[11]Contrary to the practice in some other European countries, the application of these forms of temporary or early release does not require the previous transfer of the prisoner from a closed to an open institution.

in cases with a high profile in the media, the 2006 Act provides for the possibility of the Sentence Implementation Courts to grant such prison leave themselves to prisoners who are eligible for another form of temporary or early release, such as electronic monitoring or conditional release.

After the necessary constitutional amendments, the 2006 Act transformed the Parole Commissions into Sentence Implementation Courts, which started functioning from 1 February 2007. There are now nine Sentence Implementation Courts, whose composition is multidisciplinary and comparable with the former Parole Commissions. The 2006 Act has enlarged their competence to include all forms of early release (semi-detention, electronic monitoring, provisional and conditional release) for all prisoners, irrespective of the length of their sentence. This means that, in theory, they should also decide on the provisional release of prisoners serving sentences of less than three years. However, as about 80 per cent of the prisoners released from prison every year are released under the provisional release system (see section 5), the transfer of the much swifter decision-making from the Prison Governor to the complex procedure of the Sentence Implementation Court would have had a disastrous effect on prison overcrowding, which is already creating numerous problems for prisoners and staff in Belgian prisons. This part of the Act has therefore been postponed to September 2012.

As a result, the system of conditional release is applicable in practice only to prisoners who are serving a sentence of more than three years. Conditional release is still possible after serving a third of the sentence (two thirds for recidivists) and ten years for life sentences (but 16 years now instead of 14 for recidivists). The local Prison Governor has to submit an advisory report to the Sentence Implementation Court and to the Public Prosecutor of the Court between four and two months before the prisoner is eligible for parole, including a reasoned proposal concerning the granting or refusal of the release and the appropriate individual conditions to be imposed. The Public Prosecutor sends his advisory report within one month to the Sentence Implementation Court. The possibility for the local prison to halt the procedure three times has been abolished, and the counter-indications have been slightly altered. The Act now also states that a prisoner who fulfils all the conditions must be released (see, however, section 6). The period of supervision lasts for at least the remainder of the prison sentence with a minimum period of two years, between five and ten years if the prisoner is serving sentences totalling more than five years, and ten years for life-sentence prisoners

(Art. 71). The period of supervision can therefore be longer than the remaining prison sentence.

The victims' rights to be informed and told about the appropriate victim-related conditions to be imposed have been extended to all forms of temporary or early release. In order to reinforce the symbolic importance of these changes, Parliament altered the title of the 2006 Act ('On the External Legal Position of Sentenced Prisoners') by adding 'and the Rights of the Victims in the Framework of Modalities of Implementation of Sentences' (Beernaert 2007b: 12; Daems 2007).

The authority to decide upon the special preventive detention of 'placement at the government's disposal' has theoretically been transferred by the Act of 2007 from the Minister of Justice to the Sentence Implementation Courts, and this measure has been renamed 'Placement at the disposal of the Sentence Implementation Court'. This transfer of authority has, however, been postponed until January 2012 due to the overburdening of the Sentence Implementation Courts (Verpoest and Vander Beken 2007).

4.3 Provisional release

Provisional release started as an administrative measure by the Prison Administration and was regulated by Ministerial Circulars. There were four types of provisional release: the provisional release of prisoners serving sentences of up to three years; of foreign prisoners with a view to their expulsion; for humanitarian reasons; and with a view to parole (Snacken, 2001). All forms of provisional release have in theory been transferred to the authority of the Sentence Implementation Courts by the 2006 Act. However, as lack of staff and finance would result in delays in decision-making and would increase prison overcrowding, this transfer has been temporarily suspended until 2012[12] for the release of prisoners serving sentences of less than three years. In practice, therefore, the provisional release of these prisoners is still decided by the Prison Administration, as is the provisional release of foreign prisoners serving less than three years' imprisonment.

4.3.1 Provisional release of prisoners serving sentences of up to three years
Parole had always been hampered for short-term prisoners by the length and complexity of the procedure. Hence the Prison Administration introduced in 1972 an 'alternative' early release for prisoners serving sentences of up to one year, which was called

[12]But this date could be changed again.

'provisional release with a view to pardon'. This was originally an individual decision which led to an individual pardon. Pressured by increasing overcrowding, the Prison Administration applied this tool more systematically and collectively from 1983 onwards, releasing all prisoners sentenced to up to one year after serving part of their sentence. In 1994 the application was broadened to sentences of up to three years, but the same counter-indications were used as for parole (see above). These provisional releases were renamed 'provisional releases for reasons of overcrowding', and represent more than 80 per cent of the total number of releases today (see section 5, Table 4.2).

4.3.2. Provisional release of foreign prisoners with a view to their expulsion

The same measure can be applied to foreign prisoners who do not have a legal residence permit and who will thus be expelled (1997: 3.8 per cent of releases; 2007: 6 per cent). 'Foreign' prisoners in Belgium are defined as all prisoners not having Belgian nationality. Their proportion in incarcerations ('flow') rose from 25 per cent in 1980 to 45 per cent in 1991, and their proportion in the average prison population ('stock') doubled from 21 per cent in 1980, to 40 per cent to the 1990s and 44 per cent in 2004, a figure that has remained constant since then (an index of 319 compared with 117 for Belgian nationals) (Beyens et al. 1993; Snacken et al. 2004; Snacken 2007b; Beyens 2008).

This definition, however, covers different categories. As a rule, only foreigners who are suspected of having committed an offence or who have been convicted will be imprisoned. Belgian prisons contained prisoners of no fewer than 104 nationalities in 2003, from every continent. In 2004, 76 per cent of these had no legal residence permit, 21 per cent were second- or third-generation immigrants who had not acquired Belgian nationality, and 10 per cent came from neighbouring countries (Snacken et al. 2004). In 2007, the majority were Moroccans (25 per cent of all foreign prisoners), followed by people from Eastern European countries (20 per cent) – a category that is growing rapidly – and from Western European countries (19 per cent). This growing group of foreign prisoners is confronted with many problems in respect of preparation for their early release (see section 6.3).

4.3.3 Other forms of provisional release

Provisional release may also be granted in exceptional cases – for example, for health reasons (1997: 0.13 per cent). Provisional release with a view to parole can also be granted for special social or humane reasons (1997: 17.2 per cent of releases) (Snacken 2001).[13]

5. Statistical data

Data on early release in Belgium are fragmented and not always reliable (Beyens 2006; Tubex and Strypstein 2006; Maes 2010). However, some trends can be clearly discerned.

Since the mid-1980s there has been an important decline in the number of prisoners serving their full sentence in prison: from 87 per cent in 1974 to 70 per cent in 1980, to 30 per cent in 1991 and down to 3.7 per cent in 1997 (see Table 4.2, and Figure 4.1). In the last ten years, however, we see again a small but significant increase in prisoners serving their full sentence in prison, up to 6.1 per cent in 2007 (n = 460) (Maes 2010). This evolution is explained by Strypstein and Tubex (2004) and Robert (2009) by the increasingly complex and lengthy procedures of provisional and conditional release since 1998 for all offenders, and particularly for sex offenders. Confronted with highly-demanding conditions and a higher risk of recall (for sex offenders in the system of provisional release, see Strypstein and Tubex 2004), prisoners increasingly choose to serve their full sentence in prison in order to avoid lengthy and highly controlling supervision after their release, often for a period exceeding their sentence. While the increased control was introduced after the Dutroux case in order to protect the public better, it appears to have had the reverse effect in that the group of offenders who are most in need of a supervised transition to freedom are increasingly released without any supervision or guidance.

The decline of prisoners serving their full sentence in prison is due to the enlargement of the system of provisional release of prisoners serving sentences of less than one year (since 1972), to prisoners serving up to 18 months (in 1993) and then up to three years (since 1994). This enlargement of the system was intended to tackle prison overcrowding. Since 1993, about 80 per cent of all prisoners are released under the (administrative) system of provisional release (83 per cent in 2007). It has thus become the major form of early release in Belgium and has evolved from an individualized measure to a more automatic system (except for certain categories of offenders;

[13]Data from 1997 are used here because there are no recent data.

Table 4.2 Forms of early release of sentenced prisoners, 1974–2007

Modality of early release	1974	1980	1981	1982	1983	1984	1985	1986	1987	1988	1989	1990	1991	1992	1993	1994	1995	1996	1997	2003	2006	2007
Absolute numbers																						
Full sentence	7,252	5,955	5,934	5,846	5,827	5,580	5,631	5,178	2,543	783	2,984	1,863	2,064	161	88	82	142	167	195	411	342	420
Individual pardon	7	59	40	68	69	31	16	21	4	2	6	16	19	1	1	1	1	0	1		3	1
Collective pardon	0	924	118	16	4	238	478	14	3	169	69	169	358	5	87	0	0	0	0			
Conditional release	612	679	676	688	722	872	948	935	1,073	1,161	1,108	1,351	1,198	1,026	999	872	725	758	892		605	754
Provisional release	448	863	1,049	1,288	2,212	2,078	991	1,271	3,445	4,341	2,636	3,934	3,178	3,850	4,336	5,053	4,559	4,748	4,292		5,614	5,736
Total	8,319	8,480	7,817	7,906	8,834	8,799	8,064	7,419	7,068	6,456	6,803	7,333	6,817	5,043	5,511	6,008	5,427	5,673	5,380		6,564	6,911
Percentage																						
Full sentence	87.2	70.2	75.9	73.9	66.0	63.4	69.8	69.8	36.0	12.1	43.9	25.4	30.3	3.2	1.6	1.4	2.6	2.9	3.6		5.2	6.1
Individual pardon	0.1	0.7	0.5	0.9	0.8	0.4	0.2	0.3	0.1	0.0	0.1	0.2	0.3	0.0	0.0	0.0	0.0	0.0	0.0		0.0	0.0
Collective pardon	0.0	10.9	1.5	0.2	0.0	2.7	5.9	0.2	0.0	2.6	1.0	2.3	5.3	0.1	1.6	0.0	0.0	0.0	0.0		0.0	0.0
Conditional release	7.4	8.0	8.6	8.7	8.2	9.9	11.8	12.6	15.2	18.0	16.3	18.4	17.6	20.3	18.1	14.5	13.4	13.4	16.6		9.2	10.9
Provisional release	5.4	10.2	13.4	16.3	25.0	23.6	12.3	17.1	48.7	67.2	38.7	53.6	46.6	76.3	78.7	84.1	84.0	83.7	79.8		85.5	83.0
Total	100.0	100.0	100.0	100.0	100.0	100.0	100.0	100.0	100.0	100.0	100.0	100.0	100.0	100.0	100.0	100.0	100.0	100.0	100.0		100.0	100.0
Index (1980 = 100)																						
Full sentence	121.8	100.0	99.6	98.2	97.9	93.7	94.6	87.0	42.7	13.1	50.1	31.3	34.7	2.7	1.5	1.4	2.4	2.8	3.3		5.7	7.1
Individual pardon	11.9	100.0	67.8	115.3	116.9	52.5	27.1	35.6	6.8	3.4	10.2	27.1	32.2	1.7	1.7	1.7	1.7	0.0	1.7		5.1	1.7
Collective pardon	0.0	100.0	12.8	1.7	0.4	25.8	51.7	1.5	0.3	18.3	7.5	18.3	38.7	0.5	9.4	0.0	1.7	0.0	0.0		0.0	0.0
Conditional release	90.1	100.0	99.6	101.3	106.3	128.4	139.6	137.7	158.0	171.0	163.2	199.0	176.4	151.1	147.1	128.4	106.8	111.6	131.4		89.1	111.0
Provisional release	51.9	100.0	121.6	149.2	256.3	240.8	114.8	147.3	399.2	503.0	305.4	455.9	368.3	446.1	502.4	585.5	528.3	550.2	497.3		650.5	664.7
Total	98.1	100.0	92.2	93.2	104.2	103.8	95.1	87.5	83.3	76.1	80.2	86.5	80.4	59.5	65.0	70.8	64.0	66.9	63.4		77.4	81.5

Source: Maes (2010).
Notes
1. Data unavailable for certain years.
2. Percentages may not add up to 100 per cent due to rounding.

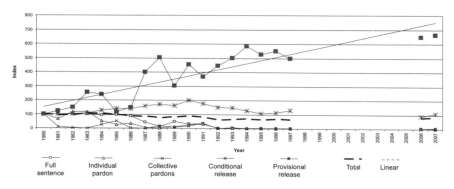

Figure 4.1 Evolution of early release of sentenced prisoners (indexes), 1980–97, 2006–07
Source: Maes (2010)

see above). It is mainly used by the Prison Administration as a means to relieve prison overcrowding. Separate times series for the different forms of provisional release are not available, but one category deserves special attention: the 'provisional release of foreign sentenced prisoners with a view to their expulsion'. In 2008, 324 foreign prisoners were released this way. The delays in the provisional release of foreigners serving sentences of more than three years are smaller than for conditional release, but still amount to an average of seven to eight months, with a high in 2004 of ten months (Deltenre 2008: 50, Table 14). This means that, where these prisoners are, on average, eligible for release after serving 38–40 per cent of their sentence, in practice between 48 and 55 per cent of the sentence is served.

Table 4.2 shows that collective pardons were used occasionally during the 1980s, also in order to reduce prison overcrowding. In 1980, for example, 924 prisoners (10 per cent) and, in 1985, 478 prisoners (5.9 per cent) were released earlier due to a collective pardon.

Although early release in Belgium is often associated with the system of conditional release, this form of release has never exceeded 20 per cent (1992: n = 1026) of the total number of releases. In 2007 only 10.9 per cent (n = 754) were released under conditional release. There is also an obvious relationship between provisional and conditional release. Since 1993 there has been a drop in the number of conditional releases, due to the enlargement of the provisional release system to sentences of up to three years: while only 24 per cent of prisoners serving sentences between one and three years were released provisionally in 1990, this number climbed to 73.5 per cent in 1998. As from 1994, conditional release was applied almost exclusively to sentences of more than three years (Deltenre 2008).

As noted earlier, the decision-making process for conditional release was changed twice (in 1998 and 2007). Under the former Act of 1888 (period 1888-1998), only positive propositions by the local Prison Board reached the Minister of Justice and, in the 1980s, more than 80 per cent of these proposals were followed by a positive decision by the Minister. However, ministerial decision-making was highly influenced by media coverage of incidents. In 1993, for example, positive decisions decreased significantly to 68 per cent, due to a stricter policy developed by the then Minister of Justice following a case of violent recidivism by drug offenders on prison leave and parole (Mary 1999). This ministerial practice, however, gradually recovered (82 per cent of proposals granted in 1997) (Beyens and Tubex 2002: 162, Figure 10).

Statistical data are available on the application of conditional release by the Parole Commissions under the Acts of 1998 (period 1999–2007), but not yet by the Sentence Implementation Courts under the new Act of 2006 (since February 2007). These data show that in the period 1999–2003, only 20 per cent of the prisoners successfully passed the first level of decision-making, which is the local Prison Board (Tubex and Strypstein 2006). Consequently, at least 80 per cent of prisoners served more than the legal minimum term, which largely qualifies the, at first sight, generous legal minimal term of a third of the sentence to be served by first offenders.[14] In general, the Parole Commissions granted parole between some 68 to 60 per cent of cases, and this percentage has declined over the years (see Table 4.3).

Table 4.3 also indicates that regional Parole Commissions varied in the proportion of granted conditional releases: for example, in 2004, 82 per cent in Antwerp, 39 per cent in Ghent and 51 per cent in Mons. The reasons for the geographical differences are not clear. They could be linked to different profiles of the respective prison populations, different policies of the local Prison Boards or a different way of application by the Parole Commissions.

It is obvious, though, that conditional release occurs increasingly late compared with the date of eligibility (Rihoux 2000; Tubex and Strypstein 2003/2005). The period that exceeds the eligibility date

[14]But the 20 per cent includes both first offenders and recidivists who have to serve two thirds of their sentence.

Table 4.3 Admission rate for conditional release per language (French, Dutch) and per Parole Commission, 1999–2004 (per cent)

	Year					
	1999	2000	2001	2002	2003	2004
Antwerp	90.0	88.4	80.6	79.0	79.4	82.0
Brussels–Dutch	77.2	66.0	69.7	62.7	70.8	62.8
Ghent	76.0	64.5	63.8	65.8	41.9	39.4
Brussels–French	63.6	54.5	59.6	61.8	67.6	63.3
Liège	54.8	51.3	47.5	49.2	51.0	57.9
Mons	42.7	59.4	58.5	41.8	49.2	51.4
Total	68.3	62.6	62.0	59.2	59.3	59.7
Dutch	80.6	72.6	71.7	69.2	63.6	63.2
French	54.3	54.8	56.1	52.0	56.2	57.4

has increased steadily from four to five months in 1990, to about eight months in 1999 (Rihoux 2000). Since then this 'surplus' period fluctuates continuously above ten months. In 2007, for example, prisoners with a sentence of more than three years served on average 14.5 months more than they should serve according to the law (Deltenre 2008: 50; Maes 2008: 9). As a result, figures for 2003–7 show that, on average, prisoners were released conditionally after serving 62 per cent of their terms, while they were eligible for parole after 45.7 per cent of their sentence (Deltenre 2008: 52, Table 15).

6. Challenges

6.1 Social reintegration as the aim of the implementation of sentences: theory and practice

The Prison Act 2005 and the 2006 Act on the External Legal Position of Prisoners are based on the principle of the relative autonomy of the aims of the implementation of sentences from sentencing. This reflects the different priorities at different stages in the criminal justice system. Whatever the aims may have been at the time of sentencing (retribution, general prevention, incapacitation), these cannot be considered automatically to determine the content of the imprisonment's execution (Dupont 1998: 135; Snacken 2004: 42; van Zyl Smit and Snacken 2009). Both new laws thus state that imprisonment and its relaxations should aim at limiting the detrimental effects of the deprivation of liberty, at reparation of the harm caused to victims and at the reintegration of prisoners into society. But what does this mean in practice?

Although the General Regulation of 1965 already stressed the official aim of the 'resocialization of prisoners through individual diagnosis, support and treatment, appropriate education and professional training, while paying due respect to human dignity and responsibility' (Introduction – Report to the King: IV), Belgium never had a truly 'scientific, treatment-oriented' prison system. A 'Penitentiary Orientation Centre' for the individual observation and classification of prisoners was established in 1963, but it had a maximum capacity of 20 prisoners and was closed in 1987. Observation and Treatment Units were introduced into 11 prisons in 1971, but they existed for a significant number of years in only five of the 32 prisons that eventually had them.

Following the Dutroux case in 1996 and the legislative reforms of 1998, each prison now has a psychosocial service. This is responsible for evaluating the possibilities for and efforts towards the social reintegration of the prisoner, his behaviour inside the prison, his attitude towards the victims and his risk of recidivism. For sex offenders, any form of early release had to be coupled to specialized advice by a psychosocial service and the acceptance of specialized treatment on release. This compulsory specialized advice was retained in the 2006 Act but, in order to counter an 'over-psychologization', this must now assess the necessity of imposing specialized treatment (Snacken 2004). However, it is claimed that the political and public climate have fostered 'zero-risk' policies, aiming more at incapacitation than at reintegration. 'Negative selection' for conditional release, which was originally meant in 1981 as a guarantee for the prisoner that he would not have to prove his possibilities for reintegration but would be granted conditional release unless there were strong counter-indications, has in practice resulted in a situation in which the prisoner not only has to prove his efforts at reintegration but the psychosocial service also investigates for the presence of any possible counter-indication as part of a 'risk-based' approach (Mary 1999; Minet and Slingeneyer 2005). Although the 2006 Act reacts against the former system in which the Parole Commissions could postpone the conditional release on the sole argument of retribution (Court Cassation 5 April 2000, Pas, I, 227; Pieters 2001: 429; Snacken 2004: 56–7) and clearly states that a prisoner who fulfils the conditions must be released, it becomes increasingly difficult for prisoners to fulfil

93

the conditions imposed upon them, leading to an increasing number of prisoners eventually opting out of the possibility of conditional release and thus serving their full sentence in prison.

Some valuable initiatives were taken, however, by the Prison Administration following a Ministerial Circular of 5 March 1975 that fosters contacts with the outside world, such as family visits and unlimited correspondence, introducing systematic prison leave (1976), telephones (1989) and unsupervised conjugal visits and special children visits. This was further developed in the Prison Act 2005 as far as contacts with the outside world are concerned, which become (qualified) rights for prisoners that can be limited only in cases provided for by law and by the 2006 Act, which considers systematic prison leave to be a 'normal' aspect of the prison regime that can be refused by the Prison Administration only in the case of counter-indications which are explicitly mentioned in the Act. The Sentence Implementation Courts can themselves grant such prison leave in the framework of a procedure concerning other interruptions of the detention or forms of early release which fall under their authority, such as semi-detention or electronic monitoring.

Moreover, following the institutional reforms of 1980 and 1988, all aspects relating to 'forensic welfare' (i.e. social aid to offenders, prisoners, victims and their families) are the exclusive responsibility of the regional authorities, which are distinguished according to their language base ('Communities'). All forms of welfare interventions that prepare for the social reintegration of prisoners hence belong to the competence of the regional Communities. As many regimes in prison can be seen as part of both the humane execution of a prison sentence (federal competence) and preparation for the social reintegration of prisoners (regional competence), 'co-operation agreements' between the Ministry of Justice and the regional Communities were reached in the 1990s (Snacken et al. 2004). The participation of the community at large in prisons, however, remains modest and has developed unevenly between regions. The Flemish Community developed a Strategic Plan for Welfare Aid to Prisoners in 2000, aiming at guaranteeing the prisoner's right of access to services available outside prison, as long as these are compatible with his imprisonment: social agencies, employment agencies, healthcare agencies, adult education agencies, etc. Starting as an experiment in seven prisons, this Strategic Plan has only recently been implemented in all Flemish prisons (since the end of 2008), resulting in great variations in the services available between different prisons. This is even more so for the two other regions (Brussels and Walloon), where such a Strategic Plan has not yet been elaborated, leaving the development of social programmes to the local prison governors and local external services.

With the prisons' psychosocial services pressed into a mainly diagnostic function and with the uneasy and unequal introduction of welfare services by the Communities, it is clear that the development of a complete package of help to prepare for prisoners' social reintegration is not yet a reality. However, prisoners still have to establish such a reintegration plan in order to be considered for conditional release.

6.2 Interaction between sentencing, prison overcrowding and the early release of prisoners

We have described how the provisional release of prisoners serving sentences of up to three years has been used since the 1980s as a strategy to overcome the problem of prison overcrowding. However, this so-called 'back-door strategy' (Rutherford 1984) has led to a pure instrumentalization of early release and to a great deal of unrest and misunderstanding among the public, politicians and sentencing judges. Due to the complexities of the different forms of early release, confusion between the systems of conditional and provisional release has steadily increased, despite their differences in nature and application. The increased use of provisional release for reasons of overcrowding, coupled with the expanding use of electronic monitoring as a way of implementing sentences for prisoners sentenced to a maximum of three years, has generated a widespread notion of impunity in society at large. It has led to the situation that a growing number of offenders sentenced to short terms of imprisonment do not have to serve one single day or only a very short period in prison. Sentencing judges regard this as an erosion of their decisions, and many are inclined to impose longer prison sentences in order to ensure that the offender will spend at least some months in prison (Beyens 2000; Beyens and Scheirs 2009; Pieters 2010). Although many judges are not very well acquainted with the different forms of release, they tend to anticipate possible release decisions in their sentencing. The wide and quasi-automatic[15] use of provisional release has overshadowed the reputation of conditional release, which is granted in an increasingly-strict manner and largely exceeds eligibility dates. Research by Beyens and Scheirs (2009) also shows that judges who are familiar with the function of

[15]However, we noted earlier that this is not true for all categories of sentenced prisoners.

the Sentence Implementation Courts are inclined to impose sentences of three years and longer (sometimes even the symbolic length of 36 months and one day) to be sure that the release decision will be taken by this Court and not by the Administration (see also Pieters 2010).[16] This leads to a spiral of punishment, with longer sentences being imposed by the sentencing judges, which increases the overcrowding, which in turn increases resort to provisional release.

6.3 Early release of foreign prisoners

Early release is fraught with difficulties for foreign prisoners in Belgium due to a combination of criminal and administrative procedures, their exclusion from certain reintegration activities, and language or cultural problems when preparing for release (for a more detailed account, see Snacken 2007b).

6.3.1 Interaction between criminal and administrative procedures

Criminal procedures of importance here are conditional release, provisional release and provisional release with a view to expulsion. As far as conditional release is concerned, the 1998 and 2006 Acts do not distinguish between Belgian and legally residing foreign prisoners. The local Prison Board must therefore discuss all admissible prisoners, including foreign prisoners, except those against whom an order to leave the country or a decree of expulsion has been issued. These latter prisoners fall under the system of provisional release with a view to expulsion. Prisoners serving between one and three years of imprisonment are provisionally released after serving one third of their sentence.[17] The problem is that many illegally-residing foreign prisoners have submitted a request for asylum or for legal residency, and that, as long as the administrative status of the prisoner as a foreigner is uncertain, it is unclear which procedure for early release must be applied. This uncertainty was found for 98 per cent of foreign

---

[16]This unwanted effect was anticipated by the Holsters Commission, who had proposed to abolish the artificial distinction between sentences of up to and more than three years and to allow the President of the Sentence Implementation Court to decide on all proposals for early release where a consensus had been reached between the prisoner, the Public Prosecutor and the local Prison Governor, which would probably have encompassed most of the shorter sentences (Snacken 2004).

[17]Prisoners serving less than one year are released after an even shorter term (see above).

prisoners in 1993, and for 65 per cent of them in 2003 (Snacken *et al.* 2004: Table 4).

The decision on the prisoner's legal status by the Office for Foreigners Affairs (OFA) of the Ministry of Interior is mostly taken after his having served one third of the sentence. As a result, the procedure for conditional release is sometimes started but cannot be finalized in the absence of a decision by the OFA, which means that the prisoner serves more than the minimum of one third or two thirds imposed by law. Sometimes conditional release was granted by the Commission, but this is then followed by a negative decision by the OFA, refusing residence. The transfer of supervision to another country is not always possible, and reintegration or treatment in the country of origin may be difficult to assess, which may hamper granting a conditional release.

Serious problems are also faced by those foreign prisoners who did not have lawful residence permission at the time of their arrest because, although these prisoners have served the required proportion of one third or two thirds of their prison sentence for the Ministry of Justice, they can be further detained in the prison on administrative grounds. On several occasions a prisoner about to leave prison on provisional release has been held back by a last-minute fax from the OFA requesting his further detention for administrative reasons, often resulting in dramatic consequences, such as hunger strikes, suicide attempts or aggressive behaviour. A new co-operation agreement between the Ministries of Justice and of the Interior should now enhance the swiftness of the OFA's decision.

6.3.2 *Exclusion from certain reintegration activities*
Participation in reintegration activities may be hampered by language problems and by the uncertainty concerning the possibility of expulsion to the country of origin. Prison governors will normally not differentiate between foreign and national prisoners when allocating work, but some types of work may require language skills or knowledge of one of the Belgian languages. Participation in training programmes in co-operation with the local community employment agency and aimed at finding work upon release may also be hampered by uncertainty about expulsion.

The 2006 Act on the external legal position of prisoners does not differentiate between national and foreign prisoners as far as the different forms of prison leave are concerned (day leave, systematic prison leave, semi-detention, electronic monitoring). However, as 76 per cent of foreign prisoners in 2004 had no legal permit to stay, it can be assumed that the assessment of possible counter-indications will probably be more negative for foreign prisoners without a legal permit (e.g. the risk of absconding). And, as these forms of prison leave are increasingly seen as important transitional tools between detention and conditional release, it can be assumed, albeit tentatively, that such leave influences the likelihood of their obtaining a conditional release.

6.3.3 *Preparation for early release by psychosocial services*
Another problem results from the fact that all these forms of early release require some preparation by the prison's psychosocial service. Language problems may arise here because of the complexity of the interaction between the different procedures. But specific cultural problems may also arise because of different attitudes towards certain forms of delinquency (for example, those linked to matters of honour or where help is provided to fellow illegal immigrants). The emphasis in the Belgian conditional release system on individual responsibility, guilt and reparation towards the victims of crime may be alien to more collectivistic cultures or to foreign prisoners who commit offences to survive. Psychological tests also raise cultural problems. Standard tests are based on Western thinking, leading to interpretation problems. Similarly, the psychologists working in prisons are trained in Western psychology, often with very little knowledge of ethno-psychiatry or psychology. These cultural problems may persist even when the language problems have been resolved.

7. Conclusions

The early release of sentenced prisoners has been the object of many legislative and regulatory reforms over the last two decades, resulting in a complex system of conditional and provisional releases and of a bifurcation of policy and practice which seem to have several unintended consequences.

The specific characteristics of the Belgian conditional release system are the transfer of decision-making from an administrative to a juridical body, the multidisciplinary composition of this body and the increased involvement of the victims of crime. The transfer of decision-making on conditional release from the Minister of Justice to multidisciplinary Parole Commissions and, later, the transfer of most forms of temporary and early release to multidisciplinary Sentence Implementation Courts was meant to increase its legitimacy by fostering its independence, professionalism and transparency. The introduction of procedural rights for prisoners, the legal enumeration of possible counter-indications for release, the introduction of the right of victims to be informed of the forms of early release and to suggest conditions that might be imposed in their own interests were meant to foster both the subjective right to the social reintegration of the prisoner and the interests of the victim and of society at large.

In the absence of research on the application of conditional release by the Sentence Implementation Courts or on the application of the placement at the disposal of the government, it is too early to come to real conclusions. The influence of the multidisciplinary nature of the Sentence Implementation Courts and of the increased attention on the victims of crime is unknown at the moment but is the subject of research that has just started.[18] Some research indicates, however, that it has become increasingly difficult for prisoners to respond to the criteria laid down in the law because of the increased emphasis on the prisoner's own responsibility for his reintegration and the enhanced strictness of the conditions for release, which may be too demanding in view of the socioeconomic and mental vulnerability of many prisoners, the increased emphasis on risk assessment and risk management by the psychosocial services and the uneven provision of preparation for release by the Communities. The increased application of different forms of temporary release, such as semi-detention and electronic monitoring, as necessary intermediate steps before conditional release may also result in the postponement of the conditional release decision. The fact is that conditional release is being granted increasingly late compared with the date of eligibility, thus seriously qualifying the apparently 'generous' legal provision of (non-legal recidivist) prisoners having to serve 'only' a third of their sentence and leading to an increasing number of prisoners opting out of the whole system. It is also clear that the complexities and restrictive application of the conditional release system stand in opposition to the provisional release system that is still applied in practice to the majority of prisoners, and that leads to feelings of impunity among politicians and the general public and to compensating sentencing practices by the judges, thus closing the vicious circle and increasing

---

[18]*The Sentence Implementation Courts at Work. Ethnographic Research into their Interactions, Decision-making and Practices* (K. Beyens and S. Snacken, Vrije Universiteit Brussel, 2009–12).

punishment trends. It is obvious that prison overcrowding needs to be tackled differently. But that is a different story...

References

Beernaert, M.-A. (2006) 'Le statut juridique externe des détenus et les tribunaux de l'application des peines. Un premier aperçu rapide', *Journal des tribunaux*, 125: 801–6.

Beernaert, M.-A. (2007a) *Manuel de droit pénitentiaire*. Louvain-la-Neuve: Anthémis.

Beernaert, M.-A. (2007b) 'Vers des tribunaux de l'application des peines et une définition légale du statut juridique "externe" des personnes condamnés à une peine privative de liberté', *Revue de droit pénal et de criminologie*, 1: 7–49.

Beernaert, M.-A., Clavie, M., De Rue, M., Hoffmann, C., Moreau, T., Spronck, V., Van Boven, B. and van der Elst, S. (2008) *L'exécution des peines privatives de liberté. Regards croisés*. Louvain-la-Neuve: Anthémis.

Beernaert, M.-A. and Vandermeersch, D. (2008) *Le tribunal d'application des peines et le statut externe des condamnés à des peines privatives de libertés de plus de trois ans*. Brussels: Kluwer.

Beyens, K. (2000) *Straffen als sociale praktijk. Een penologisch onderzoek naar straftoemeting*. Brussels: VUB Press.

Beyens, K. (2006) 'Het nakomertje in de Belgische criminografie', in E. Devroe, K. Beyens and E. Enhus (eds), *Zwart op wit? Duiding van cijfers over onveiligheid en strafrechtsbedeling in België. Handboek criminografische basisinformatie*. Brussels: VUB Press.

Beyens, K. (2008) 'Une justice pénale colorée?', *Contradictions*, 121/122: 47–62.

Beyens, K., Devresse, M.-S., Kaminski, D. and Luypaert, H. (2007) 'Over het "eigen" aardige karakter van het elektronisch toezicht in België', *Fatik*, 116: 4–15.

Beyens, K. and Scheirs, V. (2009) 'Geruchten, frustraties en verdeeldheid. Belgische strafrechters over de strafuitvoering', *Proces*, 88(2): 16–34.

Beyens, K. and Tubex, H. (2002) 'Gedetineerden geteld', in S. Snacken (ed.) *Strafrechtelijk beleid in beweging*. Brussels: VUB Press.

Beyens, K., Snacken, S. and Eliaerts, C. (1993) *Barstende muren. Overbevolkte gevangenissen: omvang, oorzaken en mogelijke oplossingen*. Antwerpen-Arnhem: Kluwer-Gouda.

Close, F. and Raneri, G.-F. (2008) 'Un an de jurisprudence de la cour de cassation relative au tribunal de l'application des peines', in A. Masset (ed.) *L'exécution des condamnations pénales*. Liège: Anthémis.

Daems, T. (2007) 'Strafuitvoeringsrechtbanken, overbevolkte gevangenissen en compatibele slachtoffers', *Panopticon*, 28(3): 41–57.

De Clerck, S. (1996) 'Oriëntatienota Strafbeleid en Gevangenisbeleid', *Fatik*, 70/71: 8–54.

Deltenre, S. (2008) *Des commissions de libération conditionnelle aux tribunaux d'application des peines: analyse de l'impact des libérations conditionnelles et des libérations en vue d'éloignement sur la population pénitentiaire*. Brussels: Cellule des données, Service ICT, DGEPI, SPF Justice.

De Rue, M. (2006) 'Le statut juridique externe des détenus', in A. Masset and P. Traest (eds), *L'exécution des peines – de strafuitvoering. Les Dossiers de la Revue de Droit pénal et de Criminologie 13*. Brussels: la Charte.

De Swaef, M. and Traest, M. (2007/2008) 'Een jaar strafuitvoeringsrecht- banken: overzicht van cassatierechtspraak', *Rechtskundig Weekblad*, 71: 1570–84.

Dupont, L. (1998) *Op weg naar een Beginselenwet Gevangeniswezen*. Leuven: Universitaire Pers Leuven.

Eliaerts, C. (1980) 'De herziening van de wet op de voorwaardelijke invrijheidstelling: op weg naar een "strafuitvoeringsrecht"'? *Panopticon*, 1: 184–96.

Eliaerts, C. and Rozie, M (1978) 'Toezicht op de uitvoering van de straf', *Rechtskundig Weekblad*, 41: 2409–28.

FOD Justitie (2009) *Justitie in cijfers 2008*. Brussels: FOD Justitie.

Hermans, C. (2007) 'Strafuitvoeringsrechtbanken uit de startblokken. De nieuwe strafuitvoeringsrechtbanken en de gedeeltelijke inwerkingtreding van de wet betreffende de externe rechtspositie van veroordeelden', *Fatik*, 113: 6–18.

Hoffman, C. and Moreau, T. (2008) 'Les droits du détenu dans l'exécution des peines privative de liberté', in A. Masset (ed.) *L'exécution des condamnations pénales*. Liège: Anthémis.

Jacobs, A. (2006) 'Le statut externe du détenu', in A. Masset (ed.) *Actualités de droit pénal et de procédure pénale*. Brussels: Larcier.

Legros, R. (1985) *Voorontwerp van Strafwetboek*. Brussels: Ministerie van Justitie.

Maes, E. (2008) 'Komen gedetineerden te vroeg vrij?', *Fatik*, 119: 4–10.

Maes, E. (2010) 'Evoluties in punitiviteit: lessen uit de justitiële statistieken', in I. Aertsen, K. Beyens, T. Daems and E. Maes (eds) *Hoe punitief is België?* Ghent: Maklu.

Mary, P. (1999) 'De l'amendement à la réduction des risques. L'évolution de la loi sur la libération conditionnelle en Belgique', in P. Mary and T. Papathéodorou (eds) *La surpopulation pénitentiaire en Belgique. De la détention avant jugement à la libération conditionnelle*. Brussels: Bruylant.

Minet, J.-F. and Slingeneyer, T. (2005) 'Chronique de criminologie – Transformations du système de libération conditionnelle en Belgique: évolution procédurale et spirale des logiques décisionnelles?', *Revue de droit pénal et de criminologie*, 3: 280–312.

Ministry of Interior, Office for Foreigners Affairs (2000) *Annual Report*. Brussels: Ministry of Interior.

Pieters, F. (2001) 'De voorwaardelijke invrijheidstelling: een tip van de sluier opgelicht', in L. Dupont and F. Hutsebaut (eds) *Herstelrecht tussen toekomst en verleden*. Liber Amicorum Tony Peters. Leuven: Universitaire Pers.

Pieters, F. (2010) 'Maar, wat als en mogelijkerwijze', in I. Aertsen, K. Beyens, T. Daems and E. Maes (eds), *Hoe punitief is België?* Ghent: Maklu.

Rihoux, A. (2000) 'Tendances passées et effets de la réforme sur les flux d'entrées, les fluxs de sorties et les durées de détention', in *La libération conditionnelle: évaluation des pratiques*. Nivelles–Louvain-la-Neuve: Conférence du Jeune Barreau, Département de droit pénal et de criminologie.

Robert, L. (2009) 'Geleidelijke terugkeer of plotse overgang naar de samenleving? Langgestrafte gedetineerden in de gevangenis van Andenne', in T. Daems, P. Pletincx, L. Robert, V. Scheirs, A. van de Wiel and K. Verpoest (eds) *Achter tralies in België*. Ghent: Academia Press.

Rutherford, A. (1984) *Prisons and the Process of Justice: The Reductionist Challenge*. London: Heinemann.

Snacken, S. (2001) 'Belgium', in D. van Zyl Smit and F. Dünkel (eds) *Imprisonment Today and Tomorrow. International Perspectives on Prison Conditions and Prisoners' Rights* (2nd edn). The Hague, London and Boston, MA: Kluwer International.

Snacken, S (2004) 'De voorstellen van de subcommissie externe rechtspositie', in I. Aertsen, K. Beyens, S. De Valck and F. Pieters (eds) *De Commissie Holsters buitenspel?De voorstellen van de commissie Strafuitvoeringsrechtbanken, externe rechtspositie van gedetineerde en straftoemeting*. Brussels: Politeia.

Snacken, S. (2007a) 'Penal policy and practice in Belgium', in M. Tonry (ed.). *Crime, Punishment and Politics in Comparative Perspective. Crime and Justice: A Review of Research. Vol. 36.* Chicago: Chicago University Press.

Snacken, S. (2007b) 'Belgium', in A.M. van Kalmthout, M.M. Knapen and C. Morgenstern (eds) *Foreigners in European Prisons*. Nijmegen: Wolf Legal Publishers.

Snacken, S., Keulen, J. and Winkelmans, L. (2004) *Buitenlanders in de Belgische gevangenissen. Knelpunten en mogelijke oplossingen*. Brussels: Koning Boudewijnstichting.

Strypstein, J. and Tubex, H. (2004) 'Voorlopige invrijheidstelling: theorie en praktijk', *Fatik*, 102: 5–10.

Tubex, H. and Snacken, S. (1999) 'Libération conditionnelle et opinion publique', in *La libération conditionnelle. Analyse des lois des 5 mars et 18 mars 1998. Les dossiers de la Revue de Droit Pénal et de Criminologie*, 5.

Tubex, H. and Strypstein, J. (2003/2005) *Evaluatie van de uitstroom van veroordeelden uit de gevangenis. Final report.* Brussels: VUB Press.

Tubex, H. and Strypstein, J. (2006) 'Grasduinen in penitentiaire bronnen en statistieken', in E. Devroe, K. Beyens and E. Enhus (eds) *Zwart op Wit? Duiding van cijfers over onveiligheid en strafrechtsbedeling. Handboek criminografische basisinformatie*. Brussels: VUB Press.

Tulkens, H.J.J. (1988) *Graden van vrijheid. Over hervormingsmogelijkheden van de vrijheidstraf* (rede uitgesproken bij de aanvaarding van het ambt van bijzonder hoogleraar in de penologie aan de Rijksuniversiteit Groningen op dinsdag 25 oktober 1988). Arnhem: Gouda Quint.

Vanacker, J. (2007) 'De strafuitvoeringsrechtbanken en de externe rechtspositie van veroordeelden: een (recht)bank vooruit?', *Panopticon*, 28: 1–7.

Van den Berghe, Y. (2006a) 'De uitvoering van vrijheidsstraffen: van nu en straks ... met de oprichting va de strafuitvoeringsrechtbanken', *Tijdschrift voor strafrecht*, 5: 249–63.

Van den Berghe, Y. (2006b) 'Een nieuwe regeling van de externe rechtspositie van veroordeelde gedetineerden en de oprichting van strafuitvoeringsrechtbanken', *Rechtspraak Antwerpen Brussel Gent*, 13/14: 1081–90.

Van den Berge, Y. (2006c) 'Een nieuwe regeling van de externe rechtspositie van veroordeelden tot een vrijheidsstraf en de oprichting van strafuitvoeringsrechtbanken', *Panopticon*, 27: 78–88.

Van den Berge, Y. (2006d) *Uitvoering van vrijheidsstraffen en rechtspositie van gedetineerden* (2nd edn). Brussels: Larcier.

van Zyl Smit, D. and Snacken, S. (2009) *Principles of European Prison Law and Policy*. Oxford: Oxford University Press.

Verpoest, K. and Vander Beken, T. (2006) 'Rechters in uitvoering. Een eerste analyse van de wetten rond de externe rechtspositie van veroordeelden en de oprichting van de strafuitvoeringsrechtbanken', *Nullum Crimen*, 1: 370–82.

Verpoest, K. and Vander Beken, T. (2007) 'Wat je doet en niet wie je bent'; De nieuwe wet betreffende de terbeschikkingstelling van de strafuitvoeringsrechtbanken', *Fatik*, 116: 21–4.

Chapter 5

England and Wales

Nicola Padfield

Summary

Early release, with and without conditions, has long been a feature of English sentencing and prison practice. A key date was 1967, when the government decided that the decision to release a prisoner could be helped by the advice of a body of experts: Parliament created a Parole Board. Initially, this body had an advisory role, but the Home Secretary decided to delegate certain decisions to it. Another important stage began in 1991, when the window of parole (conditional release) 'opportunity' shrank, but the Board gained more powers. It began oral, more court-like, hearings for some life-sentence prisoners, and over the years this expanded to cover the cases of all lifers, and those who disputed their recall to prison. But all powers of early release (now always conditional) for fixed-term prisoners have recently been returned to the executive. The system today is bifurcated: a Parole Board hearing for 'lifers', but fixed, half-time release for most determinate prisoners, with in addition up to four and a half months[1] discretionary earlier release. The cases of recalled prisoners who are not re-released within 28 days are also considered by the Parole Board. As we shall see, two other characteristics of the English sentencing and conditional release system are the frequency of change and the complexity of the rules. At the time of writing, another review of the process has been announced.

1. History

1.1 Before 1967

To understand the history of early release in England and Wales, one has to understand a variety of sentences which have existed in English law. Transportation was superseded in the mid-nineteenth century by 'penal servitude', and those subject to this had more privileges than ordinary prisoners but, unlike ordinary prisoners, they were also subject to release on 'licence' and subject to recall. This 'licence to be at large' evolved from the 'ticket of leave' which had developed to set free transported convicts after several years of labour. Under the penal servitude system, this remission, or licence, was in effect a conditional release: the sentence remained in force and the prisoner might be required to serve the unexpired part if he breached the condition (not to reoffend). The Prison Act 1898 extended this privilege of remission from penal servitude to ordinary imprisonment, but it then became an absolute, unconditional remission.

Penal servitude was abolished by the Criminal Justice Act 1948, and this system of remission without condition continued for all sentences of imprisonment of whatever length, except for young prisoners. The amount of remission on a sentence of penal servitude had been one quarter of the term for men, and one third for women. In the case of imprisonment it had been only a sixth but, during the 1939–45 war a flat rate of one-third remission was introduced. Remission was a privilege which could be lost: writing in 1952, a leading commentator wrote:

> From the days of transportation and the early penal servitude system, eligibility to earn a remission of part of the sentence by good conduct and industry has been the first and most valuable privilege accorded to prisoners, as the power to forfeit remission has been and remains one of the strongest sanctions against bad conduct (Fox 1952: 165).

However, the 1948 Act replaced 'penal servitude' with special sentences of 'corrective training' and 'preventive detention' to deal with persistent offenders. Both schemes survived only from 1948 to 1967. Prisoners serving these sentences were eligible to be released on conditional licence, subject to recall.

1.2   Conditional release on the advice of the Parole Board: 1967–91

The Parole Board was created in 1967 (for the early history, see Morgan 1983; Padfield and Walker 1996; Shute 2003). In 1967, the parole 'window' was wide: the prisoner could be considered for release after serving one third of the sentence. The Criminal Justice Act 1967 gave the Home Secretary power (but not a duty) to release a prisoner from a determinate sentence after he or she had served a third of it or 12 months, whichever was the longer (the minimum qualifying period was reduced to six months by s. 33 of the Criminal Justice Act 1982). It was still the executive (in the name of the Home Secretary) which exercised the power to release, but it could do so only in cases in which release was recommended by the Parole Board or, in certain types of case, by a local review committee of the prisoner's establishment; but such a recommendation did not oblige him to follow it, and occasionally he did not. The prisoner could refuse to apply for conditional release (parole). If paroled, he was on licence until the date on which he would have been released on remission, but with exceptions (those serving 'extended' terms and young offenders serving 18 months or more). The parole licence meant that he was released under supervision by a probation officer and would be liable to recall to prison to serve what remained of the sentence if he broke the conditions of his licence. Thus, release was conditional from the time of release until the two-thirds point in the sentence, when it became unconditional release. In the early years, parole (conditional release) was relatively rarely granted: most prisoners therefore still left prison unconditionally at the two-thirds point.

The local review committees were made up of the Prison Governor (often in practice represented by his deputy), a probation officer, a member of the prison's Board of Visitors (independent people, sometimes lay magistrates, a bit like an independent lay inspectorate) and two other people, representing the wider community. These disappeared after the reforms of 1991, but it remains an important question today whether ordinary people are adequately involved in the release decision. As McCabe put it more than 20 years ago, the point of involving ordinary citizens in prisoner release is 'that members of the community and their parliamentary representatives, not bureaucratic officials, should indicate the measure of danger which everyone must be prepared to accept' (1985: 499).

1.3   Less discretion in conditional release, and the introduction of more 'court-like' hearings for some life-sentence prisoners: 1991–2005

Over the years it became clear that substantial differences in sentence lengths often in reality disappeared with such a flexible release system. Prisoners serving 9 months or 18 months were all eligible to be released after 6 months. The government formed a committee, chaired by Lord Carlisle, to review the system applied to determinate-sentence prisoners, which reported in 1988. This Carlisle Report[1] was based on a number of key policy principles (pp. 48–50; 60–63):

1. The undesirability and impracticability of a selective system of release for shorter-term prisoners.

2. Any release system should not undermine the proportionality of sentences passed by the courts, and it should not be for the Parole Board to assess whether a prisoner has served sufficient time to satisfy desert criteria.

3. There is a strong case for attaching at least some real meaning to the whole of the sentence passed by the court.

4. There is a positive value in ensuring that very few prisoners should emerge from prison without any period of supervision by a probation officer.

5. Prisoners considered for discretionary release should have the benefit of appropriate procedural safeguards.

The government's White Paper, *Crime, Justice and Protecting the Public* (1990), accepted the main recommendations of the Carlisle Report and these principles underpinned the major reforms of the Criminal Justice Act 1991:

1. Discretionary release for anyone sentenced to less than four years was abolished (i.e. those sentenced to less than four years should come out automatically but conditionally at the half-way point in their sentences. This system remained in place until the introduction of the Home Detention Curfew in 1998; see below). The conditions continued to apply until the prisoner reached the three-quarters point in their sentence, when release became unconditional.

[1]See *The Parole System in England and Wales* (Cm 532) (London: HMSO 1988).

2. A narrower parole 'window' (i.e. between a half and three quarters of sentence) for those serving longer than four years.

3. For long-term prisoners (those serving four years or more), release had to take place at the two-thirds point, thus allowing some licence (supervision) in all cases.

4. Local review committees were abolished.

5. The process became more open: prisoners were given access to their dossiers, had the opportunity to make representations on their contents by way of an interview with a Parole Board member and were given reasons for the decisions that were taken.

6. Statutory criteria for release were enacted.

Technically, according to the Criminal Justice Act 1991, the Board only recommended release, and the Secretary of State granted it; but after December 1998 decision-making was delegated by the Home Secretary to the Board for all sentences of less than 15 years.

These changes introduced in the 1990s were subject to detailed independent research, primarily by Hood and Shute who, in a series of studies (see Hood and Shute 1994; 1995; 2000; 2002), examined the Board's approach in the 'paper panels' which considered up to 24 discretionary release cases a morning. They pointed out that the parole rate for prisoners serving four years or more fell significantly after the 1991 reforms (judged by the percentage of prisoners receiving any parole before the two-thirds point). This was for a number of reasons: the new emphasis on the risk of reoffending; the fact that parole no longer had to be granted to ensure some supervision; and the fact that prisoners got fewer reviews than under the old system (because of the one-half minimum threshold). The post-Carlisle procedural changes (especially the interview) were generally well received by prisoners. Parole Board decisions were often taken quickly, and there was a high degree of consistency and predictability in the decision-making. The main written reasons given for refusal of parole were:

1. various indicators of risk (history of offending, failure to respond to supervision, etc.);

2. failure to address offending behaviour;

3. and inadequate release plans.

We will return later to the question whether 'failure to address offending-behaviour' too often equates that criterion with formal offending-behaviour courses undertaken in prison.

Interestingly, Hood and Shute also pointed out that formal risk assessments – 'risk of reconviction' (ROR) scores – were not used by the Board, but their decision-making was strongly correlated with ROR scores, except in the case of sex offenders. The Board's cautious decision-making, especially for sex offenders, was explored further in Hood and Shute (2002): the paroling rate for sex offenders with a ROR of 7 per cent or less for a 'serious offence' (one likely to result in imprisonment) during the parole period was only 22 per cent, whereas the paroling rate for non-sex offenders with a similar ROR was 60 per cent.

The Carlisle Committee considered the release only of determinate-sentenced prisoners. Meanwhile, the European Court of Human Rights forced on a reluctant British government a more open and court-like procedure for deciding on the release (or continued detention) of life (indeterminate) sentence prisoners. Anyone convicted of murder receives a mandatory life sentence in England, but many 'dangerous' people also receive a discretionary life sentence. First, discretionary lifers won the right to an oral hearing before the Parole Board (*Thynne, Wilson and Gunnell* v. *United Kingdom* 25 October 1990). As a result, ss. 32–34 of the Criminal Justice Act 1991 created Discretionary Lifer Panels of the Parole Board: a panel of three members of the Parole Board holding an oral hearing in prison. A few years later, the decision in *Hussain and Singh* forced a similar process for those who had been sentenced as children to a mandatory life sentence for murder (detention 'during Her Majesty's pleasure') (for the history, see Padfield 2002). These Panels, chaired by a judge or other legally-qualified member, meet in the prisoner's prison and hear evidence from the prisoner and other key witnesses. Padfield and Liebling (2000) carried out a study of the decision-making at oral hearings (Discretionary Lifer Panels, as they were then known). It is particularly important to note the length of time served by lifers and their much lower percentage release rates, despite the fact that they are not being considered for 'early' release (these prisoners have already completed the 'tariff' part of their sentence). Thus, while the tariff or minimum term (largely based on proportionality principles and the need for punishment and deterrence) to be served by a lifer is fixed by the sentencing judge, the different criteria applied by the Board mean they may stay in prison for many years (indeed life) even after the proportionate part of the sentence has been served.

For determinate prisoners, the return to more flexible conditional release at the hands of the prison authorities was first signalled in the Crime and Disorder Act 1998 (the first criminal justice legislation of 'New Labour' when it took power after 18 years of Conservative government). Sections 99–100 introduced Home Detention Curfews (HDCs) – release on licence with a curfew enforced by electronic monitoring. Originally HDC was possible only for the last two months of a sentence, and the government imposed a cautious policy of release. But in 2002 it introduced a 'presumptive' HDC and increased the possible period to 90 days. In July 2003 HDC was extended from 90 days to 135 days but, at the same time, more restrictive criteria were imposed (for example, sex offenders are ineligible). The decision-making is done by employees of the prison system (see below). Early research (Dodgson *et al.* 2001) suggested worrying variations in release statistics, depending on the location of the prisoner.

Another feature of this period was a significant increase in the number of prisoners being recalled to prison during the period of supervision in the community. It was unsurprising that the House of Lords decided in *R (Smith)* v. *Parole Board; R (West)* v. *Parole Board* (2005) that prisoners who wished to challenge the factual basis for their recall should have the right to do so by way of an oral hearing, but this added considerably to the workload of an already hard-pressed and under-funded body. So, at the end of this period, many recalled offenders and life-sentenced prisoners had become entitled to an oral hearing before the Parole Board. Those sentenced to a determinate sentence of four years or more still had their cases considered by a panel of the Parole Board, but without an oral hearing, on paper only.

1.4 Conditional release for all fixed-term prisoners, determined by the prison authorities; a changing Parole Board for lifers: 2005–

The Criminal Justice Act 2003 made significant changes to release processes, changes which were brought into force in April 2005. For determinate-sentenced (fixed-term) prisoners, the government accepted the recommendations in the Halliday *Review of the Sentencing Framework* (2001) that discretionary conditional release (parole) in its existing form should be abolished for all prisoners serving determinate sentences. The Parole Board was no longer to be involved with decisions to release determinate-sentence prisoners. Interestingly, s. 238 of the Criminal Justice Act 2003 enabled a sentencing court to recommend licence conditions for those sentenced to more than 12 months, but this practice has not been encouraged: it is the prison authorities who impose the licence conditions when a determinate-sentenced prisoner is released automatically at half time, or earlier on HDC. The licence now continues to the end of the sentence (see s. 249 of the Criminal Justice Act 2003): remission has disappeared completely. The Act also confirmed the executive's powers to release early on HDC (s. 246) and to release exceptionally on compassionate grounds (s. 248). As an example of the difficulties in this area of law, ss. 263 and 264 lay down very complex rules for calculating the time offenders must spend in custody and on licence (conditional release) where several sentences are passed on the same or different occasions and are ordered to be served concurrently or consecutively.

The Criminal Justice Act 2003 introduced a new indeterminate sentence for 'dangerous' offenders – Imprisonment for Public Protection (IPP), identical to life except that, once the prisoner has been out of prison for at least 10 years, he may apply to have the conditions of his licence removed. All life-sentence prisoners (which include murderers receiving a mandatory life sentence[2] as well as discretionary lifers and IPP prisoners) are now entitled to an oral hearing before the Parole Board. The processes have been further amended by the Criminal Justice and Immigration Act 2008 (see Padfield 2009a). The rule that 'non-dangerous' fixed-term prisoners come out of prison at the half-way point in their sentence now applies also to those sentenced before 4 April 2005. And more dramatically, dangerous offenders sentenced to an extended sentence are also to be released at half time.[3] This is surprising since, to qualify for an extended sentence, the offender must have been deemed to be 'dangerous' and merit an extended sentence, made of a custodial part and an extended period of supervision in the community after they have served the custodial part of their sentence. It used to be thought that 'dangerous' offenders should be subject to review by

[2]Murderers won the right to an oral hearing only after the decision of the European Court of Human Rights in *Stafford* v. *United Kingdom* (2002) and the decision of the House of Lords in *R (Anderson)* v. *Secretary of State for the Home Department* (2002) to issue a declaration that the existing law was incompatible with the Human Rights Act 1998 (see Padfield 2006).
[3]Extended sentences have a long and complex history, and their routes can be traced to the earlier 'preventive detention' (see section 1.1 above). There were slightly different forms created in 1991 and 1998, but both were replaced by the 'new'-style extended sentence of the Criminal Justice Act 2003 (see s. 227).

the Parole Board. If the offender subject to an extended sentence is recalled to prison during the extension period, he may well serve the entirety of the remaining part of the sentence in prison, without the benefit of any supervision on release.

A new discretionary release scheme, the End of Custody Licence (ECL), was announced by the then Lord Chancellor on 19 June 2007. Under the ECL prisoners serving sentences of between four weeks and four years may be released for the final 18 days of their sentence subject to meeting strict eligibility criteria. Prisoners who would normally be subject to supervision on release (prisoners serving 12 months or more or those under 22 years of age) must meet their probation officer after release and have regular contact after that in line with their supervision plan. All prisoners released on ECL are liable to recall if they are reported to have misbehaved during the period of the licence.

2. Statistical data

The main data available in England and Wales are to be found in the annual *Offender Management Caseload Statistics*, published by the Ministry of Justice.[4] In this, Chapter 6 is on 'Receptions into prison establishments' and Chapter 7 on 'Characteristics of the prison population'. Thus, the latest volume states the following:

- There were 125,880 first receptions in 2007, a decrease of 2% compared to 2006 and the lowest annual number of first receptions since 1997 (when there were 124,170 first receptions).

- There were 90,260 receptions under sentence (excluding fine defaulters) in 2007, up 2% on the previous year and 12% higher than in 1997.

- Receptions of prisoners on indeterminate sentences (either a life sentence or an Indeterminate Sentence for Public Protection (IPP)) increased by 6% from 2,160 in 2006 to 2,280 in 2007. This rise was due to an 11% increase in IPP receptions (from 1,570 in 2006 to 1,750 in 2007) while receptions of all other indeterminate sentences fell by 10% to 530 (of which 360 were mandatory lifers).

- The number of sentenced receptions increased between 2006 and 2007 in all sentence length bands except those for 4 years or more (excluding indeterminates) which fell by 180 (3%) reflecting the

[4]See, for example, www.justice.gov.uk/docs/omcs2007.pdf

switch from long determinate sentences to IPPs (which rose by 180).

- The prison population in June 2007 reached 79,730 an increase of 2% compared to 2006. This was due to a 3% rise in the male population while the female prison population fell 4%. (The overall increase of 2% was slightly lower than it would otherwise have been as a result of the introduction of the End of Custody Licence (ECL) scheme on 29 June 2007).

- Over the longer term the prison population increased by 30% between 1997 and 2007, with the female population up 60% and the male population up 28%.

Chapter 9 of the *Offender Management Caseload Statistics* is entitled 'Releases and recalls'. In 2007, the key facts (omitting those related to escapes and self-inflicted deaths) were as follows:

- The total number of adults and young offenders discharged from determinate sentences in 2007 was 65,000 and 12,000, respectively, a fall of 1% and 4% compared with 2006. Between 2003 and 2007, the total number of discharges decreased by 6%.

- Around 21% (11,428) of potentially eligible prisoners were released on Home Detention Curfew (HDC) in 2007. The rate in 2006 was 26%. The highest release rates to date on HDC were in 2002 and 2003.

- In 2007, there were 1,654 decisions to recall from HDC, representing a decrease of 24% on 2006. The most common reason for recall, which accounted for nearly 75 per cent of all recalls, was breaching HDC conditions. Nine per cent of recalls were on the grounds of being charged with a new offence.

- Around 6,000 determinate sentence prisoners were considered for parole in 2007-08, a decrease of 13 per cent compared to 2006–07. Of those prisoners considered for parole, around 2,150 were released. The release rate remained the same at around 36%. The release rate in 1997–98 was 38%. The highest release rates to date were between 2002 and 2004.

- In 2007–08, 926 parolees were recalled, a decrease of 24% from 2006–07. In the same period, a total of 11,756 determinate sentence offenders were recalled to custody, an increase of 5% on 2006–07.

- The amount of time served by life sentence prisoners varies considerably. In addition to being released on life licence, life sentence prisoners can be discharged for other reasons, such as successful appeals, or transfers to other jurisdictions or to psychiatric hospitals. The mean time served for mandatory lifers first released from prison in 2007 on life licence was 16 years, an increase of two years for the previous three years. For other lifers the mean time served was 9 years in 2009, an increase of 2 years from 2006.

- In 2007, 146 life sentence prisoners were released for the first time. This is 11 more than those first released in 2006 and 26 more that those released in 1999. In the same year, 134 offenders on life licence were recalled to prison. This is 30 fewer that those recalled in 2006 and 100 more than in 1999.

- There were 441,167 releases on temporary licence in 2007, an increase of 10 per cent compared to 2006. Resettlement day release licences accounted for 96% of all temporary releases. Of these, 278,406 were for the working out scheme.

- Between 29 June and December 2007, there were 16,197 releases on End of Custody Licence (ECL). Of these, 71% were serving sentences of up to 6 months. In the same period, there were 564 decisions to recall prisoners whilst on ECL.

Each Chapter of the *Offender Management Caseload Statistics* contains detailed tables. Thus, for example, Chapter 9 on 'Releases and recalls' provides tables on the following:

1. The average time served in prison by adult and young prisoners discharged from determinate sentence or on licence (males and females) 2003–7
2. Home Detention Curfew release and population figures by sex; by sentence length, by age group, by ethnic group, by offence group
3. Number of releases on temporary licence by type of licence
4. Summary of determinate sentence cases considered by the Parole Board
5. Number of first releases from prison on life licence and average time served
6. Number of releases and recalls on End of Custody Licence, 29 June–31 December 2007
7. Home Detention Curfew recalls by reason
8. Recalls of determinate sentences and from life licence

Table 5.1 Home Detention Curfew

	2004	2005	2006	2007
Percentage of eligible prisoners released on HDC (men/women)	33/47	31/44	25/35	20/30
Total number	19,294	17,296	13,666	11,428
Number (and %) recalled to prison	3,003 (16%)	2,627 (15%)	2,184 (16%)	1,654 (14.5%)

Source: Compiled from data in *Offender Management Caseload Statistics* (2007: Table 9.3 and Table 9.8).

9. Number of absconds, escapes and temporary release failures
10. Numbers of deaths in custody 1997–2007

Thus, by way of example, Table 5.1 contains a summary of HDC statistics.

The Prison Service also publishes a monthly bulletin of the prison population,[5] listing every prison individually and listing not only its current population but also its operational capacity: in January 2009, the total population was 82,240 prisoners. Unfortunately the HDC release rates per prison are not published: there remains concern whether HDC is in fact applied differently across different prisons. Information on numbers released under the ECL licence scheme is published monthly in the statistics bulletin, *End of Custody Licence Releases and Recalls*.[6] As we have seen, this is a very short period of discretionary earlier-than-halftime release for those serving short sentences.

The Parole Board's annual reports are also an important source of statistical information. Table 5.2, for example, shows its caseload summaries for the last few years, revealing the dramatic increase in both the cases of recalled prisoners and those of life-sentence prisoners. This table makes clear that the dramatic increase in workload is largely due to the number of people being recalled to prison during the part of the sentence that is served in the community. The Parole Board also publishes the rate of reoffending for both determinate and indeterminate sentences (Table 5.3).

[5]See www.hmprisonservice.gov.uk/resourcecentre/publications documents/index.asp?cat=85
[6]Available online at: http://www.justice.gov.uk/publications/endof custodylicence.htm

Table 5.2 Parole Board caseload summaries

	2000–1	2001–2	2002–3	2003–4	2004–5	2005–6	2006–7	2007–8
Recalls	2,457	4,885	7,246	9,031	9,320	9,296	14,669	19,060
Oral hearings	272	466	495	1,018	1,341	1,900	2,505	2,531
Indeterminate non-oral hearings					273	249	283	397
Determinate sentence prisoners	5,576	5,514	6,012	6,038	7,297	7,528	7,857	7,594
Total caseload	8,836	11,378	14,668	17,147	18,583	19,402	25,436	31,172

Source: Compiled from a number of recent *Annual Reports of the Parole Board*.

Table 5.3 Rate of reoffending (or allegations of further offences) for determinate prisoners (based on recall rate) (per cent)

2002–3	2003–4	2004–5	2005–6	2006–7	2007–8
5.8	7.0	6.5	6.4	5.7	6.8

Source: Compiled from *Annual Reports of the Parole Board*.

In 2007–8, there were 1,751 life-sentence prisoners on conditional release (i.e. life licencees under supervision). In the same year, 114 life licencees were recalled, 50 of whom were recalled for allegations of offending. It is interesting to contrast this number with the number of recalled offenders on HDC: as we saw above, breaching HDC conditions accounted for nearly 75 per cent of all HDC recalls, and only 9 per cent of HDC recalls were on the grounds of being charged with a new offence.

3. The legal criteria applicable in 2009

3.1 Aims and objectives

The aims of the release processes for determinate and indeterminate prisoners now appear very different, although they are not clearly articulated. For determinate-sentence prisoners, half-time release allows for supervision in the community, and the aims of earlier-than-halftime release are pragmatic: reducing the problems of prison overcrowding. For indeterminate prisoners, the approach is 'plainly in tune with the public protection agenda that has driven criminal justice policy for the last 10 to 15 years, ... refocus[ing] parole on risk and risk assessment' (Shute 2007a: 22).

When parole was introduced in 1967, there were two main objectives: to reduce the prison population and to help in the rehabilitation of offenders by releasing them into the community at the 'right' time in their sentence, under the supervision of a probation officer to whom they were required to report regularly. This rehabilitative aim seems to have slid down the political agenda.

3.2 Conditional release for determinate-sentence prisoners

For prisoners serving determinate sentences, the law is currently clear that they should be released on licence at the halfway point in their sentence, with the added possibility of HDC and ECL[7] (see s. 33 of the CJA 1991, which has been amended very significantly many times, most recently by s. 26 of the Criminal Justice and Immigration Act 2008). Great effort is made to try to calculate the prisoner's release date accurately (see Prison Service Order 6650[8]). But the law is very complex, due in part to the frequency of change and to complex transitional rules. Thus, in a recent case, *R. (Noone)* v. *Governor of Drake Hall Prison*, the Master of the Rolls (the head Judge in the Court of Appeal, Civil Division), explicitly agreed with Wall LJ's comment that:

> I cannot, however, leave the case without expressing my sympathy both for the 'despair' which the judge felt when considering the statutory provisions in the case, and for the view which he expressed in paragraph 2 of his judgment: 'It is simply unacceptable in a society governed by the rule of law for it to be well nigh impossible to discern from statutory provisions what a sentence means in practice'. The argument in this court lasted for the best part of a day, and the respondent's correct

[7]Release on temporary licence (ROTL) is also very important: there were 441,167 temporary licences granted in 2007. The vast majority are resettlement day releases done under Prison Rule 9, made under s. 47 of the Prison Act 1952. Detailed rules are in Prison Service Order 2300.

[8]See www.hmprisonservice.gov.uk/resourcecentre/psispsos/listpsos/index.asp?startrow=101.

release date has only emerged in a careful reserved judgment (*ibid.* at [60]).

The case provides a useful practical example. Rebecca Noone was sentenced on 23 May 2007 for theft to 22 months' imprisonment; for three further offences of theft to four month's imprisonment concurrent with each other but consecutive to the sentence of 22 months; and for contempt of court, to one month's imprisonment consecutive. The total sentence was therefore 27 month's imprisonment. On 24 May 2007 she was given a release-date notification slip with the following information on it:

- Eligibility for HDC: 15 January 2008.
- Conditional release date: 28 May 2008.
- Sentence and licence expiry date: 13 July 2009.

On 18 July 2007 she was given a further release-date notification slip with the following revised information:

- Eligibility for HDC: 20 April 2008.
- Conditional release date: 28 May 2008.
- Sentence and licence expiry date: 10 February 2009.

She challenged this assessment by way of judicial review in the High Court in January 2008 and was released in February, but her case continued to the Court of Appeal for a detailed review of the relevant law. As a result of the Criminal Justice Act 2003 (Commencement No. 8 and Transitional and Saving Provisions) Order 2005 (Supplementary Provisions) Order 2005 sch. 2 para. 14, the sentences were partly governed by the Criminal Justice Act 1991 and partly by the Criminal Justice Act 2003. It was clear to the Court of Appeal that the 2003 Act was intended to bring into effect a new sentencing regime to replace the regime under the 1991 Act and that provisions for sentences of less than 12 months were contained in ss. 181 and 182 of the 2003 Act. However, those sections were not yet in force. The coming into force of the relevant provisions of the 2003 Act, and the repeal of the relevant provisions of the 1991 Act, were subject to the provisions contained in sch. 2 to the 2005 Order. The case serves as an excellent example of the despair faced by those implementing the system, as the quotation from the Master of the Rolls above makes clear!

The rules for the granting of the ECL were described in section 1.4 above. The detailed criteria for the granting of both HDC and the

ELC are set out in Prison Service Order 6700. It is worth noting that prisoners who have had 'additional days awarded' for disciplinary offences committed in prison will find their date of conditional release delayed. The rules on the release of young offenders are somewhat different because of the different sentences available for young offenders.

3.3 Indeterminate-sentence prisoners

This category includes those subject to mandatory or discretionary life sentences, and Imprisonment for Public Protection (IPP). The decision to release 'lifers' is taken by the Parole Board. The law itself is not easy to find: it is spread across very many different statutes, reflecting the changing status of the Parole Board. As explained above, parole was first introduced in this country by the Criminal Justice Act 1967. Over the years many changes have been made to the system, by Parliament (sweeping changes were made by the Criminal Justice Act 1991, the Criminal Justice and Public Order Act 1994, the Criminal Justice Act 2003 and the Criminal Justice and Immigration Act 2008) and by change forced onto a reluctant government by a stream of important decisions from the courts (see section 1 above).

The test to be applied by the Parole Board in satisfying itself that 'it is no longer necessary for the protection of the public that the prisoner should be confined' is whether 'the lifer's level of risk to the life and limb of others is considered to be more than minimal' (see the Directions issued by the Secretary of State in August 2004[9]). These directions specify that the Parole Board must consider:

a) all information before it, including any written or oral evidence obtained by the Board;
b) each case on its merits, without discrimination on any grounds;
c) whether the release of the lifer is consistent with the general requirements and objectives of supervision in the community, namely;

- protecting the public by ensuring that their safety would not be placed unacceptably at risk;
- securing the lifers successful re-integration into the community.

[9]Available online at www.paroleboard.gov.uk/policy_and_guidance/secretary_of_states_directions/

In assessing the level of 'risk to life and limb' presented by a lifer, the Parole Board must consider the following information, where relevant and where available, before directing the lifer's release, recognizing that the weight and relevance attached to particular information may vary according to the circumstances of each case:

a) the lifer's background, including the nature, circumstances and pattern of any previous offending;
b) the nature and circumstances of the index offence, including any information provided in relation to its impact on the victim or victim's family;
c) the trial judge's sentencing comments or report to the Secretary of State, and any probation, medical, or other relevant reports or material prepared for the court;
d) whether the lifer has made positive and successful efforts to address the attitudes and behavioural problems which led to the commission of the index offence;
e) the nature of any offences against prison discipline committed by the lifer;
f) the lifer's attitude and behaviour to other prisoners and staff;
g) the category of security in which the lifer is held and any reasons or reports provided by the Prison Service for such categorisation, particularly in relation to those lifers held in Category A conditions of security;
h) the lifer's awareness of the impact of the index offence, particularly in relation to the victim or victim's family, and the extent of any demonstrable insight into his/her attitudes and behavioural problems and whether he/she has taken steps to reduce risk through the achievement of life sentence plan targets;
i) any medical, psychiatric or psychological considerations (particularly if there is a history of mental instability);
j) the lifer's response when placed in positions of trust, including any absconds, escapes, past breaches of temporary release or life licence conditions and life licence revocations;
k) any indication of predicted risk as determined by a validated actuarial risk predictor model, or any other structured assessments of the lifers risk and treatment needs;
l) whether the lifer is likely to comply with the conditions attached to his or her life licence and the requirements

of supervision, including any additional non-standard conditions;

m) any risk to other persons, including the victim, their family and friends.

Before directing release on life licence, the Parole Board also considers the following:

a) the lifer's relationship with probation staff (in particular the supervising probation officer), and other outside support such as family and friends;
b) the content of the resettlement plan and the suitability of the release address;
c) the attitude of the local community in cases where it may have a detrimental effect upon compliance;
d) representations on behalf of the victim or victim's relatives in relation to licence conditions.

Once released, the prisoner is on licence. The standard licence is likely to look like Figure 5.1.

Additional licence conditions may include the following:

• Attendance at appointments with a named psychiatrist/psychologist/medical practitioner, and co-operation with recommended care or treatment.

• Not to work with or to take part in organized activities with people under a certain age.

• A residence condition.

• A requirement not to reside in the same household as children under a specified age.

• A requirement not to approach or communicate with named people.

• A requirement to avoid a particular area.

• A requirement to address alcohol/drug/sexual/gambling/solvent abuse/anger/debt/offending behaviour problems at a specified centre.

• A drug-testing condition.

• A polygraph condition (added by ss. 28 and 29 of the Offender Management Act 2007)

1. Under the provisions of Sections 244–253 of the Criminal Justice Act 2003 you are being released on licence. You will be under the supervision of a probation officer or a social worker of a local authority social services department and must comply with the conditions of this licence. The objectives of this supervision are to (a) protect the public, (b) prevent re-offending and (c) achieve your successful re-integration into the community.

2. Your supervision commences on_____and expires on_____ _____unless this licence is previously revoked.

3. On release you must report without delay to

Name:

Address:

4. You must place yourself under the supervision of whichever probation officer or social worker is nominated for this purpose from time to time.

5. While under supervision you must:

    (i)   keep in touch with your supervising officer in accordance with any reasonable instructions that you may from time to time be given;

    (ii)   if required, receive visits from your supervising officer at your home at reasonable hours and for reasonable periods;

    (iii) live where reasonably approved by your supervising officer and notify him or her in advance of any proposed change of address;

    (iv) undertake only such employment as your supervising officer reasonably approves and notify him or her in advance of any proposed change in employment or occupation;

    (v)   not travel outside the United Kingdom without obtaining the prior permission of your supervising officer (which will be given in exceptional circumstances only);

    (vi) be of good behaviour, not commit any offence and not take any action which would jeopardise the objectives of your supervision, namely to protect the public, prevent you from re-offending and secure your successful reintegration into the community;

    ((vii) Additional licence conditions)

6. The Secretary of State may vary or cancel any of the above conditions, in accordance with Section 250 of the Criminal Justice Act 2003.

7. If you fail to comply with any requirement of your probation supervision (set out in paragraphs 3, 4 and 5 above), or if you otherwise pose a risk to the public, you will be liable to have your licence revoked and be recalled to custody until the date on which your licence would otherwise have expired. If you are sent back to prison and released before the end of the licence period, you will still be subject to supervision.

Signed:

Status:

Date:

for the Secretary of State for the Home Department

This licence has been given to me and its requirements have been explained.

Signed:

Date:

Figure 5.1 A standard licence

Offenders may be subject to multi-agency supervision. Sections 325–327 of the Criminal Justice Act 2003 lay down the duties for Multi-agency Public Protection Arrangements, set up under the Criminal Justice and Court Services Act 2000, which require Chief Officers of Police and local Probation Boards to establish arrangements for the management of certain high-risk offenders in the community (see Kemshall 2007). There have recently been experiments with the satellite tracking of offenders (see Shute 2007b).

3.4 Special rules for foreign prisoners

Deportation and the removal of foreign prisoners are still governed by the Immigration Act 1971, s. 46 of the Criminal Justice Act 1991 (as amended) and by the Nationality, Asylum and Immigration Act 2002, although the UK Borders Act 2007 has now (in s. 32) introduced 'automatic deportation' for foreign criminals (with a plethora of exceptions to be found in s. 33). Some prisoners are sent home during their sentence under the provisions of the Repatriation of Prisoners Act 1984, which brought into effect the 1983 Council of Europe Convention on the Transfer of Sentenced Prisoners. Under the Convention, the consent of both the sentencing country and the country to which the prisoner is to be transferred, as well as of the prisoner himself, is required before a transfer may take place. The prisoner must have at least six months left to serve.

To encourage more foreign prisoners to leave, a new Early Removal Scheme was introduced in July 2004 (see Prison Service Order 6000, ch. 9; Prison Service Instruction 27/2004). It applies to all foreign prisoners sentenced to more than three months, subject to exceptions. Since 7 April 2008 (see para. 7 of PSI 19/2008) prisoners may be deported/removed earlier in their sentence, up to 270 days before half time (Council Framework Decision 2008/909/JHA of 27 November 2008 on the Application of the Principle of Mutual Recognition to Judgments in Criminal Matters Imposing Custodial Sentences or Measures involving Deprivation of Liberty for the Purpose of their Enforcement in the European Union will, of course, result in dramatic changes to the law; see Chapter 2).

4. Types of decision-making

4.1 Executive decision-making

Decisions on earlier-than-halftime conditional release for determinate-sentence prisoners (HDC and ECL decisions) are taken by the prison authorities (details are to be found in Prison Service Order 6700). The risk assessment for HDC should commence 10 weeks before a prisoner's eligibility date. The suitability assessment is normally taken by a member of the seconded probation team working in the prison (see para. 5.9.2 of Prison Service Order 6700), but the Governor may authorize other staff to do this. Information will be collected from the prisoner and from a member of the prison staff in daily contact with the prisoner. An enhanced assessment may be required, in which case the file will be considered by a board comprising a member of the governing grade of the prison and a seconded probation officer or a member of the prison throughcare team. The prisoner does not attend. The final decision whether to release a prisoner on HDC or not must be taken by an authorized Governor on behalf of the Secretary of State. The Governing Governor (or, in contractually-managed prisons, the Controller) is authorized to take this decision on behalf of the Secretary of State. They may delegate the task to a more junior governor grade. There is some confusion at the moment as to the role which the staff of privately-run prisons take in the decision-making process (see Padfield 2009: 170).

A prisoner may appeal to a more senior governor-grade employee in the prison, and from there to the area manager at Prison Service Headquarters. From there, the only further 'appeal' is by way of an application for judicial review to the Administrative Court of the High Court, where the Court will consider the lawfulness of the way the decision was made, but not the rights and wrongs of the conclusion reached. There are few reported cases: the procedure is not only unlikely to be successful but can also take both time and money.

4.2 The Parole Board

What is the status of the Parole Board? It was made a non-departmental public body in 1994, but it has never been made a genuinely independent tribunal. Whether this will change soon remains to be seen: both the previous Chairman (see Nichols 2007) and the Court of Appeal (in R (Brooke) v. Parole Board) have been loud in their criticism of the Board's supposed compliance with Art. 5(4) of the European Court of Human Rights.

The panels of the Parole Board who take oral decisions have in recent years been chaired by judges. But because of the cost and difficulty of finding enough available judges, recently panels have sometimes been chaired by lawyers. The latest amendments to the Rules (see Parole Board (Amendment) Rules 2009) remove both the requirement that all cases must be heard by a panel consisting of three members (panel membership to be at the discretion of the Chairman of the Parole Board) and the requirement that only a legally-qualified member of the Parole Board chair a panel, other than a panel convened to determine whether to release a prisoner serving a mandatory, discretionary or automatic life sentence or a prisoner detained at Her Majesty's Pleasure.

The members of the Parole Board include judges, psychiatrists, those with 'knowledge and experience of the supervision or aftercare of discharged prisoners' and those who have 'made a study of the causes of delinquency or the treatment of offenders' (see s. 239 and sch. 19 of the Criminal Justice Act 2003). The work of the Parole Board is well described in its annual reports to Parliament; it has an excellent website and it has encouraged a number of research projects.

In *R (Brooke)* v. *Parole Board* (2008) the Court of Appeal upheld the declaration of the Divisional Court that the Parole Board was not sufficiently independent of the Secretary of State, as required by both English common law and Art. 5(4) of the European Convention on Human Rights. The Lord Chief Justice concluded:

Neither the Secretary of State nor his Department has adequately addressed the need for the Parole Board to be and to be seen to be free of influence in relation to the performance of its judicial functions. Both by Directions and by the use of his control over the appointment of members of the Board the Secretary of State has sought to influence the manner in which the Board carries out its risk assessment. The close working relationship between the Board and the unit acting as its sponsor has tended to blur the distinction between the executive role of the former and the judicial role of the latter (*ibid.* at para. 78).

He was also critical of the funding restriction which stopped the Board from interviewing prisoners, contrary to its wishes:

While this did not threaten the Board's impartiality it was interference that exceeded what could properly be justified by the role of sponsor (*ibid.* at para. 80).

A Government Consultation Paper[10] on the future of the Parole Board was published in July 2009, asking wide-ranging questions, such as 'should the Parole Board's existing jurisdiction, functions and powers be clarified?'. Clearly more change lies ahead.

4.3   Indirect influences on release decisions

In relation to determinate-sentence prisoners a clear indirect influence is prison overcrowding. Release before half-time is largely motivated by the question of saving money, although the actual decisions are individualized (see Dodgson *et al.* 2001). In relation to indeterminate prisoners, the influences are more complex and more offender-based. The factors considered by the Parole Board were analysed in Padfield and Liebling (2000). Discretionary lifer panels looked for evidence of change, insight into the offence, evidence of offending behaviour work successfully undertaken and realistic release plans, with the prospect of effective supervision. They also took account of behaviour in prison, security classification, relationships with family, the nature of the index offence, attitude towards the victim and other risk factors, such as medical treatment. There was a certain 'intuition gradient' in the decision-making process. Sometimes personal characteristics or cultural factors seemed to influence decisions. There was scope for bias to be checked during the deliberations because of the composition of the panel. *Level* of risk was rarely discussed, and the Board operated with extreme caution. Given the wide range of factors considered to be relevant, it is clear that many factors considered to be administrative (for example, categorization) have an important impact on the 'judicial' decision whether or not to release.

5.   Recall procedures

Section 254 of the Criminal Justice Act 2003 gave the power to revoke a licence and recall an offender to prison entirely to the Home Secretary, whereas previously (other than in cases where immediate action was required) the Home Secretary could usually recall a prisoner only if recommended to do so by the Parole Board. Now the power to recall is initiated by the Probation Service, part of the National Offender Management Service.

[10]Ministry of Justice (2009) *Future of the Parole Board* (available online at www. justice.gov.uk/consultations/future-parole-board.htm).

Recalled offenders used to be the 'waifs and strays of the system' (Shute 2003: 430). Their cases were considered at an ordinary 'paper' panel of the Parole Board at the beginning of a meeting with an already-full agenda. Often, decisions were taken on the basis of tabled papers rather than on papers which had been circulated in advance. However, the House of Lords in *R (Smith)* v. *Parole Board; R (West)* v. *Parole Board* (2005) required the Board to provide recalled prisoners with the possibility of an oral hearing.

As has been noted, the number of prisoners recalled to prison during the period on licence has been increasing dramatically in recent years. This reflects a complex variety of factors, the most obvious of which are greater flexibility in early release rules (particularly, the introduction of HDC), greater caution and risk aversion among probation officers and their supervisors, and closer surveillance of offenders on licence (see Padfield and Maruna 2006; Padfield 2009a and b). Appleton and Roberts (2005) carried out research between 2002 and 2003 on 118 lifers released between 1992 and 1997. Remarkably, 20 cases were simply missing but, of those they studied, 45 per cent had been recalled at least once. Appleton and Roberts noted the dearth of information available in prisoners' supervision files on the courses, etc., that the prisoners had done in prison – a sign of the failure of the Prison and Probation Services to 'join up' as effectively as they should.

The increasing number of prisoners has forced the government to streamline procedures. The prison authorities now have the power to re-release recalled prisoners without recourse to the Parole Board. The hugely complicated s. 29 of the Criminal Justice and Immigration Act 2008, on the release of prisoners after recall, takes more than three pages of the statute book. Automatic re-release is hedged around with exceptions. Sexual and violent offenders, those on HDC or those previously recalled and released are not eligible for this automatic re-release. And the Secretary of State must be satisfied that all prisoners do not present a risk of serious harm if released (s. 255A(3) and (5)). It seems likely that the prison population will continue to grow, a figure inflated by the increasing number of people recalled to prison in breach of their conditions. This raises significant new problems. For example, for the judge sentencing an offender for a new offence: the prisoner may or may not have been recalled for breaching his earlier licence, and the judge has to calculate how much time spent in prison pre-sentence counts towards the new or the old sentence (see Chapter 16).

6. Practical challenges

6.1 Costs and delay

The funding of the system is clearly a major issue, as is the way costs are calculated: different agencies and bodies (private and public) are more concerned by their own budgets than the costs to the wider 'system'. Governments are more interested in short-term costs than the long term. The soaring costs of the Parole Board must have been an important factor in the government's decision to remove the release of determinate-sentence prisoners from its remit. Closely tied to the question of cost is that of delay, particularly shocking when the liberty of the citizen is at stake. In the National Audit Office's sample of 276 oral hearing cases from September 2006 to May 2007, only 32 per cent were held in the target month: an astonishing 20 per cent were held 12 or more months late (National Audit Office 2008). Another area of concern is the soaring costs of legal advice to prisoners, which has recently led the government to announce sweeping cuts to legal aid.[11] These proposed savings are very worrying, particularly given the low IQ and literacy skills of many prisoners and the complexity of the processes.

6.2 Risk assessments

A large number of risk assessment tools are used in the Prison and Probation Services in England and Wales. The Offender Assessment System (OASys) was developed in the 1990s to help measure the likelihood of reconviction and to identify the 'criminogenic needs' of offenders (i.e. to help identify suitable interventions). The Offender Group Reconviction Scale (OGRS) and Risk Matrix 2000 are also used to measure the likelihood of reconviction (for a description of these tools, see JUSTICE 2009: App. E). We have already mentioned Hood and Shute's concern that the 'clinical' way the Parole Board makes decisions may be significantly more cautious than actuarial risk predictors suggest is necessary. Kemshall (2007), too, calls for much more rigorous testing of the evidence presented to parole panels, for an increased and transparent use of actuarial risk factors and for an increased awareness of these tools by decision-makers. This last is vital: greater understanding of the reliability/unreliability of all risk assessments is essential. Even if they were accurate, there is a real danger in applying group reconviction rates to any one individual.

[11]See Legal Services Commission (2009) *Prison Law Funding: A Consultation.* London: LSE.

Many people may be detained unnecessarily. The use of risk assessment tools by probation and prison staff should be evaluated more closely. Similarly, we have already questioned whether 'failure to address offending behaviour' too often equates that criterion with formal offending behaviour courses undertaken in prison (see section 1.3 above). It would appear that we are reaching a moment in England and Wales where financial constraints may be leading decision-makers to put less emphasis on the courses which offenders have completed as a measure of lowered risk. It is, of course, vitally important to continue to attempt to assess the efficacy of various courses and treatments, and to monitor their availability in different prisons, both private and state run.[12]

6.3 Supervision in the community

Effective supervision of offenders in the community is inevitably costly. Probation services in England and Wales have been under enormous pressure in recent years. There has been a stream of management and organizational reforms, including centralization, and increasing government conviction that the private sector should be used to transform not only prisons but also probation services. Yet probation still appears as the poor relation of the prison system. Raynor and Maguire (2006) are typical of many academic commentators who suggest that 'contestability'[13] will in fact create more problems than it solves. Not only are services becoming more fragmented as they become privatized, but high-profile failures of supervision also encourage more cautious decision-making. For example, in November 2004, Damien Hanson and Elliot White murdered a London businessman in his home during a burglary, when both men were under the supervision of London Probation Area; and in August 2005, Anthony Rice murdered a woman who befriended him in her home some nine months after he was released from prison on life licence. Both cases caused much public concern, and the investigations conducted by the Chief Inspector of Probation revealed worrying failures in the effectiveness of supervision in practice (Her Majesty's Inspectorate of Probation 2006a, 2006b). Current controversies surrounding 'joined

[12]The case law provides depressing examples of the non-availability of courses which prisoners have been required to undertake: see *Secretary of State for Justice* v. *Walker and James*; *R (Lee)* v. *Secretary of State for Justice*.

[13]Contestability is the term currently much used to explain competition in the delivery of what used to be considered public services: competition between public, private and now sometimes third sector (non-profit making) providers.

up' criminal justice agencies can be no more than highlighted in this short chapter.

7. Theoretical and other conclusions

7.1 The justifications for conditional release

It remains somewhat unclear in England why prisoners are being released conditionally. Clearly for those who are not deemed dangerous, it is for largely pragmatic reasons (vacating expensive prison beds), combined with recognition that supervision by probation services on release is useful. But the focus of flexible release for those deemed 'dangerous' raises important questions about the assessment of danger, levels of acceptable risk and so on. The Secretary of State's Directions to the Parole Board under s. 239(6) of the Criminal Justice Act 2003 make clear that, where an offender is subject to a custodial sentence, the licence period is an integral part of the sentence, and compliance with licence conditions is required. In most cases the licences are combined with supervision by a probation officer, social worker or member of the youth offending team (the exception to this is the use of HDC licences for adult prisoners serving a sentence of less than 12 months).

The Directions state that the 'objects of supervision are: to protect the public; to prevent reoffending; and to ensure the prisoner's successful reintegration into the community'. Yet the large numbers of prisoners being recalled to prison, some of whom will therefore get no further supervision on their eventual release, can undermine these objects. The purposes of sentencing have been legislated (see s. 142 of the Criminal Justice Act 2003) but Parliament should also enact clear criteria for release, which should include a statement that the purposes of conditional release include not only public protection, but also the rehabilitation or reintegration of offenders into mainstream society (see also JUSTICE 2009). It is a point which needs greater emphasis.

7.2 The constitutional position of the Parole Board

We have seen how the Parole Board, in its 42-year life, has shifted from being an advisory body, advising on the release of most prisoners, to a 'court-like' body directing the release (or non-release) of life-sentence prisoners. However, it is clear that the current position is not tenable. The government is currently considering the implications of the decision of the Court of Appeal that the Parole Board is not sufficiently independent of the Secretary of State, as required by both English common law and Art. 5(4) of the European Convention on Human Rights.[14] It is high time that the Parole Board became a judicial body, totally independent of the Ministry of Justice. It is seems very unlikely that the government, not least for reasons of cost, will go so far as to create a new system of courts to review the implementation of all sentences, but this commentator would welcome a fundamental reconsideration of the current position.

7.3 The role of the victim

There has been a growing awareness of the rights and needs of victims in the English criminal justice system in recent years. The Home Office's Code of Practice for Victims of Crime[15] states that the Parole Board has the following obligations:

> The Parole Board must consider any representations that victims have offered to the Probation Service on the conditions to be included in the release licences of prisoners serving sentences subject to consideration by the Parole Board and reflect these considerations in the parole decisions. Conditions relating to the victim should be disclosed to the victim through the Probation Service, and where a licence condition has not been included, the Parole Board should provide an explanation for the non-inclusion. The Parole Board must consider any information regarding the victim that relates directly to the current risk presented by a prisoner in deciding whether or not to grant or recommend release and reflect this in the parole decision (paras. 12.1–12.2).

The courts have upheld conditions imposed at the request of victims that, for example, a released murderer should not enter a certain city without the approval of his supervising officer (see *R (Craven)* v. *Secretary of State for the Home Department and the Parole Board* (2001)). And now victims may sometimes be able to give oral evidence to a Parole Board hearing. But a parole hearing may in fact aggravate rather than ameliorate victim concerns (see Stone 2002), and current moves to encourage further victim participation need to examined

[14]See Legal Services commission (2009) *Prison Law Funding: A Consultation.* London: LSE.
[15]Available online at www.homeoffice.gov.uk/documents/victims-code-of-practice?view=Binary.

with care (see Padfield and Roberts forthcoming). The role of the victim in executive conditional release needs to be examined.

7.4 Complexity and change

It should be clear to the reader that the English system of conditional release is complex, and that complexity is exacerbated by the frequency of change. Frequent change can lead to apparent unfairness, especially when co-defendants find themselves subject to different regimes (see *R (Poku)* v. *Parole Board* (2009)). It is with some hesitation, therefore, that this review of the system concludes with a plea for further change. The *Offender Management Caseload Statistics 2007* (published in October 2008) reported that, by June 2007, there were 9,480 life-sentenced prisoners in English and Welsh prisons (out of a total population of 79,730 prisoners). By 22 May 2009 the total population had reached 82,965, and the number of lifers will undoubtedly have risen as well. Does it make sense to have such a different system in place for life-sentence prisoners? Are there (far) too many prisoners facing indeterminate sentences? The current system merits a fundamental review.

References

Appleton, C. and Roberts, C. (2005) *The Resettlement of Discretionary Life-sentenced Offenders. Home Office Development and Practice Report 44.* London: Home Office.

Dodgson, K., Goodwin, P., Howard, P., Llewellyn-Thomas, S., Mortimer, E., Russell, N. and Weiner, M. (2001) *Electronic Monitoring of Released Prisoners. Research Study 222.* London: Home Office.

Fox, L.W. (1952) *The English Prison and Borstal Systems.* London: Routledge & Kegan Paul.

Halliday, J. (2001) *Making Punishments Work: Report of a Review of the Sentencing Framework for England and Wales.* London: Home Office Communication Directorate.

Her Majesty's Inspectorate of Probation (2006a) *An Independent Review of a Serious Further Offence Case: Damien Hanson and Elliot White.* London: Home Office.

Her Majesty's Inspectorate of Probation (2006b) *An Independent Review of a Serious Further Offence Case: Anthony Rice.* London: HMIP (available online at http://www.inspectorates.homeoffice.gov.uk).

Home Office (1990) *Crime, Justice and Protecting the Public (Cm 965).* London: Home Office.

Home Office (2001) *Review of the Sentencing Framework.* London: Home Office.

Hood, R. and Shute, S. (1994) *Parole in Transition: Evaluating the Impact and Effects of Changes in the Parole System – Phase One, Establishing the Baseline. Oxford Centre for Criminological Research, Occasional Paper 13.* Oxford: Oxford Centre for Criminological Research.

Hood, R. and Shute, S. (1995) *Paroling with New Criteria: Evaluating the Impact and Effects of Changes in the Parole System: Phase Two.* Oxford: Centre for Criminological Research.

Hood, R. and Shute, S. (2000) *The Parole System at Work: A Study of Risk Based Decision-making. Home Office Research Study 202.* London: Home Office.

Hood, R. and Shute, S. (2002) 'The changing face of parole in England and Wales: a story of some well-intentioned reforms and unintended consequences', in C. Prittwitz, M. Baurmann, K. Günther, L. Kuhlen, R. Merkel, C. Nestler and L. Schulz (eds) *Festschrift für Klaus Lüderssen.* Baden-Baden: Nomos Verlag.

Hood, R., Shute, S., Feilzer, M. and Wilcox, A. (2002) 'Sex offenders emerging from long-term imprisonment', *British Journal of Criminology*, 42: 371–94.

JUSTICE (2009) *A New Parole System for England and Wales.* London: JUSTICE.

Kemshall, H. (2007) 'MAPPA, parole and the management of high-risk offenders in the community', in N. Padfield (ed.) *Who to Release? Parole, Fairness and Criminal Justice.* Cullompton: Willan Publishing.

McCabe, S. (1985) 'The powers and purposes of the Parole Board', *Criminal Law Review*, 489–99.

McCarthy, T. (2007) 'Dealing with indeterminacy: life sentences and IPP – the view from within', in N. Padfield (ed.) *Who to Release? Parole, Fairness and Criminal Justice.* Cullompton: Willan Publishing.

Morgan, N. (1983) 'The shaping of parole in England and Wales', *Criminal Law Review*, 137–51.

National Audit Office (2008) *Protecting the Public: The Work of the Parole Board.* London: HMSO.

Nichols, D. (2007) 'Who should we keep locked up?', in N. Padfield (ed.) *Who to Release? Parole, Fairness and Criminal Justice.* Cullompton: Willan Publishing.

Padfield, N. (2002) *Beyond the Tariff: Human Rights and the Release of Life Sentence Prisoners.* Cullompton: Willan Publishing.

Padfield, N. (2006) 'The Parole Board in Transition', *Criminal Law Review*, 3–23.

Padfield, N. (2009a) 'Parole and early release: the Criminal Justice and Immigration Act 2008 changes in context', *Criminal Law Review*, 166–87.

Padfield, N. (2009b) 'The administrative implementation of sentences', *Cambridge Law Journal*, 256–8.

Padfield, N. and Liebling, A. with Arnold, H. (2000) *An Exploration of Decision-making at Discretionary Lifer Panels. Home Office Research Study 213.* London: Home Office.

Padfield, N. and Maruna, S. (2006) 'The revolving door at the prison gate: exploring the dramatic increase in recalls to prison', *Criminology and Criminal Justice*, 6: 329–52.

Padfield, N. and Roberts, J. (forthcoming), 'Victim submissions at parole in England and Wales and Canada: probative or prejudicial?', in A.E. Bottoms and J. Roberts (eds) *Victims in Contemporary Society*. Cullompton: Willan Publishing.

Padfield, N. and Walker, N. (1996) *Sentencing: Theory, Law and Practice*. Oxford: Oxford University Press.

Raynor, P. and Maguire, M. (2006) 'End to end or end in tears? Prospects for the effectiveness of the National Offender Management Model', in M. Hough, R. Allen and U. Padel (eds) *Reshaping Probation and Prisons: The New Offender Management Framework*. Bristol: Polity Press.

Shute, S. (2003) 'The development of parole and the role of research in its reform', in L. Zedner and A. Ashworth (eds) *The Criminological Foundations of Penal Policy: Essays in Honour of Roger Hood*. Oxford: Oxford University Press.

Shute, S. (2007a) 'Parole and risk assessment', in N. Padfield (ed.) *Who to Release? Parole, Fairness and Criminal Justice*. Cullompton: Willan Publishing.

Shute, S. (2007b) *Satellite Tracking of Offenders: A Study of the Pilots in England and Wales*. London: Ministry of Justice Research.

Stone, N. (2002) 'Release of prisoners on licence – fears and concerns of victims and their families', *Journal of Social Welfare and Family Law*, 24.

Cases

European Court of Human Rights

Hussain *v.* United Kingdom, Singh *v.* United Kingdom 21928/93 21 February 1996 (1996) 22 EHRR 1

Stafford *v.* United Kingdom [GC] 28 May 2002 (46295/99) (2002) 35 EHRR 32

Thynne, Wilson and Gunnell *v.* United Kingdom 25 October 1990 (11787/85; 12009/86; 11978/86) (1991) 13 EHRR 666

Domestic cases

R (Anderson) *v.* Secretary of State for the Home Department [2002] UKHL 46

R (Brooke) *v.* Parole Board [2008] EWCA Civ 29

R (Craven) *v.* Secretary of State for the Home Department and the Parole Board [2001] EWHC Admin 850

R (Noone) *v.* Governor of Drake Hall Prison [2008] EWCA Civ 1097

R (Poku) *v.* Parole Board [2009] EWHC 1380 (Admin)

R (Smith) *v.* Parole Board; R (West) *v.* Parole Board [2005] UKHL 1

Secretary of State for Justice *v.* Walker and James; R (Lee) *v.* Secretary of State for Justice [2009] UKHL 22

Chapter 6

Finland

Tapio Lappi-Seppälä

Summary

In Finland, all prisoners – except those few dangerous violent recidivists who serve their sentence in full (approximately 30 prisoners on any given day) – are released on parole. In practice this means that 99 per cent of prisoners released every year are released on parole. Release on parole is based on the decision of the prison's Director. Release practice is also quite fixed. As a rule recidivists are released after they have served two thirds of their sentence, while first-time prisoners are released after they have served one half of their sentences. Offenders aged 15–20 are released either after one third (first offenders) or after one half (recidivists) of their sentences. In all cases, a further condition is that the prisoner must have served at least 14 days. Release may be postponed due to a substantial risk of reoffending. However, this has been used in only a handful of cases.

Offenders who are serving the full term of their sentence can also be released on parole after serving five sixths but at least three years of their sentence. The Helsinki Court of Appeal decides on the release. Prisoners sentenced to life imprisonment can also be released on the decision of Helsinki Court of Appeal. Release from life sentence is possible after serving 12 years and, if the offender was under 21 years of age at the time of the offence, after ten years.

In addition to regular parole, long-term offenders may be placed on supervised probationary liberty. This may take place, at most, six months before regular release times. This form of early release is supervised with global system for mobile (GSM) communications and global positioning system (GPS) techniques.

After release on parole the probation period begins. This period equals the length of the remaining sentence but, at most, is three years. Parole may be revoked because of a breach of parole conditions for a maximum period of 14 days. This decision is taken by the Court. However, this has been used annually in only around ten cases. In practice, parole is revoked only because of a new offence committed during the probation period, for which the offender is sentenced to unconditional imprisonment for three months or more. In these cases the remainder of the old sentence will be partially enforced (usually between one third and one sixth of the old sentence).

I. History

I.I   Introduction

The Finnish juridical system is manifestly rooted in Western, continental, legal culture and has been strongly influenced by neighbouring Nordic countries. The Nordic countries share a long legal and cultural history, the connection between Finland and Sweden being exceptionally close. For centuries, the same laws were in force in both Finland and Sweden because, up to 1809, Finland was part of Sweden. Between 1809 and 1917 Finland was an autonomous Grand Duchy of the Russian Empire, but it still maintained its own laws. Finland declared independence from Russia in 1917. During the last century, Finland underwent three wars (the 1918 Civil War and the two wars against the Soviet Union between 1939 and 1944). Wars and political crises, as well as exceptional postwar conditions, have also made their mark on Finnish criminal policy. In general terms, Finland's criminal justice system has been less resourceful, less flexible and more repressive than those of its Nordic counterparts.

Finland's harsh history was also reflected in the extraordinarily turbulent trends in the use of imprisonment during the last century. Prisons were often occupied not only by regular prisoners serving their sentences for ordinary crimes but, at times, also by prisoners convicted for treason-like activities after the Civil War, and for war-related crimes during the two wars against the Soviet Union. In addition, the dire economic circumstances and the extensive use of fines created a substantial group of fine defaulters – an issue that, from time to time, dominated the penal policy debate about the use

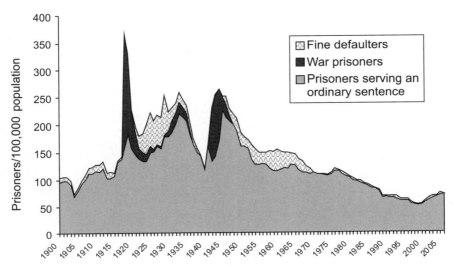

Figure 6.1 Imprisonment rates in Finland, 1880–2005 (annual averages)
Source: Criminal Sanctions Agency

of imprisonment. Figure 6.1 highlights the changes in the use of imprisonment with different categories of prisoners.

Under these conditions the system of parole and early release served different purposes at different times, being influenced by ideological as well as by social, economic and political changes.[1] In the history of parole one may distinguish three distinct phases: the introduction of the parole system in connection with the enactment of a new criminal code for Finland during the late 1800s; the period of rapidly changing prisoner rates under the pressures of political and economic crises (the early and mid-twentieth century); and the period of penal liberalization (the late twentieth century). Throughout these periods the dominant trend was a gradual increase in the application of early release programmes, with varying motivations and with different techniques. Figure 6.2 shows the total number of prisoners released each year (in absolute terms) as well as the number of prisoners released on parole in 1885–2005. Sections 2–4 below discuss in more detail the changes that took place during this period.

[1]The overall changes in the use of imprisonment in Finland are discussed in more detail in Lappi-Seppälä (2009).

Release from Prison

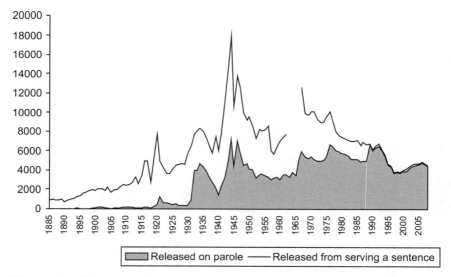

Figure 6.2 Prisoners released on parole, 1885–2005 (prisoners serving an ordinary sentence only)
Source: Criminal Justice Agency

1.2 The introduction of early release

1.2.1 1870 and the partial reforms of the sanctions system

Imprisonment came to occupy a central role in the Finnish sanctions system through a major, though partial, reform that was approved by the estates[2] in 1866 and that came into force in 1870. This enforcement was arranged following Irish enforcement principles and the 'progressive principle' current in Europe at the time. The estates' original proposal also contained provisions for early release. However, this part of the proposal was rejected, partly on formal grounds and partly with reference to the adverse effects of such a system on public security.

1.2.2 The Criminal Code 1889

In 1865 a new committee was set up to prepare for the total reform of the Criminal Code. Despite its recent rejection by the estates, the committee proposed the adoption of an early release system as an

[2]The estates were the two higher estates (the nobility, clergy) and the two lower estates (burghers and land-owning peasants). Each had specific rights and responsibilities and the right to send a representative to the Governing Assembly.

essential part of the progressive principle (although the substantive parts of the Code reflected the ideas of the classical German school). This time the proposal met no resistance. The new Criminal Code, with provisions on early release, was enacted in 1889 and came into force in 1894. The formal requirements established by the Code for early release were strict. It could be applied only to prisoners sentenced to at least for three years' imprisonment. Only after three quarters of a sentence had been served could the Court have the discretion to grant early release. Early release was also reserved purely for prisoners with good prognoses, based on their behaviour in prison and their prospects when released (i.e. a steady job). Parole could be revoked on the basis of behavioural infractions or a new offence. Those whose parole was revoked had to serve their original sentence in full.

The actual use of early release during the last years of the nineteenth century was very restricted, covering about 2 per cent (30–50) of the 1,500 persons released annually from prison.

1.3 Managing prisoner rates in a political and social crisis

1.3.1 Civil War, 1918

By the early 1900s the prevention-oriented ideology of the modern German (sociological) school had reached Finland. The adoption of this ideology into the criminal sanctions system was substantially promoted by an internal political crisis. The Finnish Civil War of 1918 had created an immense prisoner problem: by the early 1920s, prisoner rates tripled from 100 to 350 per 100,000 of the overall population. About half these prisoners were convicted for treason-like activities.

After a series of amnesties prisoner rates fell by a third in two years. The situation was also eased by the adoption of conditional imprisonment in 1921. Early release provisions were also relaxed. Similarly, different rules applied to ordinary prisoners and to prisoners whose offences related to the Civil War. According to a reform carried out in 1918, Civil War prisoners were released automatically after half their sentence and at least one year had been served. In addition to early release procedures, the number of Civil War prisoners was reduced by the massive use of presidential pardons.

In 1921 the general rules on parole were also amended. The formal restriction relating to the length of the original sentence was replaced by a general minimum period of two years to be served in prison before parole could be granted. Prisoners were released after three quarters of the sentence and at least two years had been served. In this way, the decision-making powers were removed from the Court to the prison authorities. These reforms thus increased the use of parole from 2 to 10 per cent of all released prisoners.

1.3.2 Prohibition, recession and severe overcrowding, from the mid-1920s to the 1930s

Prohibition and fine defaulters As a result of the prohibition of alcohol and an economic recession, the crime problem worsened considerably in the mid-1920s. Between the years 1922 and 1930, for example, the number of prisoners increased by almost 50 per cent, taking prisoner rates back again to 250 per 100,000 of the overall population. During the period 1920–30, almost a third of the whole prison population consisted of fine defaulters, which was a side-effect of the economic recession.

The repeal of prohibition in 1932 removed a large number of prisoners sentenced for alcohol-related offences. Rigid fine-default rules were also relaxed. However, notwithstanding the short decline in prisoner numbers in 1931 related to fine defaulters and prohibition offences, overall imprisonment rates continued to climb. This increase was mainly due to an increase in theft. The increase in property offences and the resulting prison overcrowding led to a series of inter-related law reforms.

Property offences and recidivism Repeat offending became a major criminal policy issue and several laws were enacted to tackle this problem. These included a system of preventive detention for chronic recidivists and aggravated recidivism rules. Most of these tougher measures dealt with property offences where recidivism rates were generally high. These reforms, together with the overall increase in property offences, were the over-riding reason for the overall increase in imprisonment rates, which continued until the mid-1930s. To a small extent this increase was also the result of a rise in the number of political prisoners (the so-called communist laws), which reflected the political tensions of the 1930s and the rise of right-wing extremism in Finland.

To ease prison overcrowding, the enforcement rules were changed through the adoption of a qualified form of imprisonment (water-and-bread-imprisonment), which shortened sentences by four fifths by replacing the normal conditions of enforcement with a penalty akin to corporal punishment: meagre nutrition and hard discipline.

Parole reform: 1931 At the same time the application of the parole system was expanded. A major reform of 1931 had two intentions.

First, it was pointed out that early release had beneficial effects on recidivism. It was reported that only 5 per cent (387) of the 7,996 prisoners conditionally released had returned to prison within five years of their release. This encouraged the relaxation of the conditions for the early release. The minimum time served before release was reduced from two years to six months and the proportion that had to be served from three quarters to two thirds. At the same time, however, the probation period was extended. Until then the probation period had been determined solely on the basis of the rest of the sentence to be served at the time of release. In 1931 this period was extended by adding one year to the remainder of the sentence. For those prisoners who would not be eligible for regular (discretionary) parole, a new form of parole was created. In order to ensure that all prisoners would be placed under supervision, it was provided that prisoners should be paroled at the latest when a twelfth of their original sentence remained to be served. The power to decide on parole was moved to the Ministry of Justice (more precisely, to the Prison Administration within the Ministry of Justice).

Rules concerning life imprisonment were also changed. According to the original provisions of the 1889 Criminal Code, prisoners serving life sentences could be paroled after 12 years. In 1931 the release of prisoners serving life sentences was left solely to the pardoning discretion of the President of the Republic. This, however, did not have any substantial effect on release practice.

The 1931 parole reform also brought other important changes. Earlier, parole supervision had been carried out solely by the police. This was deemed to be too formal and inefficient. Those released on discretionary parole were to be supervised either by volunteer workers or the Prison Association, whereas those released on compulsory parole were still placed under police supervision.

The 1931 reform had an immediate impact on the number of parolees. Prior to the reform one out of ten prisoners (at most) was released on parole. During the early years of the reform, this proportion grew substantially and, by the mid-1930s, around a half of prisoners were granted parole.

1.3.3 Easing the tensions: the late 1930s

During the latter half of the 1930s the economy was recovering. The side-effects of prohibition had vanished and imprisonment rates were falling. Law reforms related to general recidivism rules, juvenile justice and open prisons were under consideration. These plans were, however, interrupted by the Winter War that broke out between the Soviet Union and Finland in 1939, as well as by the subsequent Continuation War of 1941–4. When the war commenced with the Soviet Union, men were needed at the front and, consequently, about 20 per cent of prisoners received an amnesty. During the Continuation War imprisonment rates rose once more to 250 per 100,000 of the overall population. These figures included a large number of war prisoners and those kept in isolation for reasons of national security. Early release programmes were expanded to ease the prison overcrowding, but the exceptional postwar conditions and a steep increase in crime still kept the figures high. Between 1940 and 1945 homicide and assault rates doubled, theft offences tripled and robberies increased almost tenfold. This surge in crime was addressed by increased penalties.

1.3.4 The postwar years

The postwar years included some rapid social and economic changes, with sometimes dramatic effects on both crime and crime control. The postwar increase in crime was met in 1946 by increased punishments for property crimes and, as a result, imprisonment rates rose rapidly. However, other parts of the penal system were relaxed due to the abolition of the system of wartime courts martial, and the overall Zeitgeist was becoming more lenient after the harshness of wartime. Two committees were established in 1945–7 to investigate order inside prisons, and this led to the exposure of some of the malpractices that took place during the war. The loudest critics of prison conditions were those held captive during the war as political prisoners. The fact that at least one of the committee members was a former political prisoner obviously left its mark on the report.

The next parole reform took place in 1944, immediately after the war with the Soviet Union. This reform was inspired by the beneficial effects of previous reforms. It was reported that only about 4 per cent of those released on parole in 1938 had had their parole revoked during the following year. This encouraged the further expansion of parole. This reform was also motivated by the need to humanize the criminal justice system, with more flexible parole rules. The 1944 parole reform similarly reflected the concept of more lenient treatment for first offenders. The 1944 reform therefore introduced different rules for first offenders and recidivists. First offenders (or offenders with a 'clean period' of five years after their last release from the prison) could be released after serving half of their sentence and recidivist after serving two thirds. Those released under the rules of compulsory early release could be released after serving five sixths. The minimum time to be served in both cases remained six months.

1.4 Parole and the criminal political turn of the 1960s and 1970s

1.4.1 Parole under the neoclassical framework

The system of parole, as adopted in 1889, was founded on progressive thinking and on the assumption that parole represented the last step on the long road of turning a hardened criminal into a fully-rehabilitated member of society.

However, during the 1960s new winds had started to blow. Within the Nordic countries there was a heated debate about the results and justifications of involuntary treatment in both penal and other institutions (such as in healthcare and the treatment of alcoholics). In Finland this criticism of treatment ideology merged with a criticism of the overly-severe Criminal Code and the excessive use of custodial sentences. The resulting criminal policy ideology was labelled 'humane neoclassicism', which stressed both legal safeguards against coercive care and the goal of less repressive measures in general.[3] In sentencing, the principles of proportionality and predictability became central values, with individualized sentencing and sentencing for general preventive reasons or on the grounds of perceived dangerousness placed in the background.

The fall of the rehabilitative ideal seriously damaged the underlying justifications of the early release system. During the early years of the 1970s there were serious discussions about whether the parole system should be abolished altogether and replaced by 'real time' sentencing. Unlike in many other countries, these proposals were not motivated by the need to increase the credibility of the system or by a desire to increase sentencing levels. The over-riding motive was to expose the hidden coercive elements behind the treatment orientation, to enhance legal safeguards, to separate coercion from care and to reduce the overall level of penal severity.[4]

In 1978 the Nordic Criminal Law Committee published its report on conditional release.[5] This report discussed the arguments for and against the parole system. Most of the reasons for abolishing

[3]The topics in the following sections have been dealt with in more detail in Lappi-Seppälä (2001; 2007). On the trends and changes in Finnish penal policy, see also Anttila and Törnudd (1992) and Lahti (2000). The more extensive texts on parole have been published in Finnish only (see, for example, Pellinen 1991).

[4]The collected essays of both Anttila (2001) and Törnudd (1996) provide excellent overviews on this debate.

[5]See Villkorlig frigivning/Nordic Criminal Law Committee (1978); for a proposal to replace parole and probation with voluntary-based social services. See also Anttila (1975b).

parole related to the transparency of the system and the risks of the administrative misuse of wide discretionary powers. If parole was to be retained, it should contain as little discretion as possible. Furthermore, it was deemed to be unjust to imprison someone because of behavioural infractions that, in other circumstances, would have no legal consequences whatsoever. If parole was to be retained, it should not be revoked merely because of behavioural misdemeanours that do not constitute an offence. Thirdly, as the critics pointed out, the supervision of parole had remained highly formal in nature, and it would be unrealistic to assume that any sort of police supervision would have tangible preventive effects. Furthermore, the current arrangements were unsuited to generating the required support and treatment. To the extent that released prisoners should be given such support, this should be provided by the general social service system based on voluntariness, not coercion. As the Committee concluded, the final decision would depend on how to balance these arguments with each other. The Committee was also divided on whether, in the future, parole should be abolished altogether. However, an agreement was reached that such a reform was not possible at that point. The main argument for retaining the system related to the risk of increased penalty levels. It was agreed that, if parole was abolished, this could be done only if accompanied by a concomitant overall reduction in sentencing levels. This, in turn, was deemed to be unrealistic as it was assumed that the abolition of parole would lead to a serious increase in the level of penalties.

The conclusion of all these deliberations was to retain the system of early release, not so much because of its rehabilitative potential but for its ability to function as a practical tool for regulating the prison population. In other words, the key justification for early release had changed. Furthermore, it was pointed out that this system also reflected our everyday moral judgments: the urge to punish is strongest immediately after the commission or detection of a crime but, as time passes, this need for 'retributive atonement' slowly dissipates, allowing room for a subsequent shortening of the sentence. Other arguments were put forward: the parole system was seen to help maintain prison order, provided the system was not 'completely automatic'. And, despite the decline of the rehabilitative ideal, there were still those who were of the opinion that parole provided a workable framework for organizing assistance and support for released prisoners, even if sanctions for breaches of parole remained fairly nominal.

1.4.2 Legislative changes

Reform of 1966 The first major change in 1966 was still motivated partly by rehabilitative ideals, although the fundamental arguments related to efforts to ease the problems created by serious overcrowding in Finnish prisons. The minimum time to be served was shortened, this time from six to four months. Release after half the sentence was now reserved not for first offenders but for prisoners for whom there were specific reasons for early release. Most of these changes were motivated by the need to decrease the number of prisoners in order to allocate the remaining resources to those prisoner groups who would benefit the most from the treatment available in prisons.

Reform of 1975 The major prison reform of 1975 was influenced strongly by neoclassical criminal policy thinking. The leading progressive principles of enforcement were replaced by the principle of normality. Optimistic rehabilitative goals were similarly replaced by more realistic aims, such as the minimization of harm caused by the loss of liberty. The 1974 reform introduced several improvements in the Finnish prison system. However, the changes to the parole system were fairly modest. The minimum time to be served before parole was granted was reduced from four to three months. The probation period was also shortened to consist only of the remainder of the sentence to be served at the time of release. In addition, the general maximum length of the probation period was fixed at three years. The use of supervision was reduced, especially in connection with shorter sentences.

Reforms of 1989 and 1990 Originally, early release was possible only after the exercise of discretion based strictly on criteria as defined in the law. However, by the 1980s these discretionary elements had largely disappeared from the system. In the 1980s less than 10 per cent of decisions to grant parole were postponed beyond the minimum period. In 1995 the Ministry of Justice issued new guidelines for early release. As a result, the postponement of parole became a statistical rarity and early release a semi-automatic practice. This led to some criticism of a lack of transparency in the sentencing process. However, proposals for the abolition of parole were rejected, citing the risk of increased prison terms (see above). Parole remained a fairly low-profile issue, and no major changes were made. The minimum time to be served before parole, however, was reduced in 1989, this time from 3 months to 14 days. The provisions of compulsory parole were abolished because these rules had not had any practical relevance for years. Furthermore, the rules covering the serving of revoked parole were changed, and the time to be served from the initial prison term was also reduced.

In 1990 the rules concerning the decision-making procedures about parole revocation were changed. This reform was motivated by the requirements of Art. 4 of the European Convention on Human Rights (ECHR). Until 1989 parole could be revoked by a decision of the prison authorities, without the possibility of an appeal to a court. After Finland ratified the ECHR, the power of revocation was transferred to the courts. The practical relevance of the reform was fairly limited, however, because there were only isolated cases of revocation based solely on behavioural misdemeanours.

1.5   Releasing the high-risk recidivists: preventive detention

1.5.1   The adoption of preventive detention in 1931

The risk of reoffending remains a central criterion in most early release systems. Consequently, release procedures for recidivists usually differ from those applied to first offenders. In the history of criminal law, recidivism is linked partly with mental health problems. The solutions to recidivism differ, depending on whether the emphasis is on mental health problems or the risks of reoffending. During the 1920s most Scandinavian countries established special institutions for mentally disturbed offenders and recidivists (Anttila 1975a). Similar proposals were put forward in Finland but, during parliamentary hearings, the system that was agreed on was incapacitation based on a high-risk of reoffending. Preventive detention thus allowed for the prolonged isolation of recidivists. This represented a form of indeterminate sentencing based on estimated dangerousness. Detention could exceed the original prison sentence imposed by the courts, the cases were reviewed at six-monthly intervals.

1.5.2   Expanding the scope of preventive detention: 1953

After the war there was growing pressure for the wider application of preventive detention. This was partly due to the steep increase in crime. Also emerging was an increased interest in the psychiatric background of offending. The focus on 'abnormal' offenders justified demands for the prolonged imprisonment of psychopaths who lacked full moral responsibility. When the requirements for detention were relaxed in 1953, there was an increase in the annual average number of prisoners held in preventive detention, from around 100 to almost 400 per 100,000 of the overall population, representing about 6 per cent of the whole prison population (see Figure 6.3).

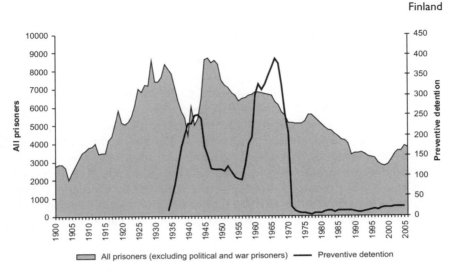

Figure 6.3 Imprisonment rates in Finland, 1900–2005
Source: Criminal Sanctions Agency

1.5.3 Restricting the use of preventive detention: 1971

During the 1960s institutions for mentally-disordered offenders became the target of increasing criticism. This criticism was reinforced by a more general criticism directed against any sort of institutional treatment and – especially in Finland – against the overuse of imprisonment. Long periods of incarceration for habitual property offenders were seen as breaches of the proportionality principle, particularly as there was little or no evidence of the effectiveness of such treatment. Indeterminate sentencing was seen as a breach of fundamental legal safeguards. The scope of preventive detention was drastically reduced by a reform of 1971, which restricted the system to repeat serious violent offenders only (Anttila 1975a). As a result, the absolute number of prisoners in preventive detention decreased from 250 to below 10.

This reform still allowed for prolonged imprisonment beyond the length of the original sentence on preventive grounds. However, since 1971 no one has been held in prison beyond the originally imposed prison sentence. Thus preventive detention had been reduced to a system under which a restricted number of high-risk, violent recidivists were excluded from the normal parole system.

1.6 Early release and the 2006 prison reform

1.6.1 The 2006 prison reform and the parole rules

In 2006 Finland carried out a total reform of its prison law. This reform was very much influenced by the constitutional reforms carried out in 1995 and 2000, which required a much more detailed definition of a prisoner's rights and responsibilities than before.[6] This new Prison Act also aimed to reorganize the imprisonment process (making it more structured and planned), to increase investment in rehabilitative programmes and treatment and, thereby, also to reduce recidivism. All prisoners should be provided with a sentence plan that includes preparation for release. This preparation is made in co-operation with the Probation Service and the social service and employment authorities. Thus networking, which aims to ensure that the rehabilitation started in prison continues after release, is at the core of the plan process.

The parole system as such was therefore not at the centre of the 2006 reform. Substantial parts of the parole system had been reformulated during preceding decades and the rules seemed to function without defects or drawbacks. However, in the event parole and the release rules also underwent a number of important revisions. The system of preventive detention was abolished and replaced by a system that enables the courts to order serious violent offenders to serve their sentence 'in full'. This was meant to be used as restrictively as the earlier system of preventive detention and was thus intended to have no actual effect on imprisonment rates.

A new form of early release (a supervised probationary liberty) was designed for long-term prisoners who needed more support and more intensive programme work. Provisions concerning release from life sentences were also renewed. In addition, the recall procedures were changed, as well as the provision related to supervision.

The basic arrangements that affected the use of parole, however, remained more or less the same. The proportions of the sentences to be served before prisoners were eligible for parole were retained at the existing levels, with a reference to 'general penal policy and economic considerations'. The prison authorities retained the decision-making powers (but with a right to appeal to a Court), again with reference to the fact that the system in Finland is 'very predictable'.

---

[6]For the background to this prison reform, see Lappi-Seppälä (2008; 2009).

1.6.2 The organization of the Probation Service and the aftercare

As part of a larger organizational reform, in 2000 probation work was moved to the Ministry of Justice. Prior to this, probation work had been conducted by a semi-official Probation Association. This change was based largely on constitutional reasons. According to the Constitution, functions that consist of a 'substantial exercise of public power' should be taken care of by state officials. A result of the expansion of community sanctions, the tasks of the former Probation Association had become more akin to the actual enforcement of criminal sanctions. This had led to the conclusion that this work should be done by state officials. Consequently, the major functions of the Probation Association were relocated to a newly-founded Criminal Sanctions Agency and, more specifically, to the Probation Service within that agency.

The Probation Service is responsible for the enforcement of community sanctions, including community service, juvenile punishment, and the supervision of conditionally-sentenced young offenders and conditionally-released prisoners (parolees). It has an official role as the Agency responsible for the supervision of parolees. The Service has 15 district offices and five local offices. Along with the establishment of the Probation Service, probation work received a more official label and became more control oriented. However, the Service is still responsible for supportive work, in co-operation with municipal social welfare services. In addition, several other organizations are involved in supportive aftercare work.

Among these, the Probation Foundation of Finland has a central position. This Foundation was created during the organizational restructuring under which the Probation Association was merged with the Criminal Sanctions Agency. The Foundation's purpose is 'to support the Probation Service and its development, to foster the measures that reduce recidivism and its side effects, and to organize and to make available services that reinforce the aims of the Foundation'. It has comprehensive support programmes for released prisoners. It also aims to help people who have been convicted of a crime, are in a crisis situation because of a crime or are facing social ostracism.

Even though the Probation Service and the Probation Foundation hold the key roles in arranging post-release conditions, much of the aftercare work is left to other organizations and associations.[7] It seems

[7]Other agencies in the field include the Bridge Support Organization. This provides some nationally-significant services in the fields of rehabilitation, education and work–life oriented services for people in danger of becoming

that prisoners drop out too easily from the control of community social welfare services, for which the municipal and communal authorities have responsibility. All in all, therefore, aftercare is still largely underfunded and in constant need of support from a wide range of voluntary organizations.

2. Forms of early release

According to the new provisions, release from prison may take the following forms:

- *Regular parole* (the normal route for release), according to the rules defined in the Criminal Code.

- *Supervised probationary liberty* – an extension of, and more lenient form of, parole.

- *Serving the entire sentence*, replacing the previous system of preventive detention. In essence, this is a denial of regular parole and is reserved for a restricted group of high-risk, violent offenders (release from a life sentence is regulated separately).

- *Temporary release*, which can be granted for educational study, treatment, work, training and for prison leave.

2.1   Release on regular parole

Release on parole refers to the release of a prisoner serving an unconditional sentence of imprisonment so that they can serve the remainder of their sentence at liberty. The time spent on parole is counted as part of the sentence. This has certain implications in cases where conditional release is revoked due to a new offence.

socially ostracized, such as prison inmates and clients of the probation and aftercare services. Prison Fellowship Finland is operated by the Finnish Evangelic Lutheran Church. It assists ex-prisoners, victims and their families and promotes the advancement of restorative justice. KRIS-Finland and Support for Released Prisoners helps ex-criminals and addicts who have decided to start a new life and to get back into society. The Back to Life Association does supportive and preventive work with children, young people and young adults who have become alienated or who run the risk of becoming alienated. The Guarantee Foundation helps people who have problems as a result of heavy debts to manage their debts independently.

2.1.1 Time of release

The time of release depends on the offender's age at the time of the offence and any previous prison sentences. The law identifies four groups:

1. Persons at least 21 years of age at the time of the offence and who have not served a sentence of imprisonment within three years preceding the offence. As a rule, these people are released after having served half of their sentence.

2. People who have served a sentence of imprisonment within three years preceding the offence. These people will be released after serving two thirds of their current sentence.

3. Offenders under the age of 21 when the offence was committed. First-time offenders who have not served a prison term during the last three years prior to the new offence will be released after serving one third of their sentence.

4. Juveniles under the age of 21 who have served a term of imprisonment during the last three years prior to the new offence. These will be released after serving half of their sentence.

The minimum period to be served is in all cases 14 days. This is also the general minimum length of any prison sentence in Finland.

In addition, the law has detailed provisions regarding cases where the prisoner is serving a sentence made up of several different sentences from different courts (a consecutive sentence) or where a sentence is imposed for several offences committed at different times and in a manner that would lead to the application of different fractions under the calculation rules (a joint sentence). In the latter case, the *dubio mitius* principle is applied. If the prison sentence is imposed for several separate offences (a joint sentence) and if the different offences would lead to the application of different fixed fractions, the person is paroled according to the most beneficial fraction. If the sentence has been calculated from different sentences imposed by different courts (a consecutive sentence), the fixed fractions will be counted individually for each sub-sentence following the normal rules.

2.1.2 Postponement of parole

Release terms are fixed strictly in Finland. Annually, some 4,700 prisoners are released from prison. Of these, some 4,600 cases of parole follow the rules described above. There are, however, exceptions.

Supervised probationary release is more lenient whereas serving a sentence in full is the least lenient. The postponement of parole is also possible, and this can be either consensual or non-consensual.

Parole may be postponed with the prisoner's consent if new sentences of imprisonment or conversion sentences for unpaid fines are to be enforced or if the prisoner wants to postpone release on parole for another justified reason. Release on parole may be postponed without the prisoner's consent if, on the basis of the prisoner's conduct or on threats made by the prisoner, there is an evident danger that, on release, he would commit an aggravated offence against life, health or liberty. Postponement of the release is necessary in order to prevent the offence. Non-consensual postponement of parole must be reconsidered at intervals of, at most, six months. The decision to postpone parole non-consensually can be subjected to an appeal.[8]

2.1.3 The parole period and the remaining sentence

The law makes a distinction between the 'parole period' and the 'remaining sentence'. Usually these terms refer to the same time span but they may be of different lengths. The parole period refers to the period during which the parolee's behaviour may lead to a revocation of the parole. The remaining sentence refers to that part of the sentence that had not been served at the moment the prisoner was released on parole. This part of the sentence becomes relevant in cases when the Court decides to revoke parole due to a new offence (see below).

The length of the parole period is equivalent to the length of the sentence remaining at the time of release. The maximum length of the parole period is three years. Prior to 2006, the minimum length of the parole period was three months, which was intended to prevent too short a period of supervision. This limitation was removed because placement under supervision is at the discretion of the prison authorities and because short sentences (that is, of less than three months) hardly require supervision.

The parole period and the remaining sentence for a person sentenced to life imprisonment is three years. This means that a life sentence can be revoked if a new offence is committed during the

---

[8]Statistics on the postponement of parole from the late 1990s indicate that this option had been used in around 0.3 per cent of all parole cases. All these postponements were consensual and made at the prisoner's request. No later data are available.

first three years after the release. However, the maximum time in which it can be revoked is three years.

2.1.4 The decision-making process

The decision-making powers have been regulated by ch. 22 s.2 of the Prison Act 2006. In regular parole matters these powers are, in the first instance, in the hands of the Prison Director. He or she decides on a conditional release in accordance with the provisions of ch. 2(c), s. 5 of the Criminal Code. This applies also to the postponement of a conditional release where the postponement is either consensual or based on the fact that there are new sentences waiting to be enforced. The postponement of a conditional release without the prisoner's consent because of the imminent risk of reoffending is decided by the Criminal Sanctions Agency. The Prison Director also decides both whether the prisoner will be placed under regular supervision and the consequences of a violation of probationary release under supervision. However, a revocation of conditional release is always a matter for the Court to decide.

A prisoner has the right to appeal to the District Court against a decision postponing conditional release, either by the decision of the Prison Director or by the Criminal Sanctions Agency. An appeal should be lodged in writing within one week of the date on which the prisoner was served the notice of the decision. When parole is postponed, the prisoner is simultaneously issued with written appeal instructions indicating the appellate Court and the date set for lodging the appeal, as well as explaining the procedure to be complied with when lodging the appeal. The Prison Director also ensures that the prisoner has the opportunity to draw up a letter of appeal and that he can participate in the handling of the appeal in court. The decision-maker or an official representing him will be present in the District Court handling the appeal. The appellant also has the right to be present in the District Court. The District Court ensures that the matter is considered thoroughly. Appeals are handled as urgent and, where applicable, are governed by provisions on procedure in criminal cases. The District Court's decision is not subject to appeal.

2.2 Repeat violent offenders and serving the sentence in full

2.2.1 The abolition of the system of preventive detention

The system of preventive detention remained in Finnish law, despite its critics, until 2006. It had, however, been applied only to serious violent recidivists. In practice preventive detention meant that offenders were not released before they had served their full sentence. The use of this system had been relatively restricted (the annual number of prisoners in preventive detention was around 20–25).

However, even the limited use of preventive detention contradicted the prevailing sentencing ideology, which was very reluctant to accept any assessments of dangerousness as a basis for criminal sanctions. The reliability of such predictions was questioned by the Committee preparing the 2006 reform. Confinement 'for crimes never committed' had also been criticized on ethical grounds (Anttila 1975a). In the totally-reformed Prison Act 2006, preventive detention was abolished and replaced by a system that allows the courts the right to order serious violent offenders to serve their sentence 'in full'. This option was meant is to be used as restrictively as the earlier system of preventive detention. This has more or less been the case in subsequent practice.

2.2.2 Requirements and the process

Decision to serve the sentence in full   This new option has two stages. First, the District Court issues a statement that the person should serve the sentence in full. This decision is taken only at the request of the Prosecutor and provided three criteria set by the law are met:

1. The offender is to be sentenced to a term of least three years for a serious violent offence.[9]

2. Either during the ten years preceding the offence the offender has been guilty of similar serious violent crime or the offence was committed within three years of his release (after having served the full sentence in prison or after having served a sentence of life imprisonment).

---

[9]These offences include murder, homicide, killing, an aggravated assault, aggravated rape, the aggravated sexual abuse of a child, aggravated robbery, aggravated criminal mischief, genocide, a crime against humanity, an aggravated crime against humanity, a war crime, an aggravated war crime, aggravated human trafficking, the taking of a hostage, the aggravated endangerment of health, an offence relating to a nuclear device, hijacking, an offence committed with terrorist intent or an attempt to commit, or complicity in, such an offence.

3. On the basis of the factors apparent in the offences and following on from an investigation of the offender, he is deemed particularly dangerous to the life, health or liberty of others.

Decision to release the prisoner In the second phase the order to serve the sentence in full must be confirmed by the Helsinki Court of Appeal. The presumption is that a prisoner ordered to serve his entire sentence shall be released on parole after he or she has served five sixths of the sentence if he or she is no longer deemed particularly dangerous to the life, health or liberty of another. Release on parole may occur at the earliest when the prisoner has been in prison for three years. However, if the Court of Appeal still deems the prisoner to be particularly dangerous, the enforcement continues.

However, there is an absolute limit for any detention under this system. All prisoners must be released on supervised probation at the latest three months before their term has been served completely. The rationale behind this provision is the fact that releasing high-risk prisoners into society without any form of supervision or support is impractical, inhumane and unwise. For example, a prisoner is sentenced to serve the full term of a six-year sentence. If the Court of Appeal subsequently decides that the prisoner no longer presents a particular danger, he will be released after serving five years. If the prisoner is still deemed to be particularly dangerous, however, he will be released on supervised probation after serving five years and nine months.

2.3   Supervised probationary release

The Prison Act 2006 also introduced a new form of early release: 'probationary liberty under supervision'. This system was designed particularly for long-term prisoners who need more support and more intensive programmes. Probationary liberty may be available at the most six months prior to normal conditional release (see above).

2.3.1   Conditions

The conditions for probationary release are defined in detail in the law. According to the Criminal Code (ch. 2(c) s. 8), 'a prisoner may, for the promotion of his or her social adjustment, be placed outside the prison on parole supervised through technical means or otherwise through special means for at most six months before release on [regular] parole'. Further conditions for supervised parole are as follows:

- The sentence plan drawn up while in prison should be implemented.

- On the basis of information gathered about the prisoner's conduct during his sentence, about his personality and criminality, it is deemed probable he will meet the conditions of parole.

- The prisoner undertakes to refrain from using any illegal substances and to agree to being supervised in his abstinence from from intoxicants.

- The prisoner undertakes to stay in contact and to obey other necessary written conditions connected with moving outside the prison and participating in activities.

- Adherence to the conditions of the parole is to be be supervised in a suitable manner.

Probationary liberty requires a release plan that includes information on, for example, housing and the parolee's subsequent livelihood, his obligation to participate in activities, his daily programme and the supervision of his probationary liberty. As a rule, supervision is carried out by means of a global system for mobile (GSM) communications monitoring system (see below).

2.3.2 Target groups
Supervised probationary liberty is targeted at long-term prisoners. This includes prisoners serving sentences of over four years, typically for serious violent offences (homicide) or aggravated drug offences. The average prison term to be served by such prisoners is around three years. In addition to 'regular' prisoners, supervised probationary liberty is a compulsory intermediate step in releasing a prisoner serving his sentence in full (unless he is released after serving five sixths of his sentence). Supervised probationary release may also be applied to prisoners serving life imprisonment (see below).

On 16 December 2009 there were 93 prisoners on supervised probationary liberty. This figure includes two prisoners serving their sentences in full and seven prisoners released from life imprisonment.

2.3.3 Decision-making powers
The decision-making powers vary according to the prisoner group in question. In regular cases the decisions are taken by the Director of the placement unit (a regional institution responsible for placing

prisoners in the different prisons in its region). Decisions concerning prisoners serving their sentence in full and prisoners serving a life sentence are taken by the Criminal Sanctions Agency.

The decision to release or not to release a prisoner on supervised probationary liberty is not subject to appeal. This has been justified on the basis that release on probationary liberty is a discretionary decision by which a prisoner has been granted an exceptional benefit, comparable with prison leave (which also falls outside appeal procedures).[10] A revocation of supervised probation may, however, be subject to appeal. A prisoner can appeal for a reconsideration of his case if the decision was taken by the Prison Director. Such an appeal will be handled by the Director of the regional prison. An appeal against a decision made by the Director of a regional prison may be lodged with the Administrative Court. Decisions made by the Criminal Sanctions Agency may also be subject to appeal in the Administrative Court. The decision of the Administrative Court is not subject to appeal.

2.4 Release from life imprisonment

2.4.1 General provisions

All prisoners serving a life sentence are either released on parole or pardoned by the President of the Republic. For adult prisoners, release on parole may take place at the earliest 12 years into the term being served. If the offence was committed before the age of 21, on the other hand, the prisoner may be released on parole at the earliest when he has served ten years in prison.

Because this decision is discretionary, the law contains further guidance. According to the Criminal Code (ch. 2(c), s. 10.2), in considering release on parole, attention should be paid to the nature of the offence or offences that led to the sentence of life imprisonment, to the possible subsequent criminality of the convicted person and to those factors that justify the postponement of early release on the basis of the prisoner's own behaviour. In the consideration of release, 'attention shall also be paid to the implementation of the sentence plan and also to the conduct of the prisoner while in prison'.

Before a person sentenced to life imprisonment is released on parole, he may be released on supervised parole. If the Criminal Sanctions

[10]A prisoner claiming he has been denied the supervised probationary liberty to which he would have been entitled can file a complaint either to a higher prison authority or to the Parliamentary Ombudsman.

Agency decides that, due to the nature of the offence committed during parole, the release should be reconsidered, it will submit the matter for reconsideration to the Helsinki Court of Appeal.

2.4.2 The process

The application is heard by the Helsinki Court of Appeal. The provisions of the procedure are set out in the Procedure for the Release of Long-term Prisoners Act (781/2005). According to these provisions, the Criminal Sanctions Agency presents its report based on the application. This report must include a statement of the prospects for early release and any other necessary information about the prisoner, as well as the Agency's view about whether the prisoner should be placed under supervised probationary release.

If the application is rejected, the matter can be reconsidered after one year. The prisoner has the right to present evidence to support his application. Furthermore, the prisoner may appeal to Supreme Court.

Prior to 2006, prisoners serving a life sentence were released only by a pardon of the President of the Republic. Since 2006, the release of life prisoners was redefined as a form of ordinary parole procedure. However, the possibility of using a pardon still remains for exceptional cases, for example, when the prisoner's personal circumstances or health have changed radically during his sentence.

The number of such prisoners who are released annually is fairly small (on average two to three a year). The average length of the prison term served before release is around 12–13 years (see Table 6.1).

Table 6.1 Release of life prisoners in Finland, 1992–2009

Year	Average term served (years)	Number of released prisoners
1992–6	10.1	13
1999–2004	13.4	17
2005–9	12.4	21

Source: Prison Administration.

3. Supervision

3.1 Regular parole

3.1.1 General remarks

Prisoners released on parole can be placed under supervision by the decision of the Prison Warden. The implementation of supervision, however, is the responsibility of the Criminal Sanctions Agency and the Probation Service.

Parole supervision has many aims. At a social level it aims to 'increase public safety'. This occurs 'by supporting the supervised person in order to promote his social coping and by preventing him from committing new offences' (Supervision of Conditional Release Act 2005 s. 1).

Only officials of the Probation Service can be appointed as supervisors. However, for resource reasons this requirement cannot be implemented fully. Therefore, the law acknowledges the possibility of appointing social workers and people with the training and experience appropriate to the task of supervising parolees. Lay people may also be allowed to do so 'for a special reason'. As supervisors and their assistants are performing an official duty, their actions are governed by the provisions of the Criminal Liability for the Public Act. The provisions of the Language Act 2003 similarly apply, which means that the service must be available both in Finnish and in Swedish.

3.1.2 Placement under supervision

Whether the prisoner is placed under supervision or not depends on the length of the remaining sentence and the prisoner's age when he committed the offence. Prisoners released on parole are placed under supervision if the probation period is longer than one year or if the offence was committed when the offender was under 21 years of age. Supervision is also possible if the prisoner requests it.

In order to lend flexibility to these fairly formal conditions, placement under supervision may be waived if the prisoner is about to leave the country, has a serious illness or for any other special reason. This waiver is used mainly with young offenders (who would otherwise be placed under supervision due to their age) who have very short remaining sentences.

3.1.3 The contents of supervision

Supervision includes regular meetings between the supervisor and the supervised person in order to monitor his circumstances and any changes therein. These meetings aim to improve the person's ability to accept his responsibilities and to act in an acceptable manner.

The supervision may also include tasks or programmes designed to enhance the supervisee's ability to function in society. The meetings, tasks and programmes may take up at most 12 hours monthly. This legal specification was added at the insistence of Parliament's Constitutional Committee on the grounds that supervision is part of criminal punishment and, thus, should be defined in a precise enough manner to fulfil the demands of the legality principle.

The detailed contents of the supervision are included in the supervision plan. This plan is prepared by the Probation Service prior to release and in co-operation with the supervisee. The plan should, to the extent necessary, also be drawn up in co-operation with the prisoner's municipality of residence (or the municipality where he is staying) as well as with other relevant authorities and private organizations. The plan must include details of the number of contacts and meetings with the supervisor, information about the parolee's place of residence, his work, studies and economic situation, and the consequences of any breaches of these conditions. The plan may be amended or supplemented when necessary.

The supervisee's duties are defined in law and in the supervision plan. He is liable for participating in the drawing up of the plan and for keeping in contact with his supervisor in the manner specified in plan. He may not be under the influence of alcohol or other intoxicants at supervision appointments. If the supervisee is under the influence of alcohol or another intoxicant at a supervision appointment, his supervisor must record their observations regarding the intoxication. Supervisors have been granted the powers to carry out a breathalyser test should they suspect the intoxication is caused by alcohol.

Supervisors must treat their supervisees with dignity: 'The supervisor must treat the supervised person in a proper manner and aim at creating a confidential relationship with the supervised person.' The supervisor must also conduct the supervision in a manner that ensures that 'the supervised person does not therefore become the centre of attention and that the supervision does not otherwise unnecessarily complicate the life of the supervised person' (Supervision of Conditional Release Act 2005 s. 3).

3.1.4 Breaches of conditions

If the supervised person breaches his obligations, the Probation Service will issue him with a written warning. If the person fails to arrive at a supervision appointment without an acceptable reason, he may be brought to the next appointment by the police. He may be apprehended and taken into custody at most six hours before the next supervision appointment. If the supervisee fails to comply with his duty to keep in contact with his supervisor even after having been apprehended by the police, or if he is otherwise guilty of a gross violation of his obligations, the Probation Service will notify the Public Prosecutor of this without delay. If the Public Prosecutor decides that the recall process should be initiated on the basis of such breaches, they may take the case to court (see below). If the Prosecutor decides not to take the case further, they must inform the Probation Service of this decision.

3.1.5 Termination of supervision
If the probation period has lasted for at least six months and if it has become evident that the continuance of supervision is not necessary, the Probation Service may, on the supervisor's suggestion, terminate the supervision.

3.1.6 Practice
Practically all prisoners (99 per cent) are released on parole. About one out of four of those released on parole are placed under supervision (see Table 6.2).

Table 6.2 Prisoners released on parole and placed under supervision, 1998–2007

	1998	1999	2000	2001	2002	2003	2004	2005	2006	2007
All released	3,898	3,859	3,984	4,086	4,410	4,546	4,637	4,662	4,844	4,627
On parole	3,814	3,785	3,877	3,930	4,237	4,430	4,510	4,579	4,767	4,567
Under supervision	914	878	852	865	878	895	1013	978	1154	1142
Under supervision (%)	24	23	22	22	21	20	22	21	24	25
In supervision	1,197	1,247	1,310	1,283	1,426	1,296	1,397	1,448	1,456*	1,751*

Source: Criminal Sanctions Agency.
Note:
*1 May 2006 and 1 May 2007.

3.2 Supervised probationary liberty

Supervision for those placed under supervised probation differs markedly from the supervision attached to regular parole. All parolees are given a specific programme, with which they should comply. This may include an obligation to work, study or join a training programme or a course. In addition, all supervision plans include the requirement to abstain from any use of alcohol or drugs. Some programmes also include restrictions on movement in certain areas or at certain times.

However, the most distinctive feature of supervised probationary liberty is that it always includes supervision in the form of electronic monitoring. Monitoring is carried out using mobile phones and global positioning system (GPS) technology. Prisoners carry a GSM mobile phone which enables their surveillance via the prison's computer. The prisoners are required to make regular calls, which allow their location to be traced. The prison, in turn, makes random calls with similar results. The prisoners may use the phones only for contacting the prison and the alarm centre. This method is less stigmatizing and considerably cheaper than traditional electronic-monitoring techniques. The prisoners have demonstrated a positive attitude towards this method of surveillance and no improper use has occurred. In addition to mobile techniques, other and more personal forms of supervision are used.

The first steps in GMS supervision were taken in 2001 with the supervision of prisoners working outside the prison. The prisoners were placed in a small, open prison unit and were given the opportunity to work or study outside the prison on the condition that they carried with them a GSM mobile phone that enabled their surveillance from the prison. On the basis of the success of this scheme, the system was expanded to all prisons as a means of supervising high-risk prison leave. Subsequently it was extended to early release procedures. At the moment a working group is considering whether and to what extent similar techniques could be used in connection with other community sanctions.

Between 1 October 2006 and 31 December 2008, a total of 272 prisoners completed their supervised probation. In all, 35 breaches of conditions were reported, 7 warnings were issued and 25 parolees had their parole revoked.

4. Recall procedures

The revocation of parole may take place either owing to a breach of the supervision order or, as a rule, owing to a new offence committed during the probationary period. The process usually starts by a notification from the Probation Service.

4.1 Breach of the supervision order

Prior to 2006, a breach of a supervision order could lead technically to a revocation of the full remaining period of the sentence. However, this was not done in practice. Since 2006 a breach of a supervision order may, in serious cases, lead to a partial revocation. This is restricted at most to 14 days. If the court finds that the supervisee has grossly breached his order and that there are serious reasons to call for it, the Court may order at least 4 days and at most 14 days of the remaining sentence to be enforced.

Since 2006, the prosecutors have received around 30 requests for revocation, but the number of actual revocations is lower. In 2008 there were, in all, nine such cases. The length of the revocation varied from 8 to 14 days (an average of 11 days). It may be assumed that some of these cases were revoked owing to a new offence being committed while on parole.

4.2 Recall owing to new offences

Until 2006 the procedures for recalling parole followed a very formal pattern. The prisoner was ordered to serve at least one month of the remaining sentence (in addition to the penalty incurred for the new offence, as defined by the general parole rules). This decision was taken by the prison authorities. The procedure was, therefore, guided by instructions from the Prison Administration. According to these guidelines, one month was the minimum general rule, to be followed without any exceptions.

This practice was, however, deemed to be too formal. Furthermore, it made no distinction between prisoners with short and long remaining sentences. To address this problem the provisions on the enforcement of the remaining sentence period were amended in 2006. The decision-making powers were removed from the prison authorities to the Courts. The Courts were ordered to form a joint sentence from the remaining sentence and the sentence imposed for the new offence. This, in effect, turned the issue of parole revocation into a sentencing issue. The remaining sentence can be enforced only at the request of the Prosecutor, and the charges must be brought within one year of the termination of the parole period.

Parole can be revoked only as a result of offences that would lead to an unconditional prison sentence. The Courts, however, can still exercise discretion in such cases. The Court may withdraw the enforcement of the remaining sentence altogether or revoke only part of the sentence. Enforcement of the remaining sentence may be waived in particular if:

- most of the parole period had been served before the new offence was committed;
- the remaining sentence is brief; or
- the sentence to be imposed for the offence committed during the parole period is short.

In practice the limit is around three months (shorter remaining sentences are usually not revoked). The same applies if the new sentence is less than three months.

As noted above, should the Court choose to enforce the remaining sentence, it must form a joint sentence. This is done according to the general principles for the calculation of a joint punishment in cases of multiple offences. In practice this means that the Courts add a fraction (on average around a quarter or a fifth of the remaining sentence) onto the new joint punishment. Much, however, depends on the composition of the old remaining sentence.[11]

The aim of the 2006 reform was to differentiate between cases with different lengths of remaining sentences: longer remaining sentences should have more of an impact. On the other hand, there was a desire to reduce the number of revocations in minor cases. Thus there was no intention to increase the general level of sanctions. First reports indicate that these aims have been achieved. The annual number of parole revocations thus declined from, for example, 1,500 in 2005, to around 600–700 from 2007 onwards.

[11]If the remaining sentence consists of very old and minor sentences that have been added together, the Supreme Court has made provisions for much smaller fractions, such as a seventh or tenth of the remaining sentence (see Supreme Court Decisions 2008: 70–2).

4.3   Parole revocations in specific cases

4.3.1   Offenders serving their sentence in full
The consequences of reoffending during the parole period are
regulated by the revocation rules. But, for offenders serving their
sentence in full, there may be neither any remaining sentence nor
any parole period. Consequently, reoffending might incur no further
consequences. It was therefore deemed inconsistent to increase the
penalties resulting from new offences committed by those offenders
who were released on parole, but not for those who had served their
sentences in full. To avoid this situation, a specific provision was
added stating that if a person who has served his entire sentence
in prison commits an offence that leads to an unconditional prison
sentence within three years of being released, then this will be
considered as an aggravating factor in sentencing. Whether this
provision was actually needed is a matter of dispute since recidivism
is already defined as an aggravating factor to be taken into account
in the general sentencing rules, as defined in ch. 6 of the Criminal
Code (for more details, see Lappi-Seppälä 2001).

4.3.2   Revoking and withdrawing supervised probationary release
Unlike regular parole, a period of supervised probation is granted
only under specific conditions. Therefore changes in these conditions
must be monitored in detail.

According to a general provision in the Criminal Code (ch. 2(c) s.
8.s), if the conditions for supervised parole no longer exist, the parole
shall be withdrawn. This typically applies to reoffending. Unlike the
revocation of regular parole, the withdrawal of supervised parole
places no further requirements on the seriousness of the offence.
However, this is at the discretion of the prison authorities. More
detailed guidance is given concerning breaches related to the parolee's
duty to abstain from intoxicants and to participate in meetings. If the
parolee violates these conditions, he is issued with a warning or the
parole is withdrawn for a determinate period of at least one month
or completely. The period when the prisoner is in violation of his
contact obligations is not counted as part of his sentence.

5.   Discussion

The functions and procedures of parole and early release have varied
over time. While originally motivated by rehabilitative and preventive

goals, the system of parole and early release was seen, especially from the 1970s onwards, mainly as tool for controlling prisoner rates. This view was dominant during the 1980s and early 1990s, when expectations about the rehabilitative effects of community supervision were at their lowest. However, in the 2000s the preventive and rehabilitative potential of parole has once more received attention, as reflected in the 2006 reforms to the system.

Regular parole has remained the backbone of the system as the semi-automatic form of early release. Around 4,600–4,700 prisoners (99 per cent) are released annually on parole under these rules. Release is based on the decision of the prison's Director. Depending on the offender's age and any previous prison terms, release may occur after he has served a third, a half or two thirds of the sentence. Regular parole provides a means for the controlling imprisonment rates. It also provides a framework under which supervision and support can be organized.

The release of high-risk, dangerous recidivists is regulated under the system of serving the sentence in full. The final decision to release dangerous recidivists is taken by the Helsinki Court of Appeal. This form of release is undertaken in the interest of public protection. When compared with many other countries, the application of this type of release is fairly restricted. At the moment there are around 30 prisoners serving their sentence in full (out of a total number of around 3,600 prisoners). Those serving their sentences in full are released on parole at the latest three months prior to the end of their sentences.

The third form of early release – supervised probationary liberty – emphasizes the more rehabilitative and reintegrative aims of the system. Long-term offenders may be released at most six months earlier than the normal rules of parole indicate, provided they agree to submit themselves to extensive supervision. This form of release is designed to help offenders acquire the extra help and support they need in their efforts to adjust to normal life after a long prison term. Those released on supervised probationary liberty are usually monitored electronically.

The 2006 reform of the revocation of parole had two aims: to increase the impact of parole revocation on longer sentences and to restrict the use of revocation in minor cases. Both aims seem to have been accomplished. The number of revocations has more than halved (from 1,500 to around 600–700). Parole is, as a rule, revoked only as a result of a new offence leading to an unconditional prison sentence of at least three months. When parole is revoked, on average a quarter to a fifth of the remaining old sentence will be added to the sentence imposed for the new offence.

No major changes to the existing system are under consideration at the moment. However, the effects of the 2006 reform are now being monitored, and future actions will depend on the findings. The experiences gained from GSM monitoring may influence current plans for the adoption of electronic monitoring as an independent sanction imposed by the Courts.

References

Anttila, I. (1975a) *Incarceration for Crimes Never Committed? The Rise and Fall of Preventive Detention*. Helsinki: National Research Institute of Legal Policy.

Anttila, I. (1975b) 'Probation and parole: social control or social service?', *International Journal of Criminology and Penology*, 3: 79–84 (reprinted in Anttila 2001).

Anttila, I. (2001) (ed. R. Lahti and P. Törnudd). *Ad Ius Criminale Humanus: Essays in Criminology, Criminal Justice and Criminal Policy* Helsinki: Finnish Lawyers' Publishing Company.

Anttila, I. and Törnudd, P. (1992) 'The dynamics of the Finnish Criminal Code reform', in R. Lahti and K. Nuotio (eds) *Criminal Law Theory in Transition: Finnish and Comparative Perspectives*. Tampere: Finnish Lawyers' Publishing Company (reprinted in Törnudd 1996).

Falck, S., von Hofer, H. and Storgaard, A. (2003) *Nordic Criminal Statistics, 1950–2000*. Stockholm: Department of Criminology, Stockholm University.

Greve, V. (2007) 'Trends in prison law', in K. Nuotio (ed.) *Festschrift in Honour of Raimo Lahti*. Helsinki: Publications of the Faculty of Law, University of Helsinki.

Lahti, R. (2000) 'Towards a rational and humane criminal policy – trends in Scandinavian penal thinking', *Journal of Scandinavian Studies in Criminology and Crime Prevention*, 1: 141–55.

Lappi-Seppälä, T. (2001) 'Sentencing and punishment in Finland: the decline of the repressive ideal', in M. Tonry and R. Frase (eds) *Punishment and Penal Systems in Western Countries*. New York: Oxford University Press.

Lappi-Seppälä, T. (2007) 'Penal policy in Scandinavia', *Crime and Justice*, 36: 217–97.

Lappi-Seppälä, T. (2008) 'Politics or policy – fluctuations in the Finnish penal policy', in T. Elholm, P. Asp, F. Balvig, B. Feldtmann, K. Nuotio and A. Strandbakken (eds) *Ikke kun straf... Festskrift til Vagn Greve*. Copenhagen: Juris-og Ökonomiforbundets Forlag.

Lappi-Seppälä, T. (2009) 'Imprisonment and penal policy in Finland', in P. Wahlgren and C. Lernestedt (eds) *Scandinavian Studies in Law. Vol. 54.* Stockholm: Stockholm Institute for Scandinavian Law.

Nuotio, K. (2003) 'Finland', in M. Delmas-Marty, G. Giudicelli-Delage and E. Lambert Abdelgawad (eds) *L'Harmonisation des sanctions pénales en Europe. Unité mixte de recherche de droit comparé de Paris. Vol. 5.* Paris: Société de Législation comparée.

Pellinen, T. (1991) *Ehdonalaisen vapauden kehitys Suomessa.* Helsinki: Helsingin yliopisto.

Törnudd, P. (1996) *Facts, Values and Visions: Essays in Criminology and Crime Policy. Research Report 138.* Helsinki: National Research Institute of Legal Policy.

Villkorlig frigivning/Nordic Criminal Law Committee (1978) *Betänkande avgivet Nordiska straffrättskommittén A (No. 6).* Helsinki: Nordic Criminal Law Committee.

Chapter 7

France

Kim Reuflet

Summary

In France, the system of release from prison has been subject to much legislative amendment in recent years. Prisoners still benefit from significant periods of remission, yet conditional release (*libération conditionnelle*) is not as common as it should be, remaining a favour granted by a judge in recognition of the effort the prisoner has made to facilitate his rehabilitation. Politicians are nervous of promoting it, despite the evidence of its effectiveness, for fear of appearing 'soft' on criminals and of being seen to increase the risk that released prisoners may reoffend. Despite the strengthening of the judicial process, judicial practices have not been able to develop significantly the use of early conditional release as a safe way to return prisoners to society. Driven by a rising prison population, the government apparently prefers to revert to automatic early release on electronic monitoring – a move away from the traditional individualization of penalties.

I. Introduction

In 1994, a new Criminal Code was adopted in France, ending earlier sentencing rules which included provision for mandatory minimum and maximum sentences. In 1994, France adopted a highly discretionary system of sentencing. At the time it was a move against automatic sentencing rules. However, the 1994 reforms are themselves now under a challenge: in August 2007, a law[1] reintroduced mandatory minimum sentences for some categories of offenders (reoffenders).

A key principle in French criminal legislation, also applicable post-sentence, is the individualization of sentences. At the original point of sentence, this principle means the sentence must be proportionate to the gravity of the offence and the personal circumstances of the offender. During the execution of the sentence, the principle means that the personality, behaviour and rehabilitative capacities of the prisoner are taken into consideration when granting him remission or conditional release.

Post-sentence, the decision still belongs to the judiciary authority. In France, there is a specific judge in charge of the execution of sentences: the Execution Judge, the *juge de l'application des peines*. Judicial practice demonstrates that a finding of 'merit' is essential before a convicted person will be released early. Because of this principle of the individualization of sentences, France employs a wide variety of measures which make the implementation of the sentence less repressive. Yet, paradoxically, it is only recently (in 2000) that a fair adversarial post-sentence procedure became a reality.

France has a large set of early release measures (*aménagement de peine*). A majority of them is reserved for short-term sentenced prisoners: electronic monitoring (*placement sous surveillance électronique*), work release (*placement à l'extérieur*) and day release (*semi-liberté*). Long-term prisoners are eligible for conditional release, which might be called parole (*libération conditionnelle*). The rules are different for those on whom a sentence of one year or less is imposed and those serving longer than a year (see Table 7.1).

As well as these measures, it is important to note that, in France, no prisoner actually serves the full sentence imposed by the courts. Different rules allow prisoners to obtain various kinds of penalty remissions, either because of the absence of bad behaviour or owing to their efforts at rehabilitation. There are also specific rules for prisoners suffering from serious illness, which allow the suspension of their sentence (*suspension de peine médicale*).

[1]Law of 10 August 2007, Journal officiel, 11 August, introduced mandatory minimum sentences (*peines plancher*).

Table 7.1 Rules for early release

Sentence or time remaining to be served	< 1 year	> 1 year
Day release	Yes	Possible only as a trial period before a conditional release
Work release	Yes	Possible only as a trial period before a conditional release
Electronic monitoring	Yes	Possible only as a trial period before a conditional release
Conditional release	Yes (time served = half or two thirds of the sentence)	Yes (time served = half or two thirds of the sentence)

2. History

Parole was first introduced in a Law of 14 August 1885. This Law initially entrusted decisions on parole to the Minister of the Interior (who was in charge of the Prison Service). Initially, the measure was a favour granted by the Prison Service, and the main condition for release on licence was good conduct in prison. In 1911, when the Minister of Justice was assigned responsibility for the Prison Service, he became the Minister in charge of granting release on licence.

In 1958, the Code of Criminal Procedure created the 'judge for the execution of sentences' who considered applications for release on licence, and supervised the implementation of this measure. The Laws of 17 July 1970 and 29 December 1972 removed the requirement of good conduct in prison, making 'serious evidence of readjusting to society' the criterion for release on licence, and they empowered the judge responsible for the execution of sentences to decide whether to grant a licence to prisoners serving sentences not exceeding three years, a power which was extended to sentences not exceeding five years by the Law of 1993.

Nevertheless, in the 1970s, the prison authorities were faced with what was seen as a worrying decline in the number of licences granted, particularly in the case of longer sentences. This problem has continued. In 1997–8, a study of long-term sentenced prisoners showed that, among prisoners eligible for licence, only 10 per cent had applied for parole.[2] And of those who had applied, only a

[2]*Etude concernant les détenus incarcérés en centre de détention national et en maison centrale en 1997 et 1998* (annexe IV du rapport Farge).

minority were granted release on licence. For instance, in 1997, in the prisons for long-term sentenced prisoners, of 4,872 convicted prisoners eligible for release on licence, the cases of 442 were referred to the Minister of Justice by the Execution Judge and only 130 (that is, 3 per cent of the total) were granted early release on licence. At this time, the Judge simply made a proposal to the Minister. The proposal was not a judicial decision, for the power to make the decision lay with the Minister.

In 1999, the rate of convicted prisoners recommended for release on parole by the Execution Judge was 15 per cent of those eligible. That is why, in 1999, the Minister of Justice decided to appoint a commission to make proposals for revitalizing the parole system.

In February 2000, the Commission on Parole, chaired by M. Farge, a Judge of the Court of Cassation, submitted its report.[3] The report concluded:

- The criteria for release on licence (that a prisoner should get a job and housing) were both overly restrictive and unrealistic. Both were very difficult for inmates to obtain when preparing for their release.

- The consequence of the automatic shortening of prison sentences (linked to free pardon or remission of sentence) was that prisoners, in order to reduce their sentences, would rather stay in prison and await the quasi-automatic reduction than make the rehabilitative efforts required to apply for early release, which would mean that they were required to stay under control during the probation period.

- Some dangerous people, who used to be taken care of by medical services, were now ending up in prison. For these people, release on licence was totally inadequate

- The increasing feeling of insecurity, fed with the media's partiality for *fait divers*, such as repeat sexual offences on children, reinforced people's aversion to taking risks. Consequently, the release authorities were extremely careful, and even more so if they were a political authority.

The Law of 15 June 2000 enacted many of the Farge Report's proposals. It made radical changes to the law on parole, removing

[3]*La libération conditionnelle: rapport à madame le garde des sceaux* (Ministre de la justice, Paris: 2000).

the Minister's powers and replacing them with an adversarial judicial procedure, and widening the release criteria. In 2001, the number of releases increased by 11 per cent. The Law of 9 March 2004 then completed the process of transferring post-sentencing powers to the judicial system by establishing the post-sentencing Courts as ordinary Courts.

But these two laws, which relaxed the requirements, were followed by two laws which toughened the criteria for early release:

- The Law of 12 December 2005, which toughened the criteria for the release on licence of repeat offenders.

- The Law of 10 August 2007, which reinforced the obligation to undergo medical supervision for some categories of offenders, principally those convicted of sexual offences.

At the same time that the parole rules were evolving, the rules governing the remission of a sentence were also changed. Based on the English model, remission was established in 1972[4] as a way of supplementing the 'blind and collective' action of the free pardon decree. For the first time, the only criterion was the prisoner's 'good behaviour'. As well as this form of remission, based only on behavioural criteria, another form of remission was added in 1975,[5] based on rehabilitative efforts. The almost-automatic grant of remission could result in a reduction of nine months per year, which meant that a convict serving four years would serve only one. A limit was therefore established in 1986: remission could not exceed five months per year of detention. The almost-automatic remission was also criticized for not providing prisoners with a good incentive for working towards their rehabilitation. So the Law of 9 March 2004 also modified the rules of sentence remission.

3. Legal criteria for early release

3.1 Remission

Currently two systems of remission are mainly in use. A remission credit (*crédit de réduction de peine*, CRP) is given on the day of

---

[4]Law 72-1226, 30 December 1972, Journal officiel, 30 December.
[5]Law 75-624, 11 July 1975, Journal officiel, 13 July.

incarceration. This credit is the equivalent to the remission of a sentence for good behaviour. It is automatically granted to every prisoner and is taken back in the case of bad behaviour. It amounts to three months for the first year of detention and two months per year in subsequent years. Thus, for example, in the case of a four-year sentence, on the day of incarceration, the date of release is set at three years and three months from that day. For short sentences the CRP is seven days per month.

Supplementary remission (*réduction de peine supplémentaire*, RSP) can also be granted, but not automatically. The criteria are mainly oriented towards encouraging social rehabilitation and reintegration. For example, passing an examination or completing some training or work while in jail, or attempting to compensate the victim, can be rewarded in this way. The RSP amounts to three months per year or seven days per month. For example, if the RSP is granted fully, a four-year sentence will actually last two years and three months.

A large majority of prisoners benefit from both these remissions. If an offender behaves badly while still in prison, the Judge can change their decision on remission and withdraw part of the credit. Supplementary remission can be withdrawn if the prisoner reoffends.

3.2   Early release

Each measure has its own rules but, since the Law of 9 March 2004, none of these measures can be granted to a prisoner convicted of a sexual offence, unless he has been examined by one or more psychiatrists and they have made a specific risk assessment.

3.2.1   Day release, work release

These measures allow the prisoner to spend part of the day outside the prison in order to take part in such activities as work, study, hunting for a job or medical treatment. When granted, the week's timetable takes into consideration the place of the activities or the prisoner's personal circumstances: some prisoners spend the day outside the prison and sleep there every night, while others just return to the prison at the weekend. These measures can be granted to any convicted prisoner serving a sentences of up to one year, and to any other sentenced prisoner, whatever the length of their sentence, provided that less than one year remains to be served. The prisoner can be released on day release or work release in order to take part in resocialization activities or if his family needs his contribution.

He must have a serious project in order to apply for such an early release.

3.2.2 Electronic monitoring

This measure[6] allows the prisoner to serve his detention time at home (home detention) under electronic control. During the day, the prisoner generally takes part in the same resocialization activities applicable to other early release measures. It can be granted to any convicted prisoner sentenced to imprisonment of up to one year. It can also be granted to any other convicted prisoner, whatever the length of their sentence, provided again that they are in the last year of their sentence. The prisoner is under electronic surveillance and has to keep strictly to a daily timetable.

3.2.3 Conditional release

In France, this measure is the only one that might allow prisoners serving long sentences to be released relatively early – that is, a long time (several years) before the end of their prison sentence. Conditional release leads to the release of the offender, whereas the prisoner who benefits from a work release, a day release or an electronic monitoring release remains, formally, under the control of the prison. The prisoner who benefits from a conditional release is no longer a prisoner and recovers his complete freedom (with, of course, some conditions). Conditional release can be defined as a penal measure whereby a convicted person is released into the community before the end of his prison sentence, under supervision, until the sentence expiry date or even one year more, with the obligation to respect certain conditions, among which is always included the condition not to reoffend.

As regards temporal requirements, Art. 729 of the Code of Criminal Procedure provides that prisoners may not apply to be released on licence until a certain period has elapsed. The common rule is that conditional release may be granted if the part of the sentence already served is, at least, equal to the part of the sentence remaining to be served, with a minimum of 18 years for prisoners sentenced to life imprisonment. Recidivists are not eligible for release on licence until they have served two thirds of their sentence, with a minimum of 22 years for such prisoners sentenced to life imprisonment.

Other rules on eligibility include taking into account remission already granted at the moment when the eligibility for early release

[6]Set up by Law 97-1159 of 19 December 1997, Journal officiel, 20 December.

is examined. This allows many prisoners to apply for release on licence before they have served half their sentence. The impact of this rule can be illustrated by again considering a four-year sentence. In such a case the automatic remission is nine months, with three more months if the prisoner makes a serious effort to rehabilitate himself. As half this credit is accumulated in the first half of the sentence, this means that the prisoner may apply for conditional release after a period of 18 months has been served.

For all sentences over ten years, there is a safety period, a minimum term during which release on licence is not possible. This period is generally half of sentence but can exceptionally be a 22-year period, as is the case with repeat offenders sentenced to life imprisonment.

In addition to the temporal requirements there are other requirements for conditional release. The prisoner must also have made serious efforts to readjust to society. There are no mandatory or precise requirements in this regard, but the prisoner might have to show that he is engaged in occupational activities or has taken part in a work experience scheme, that his presence is essential to the life of his family, that he has to undergo treatment or that he has made efforts to compensate his victims.

A specific rule relating to conditional release, inspired by the Italian sentencing rules, is that conditional release can be granted, without any temporal requirements, to any person responsible for a child younger than ten years (*libération conditionnelle parentale*[7]). This is possible only for sentences of less than four years. If all the requirements are fulfilled, conditional release might be granted *ab initio*, which means the convicted offender will totally avoid any detention period. Currently, in France, a law providing for a new category of conditional release is being discussed by Parliament. This law provides that prisoners older than 70 are eligible for a conditional release without any temporal requirements.[8]

After release, the parolee must respect some supervisory measures and perform some obligations: work or live in a particular place, undergo medical treatment or compensate his victim. Work release or electronic monitoring for a maximum one-year period can also be a pre-release measure aimed at assessing the prisoner's suitability for early release. If this probation period is incident-free, the conditional release can become effective.

---

[7]Law 2000-516 of 15 June 2000, Journal officiel, 16 June.
[8]Projet de loi no. 59 adopté par le sénat le 6 mars 2009.

Release on licence normally ends when the theoretical sentence term has been completed. This means that the probation periods may last several years. For instance, someone who has been sentenced to ten years of imprisonment might be released early after serving half his sentence. In that case, the probation period will last about four years (providing the penalty remissions have shortened the sentence). In any case, if necessary, supervisory measures can be extended by the Judge for a maximum period of one more year after this term.

4. Statistical data[9]

4.1 Prison population rate

In March 2009, there were 62,700 prisoners (100 prisoners per 100,000 inhabitants). In 1988, there were only about 50,000 prisoners but, by 1996, the number was up 10 per cent to 55,000. This increase, greater than the general population growth, is mostly due to the stiffening of both criminal laws and punishment policy, which has led both to longer sentences and to the greater use of prison sentences.

In 2005, the average time served of a prison sentence was 8.3 months. Underlying this number is a combination of several factors, not least of which is the reality that a very large majority (about 80 per cent) of sentences are for less than one year. Nevertheless, the general trend is towards the lengthening of sentences. For instance, in 1980 the average length of terms of imprisonment was 4.6 months – that is, half of what it is today. There has also been an increase in the number of prisoners who serve very long sentences: currently about 1,500 detainees are serving sentences of over 20 years and about 500 prisoners are serving life sentences.

At the same time, France has persistent prison overcrowding: there is a total of 52,535 jail places available for 62,700 prisoners. Moreover, it is inevitable that prisoners are not distributed equally across this system. This means that, among the 194 penitentiary establishments in France, there are 15 prisons with an occupancy rate greater than 200 per cent and a further 44 prisons with over 150 per cent occupancy.

4.2 Early release measures

Early release measures have increased in the last three years, mostly due to the development of electronic monitoring (see Table 7.2). In 2008,

[9]Statistical data from the Ministry of Justice.

Table 7.2 Early release measures, 2005–08

Year	Work release	Electronic monitoring	Day release	Conditional release	Total early release*	Total incarcerations
2005	1,944	3,575	4,128	5,848	15,495	85,540
2006	1,980	5,562	4,655	5,897	18,094	86,594
2007	2,289	7,900	5,283	6,436	21,908	90,270
2008	2,608	11,259	5,928	7,494	27,289	89,054

Note:
* This figure includes both temporary release, where prisoners are returned to prison after a short period, and other forms of early release, which have the effect of releasing prisoners permanently unless they are returned to prison for breaching the conditions of their release.

of the 89,054 people sentenced to imprisonment who were actually incarcerated, 27,289 were released temporarily or conditionally. An important proportion of those sentenced to imprisonment benefit from an alternative to imprisonment that comes into effect immediately after the trial. This means that they do not spend any time fully in prison (*aménagement ab initio*).

5. Decision-making

Today in France, all decisions on early release are taken by judicial authorities, except for the free pardon decree, which is a decision made by the President of the Republic. But since 2007, the new French President has taken a position against the collective and automatic pardon and so it is no longer in use. This may or may not be a definitive renunciation of this power.

Work release, day release and electronic monitoring release can be granted by:

- the Trial Judge (a single Judge or three Judges depending of the offence) who decides that the prison sentence is to be executed *ab initio* by an alternative measure to imprisonment; or

- the Execution Judge, who decides, according to the personal circumstances of the convicted offender and the length of the sentence or the remaining sentence to be served (maximum one year) that the sentence should be converted into an alternative to imprisonment.

Two types of judicial authorities are empowered to decide about conditional release:

- The Judge responsible for the execution of sentences (*juge d'application des peines*) is responsible for prisoners serving sentences of under ten years' imprisonment, with less than three years remaining to be served.

- The post-sentencing Court (*tribunal de l'application des peines*; three judges) is responsible for release on licence that falls outside the sphere of responsibility of the Judge responsible for the execution of the sentence.

These Judges are career judges: they may have been recently nominated or be more experienced. All decisions made by these first-instance Courts may be challenged in a Court of Appeal, where all the aspects of the case, both factual and legal, are re-examined. The Courts of Appeal for the post-sentencing decisions (*chambre de l'application des peines*) are composed of three judges. Nevertheless, for some categories of decisions (remission and authorization to leave the prison for a few days), the President of the *chambre de l'application des peines* alone takes the decision. For some other decisions (conditional release granted by the post-sentencing court), the Court of Appeal is constituted, by, in addition to the three judges, one representative of rehabilitation associations and one representative of victims' associations.

Decisions rendered by the Appeal Courts may themselves be the subject of an appeal before the Court of Cassation. The action of submitting a case to the Court of Cassation is called the *pourvoi en cassation*. The Court of Cassation is not a Court of third instance after the appeal courts (and thus not equivalent to Supreme Courts in most common law systems). Its purpose is simply to state whether the law has been correctly applied. In general, a Court of Cassation's judgment setting aside a decision refers the case back to another Appeal Court for another ruling.

5.1 Procedure

As soon as he fulfils the legal criteria, the prisoner can apply for early release. Moreover, the Criminal Code provides that, even when the prisoner does not apply for early release, his situation must be reviewed at least once a year. This is so that the judiciary reviews the cases of prisoners who are not being helped by the Probation

Service, for whatever reason. In this case, the Judge still has the power to order the prisoner's release. In addition to the prisoner's file, the application will include a report from the rehabilitation and probation section of the Prison Service (*service pénitentiaire d'insertion et de probation*, SPIP). This report describes the efforts made by the prisoner during the period already in detention – in particular, whether the prisoner works, compensates his victims or takes part in an addiction-recovery programme or psychotherapeutic or medical treatment that he is free to continue after release. It also gives details which allow the Court to assess whether the prisoner's plans for accommodation and employment are realistic.

Usually, and particularly for long-term prisoners, a psychiatric assessment is made to assess dangerousness. The psychiatric expert must assess the risk of criminal recidivism. To do this, experts do not use risk prediction tools or actuarial risk scores. They assess risk of reconviction clinically, after one or several confidential interviews with the convict. When the dossier is complete, a hearing takes place with the Execution Judge (JAP or TAP), the Prosecutor, representatives of the prison staff (Prison Director and warders) and members of the Rehabilitation and Probation Service. The prisoner can present his case: he can explain his plans and the reasons why he is applying for early release. The opinions of both the prison staff in charge of supervision and rehabilitation and the Public Prosecutor are presented. The Judge or the Court then exercise their discretion in making a decision. This decision can be challenged either by the prisoner or by the Prosecutor before the Court of Appeal.

When granting early release, the Judge must set, in addition to the general conditions prescribed by law,[10] all the specific conditions the prisoner will have to fulfil during the parole period. There are several possible conditions concerning matters such as work, place of residence, medical treatment, contributions to family support, compensation to victims, repayment of debt to the public treasury, driving bans, bar exclusions and not contacting specified people, such as partners in crime. The Execution Judge can modify these obligations during the parole period if they consider, for instance, that a restrictive obligation is no longer necessary. The Execution Judge then takes their decision, which is notified to the parolee who can always contest it.

[10]Article 132-44 of the Criminal Code. The convict must respond to any summoning delivered by the Judge or the Probation Service, he must give information about any change of job or address, and he must be allowed by the Execution Judge, if he so wishes, to go abroad.

6. Recall procedures

All measures of early release can be revoked if the offender is convicted again during the probation period or if he does not respect any of the obligations set by the Execution Judge. Conditional release can also be revoked for notorious bad behaviour (*inconduite notoire*). The judicial authority makes revocation decisions after an adversarial hearing. The decision to revoke the licence can be challenged before a Court of Appeal. As well as revocation proceedings, the prison administration may, in some cases, revoke the measure for a short period until a judicial authority examines the case. For prisoners under work release, day release or electronic monitoring, if the prison administration records a breach of a condition (the breach usually concerns the failure to be at home or to go to the day release centre), it has the power to recall the person to prison. After a few days, the judicial authority will examine the case. After a revocation, the prisoner must serve the sentence in prison, but may apply again for an early release. If an offender tampers with his electronic monitoring device, this is itself an offence which can result in a sentence of imprisonment of up to three years.

7. Conclusion

Despite many changes, France still has an early release system based on rehabilitation, grafted onto a largely retributive sentencing structure. All judicial practices are aimed at evaluating and encouraging the prisoner's efforts to obtain early release. Early release thus remains a way to reward rehabilitative efforts and to help convicted prisoners reintegrate into society.

Risk assessment is today an important element in decision-making. But the aim of developing risk assessment is not so much to supervise the return to society of the most dangerous prisoners but more to limit the early release of those who are identified as dangerous and to exclude dangerous people from any alternative measure to imprisonment.

Early release measures are still at the heart of a paradox. All reports on this topic suggest year after year that adapted sentences, notably alternatives to imprisonment, such as conditional release, are the best tool to fight the risks of reoffending. For instance, a study in 2005 of reconvicted prisoners showed that, in every category of offenders, including robbery, assault and sexual offences, the majority of those who were reconvicted had served their previous sentence without any alternative to prison.[11] So in France, the idea that prisoners can be integrated into society more easily if they are subject to a period of supervision in the community is well known among professionals. And at an international level, the Council of Europe Recommendation on Conditional Release of 2003 stated that release on licence is one of the most efficient measures to prevent reoffending and to ensure a gradual return to life in society (see Kensey 2004, 2007).

However, the promotion of early release is not regarded as a priority by politicians, for it is synonymous with a 'free and easy' attitude. Until now, society has had a dichotomous approach to delinquency: on one side are irredeemable repeat offenders and, on the other, the 'adaptable' ones. Thus, when a penalty management device is set up, it is aimed at the second category, with the fear that, at the same time, the first category may benefit from it. Worse, data show that, except for a small burst in 2008, conditional release is going through difficult times and is granted less and less. While 13 per cent of eligible prisoners were released on licence in 2001, only 7.5 per cent in 2007. If the Recommendation of the Council of Europe had been followed, however, it should have been granted to a majority of prisoners.

Thus one has to conclude that the radical changes to the laws on parole enacted in 2000 have been unable to change practice. Today the question of mandatory systems of early release provokes debate in France, whereas this question was totally taboo a few years ago, being considered as the opposite of the individualization of sentences. The law about the functions of the Prison Service, recently adopted by the Senate,[12] provides for automatic release under electronic control for a majority of prisoners four months before the end of their sentence. In reality the Judge will no longer have a decision to make, but simply to check that all the conditions qualifying a prisoner to be awarded it have been fulfilled. Paradoxically, this issue is also being discussed for a very pragmatic reason: the prison population is increasing and prison capacity is not growing at the same speed. Politicians are seeking solutions to this problem by releasing convicted prisoners more readily than the law and judicial practice currently allow.

---

[11]*Sortants de prisons: variabilité des risques de retour. Cahiers de démographie pénitentiaire du ministère de la justice* 17 (mai 2005).
[12]Projet de loi no. 59 adopté par le sénat le 6 mars 2009.

References

Boulay, A. (1997) 'Le juge de l'application des peines et les victimes (RAP 1997, juin 1997); quelle place pour la victime dans le processus de liberation conditionelle', *AJ pénal*, 2005: 318.

Desportes, F. and Le Gunehec, F. (2006) *Droit pénal général* (13th edn). Paris: Economica.

Cabanel, P.-G. (1996) *Pour une meilleure prévention de la récidive, rapport au Premier ministre* (La Documentation française, collection 'rapports officiels').

Canivet, G. (2000) A*mélioration du contrôle externe sur les établissements pénitentiaires: rapport* (La Documentation française).

Cartier, M.-E. (2001) 'La judiciarisation de l'exécution des peines', *Revue de sciences criminelles*, 1: 87–90.

Céré, J.-P. (2000) 'L'avancée de la juridictionnalisation de l'application des peines avec la loi n° 2000-516 du 15 juin 2000', *Revue pénitentiaire*, 555–62.

Danet, J., Grunvald, S., Herzog-Evans, M. and Le Gall, Y. (2006) *Prescription, amnistie et grâce en France*. Paris: Mission de recherche Droit et Justice.

Dinthillac, J.-P. (1998) 'Libération conditionnelle. Quel avenir?', *Revue pénitentiaire*, 287–300.

Ecole Nationale de la Magistrature (2009) *Nouveau mémento de l'application des peines*. Paris: ENM.

Farge, D. (President) (2000) *La libération conditionnelle: rapport à madame le garde des sceaux. Ministre de la justice/commission sur la libération conditionnelle sous la présidence de Daniel Farge* (La Documentation française).

Faucher, P. (2001) 'La juridictionnalisation de l'application des peines. Une révolution tranquille', *Revue pénitentiaire*, Jan–March, 215.

Hazard, A., Kensey, A. and Lévy, R. (2005) *Le placement sous surveillance électronique: une mesure désormais prise en compte. Cahiers de démographie pénitentiaire no. 20 du ministère de la justice*. Paris: DAP.

Herzog-Evans, M. (2007) *Droit de l'exécution des peines*. Paris: Dalloz.

Kensey, A. (2003) *L'aménagement des peines dans sa diversité. Cahier de démographie pénitentiaire no. 13 du ministère de la justice*. Paris: DAP.

Kensey, A. (2004) 'Conditional release and the prevention of re-offending', in Council of Europe (ed.) *Crime and Crime Policy in Europe*. Strasbourg: Council of Europe.

Kensey, A. (2005) *Durée effective des peines perpétuelles. Cahiers de démographie pénitentiaire no. 18 du ministère de la justice*. Paris: DAP.

Kensey, A. (2007) *Prison et récidive*. Paris: Armand Collin.

Kensey, A. and Tournier, P.-V. (2000) *Placement à l'extérieur, semi-liberté, libération conditionnelle... Des aménagements d'exception*. Paris: Ministère de la justice.

Kensey, A. and Tournier P.V. (2005) *Prisonniers du passé? Cohorte des personnes condamnées, libérées en 1996–1997: examen de leur casier judiciaire 5 ans après la levée d'écrou (échantillon national aléatoire stratifié selon l'infraction).* Paris: Ministère de la Justice, Direction de l'administration pénitentiaire (Collection Travaux et Documents no. 68).

Poncela, P. (1999) 'Le fait du prince: la libération conditionnelle accordée par le ministre de la justice', *Revue de sciences criminelles*, Jan–March, 1: 139–44.

Poncela, P. (2001) *Droit de la peine*. Thémis: Presses universitaires de France.

Tournier, P.-V. (2008) *Quand nécessité fait loi. Alternatives à la détention: faire des mesures et sanctions privatives de liberté l'ultime recours? contribution au débat sur le projet de loi pénitentiaire*. Marseille: Université Aix-en-Provence.

Chapter 8

Germany

Frieder Dünkel and Ineke Pruin

Summary

Early release in Germany is based on discretionary decisions – that is, conditional release from determinate prison sentences after prisoners have served (exceptionally) half or (routinely) two thirds of their sentences (of up to 15 years), or from life sentences after having served at least 15 years. Conditional release is granted to prisoners with good prognoses, but the exclusion of all risk is not required – a 'justifiable' degree of risk is accepted. There are more detailed regulations for the young inmates of youth prisons (aged 14–24 years). For those conditionally released from mental hospitals and preventive detention, special regulations for prognostic criteria and supervision are provided. The competent authority for conditional release is always a judge (special chamber of the District Courts), which is a requirement of the Constitution (Art. 104(2) of the Basic Law).

Statistical data about conditional release are not very accurate but, in practice, such release seems to have become less frequent over the last 10–15 years. A major law reform in 1998 provided more restrictive legal requirements for detainees in preventive detention and forensic psychiatric hospitals. The system of early release includes supervision by the probation services, but case loads are very high: on average about 70 clients per probation officer. The results concerning revocation are, nevertheless, very positive. Less than half of all conditional releases from prisons are revoked. There are also numerous new management systems and programmes of networking that link social services in prison with probation and aftercare services, with the aim of improving the prisoner's preparation for release and aftercare.

I. History

Historically, early release emanates from the Sovereign's 'prerogative of mercy' (*Gnadenrecht*), which was exercised as an exceptional power to pardon in the kingdoms and duchies of pre-unification Germany (von Stockhausen 2008: 17 ff.). After the foundation of the united German State in 1871, early release became legally regulated in the Imperial Penal Code (*Reichsstrafgesetzbuch* ss. 23–26). After the Second World War the West German Penal Code (*Strafgesetzbuch*, StGB) provided for discretionary conditional release after two thirds of the sentence had been served if 'it could be expected that the offender will lead a law-abiding and virtuous life'. A major step towards reforming the Penal Code was taken with the introduction of the Probation Service by the Juvenile Justice Act (JGG) in 1953 and the General Penal Code (StGB) in 1954. These laws also provided for support and aftercare for released prisoners. In the 1970s and 1980s major law reforms were driven by the principle of resocialization and the further development of alternative sanctions. These included, in substantive criminal law, the extension of conditional release. Under certain conditions (that is, if there was a good prognosis) mandatory early release was introduced. In 1986 the possibility of exceptional conditional release after the completion of half the sentence was introduced. For first offenders with sentences of up to two years it could even be the regular form of conditional release (see s. 57[2] of the Penal Code and below).

There were also some less progressive developments. As a result of the impact of a few serious cases of recidivism by ex-prisoners and the general, media-fuelled moral panics of the 1990s, a new law was adopted in 1998 (the law 'for fighting against sexual and other dangerous offences') which made the legal requirements for release from psychiatric and preventive detention more restrictive. The wording of the criteria for conditional release was changed only to clarify their meaning, but this led to uncertainty and misunderstandings by the judiciary and possibly contributed to more restrictive release practices, particularly with regards to violent and sex offenders.

Although criminology in Germany has developed since the late 1960s into an important discipline, there has been relatively little empirical research on conditional release. The embarrassing reality is that the German Statistical Bureau collects data on the practice of conditional release in a marginal rather than a meaningful way. There is no significant information about who has been released after what period of time. Therefore, empirical data can be drawn only from individual and regionally-limited empirical studies (Dünkel and Ganz 1985; Dünkel 1981, 1992; Cornel 2002b).

2. Legal criteria

The law provides several possibilities for an early release from prison or preventive detention. Which law has to be applied depends on different criteria, such as the age of the offender, the length of the prison sentence, the type of offender (first offender or recidivist) or the type of his prison sentence: determinate or life sentence, youth imprisonment and preventive (security) detention (*Sicherungsverwahrung*). Early release in Germany is always conditional. If the released offender commits further crimes or does not comply with directives or obligations, the suspended part of the sentence can be revoked. Therefore we use the term 'conditional release' instead of 'early release'. Early release in the form of the remission of the sentence plays only a marginal role (see section 3 below).

2.1 Early release from a determinate prison sentence

2.1.1 Early release after having served two thirds of the sentence (s. 57(1) of the Penal Code)
The basic provision governing the early release of adult prisoners is s. 57(1) of the Penal Code. According to this provision, determinate prison sentences as provided in s. 38 of the Penal Code (a maximum of 15 years) can be suspended after the prisoner has served two thirds of the sentence. The minimum term to be served is two months. The two-thirds requirement is related to the prison sentence as imposed by the Court, including the period of pre-trial detention (s. 57(4) of the Penal Code). As a precondition it is prescribed that the release can be justified with regards to the interests of public safety. The prognosis that is required for this raises certain problems (Dünkel 2010: s. 57 notes 14 ff.). The legislation has been interpreted as recognizing that a degree of risk of reoffending has to be accepted. The danger of recidivism in the form of petty offences does not exclude conditional release. The above-mentioned law reform of 1998 reformulated the

criteria ('with regards to the interests of the public'), but this was only a clarification, not a restriction of the conditions for early release. Nevertheless, some courts misunderstood the amendment as a signal from the legislator to be more cautious in granting conditional release (Dünkel 2010, s. 57 note 15).

Release is mandatory if all the requirements are met. Section 57(1) of the Penal Code reads as follows:

> The court suspends the remainder of a determinate prison sentence if
>
> 1. the prisoner has served two thirds of the sentence, minimum two months,
>
> 2. it can be justified with regards to the interests of public safety, and
>
> 3. the prisoner agrees.
>
> The court when deciding on early release has to consider amongst others the personality of the detainee, his prior life, the circumstances of the criminal act, the seriousness of the infringement in case of recidivism, the behaviour of the convicted in prison, his living conditions and the impact that release would have on him if he were to be released.

A negative decision has to be based on concrete facts, which result in an assessment that the risk is too great to justify a release. Even in cases of serious violence a theoretical risk does not justify a refusal of conditional release.

One of the requirements is the prisoner's consent. Why is such consent requested? The answer is connected to the specific conditions applicable to conditional release. The probation term is, in any case, at least two and a maximum of five years. This is not necessarily equivalent to the remainder of the sentence as is the case in other countries. If a prisoner serves a rather short prison sentence or if the remainder of the sentence (because of delays in the decision-making procedure) is only a few months, he may prefer to serve the full sentence in order to avoid a long period of supervision by the Probation Service or having to live with the risk of revocation for years. From their point of view, prisoners may have good reasons to serve the full sentence in order to avoid a two- to five-year term of probation.

If the requirements of s. 57(1) (1–3) are met, conditional release is obligatory. Considerations other than special prevention are to be excluded in making decisions on conditional release. This means that, even in very serious murder cases – such as, for instance, Nazi murders – other aims of punishment, such as retribution or deterrence, are not to be considered. The same applies for considerations of individual deterrence (negative special prevention) which are excluded in the decision-making on early release (OLG München *Strafverteidiger* 1999, 550). The legislator has deliberately left out similar considerations, such as the protection of the public (general deterrence), which is relevant only to the original decision to impose a suspended instead of an unconditional prison sentence (see s. 56(3) of the Penal Code [*Verteidigung der Rechtsordnung*]). Much the same has been outlined by the Federal Constitutional Court (*Bundesverfassungsgericht, BVerfG*), which has emphasized that 'It is generally accepted that the gravity of guilt, retribution and aspects of general deterrence may not lead to a denial of an early release according to s. 57 of the Penal Code' (BVerfG *Neue Zeitschrift für Strafrecht* 1994, 53). Conditional release may, however, be denied if the offender has refused to give adequate information about the goods of the criminal act (and thus impedes or even prevents the victim's compensation; see s. 57(5) of the Penal Code).

2.1.2 Release after having served half the sentence, (s. 57(2) of the Penal Code)

Another possibility of release from determinate sentences is laid down in s. 57(2) of the Penal Code. According to this provision, release is possible after the prisoner has served half the sentence, with a minimum of six months, if he: 1) is serving for the first time a prison sentence not exceeding two years; or if 2) a comprehensive review of the offence, the offender's personality and his development during the execution of the prison sentence reveals particular circumstances. Furthermore, this alternative – as with s. 57(1) of the Penal Code – requires that the release must be justifiable with regards to the interests of public safety and that the prisoner agrees to it. It is important to look at this difference with regards to the discretionary power of the Court: in the case of s. 57(1) (release after two thirds) release is obligatory if the legal prerequisites (good prognosis, etc.) are met. In the case of a release after half the sentence, release is still at the discretion of the Court, although academic commentaries stress that there are not really substantive aspects for discretion and particularly no retributive or general preventive aspects that would justify a denial of conditional release if, for example, special circumstances according to s. 57(2)2 of the Penal Code exist (Dünkel 2010: s. 57 note 61ff.). Furthermore, in the case of offenders serving a prison sentence for the first time, the general view expressed in the literature and the jurisprudence is that discretion normally inherent the wording 'can' is not applicable and that – if all other conditions are met – conditional release after half the sentence should regularly be granted.

2.1.3. Conditional release from youth prison (s. 88 of the Juvenile Justice Act)

The German juvenile justice system applies to persons aged between 14 and 21 years – that is, juveniles (14–18) and young adults (18–21). Since the reform of 1953 a young adult falls under the jurisdiction of Youth Courts which apply the sanctions of the Juvenile Justice Act 1953 (in German: *Jugendgerichtsgesetz*, JGG) if the young adult, in terms of his personal development, is closer to a juvenile than to an adult over the age of 21, or if the motives for committing the offence and the surrounding circumstances are those of a typical juvenile crime (see s. 105(1)(1,2) JGG). In practice the Youth Courts apply the sanctions of the JGG in more than 60 per cent of cases and particularly in more than 90 per cent of the most serious cases, such as murder, rape, robbery or other violent or sexual offences (see Dünkel 2006, 2010). The result is that, instead of prison sentences of up to 15 years, the range of youth prison sentences is limited to between six months and ten years, which is much more favourable for young offenders. The maximum penalty for juveniles under the age of 18 years is normally five years and, exceptionally, 10 years for very serious crimes.

Young offenders are also 'privileged' in respect of conditional release. Section 88 of the JGG stipulates that release is already possible after the prisoner has served one third of the sentence, or a minimum of six months, if the youth prison sentence is more than one year. A youth prisoner serving a sentence of six months up to one year can be released at any time after the minimum period of six months.[1] The decision has to be made in the light of the interests of public safety and the juvenile's development. The decision is made by the Juvenile

[1] The more friendly regulation of s. 88 JGG, compared with s. 57 of the Penal Code, is even applied if a young adult youth prisoner is transferred to a general prison for adults when he has been judged by the prison administration as not being suitable for a youth prison (see s. 91(2) JGG).

Judge, who has to decide as early as possible in order to ensure that the Probation and Aftercare Services can prepare for the release on time (see s. 88(3) JGG). The laws on the execution of youth prison sentences, which are not identical in the 16 Federal States, emphasize the early involvement of the Probation and Aftercare Services. Some States (Baden-Württemberg, Berlin, Hesse and Rhineland-Palatinate) prescribe that these services are obliged to co-operate in preparing release at least six months before the expected date of release (see Dünkel 2007; Ostendorf 2008).

The prognostic criteria are generally the same as in the Penal Code. However, the criterion with regard to the juvenile's personal development must be understood in the light of the principle of education, which the JGG lays down as a guide to all decision-making involving juveniles (s. 2). This means that conditional release should be granted not only when a definite good prognosis can be given but also in the case of doubt (Eisenberg 2009: s. 88 note 9a). Another important difference to the general Penal Code is that the consent of the young prisoner is not necessary. Conditional release is to be preferred, particularly because of the obligatory aftercare by the Probation Service, which is seen as an integral part of the resocialization process.

In practice, Juvenile Judges – with few exceptions – are very reluctant to orient their release practice towards the one-third or even half-way point. Instead, they regularly release juvenile offenders only after two thirds of their sentences have been served.

2.1.4 Early release because of good behaviour ('good time')
In Germany there is almost no provision for a remission of prison sentences outside the system of conditional release. So-called 'good-time' – early release in return for good behaviour or for participation in rehabilitative programmes – exists only for prisoners who work, and then only to a very limited extent.[2] After two months of regular work such prisoners can be granted one day of further prison leave, or the date of release can be brought forward by the same amount. If a prisoner works for a year he can therefore be released six days earlier than would otherwise have been the case. Compared with other countries that have 'good-time' provisions, the German scheme is very restricted. Even so, many scholars see it as highly problematic, as prison work cannot be offered to all prisoners and therefore the

[2] Time spent in school education or vocational training programmes is legally equivalent to ordinary prison work.

question of equal treatment becomes an issue. Some even doubt the constitutionality of the provision (Calliess and Müller-Dietz 2008: s. 43 note 5). On the other hand, it was in fact the Federal Constitutional Court that proposed the introduction of such a non-monetary scheme of remuneration, if the State were unable to increase prisoners' wages significantly (BVerfGE 98, 169 of 1 July 1998). In a subsequent decision the Federal Constitutional Court held that an increase of prisoners' remuneration from 5 to 9 per cent of the average salary of workers outside prison was constitutional, if it was combined with the possibility of additional remission of the sentence as an extra reward for work performed (BVerfG *Neue Juristische Wochenschrift* 2002, 2023). The Federal States, in drafting their new Youth Prison Acts, have retained this system of monetary and non-monetary remuneration. Only Berlin increased the period of 'good-time' to 12 days per year.

Another form of early release granted by the Prison Governor is related to the possibility that the scheduled date for release might fall on a weekend or a public holiday, particularly the Easter or Christmas holidays. Section 16 of the Prison Act (*Strafvollzugsgesetz*, StVollzG) allows the Prison Governor to bring forward the date of release to the Friday before the weekend. If the date of release falls between 22 December and 2 January (in the case of young prisoners the Youth Prison Laws set the latter date as 6 January), the release will normally be brought forward to 21 December. Thus, if ordinary release was due on 2 January, the prisoner would be released 12 days earlier. This form of early release is unofficially called the 'Christmas amnesty'. This rule is designed to avoid a release on days where social services or the Probation Service are not available or can be contacted only with difficulty, which may hamper the reintegration process.

2.2 Conditional release from life imprisonment

Life imprisonment in Germany is mandatory for murder and genocide and may be imposed for a number of very serious crimes, such as particularly serious forms of manslaughter, robbery resulting in fatality or sexual coercion with fatal consequences (for details, see van Zyl Smit 2002: 135 ff.). The numbers of convictions per year are between 60 and 120 and have been relatively stable since the 1970s (van Zyl Smit 2002: 136 ff.; Dünkel 2009a: s. 57a note 52). In spite of this rather stable sentencing practice, the daily number of prisoners serving a life sentence has increased considerably: from 989 in 1977 to 1,973 in 2007. The reasons may be that the practice of conditional release has become more restrictive or that more particularly serious cases are held in prisons. Such life prisoners serve more than 15 years because of the legal requirements of s. 57a of the Penal Code (see below).

Until 1981 there was no statutory framework for the release of life prisoners, but only the possibility of pardon by the Premier of each Federal State. In 1977 the Federal Constitutional Court (FCC) ruled this legal situation to be unconstitutional as it violated fundamental human rights, such as human dignity, and the principles of the *Rechtsstaat* (a state bound to the rule of law) and the *Sozialstaat* (social welfare state). On the one hand, the sentence of life imprisonment was seen as 'constitutional', but only if the prisoner was given a realistic and legally-based opportunity to be released (BVerfGE 45, 177; for details of the FCC judgment, see van Zyl Smit 2002: 145 ff.). The consequence of that decision was that the German legislator had to pass new legislation governing the early release of prisoners serving life sentences. In 1981 the new s. 57a of the Penal Code was enacted. It reads as follows:

(1) The court shall suspend the remainder of a life sentence on probation, if

1. the offender has served 15 years of his punishment,
2. the gravity of the offender's guilt does not necessitate that he continues to serve his sentence, and
3. the conditions of s. 57(1) sentence 1, numbers 2 and 3 are met.

(2) Section 57 (1) sentence 2 is to be applied correspondingly.

The conditions referred to are that the offender's release is justified with respect to the interests of public safety and that the offender agrees. Furthermore, the circumstances enumerated in sentence 2 of s. 57(1) have to be considered (the detainee's personality, the detainee's behaviour in prison, his living conditions and the impact that release would have on him). The main conditions for release therefore are that a minimum period of at least 15 years has to have been served, and a good prognosis. The definition of the 'exceptional gravity of the guilt' (*besondere Schuldschwere*) was the subject matter of numerous court decisions and, again, the FCC had to decide whether the clause is constitutional at all (BVerfGE 86, 288). The FCC upheld the legal provision but stated that the exceptional gravity of the guilt has to be the subject of the original decision of the sentencing Court and not of the Court deciding on conditional release (*Strafvollstreckungskammer*).

The principle of legal certainty requires that the offender must be able to foresee what he can expect after 15 years. The lower courts have tried to clarify the legal concept of an 'exceptional gravity of guilt'. Guilt is found to be 'exceptionally grave' only if it is considerably more than that which is necessary to qualify a killing as murder and therefore to apply the life sentence. Cases of exceptional gravity of guilt are, for example, when more than one person was killed; additional suffering by the victim; special circumstances of the crime (such as particularly cruel, brutal actions by the offender); reckless endangering of the lives of many others; and particularly anti-social motives (Dünkel 2009a: s. 57a notes 9–14). The Federal Supreme Court (*Bundesgerichtshof*, BGH) has remained quite vague, stating only that a finding of exceptional gravity would depend on the individual case, but that 'circumstances of major importance' should be established before such a finding can be made (BGHSt 40, 360 at 370).

If the Court deciding on release refuses to grant release after 15 years it must decide how long the life prisoner has to serve because of the exceptional gravity of the offence (BVerfGE 86, 288 at 331). In practice, most prisoners whose guilt is so exceptionally grave will serve 18 or 20 years.

2.3 Conditional release from preventive detention, and from psychiatric and alcohol treatment measures

German penal law is based on the principle of guilt (see s. 46 of the Penal Code: the basis of sentencing is the offender's guilt). There are cases where an offender has committed a serious crime under circumstances where he cannot be deemed guilty because of mental illness, severe drunkenness or other temporary or continuous psychiatric diseases. If, furthermore, he seems to be dangerous, the problem of how to protect society becomes relevant. Since 1933 German penal law has developed a so-called double-track system of punishments and measures for improvement and security (*Maßregeln der Besserung und Sicherung*). Dangerous offenders who are not (fully) responsible according to ss. 20 and 21 of the Penal Code can be sent to a psychiatric hospital if they exhibit mental illness and are deemed on this ground to be dangerous (s. 63 of the Penal Code). The stay is of an indeterminate length – that is, possibly for life. Release will be granted if the offender is assessed as no longer posing a threat (s. 67d(2) of the Penal Code; see below).

If the offender has serious alcohol or drug problems (addiction with the danger of committing serious crimes because of this addiction), he can be sentenced to detention in an alcohol- or drug-treatment institution for up to two years. Again, the prognosis of concrete dangerousness is required (s. 64 of the Penal Code).

As with the measure of alcohol- or drug-treatment, the security measure of preventive detention does not require that the offender could not be found guilty. Preventive detention is predominantly imposed on offenders with a previous history of serious offending, if they are assessed to be dangerous (s. 66 of the Penal Code).[3] Such preventive detention is served after the determinate sentence, which has been imposed for the specific crime, has been fully served. It is of indeterminate length and can possibly last for life. However, its enforcement is reviewed at least every two years. The inmate will be released from preventive detention after ten years, except if he continues to be dangerous, which has to be proven by the institution (s. 67d(3) of the Penal Code).

[3] In 2002 and 2004 the German legislator introduced further forms of preventive detention which can be imposed even after the original sentence – that is, during the stay in prison for a determinate period (see ss. 66a, 66b of the Penal Code). Both measures of subsequent preventive detention are heavily criticized in the academic literature (for the various arguments around the 2004 law reforms, see Dünkel and van Zyl Smit 2004). The European Court on Human Rights in its decision of 17 December 2009 (*M. v. Germany*, no. 19359/04) stated that the preventive detention of a prisoner lasting longer than ten years and thus longer than the maximum period provided before the law reform in 2004 (which abolished the former ten-year limit) in the concrete case violated Arts. 5 (1) and 7 (1) of the Convention (unlawful deprivation of liberty and violation of the principle of prohibition of retrospective penalties). The prisoner had been sentenced to preventive detention in 1986. The ECHR stated that preventive detention – although seen in German doctrine as a measure and not a penalty – has to be considered as an additional penalty, particularly 'having regard to the realities of the situation of persons in such detention' (see paragraph 128 of the decision). The jurisprudence of the Federal Supreme Court, as well as of the Federal Constitutional Court, has interpreted the conditions that have to be met before subsequent preventive detention can be imposed very strictly. Therefore, fewer than 10 out of more than 400 offenders currently in preventive detention are being held under s. 66 of the Penal Code, which authorizes this special form of subsequently ordered preventive detention (Dünkel 2008).

In 1998 the Law for the Prevention of Sexual Offences and other Dangerous Criminal Acts increased the possibilities for imposing preventive detention (s. 66(3) of the Penal Code). The same law also changed the prognostic criteria for conditional release. Section 67d(2) of the Penal Code reformulated the conditions by restricting the release of offenders in preventive detention to those for whom an assessment resulted in the 'expectation' that they would not reoffend. As is also the case with life sentences, a risk assessment by two expert psychiatrists or psychologists is obligatory for preventive or psychiatric detention (s. 463(3) sentence 3 and s. 454(2) of the Criminal Procedure Act, *Strafprozessordnung*, StPO). Section 454(2) of the Criminal Procedure Act repeats the formulation that the expert is requested to state clearly that there is no longer any danger. The intention was to make this formulation stricter than the formulation in s. 57(1)(2) of the Penal Code, where release is possible when it can be 'justified'. Justification of release means that a certain risk is inevitable and even that minor forms of recidivism are to be tolerated. The formulation in s. 67d(2) of the Penal Code instead requires the prognosis that further recidivism can be ruled out entirely. Academics argued in hearings on the legislation that such prognoses are not possible and therefore strongly criticized the legislation for proposing them. Nevertheless, the law was adopted in 1998 (Schöch 1998; Nedopil 2002).

The results can be termed disastrous, as the release practice of psychiatric hospitals has become more restrictive than ever before. The number of offenders held in psychiatric institutions has increased from 3,600 in 1991 to 8,664 in 2007 to 8,943 in 2008. This increase is more than the annual growth in the number of offenders admitted to psychiatric hospitals, which increased from 432 in 1990 to 796 in 2006.[4] Data from North-Rhine Westphalia indicate that the average number of releases declined by about half after 1998, while the Ministry of Justice of Lower Saxony reported that the average length of stay of offenders in psychiatric hospitals increased from 4.2 years in 1990 to 6.5 years in 2003 (Dünkel and Morgenstern 2010). Dessecker (2008: 35, 88) has shown that, for the whole of Germany, the average stay of those released from a psychiatric hospital increased from 5.4 years to 7.1 years in 2006 (the median from 4.5 to 5.9 years).

The restrictive formulations in s. 67d(2) of the Penal Code and s. 454(2) of the Criminal Procedure Act inevitably increase the risk of

---

[4]All data refer to the states of the former Federal Republic of Germany – that is, West Germany (for details, see Dünkel and Morgenstern 2010).

non-dangerous offenders staying longer in institutions (the problem of the so-called 'false positives' in contrast to the so-called 'false negatives' who had been assessed as not being dangerous but have committed further crimes; see Chapter 2). In public debates, only the false negatives are viewed as problematic, and not the fact that far more inmates with a wrong negative prognostic assessment are kept in institutions (for an estimate of the ratio of false positives to true positives, see Kunz 2004: s. 35 notes 25–28; Dünkel 2010: s. 57 note 111).

2.4 Probation terms, the Probation Service, obligations and directives

According to s. 57(3) of the Penal Code (read together with s. 56a(1)), the probation term is at least two years and at most five years. It shall not be less than the remainder of the sentence. The probation term can be shortened if the offender shows positive developments, and can be prolonged in order to avoid a revocation (see s. 56f(2), sentence 2 of the Penal Code and section 6 below). Conditionally released offenders are not always subject to the supervision of a Probation Officer. The law stipulates that this shall be the case only 'if this is indicated to restrain the offender from reoffending' (s. 56d(1) of the Penal Code). This general rule in the penal law for adults[5] is, however, modified in the case of conditional release: s. 57(3) (sentence 2) of the Penal Code stipulates that 'regular' supervision by the Probation Service should be ordered when the offender has served at least one year of the sentence in prison. The period of supervision might be shorter than the probation term (s. 56d(1) of the Penal Code). This rule reflects the fact that the first few months after release are the most critical ones and that, after one or two years, further support and control by the Probation Service is not necessary.

Conditional release may be combined with so-called directives (*Weisungen*) or obligations (*Auflagen*). Directives are imposed in order to influence the offender's behaviour and living routines (see s. 56c of the Penal Code) and, in this way to prevent reoffending. They can consist of an instruction to avoid contacts with persons who might negatively influence the released offender or to avoid certain places, to try to find work or – with the offender's consent – to undergo alcohol or other treatment (for details, see s. 56c(2), (3) of the Penal Code).

[5]In contrast to the JGG, where supervision by the Probation Service is obligatory for all cases of a suspended sentence or conditional release (see s. 24).

Obligations are meant to fulfil the victim's or society's desire for satisfaction. According to s. 56b(2), the obligation can consist of compensating the victim, of a payment to a non-profit organization or the state, or of community service.

3. Statistical data

3.1 The proportion of prisoners granted conditional release

The German prison statistics (*Strafvollzugsstatistik*) reveal a fairly consistent proportion of early releases (including pardons) of around 30 per cent during the last decades. However, these data are not usable as they refer to all persons who are released each year, among whom is an unknown number of released fine defaulters (normally serving less than 90 days) who – according to almost unanimous jurisprudence – are not eligible for conditional release. In the late 1990s these accounted for about 40,000 of all detainees in Germany. The number of released prisoners who have served more than three months of imprisonment is also unknown. If one considers only the offenders who are released each year after having served a prison sentence, a proportion of 60 per cent of conditional releases seems to be realistic (see Schöch 1999: 232, with further references on some Federal States). Conditional release in practice is granted after two thirds of the sentence. Release after having served half the sentence remains rare, accounting for less than 1 per cent of all conditional releases (Meier 2006: 137).

Therefore, the only significant available data result from individual and regionally restricted empirical research. They indicate large variations between Federal States and even within regions. According to empirical studies (for example, in the Federal States of Hesse, Schleswig-Holstein or Berlin), about two thirds of prisoners serving prison sentences of more than one year are granted conditional release. The longer the sentence, the higher the proportion of conditional release will be (Dünkel 1992; see also Dünkel 1981; Dünkel and Ganz 1985). In a study of prisoners released 1989 in Schleswig-Holstein and from a women's prison in Berlin, 63 per cent of male adults and 94 per cent of women (Schleswig-Holstein) and 61 per cent of women in Berlin were granted conditional release (Dünkel 1992: 287, 418). Böhm found similar results in the 1980s in Hesse (about 60 per cent conditional releases). Only 10 per cent received a negative decision from the Court for the Execution of Sentences

(*Strafvollstreckungskammer*), 12 per cent had explicitly refused to give their agreement (often due to the short remainder of the sentence which was felt to be out of proportion compared with the probation term of at least two years). The remaining cases were those of revoked suspended sentences, longer sentences for fine defaulters, etc. (Böhm and Erhard 1984: 21 ff.).

A statistical analysis by Cornel showed no substantial changes before and after 1998 (2002a: 430 ff.). This is not surprising as, with the reformulation of s. 57 of the Penal Code, the legislator did not want to restrict conditional release other than for measures of improvement and security (see section 2.3 above), but only to clarify the criteria. Nevertheless, the statistical data do not give information about when conditional release is granted (it could have changed to four fifths instead of two thirds, particularly for violent or other serious offenders) and about whether certain groups of offenders, such as sex offenders, are discriminated against.

Juvenile prisons' release practice seems to have become more restrictive in the last 10–15 years (Röthel 2007).[6] One explanation could be that the proportion of violent offenders, particularly in youth prisons, has increased. Such offenders are disadvantaged by internal administrative rules that impede the granting of prison leave. Being granted such leave is an important element in the preparation for conditional release and influences the decision on whether to grant such release.

Altogether the empirical database is very limited – surprisingly so for a country that is one of the richest in Europe. There is some hope for change as most Federal States are introducing computerized data files for prisoners, which will allow evaluation of who has been released after which part of the sentence and why. So, for example, first data in Mecklenburg-Western Pomerania show that, in 2007, 21 per cent of those released from the youth prison were granted conditional release compared with between 16 and 58 per cent in different prisons for adults (with higher proportions in prisons where longer sentences are executed).[7]

[6] In the Mecklenburg-Western Pomerania youth prison, the proportion of conditional releases was 51 per cent in 1993 and 71 per cent in 1996. Since then it dropped to only 23 per cent in 2007 (see Lang 2007: 145 ff.; data communicated by the Ministry of Justice of Mecklenburg-Western Pomerania in 2009).

[7] According to the data of the Ministry of Justice of Mecklenburg-Western Pomerania, the overall rate of conditional releases was 35 per cent in 2007;

3.2 Conditional release and recidivism

Empirical knowledge of recidivism among offenders who are conditionally released compared with those offenders who serve their sentences in full is based mainly on studies from the 1980s. The methodological problem is that, because conditional release is normally granted to those offenders who have a good prognosis, it is difficult to find a comparable control group of offenders who were not granted such release. Normative selection renders the two groups practically incomparable. However, regional disparities provide the opportunity to identify cases for which one region grants conditional release, while others do not. A comprehensive study of the data of the Federal Register of Convicted Offenders (*Bundeszentralregister*) from 1984 to 1990 revealed that those persons conditionally released and whose conditional release was not subsequently revoked were reconvicted in 40 per cent of cases, whereas for those serving their sentences in full it was 72 per cent. Offenders who were conditionally released but whose conditional release was revoked were reconvicted in 71 per cent of cases, with four out of five reoffending offenders receiving an unconditional prison sentence (Kerner 1996: 73).[8] In a study of reoffending in North Rhine-Westphalia, the recidivism rate for conditionally released prisoners was 63 per cent, compared with 75 per cent of those serving their sentences in full (Baumann *et al.* 1983: 146 ff.).

In Germany since 2003 we have had at our disposal a large federal database on recidivism, which was established by the Federal Ministry of Justice. This tracks all 947,000 cases convicted in Germany in the year 1994 for the following five years (until 1999; see Jehle *et al.* 2003). According to these data, 40 per cent of the conditionally released young prisoners (that is, those on whom youth imprisonment

only 16 per cent of prisoners in Stralsund (a prison where sentences of up to three years are served) received a conditional release compared with 47 per cent in Bützow, a prison where longer sentences are served. The rather restrictive practice of conditional release may partly be explained by the fact that about one third of the released prisoners served a revoked suspended prison sentence (i.e. have been on probation before). In these cases, the Courts for the Execution of Sentences are reluctant to award another probation term by means of conditional release.

[8]Revocation is not necessarily identical with recidivism defined as a new conviction for further crimes. Revocation can be imposed because of non-compliance with obligations or directives; on the other hand, reconviction must not necessarily have the consequence of revocation (see section 6 below).

had been imposed) were reconvicted and received an unconditional prison sentence, compared with 52 per cent of those who served their sentence in full. In the prison system for adult offenders the proportion was 22 per cent as opposed to 33 per cent recidivism (Jehle *et al.* 2003: 125 ff.).

These numbers say nothing about the effectiveness of the different strategies, because the selection of persons for conditional release is a key determinant of the outcome. In this respect studies with a control group are more significant. One essential issue in this context is that the conditional release group and the group of offenders serving full sentences are matched according to criteria regarding their legal (prior convictions, nature of crimes committed) and biographical (age, gender, anti-social attitudes and socioeconomic conditions, such as unemployment, vocational skills, etc.) history, which influence offending and reoffending. A study by Dünkel (1981) of 1,503 offenders in Berlin-Tegel prison realized such a design by controlling for prior convictions, nature of the crime, age and other legal biographical criteria. Therefore, comparable cases of conditionally and unconditionally released ex-prisoners could be compared after a risk period of about five years. The conditionally released group showed a 13 per cent lower reconviction rate (reconviction to an unconditional prison sentence) than the control group (Dünkel 1981: 289 ff.). The differences were greater for robbery and sexual offenders (17 and 21 per cent) and lower for non-violent property offenders and perpetrators of bodily injury (11 and 9 per cent). In no case did conditionally released offenders exhibit higher recidivism rates than offenders who had served their sentences in full.

The most effective strategy was to combine conditional release with so-called socio-therapeutic treatment, including intensive preparation for release through social training programmes. The difference in favour of the social therapy group was a 18–20 per cent lower reincarceration rate (Dünkel 1981: 291). Twice as many of the social therapy group had received conditional release compared with the untreated control group (see also Dünkel and Geng 1994 for similar findings about 500 career offenders after a risk period of ten years).

These results are similar to a study conducted by Böhm in Hessen (Böhm and Erhard 1984, 1988). Böhm could show that, in a comparison of the more liberal and more restrictive practices of different prisons, the former did not increase crime rates and therefore seemed to be an effective and justifiable strategy (Böhm and Erhard 1988: 106, 150 ff.).

3.3   General aspects of the effectiveness of the Probation Service

As indicated above, most prisoners who are conditionally released are subject to supervision by the Probation Service. There are no statistics differentiating between probationers with an immediate suspension of their prison sentences (s. 56 of the Penal Code) and those conditionally released (ss. 57, 57a, 67d(2) of the Penal Code), as they are both under the same supervision structures of the Probation Service. Nevertheless, data from the Federal Statistics Bureau (*Statistisches Bundesamt*) give indications of the effectiveness of the Probation Service's work in general. These data report annual cases of revocations, on the one hand, and of successful completions of the probation period, on the other.

Since the mid-1980s revocation rates for adult offenders have been between 30 and 35 per cent (after a period of being between 45 and more than 50 per cent in the 1960s and 1970s). In the age groups covered by the JGG (14–21-year-old offenders), revocation rates were more than 40 per cent until 1975 but, since the mid-1980s, they have dropped to only slightly more than 20 per cent.

A remarkable 'success story' in the German history of sentencing practice is the development and increase of suspended sentences in general and of supervision by the Probation Service in particular. When the Probation Service was introduced in 1953–4, suspended sentences were intended to be used only in exceptional cases. However, suspended sentences were accepted in practice in an astonishing way and these sentences became the rule rather than the exception. The number of probationers per day in the old Federal Republic of Germany increased from about 26,000 in 1965 to 140,000 in 1990. Interestingly, this increase was particularly due to a rise in the number of probationers who were the subject of supervision for a second or even a third time while the original probation term had not yet been completed ('repetitive probationers'). Another group of probationers who increased in numbers were the probationers with prior convictions ('recidivist probationers'). Consequently the proportion of first-time offenders under probationary supervision dropped from 41 per cent in 1963 to only 15 per cent in 1990 (Spieß 1996: 35 and Table 1). On the other hand, the proportion of prior probationers or offenders in 1990 with previous convictions increased to 85 per cent (from 59 per cent in 1963, 72 per cent in 1970, 76 per cent in 1975, 78 per cent in 1980 and 81 per cent in 1985).

This means that the proportion of probationers with higher risks of reoffending increased. When one considers traditional (risk-factor

Table 8.1 Success rates according to different groups of probationers, 1963–90 (per cent)

	1963	1990	Difference
Probationers without prior convictions (first offenders)	70	84	+ 14
Probationers with prior convictions	45	69	+ 24
Of these: with prior supervision by the Probation Service	39	65	+ 26
Total	*55*	*71*	*+ 16*

oriented) prognostic instruments, one would expect revocation rates also to increase. However, the judicial practice of revocation showed an astonishing trend in the opposite direction.

Whether probation was revoked or completed successfully, however, it is clear that the Probation Service's work led to an unexpected increase in the general success rate, from 55 to 71 per cent (an increase of 16 per cent; see Table 8.1). The most remarkable result, however, is that those groups of probationers who should be seen as special risk groups profited the most from the more liberal sentencing practice. Whereas the increase of success rates was 15 per cent for first offenders, it was 24 per cent for those with prior convictions, and even 26 per cent for those recidivists who had been under the supervision of the Probation Service before (see Spieß 1996: 36). The same result is obtained when looking at the revocation rates for juvenile and young adult offenders.

The 'natural experiment' to open the field of probation to the traditional target group for imprisonment has been successful in the sense that the judiciary has approved this extension by revoking fewer suspended sentences than before (Dünkel and Spieß 1992: 122; Spieß 1996: 35): 'If the judicial sentencing practice had followed the traditional pattern of excluding recidivist offenders from probation (based on prognostic instruments taking prior convictions as a major risk factor), it would have excluded the very group that profited most from the more liberal practice' (Spieß 1996: 35).

The 'experiment' with extending the proportion of suspended sentences confirms impressively the empirical evidence that the replacement of prison sentences by less intrusive sanctions, such as probation, does not have any negative consequences for public safety. It also underlines the fact that a wide range of sanctions are interchangeable (see Albrecht *et al.* 1981; Dünkel and Spieß 1992: 123; for further references, see Kaiser 1996: 978 ff.).

4. Types of decision-making: judicial and executive

Article 104(2) of the Basic Law (*Grundgesetz*) requires that the imposition and also termination of any form of deprivation of liberty must be decided by a Judge. Therefore the decision on conditional release is assigned to the Court for the Execution of Sentences (s. 462a of the Criminal Procedure Act). This Court was established in 1975 with the intention that, in each District Court (*Landgericht*), there should be a chamber of Judges who would be familiar with the conditions in the prisons of their district. Such Judges specialize and build up experience of prison matters. In cases of a decision on conditional release from a life sentence, from detention in a psychiatric hospital and from preventive detention, the Court for the Execution of Sentences consists of three professional Judges. In all other cases (that is, of determinate prison sentences) it is only one Judge who decides (s. 78b of the Law on the Organization of the Court System – *Gerichtsverfassungsgesetz*).

In cases arising under the terms of s. 57 (1), (2) (1) of the Penal Code (after two thirds of the sentence or half for offenders imprisoned for the first time), the Court has to decide *ex officio* – i.e. without the prisoner's application. In other cases (half-time release according to special circumstances; see s. 57(2) (2) of the Penal Code), an application by the prisoner has to be submitted.

An oral hearing of the prisoner is obligatory (see s. 454(1) (sentence 3) Criminal Procedure Act), and the prisoner's lawyer has the right to be present. The Court's decision can be appealed.

The decision is largely based on the expert opinion of the Prison Governor, who himself is dependent on the (written) statements of a conference held with the social workers, psychologists and staff members responsible for supervising the prisoner at work and on the wings. The psychologist's statement is particularly important as they may provide some risk assessment. The Court's decision is strongly influenced by these statements, but it may be that the Judge obtains a different impression from the hearing with the prisoner than from the Prison Governor's statement. The Prosecutorial Office (*Staatsanwaltschaft*) is also asked for a written statement, but it does not take part directly in the decision-making process. A negative statement by the prison can hardly be disregarded by the Court (Dünkel and Ganz 1985), while neutral and positive statements make it easier for the Judge to come to a positive decision in favour of conditional release.

If an offender is serving a life sentence or a determinate sentence of more than two years following a conviction for a sexual offence, a psychiatric assessment must be submitted to the Court (s. 454(2) (1 and 2) of the Criminal Procedure Act). The expert has to present this assessment at an oral hearing. The prisoner, his lawyer, the prison administration and the prosecutor all have the right to be present at this hearing.

5. Recall procedures

Conditions for recalling a decision of conditional release are prescribed by law in s. 57(3) (sentence 1) in conjunction with s. 56f of the Penal Code. The sentence's suspension can be revoked if the conditionally released offender commits a new offence which shows that he is not able to fulfil the expectations of the Court for releasing an offender. This means that the original prognosis has turned out to be incorrect. Close interpretation of the legal rules reveals that not every further offence will automatically disqualify an offender from remaining on conditional release. Petty offences that have no connection to the offence for which the prison sentence was initially imposed will rarely prove sufficient to establish that a good prognosis was, in fact, wrong (Stree 2006: s. 56 ff. note 4).

Another reason for a recall is if the released person deliberately or persistently violates the Court's instructions concerning his daily life (directives; see section 2.4 above), or if he defies the Probation Service's control and thereby gives cause for concern that he may commit new offences. This likewise requires that the violations must be sufficiently serious. The same is true for yet another alternative described by law: conditional release can be recalled if the released person deliberately or persistently violates the obligations set up by the Court for the reparation of the damage caused, etc. (see section 2.4 above). Even if one of these conditions for a revocation exists, the Court is still not allowed to revoke the suspension of the rest of the sentence if it would be sufficient to issue new directives or obligations or to prolong the probation period (see s. 56f(2) of the

Penal Code). This legal requirement is an expression of the principle of proportionality.[9]

6. Practical challenges

The success of conditional release, particularly with regard to the offender's rehabilitation, depends crucially on the transfer from imprisonment to liberty. The first step for the preparation of this transfer is the work done inside prison with regard to the prisoner's individual deficiencies. This means providing him with the opportunity to obtain an educational qualification, receive vocational training and, if needed, attend anti-aggression training courses or therapies, etc. Another step in the preparation for release should be the prisoner's transfer to an open prison, as provided by ss. 15, 147 of the Prison Act (StVollzG). Nevertheless, offenders who adjusted well to prison structures will usually still have to learn how to organize their lives after release. The danger of recidivism is extremely high immediately after release (National Research Council 2007: 42 ff.). Therefore a successful transfer usually requires considerable support and the involvement of aftercare services, especially in the first days and weeks after release.

According to s. 74 of the Prison Act, each prisoner shall receive support for his release from the social services inside prison, which shall work together with other services outside prison (see also s. 154(2) of the Prison Act). In practice, the quality of this support is often in need of improvement. Social services inside prisons struggle with the problems of an exorbitant workload. Therefore, they are often unable to provide support for finding a job or making arrangements for life on the outside to the extent required.

The results of the German Probation Service, which is responsible for the prisoner after early release, demonstrate that the reintegration of released prisoners who usually struggle with various problem situations is, in fact, possible (Schöch 2003: 216 ff.). However, the German Probation Service also suffers from heavy workloads. In some

[9]A special regulation deals with the situation that, after a positive decision by the Court but before the day of release, new facts have emerged that give evidence that a suspension would be irresponsible with regard to the interests of public safety. In this case the Court is competent to revoke the suspension of the remainder of the sentence before the appointed day of release (see s. 454a(2) sentence 1, of the Criminal Procedure Act).

Federal States each probation officer deals with 100 clients (Schöch 2003; on average, 70 clients per probation officer). As a consequence, released prisoners often have to wait for long periods before their first contact with the probation officer takes place. Moreover, contact is not possible as often as the client requires, and sometimes the responsible probation officers change. Other social services, such as debt regulation advisers, have excessive waiting periods. Therefore, sufficient personnel is one of the major challenges that has to be met if conditional release is to be successful. Although the law provides for engaging voluntary probation officers, this possibility is seldom used, primarily because the complex problems that prisoners face often require professional help.

Besides these problems of capacity, co-operation between the social services in prisons and the (overburdened) probation or other social services outside the institutions is often difficult to arrange. Promising projects in some Federal States,[10] however, have committed themselves to networking between the social services inside and outside prison. Contact between the prisoner and a responsible member of the aftercare service organization from the city where the prisoner will be living after his release should already have been made during the execution of the sentence. Job application training inside prison is best combined with contacts with schools and companies outside prison so that, ideally, prisoners, when they are released, have already signed a contract of employment for work on the outside. Special help with personal problems, such as the settlement of debts or relationship conflicts, is likewise part of the project objectives. It should be emphasized that these arrangements are available only for some prisoners in some Federal States and that some programmes specify the types of prisoners who can attend them. In Baden-Württemberg, for example, such programmes are offered only to juveniles and young adults.

In this regard the new prison laws for juveniles have taken a step forward because they often stipulate the Probation Service's involvement 'as early as possible'. Some Federal States even prescribe that this involvement has to take place at least six months before the day of release from prison (Ostendorf 2008).

---

[10]Baden-Württemberg, Bremen, Mecklenburg-Western Pomerania, Schleswig-Holstein and Thuringia; see the reports by Walter and Fladausch-Rödel, Matt and Henschel, Hellpap and Welchner, Jesse and Kramp, Sandmann, and Kilian-Georgus and Stein, in Dünkel et al. (2008).

7. Theoretical and other conclusions

Conditional release in Germany has been the subject of further reform proposals since the last amendments in 1998. The legal provisions for release from psychiatric or other measures for improvement and security are particularly problematic as they are too restrictive (s. 67d(2) of the Penal Code; see above). Regarding determinate prison sentences, a rule that would open the door for all prisoners to be released after they have served half their sentence (not simply first offenders with sentences of up to two years) would be beneficial.[11] The political climate is not conducive, however, to such liberalizing reforms. The 'grand coalition' of the Social Democrats and Conservatives was stultifying initiatives in both parties. Also under the new government of Conservatives and Liberals (since September 2009) it is unlikely that any legislative change will happen in the near future.

This also applies to another important reform proposal, which aims to eliminate the discretionary power of the court by replacing it with quasi-automatic conditional release, unless concrete facts give evidence of serious danger to the public (Dünkel 2009a: s. 57 note 136). There is some hope that practice might be developing in this direction as a result of the projects discussed in section 6 above. It will be interesting to observe the practical changes in the field of juvenile imprisonment, where new legislation in the Federal States has created stricter obligations for preparation for release and for co-operation between prisons and aftercare services, which should increase the proportion of inmates who are conditionally released.

From a scientific point of view, the lack of statistical and empirical information is of major concern, and therefore further research is urgently needed. The Federal Constitutional Court (in its decision on the constitutionality of youth imprisonment legislation in 2006) clearly held that the legislator has a constitutional duty to take account of research findings:

> The statutory requirements for the implementation of youth imprisonment should be based on a careful analysis of assumptions and prognoses about the effectiveness of different ways of organizing youth imprisonment and the treatment

[11]See the proposals of a law reform commission on the sanctions system of the Federal Ministry of Justice in the year 2000, and Dünkel (2010, s. 57 note 136).

measures [that form part of it]. The legislator must exhaust available sources of knowledge, to which the experiential knowledge about imprisonment practice belongs, and must orient itself to the state of scientific knowledge (BVerfG *Neue Juristische Wochenschrift* 2006, 2093 ff.; see also Dünkel and van Zyl Smit 2007).

The same approach should be adopted in respect of conditional release and aftercare. This would greatly increase knowledge about what works to reintegrate prisoners and would indicate to whom and under what conditions it would best be applied.

References

Albrecht, H.-J., Dünkel, F. and Spiess, G. (1981) 'Empirische Sanktionsforschung und die Begründbarkeit von Kriminalpolitik', *Monatsschrift für Kriminologie und Strafrechtsreform*, 64: 310–26.

Baumann, K.-H., Maetze, W. and Mey, H.-G. (1983) 'Zur Rückfälligkeit nach Strafvollzug', *Monatsschrift für Kriminologie und Strafrechtsreform*, 66: 133–48.

Böhm, A. and Erhard, C. (1984) 'Die Praxis der bedingten Strafrestaussetzung – Eine Untersuchung zur Anwendung des § 57 StGB in Hesse', *Monatsschrift für Kriminologie und Strafrechtsreform*, 67: 365–78.

Böhm, A. and Erhard, C. (1988) *Strafrestaussetzung und Legalbewährung*. Wiesbaden: Ministry of Justice.

Calliess, R.-P. and Müller-Dietz, H. (2008) *Strafvollzugsgesetz*. Munich: C.H. Beck.

Cornel, H. (2002a) 'Klarstellung oder Verschärfung der Bedingungen zur Strafrestaussetzung zur Bewährung. Eine Untersuchung zu den Konsequenzen der Gesetzesänderung von 1998 in der Praxis', *Monatsschrift für Kriminologie und Strafrechtsreform*, 85: 424–38.

Cornel, H. (2002b) *Die Praxis der Strafrestaussetzung zur Bewährung nach der Änderung des § 57 StGB vom Januar 1998*. Berlin: Alice-Salomon-Fachhochschule für Sozialarbeit und Sozialpädagogik.

Dessecker, A. (2008) *Lebenslange Freiheitsstrafe, Sicherungsverwahrung und Unterbringung in einem psychiatrischen Krankenhaus. Dauer und Gründe der Beendigung im Jahr 2006*. Wiesbaden: Kriminologische Zentralstelle.

Dünkel, F. (1981) 'Prognostische Kriterien zur Abschätzung des Erfolgs von Behandlungsmaßnahmen im Strafvollzug sowie für die Entscheidung über die bedingte Entlassung', *Monatsschrift für Kriminologie und Strafrechtsreform*, 64: 279–95.

Dünkel, F. (1992) *Empirische Beiträge und Materialien zum Strafvollzug. Bestandsaufnahmen des Strafvollzugs in Schleswig-Holstein und des Frauenvollzugs in*

Berlin. Freiburg: Eigenverlag des Max-Planck-Instituts für ausländisches und internationales Strafrecht.

Dünkel, F. (2006) 'Juvenile justice in Germany: between welfare and justice', in J. Junger-Tas and S.H. Decker (eds) *International Handbook of Juvenile Justice*. Berlin, New York: Springer, 225–262.

Dünkel, F. (2007) 'Die Farce der Föderalismusreform – ein Vergleich der vorliegenden Gesetzesentwürfe zum Jugendstrafrecht.' *Stand*: 24. September 2007 (available online at http://jura.uni-greifswald.de/duenkel/publikationen/internet/jugend-strafrecht.html).

Dünkel, F. (2008) 'Aktuelle Daten zur Sicherungsverwahrung', *Forum Strafvollzug – Zeitschrift für Strafvollzug und Straffälligenhilfe*, 57: 76–9.

Dünkel, F. (2010) 'Kommentierungen von §§ 38, 39, 57, 57a, 57b StGB', in U. Neumann, I. Puppe and W. Schild (eds) *Nomos Kommentar zum Strafgesetzbuch* (3rd edn). Baden-Baden: Nomos Verlag.

Dünkel, F. (2010) 'Germany', in F. Dünkel, J. Grzywa, P. Horsfield and I. Pruin (eds) *Juvenile Justice Systems in Europe – Current Situation and Reform Developments*. Mönchengladbach: Forum Verlag Godesberg, 547–622.

Dünkel, F., Drenkhahn, K. and Morgenstern, C. (eds) (2008) *Humanisierung des Strafvollzugs – Konzepte und Praxismodelle*. Mönchengladbach: Forum Verlag Godesberg.

Dünkel, F. and Ganz, G. (1985) 'Kriterien der richterlichen Entscheidung bei der Strafrestaussetzung nach § 57 StGB', *Monatsschrift für Kriminologie und Strafrechtsreform*, 68: 157–75.

Dünkel, F. and Geng, B. (1994) 'Rückfall und Bewährung von Karrieretätern nach Entlassung aus dem sozialtherapeutischen Behandlungsvollzug und aus dem Regelvollzug', in M. Steller *et al.* (eds) *Straftäterbehandlung. Argumente für eine Revitalisierung in Forschung und Praxis*. Pfaffenweiler: Centaurus Verlag, 35–59.

Dünkel, F. and Morgenstern, C. (2010) 'Deutschland', in F. Dünkel, T. Lappi-Seppälä, C. Morgenstern and D. van Zyl Smit (eds) *Kriminalität, Kriminalpolitik, strafrechtliche Sanktionspraxis und Gefangenenraten im europäischen Vergleich*. Mönchengladbach: Forum Verlag Godesberg (in preparation).

Dünkel, F. and Spieß, G. (1992) 'Perspektiven der Strafaussetzung zur Bewährung und Bewährungshilfe im zukünftigen deutschen Strafrecht', *Bewährungshilfe*, 39: 117–38.

Dünkel, F. and van Zyl Smit, D. (2004) 'Preventive detention of dangerous offenders reexamined: a comment on two decisions of the German Federal Constitutional Court (BVerfG – 2 BvR 2029/01 of 5 February 2004 and BVerfG – 2 BvR 834/02 – 2 BvR 1588/02 of 10 February 2004) and the Federal Draft Bill on Preventive Detention of 9 March 2004', *German Law Journal*, 5: 619–37.

Dünkel, F. and van Zyl Smit, D. (2007) 'The implementation of youth imprisonment and constitutional law in Germany', *Punishment & Society*, 9: 347–69.

Eisenberg, U. (2009) *Jugendgerichtsgesetz*. Munich: C.H. Beck.

Jehle, J.-M., Heinz, W. and Sutterer, P. (2003) *Legalbewährung nach strafrechtlichen Sanktionen. Eine kommentierte Rückfallstatistik*. Mönchengladbach: Forum Verlag Godesberg.

Kaiser, G. (1996) *Kriminologie. Ein Lehrbuch* (3rd edn). Heidelberg: C.F. Müller Verlag.

Kerner, H.-J. (1996) 'Erfolgsbeurteilung nach Strafvollzug. Ein Teil des umfassenderen Problems vergleichender kriminologischer Sanktionsforschung', in H.-J. Kerner, G. Dolde and H.G. Mey (eds) *Jugendstrafvollzug und Bewährung. Analysen zum Vollzugsverlauf und zur Rückfallentwicklung*. Bonn: Deutsche Bewährungshilfe e. V., 3–95.

Kunz, K.-L. (2004) *Kriminologie* (4th edn). Bern, Stuttgart and Wien: Haupt.

Lang, S. (2007) *Die Entwicklung des Jugendstrafvollzugs in Mecklenburg-Vorpommern in den 90er Jahren*. Mönchengladbach: Forum Verlag Godesberg.

Meier, B.-D. (2006) *Strafechtliche Sanktionen* (2nd edn). Berlin, Heidelberg, New York: Springer.

National Research Council (2007) *Parole, Desistance from crime and community reintegration* (Committee on Community Supervision and Desistance from Crime). Washington, DC: National Academy Press.

Nedopil, N. (2002) 'Prognostizierte Auswirkungen der Gesetzesänderungen vom 26.01.1998 auf die Forensische Psychiatrie und was daraus geworden ist', *Monatsschrift für Kriminologie und Strafrechtsreform*, 85: 208–15.

Ostendorf, H. (ed.) (2008) *Jugendstrafvollzugsrecht*. Baden-Baden: Nomos Verlag.

Röthel, J.C. (2007) *Vorzeitige Entlassung aus dem Jugendstrafvollzug*. Frankfurt: Peter Lang.

Schöch, H. (1998) 'Kriminologische Grenzen der Entlassungsprognose', in H.-J. Albrecht, F. Dünkel, H.-J. Kerner, J. Kürzinger, H. Schöch, K. Sessar and B. Villmow (eds) *Internationale Perspektiven in Kriminologie und Strafrecht. Festschrift für Günther Kaiser zum 70. Geburtstag*. Berlin: Duncker & Humblot, 1239–56.

Schöch, H. (1999) 'Individualprognose und präventive Konsequenzen', in D. Rössner and J.-M. Jehle (eds) *Kriminalität, Prävention und Kontrole*. Heidelberg: Kriminalistik Verlag.

Schöch, H. (2003) 'Bewährungshilfe und humane Strafrechtspflege', *Bewährungshilfe*, 50: 211–25.

Schönke, A. and Schröder, H. (2006) *Strafgesetzbuch. Kommentar* (27th edn). Munich: C.H. Beck.

Spieß, G. (1996) 'Prophetie oder Prognose? Prognostische Fragen bei der Straf(rest)aussetzung – oder: Was kann die Strafrechtspraxis aus der Prognoseforschung lernen?', *Neue Kriminalpolitik*, 8: 31–6.

Stree, W. (2006) in A. Schönke and H. Schröder (eds) *Strafgesetzbuch. Kommentar* (27th edn). Munich: C.H. Beck.

van Zyl Smit, D. (2002) *Taking Life Imprisonment Seriously in National and International Law.* The Hague, London and New York: Kluwer Law International.

von Stockhausen, H.-C. (2008) *Die Methamorphose der Strafrestaussetzung.* Berlin: Duncker & Humblot.

Decisions

BGHSt 40, 360 = BGH-GS *Neue Zeitschrift für Strafrecht*, NStZ, 1995, 124

BVerfG *Neue Juristische Wochenschrift* 2002, 2023

BVerfG *Neue Juristische Wochenschrift* 2006, 2093

BVerfG *Neue Zeitschrift für Strafrecht*, NStZ, 1994, 53

BVerfGE 45, 177

BVerfGE 86, 288 = *Neue Zeitschrift für Strafrecht*, NStZ, 1992, 484

BVerfGE 98, 169 = *Zeitschrift für Strafvollzug und Straffälligenhilfe* 1998, 242

OLG München *Strafverteidiger* 1999, 550

European Court of Human Rights

M *v.* Germany 17 December 2009 (19359/94)

Chapter 9

Greece

Leonidas K. Cheliotis
with the assistance of
Ioannis Papageorgiou

Summary

The introduction of conditional release in Greece dates back nearly a hundred years.[1] As one might expect, the pertinent laws have been subjected to a number of reforms ever since. What is less expectable, perhaps, is that none of those reforms has brought about any fundamentally progressive large-scale change to the ways in which conditional release is applied on the ground. Indeed, amid pompous rhetoric of the rehabilitative and humanitarianist varieties, conditional release in Greece has always been hostage to conservative control imperatives. This may be understood in two seemingly contradictory but eventually complementary senses. On the one hand, conditional release has been deployed as a no-cost tool for curbing overcrowding in the antiquated prisons of the country and a 'carrot-and-stick' mechanism of incentivizing orderly behaviour among prisoners.[2] Both are functions which Rothman (1980/2002) characterizes under the catch-all term 'administrative convenience'. On the other hand, owing to political considerations of the elites in office and the centralization of decision-making powers in the hands of a traditionally punitive judiciary, harsh legal and practical restrictions have been placed upon the granting of conditional release. This has not simply crippled the

---

[1] The terms 'conditional release', 'parole' and 'release on licence' are used interchangeably throughout the chapter.
[2] The same holds true in relation to similar schemes, such as temporary release (see Cheliotis 2005, 2006a, 2009).

capacity of the scheme to bring down overcrowding. The attendant frustration among prisoners over the degrading conditions of captivity combines with resentment for the lack of promised rewards in exchange for compliant conduct, to erode the effectiveness of conditional release as a means of pre-empting prison unrest. But again, as Cohen (1985) notes well, disorders caused by penality itself operate subtly to legitimate the ongoing and continuing neglect of decarcerative alternatives. Never has this paradox been more pronounced in Greece than today.

I. The early history of conditional release in Greece[3]

As a temporary scheme planned to last two years only, conditional release was first introduced in Greece in 1911 under the broader category of 'early release'. Local judges presiding in Courts of Misdemeanours were responsible for assessing applications and determining the length of the licence period, which could vary between three and five years. Prisoners serving over five years could be released after completing three quarters (or, in exceptional cases, two thirds) of their sentence, while lifers needed to have served at least 20 years. Unless their custodial sentence was converted into a monetary penalty at two thirds of the former, prisoners serving between one and five years were eligible to apply for conditional release. Licences were suspended and prisoners returned to custody in the event of a further offence at any point before the expiry of the full sentence, but no provisions were made as to their supervision.

Whereas its European counterparts evoked offender rehabilitation as the driving force behind the introduction of conditional release, the Greek government spoke only of an 'exceptional' measure of 'leniency' that aimed to lessen the duration of exposure to inhumane conditions of overcrowded captivity and, even more so, to curtail the length of short-term sentences imposed systematically by the Courts. Practice, however, belied the rhetoric. For one, no provisions were made as to the minimum of stay in prison required of those serving between three months and one year. Furthermore, in the light of public and academic criticism against the granting of clemency to so-alleged dangerous offenders, the implementation of conditional release

---

[3]No legal history of conditional release in Greece can afford to ignore the account by Massouri (2006), which also provides the basis of this section.

was subordinated to the 'law and order' ideology espoused by the Courts themselves. On the one hand, a number of what would now be called 'static' eligibility criteria were put in place (excluding, for example, animal thieves, brigands and, more generally, previously-convicted offenders) to ensure that the scheme would be reserved for a small minority of 'low-risk' prisoners. In the absence of social services, on the other hand, 'dynamic' risk classification criteria (for example, the 'character' of the prisoner) were left open to judicial interpretation, which meant in essence that the use of conditional release would remain minimal regardless. All the while, and perhaps more pragmatically, the prospect of conditional release became the first formal mechanism for incentivizing conformity among prisoners detained in Greek establishments. In fact, a ministerial circular directed the judiciary to base their assessment solely on the applicant's custodial behaviour, for this was the only risk factor that could be assessed in practice (for example, by recourse to pertinent prison reports). Albeit limited, the historical evidence demonstrates that judgments by the case-study method (today also referred to as 'clinical judgments') gave rise to an idiosyncratic and unfair system.

No sooner did the measures taken in 1911 expire, than the intertwined practical problems of prison overcrowding and institutional order came back to the surface. So much so that, in 1917, the Greek government was forced to reintroduce conditional release, this time explicitly titled as such and on a permanent basis. Although not in an instructive manner, the core law now provided that the main criterion to be assessed consisted of the applicant's custodial conduct. As that was not an essential change which would ensure wider use, decision-making responsibilities shifted from the local judiciary to a newly established Parole Board based at the Ministry of Justice and to the Minister himself. In addition, eligibility was extended to the ever-swelling cohort of prisoners serving sentences longer than three months and up to five years. While the maximum term before eligibility remained at the same high levels as previously – 20 years for lifers and three quarters or two thirds of the sentence for the rest – a low minimum of three months was set to benefit short-term prisoners. Little wonder that the granting of parole quickly underwent a notable expansion. During the period 1917–23, for example, applications were successful at an 88 per cent rate (9,471 out of 10,799).

Among others, conditions imposed on licensees included a specified place of residence and abstinence from troublesome behaviour. Licences were suspended if, during the licence period or within five years following its expiry, licensees committed a further offence and were sentenced to imprisonment for a term longer than three months. Once again, however, the supervision of licensees was not entrusted to a specialized body. In a knee-jerk effort to remedy the public concerns thus raised over security, the law reduced the length of the licence period, providing that it could not exceed a quarter of the sentence, or a third in the case of prisoners older than 70 or younger than 18 years of age. In the case of lifers, the licence period was seven years. Operational difficulties led the then Minister of Justice implicitly to gainsay official references to the rehabilitative mission of parole and explicitly to acknowledge its primary function as that of enforcing discipline among prisoners, if still with allusions to humanitarianism on the part of state elites.

The discourse of humanitarianism gained momentum especially after 1922, as parole came increasingly to be conflated with mass amnesty and clemency to the satisfaction of political clienteles (Kokolakis 1994). This practice, however, soon resulted in virulent political fury. Resolution was found in the blanket adoption of an unprecendently punitive rhetoric premised on general deterrence and institutional discipline. Unsurprisingly, and while not bereft of rehabilitatative and humanitarian proclamations, subsequent reforms signalled the decline of conditional release. Among the hardest hit were the thousands of communists and trade unionists banished under the *Idionymo* Law (*idionymo* standing for 'special crime'), which was passed by the Liberal government in 1929. Massouri (2006: 190) reports that political prisoners were strictly excluded from conditional release, while Voglis argues that they could be released only at the one-quarter point of sentence after signing a declaration that they had 'repented' and would abstain from activities 'whose manifest purpose [was] the overthrow of the established social order by violent means or the detachment of part from the whole of the country' (2002: 36; see also Panourgiá 2008).

In 1933, the granting of parole was restricted to the incongruous category of 'no-risk' prisoners, the required minimum of stay in prison rose to six months, and the maximum term before eligibility moved upwards to two thirds of the sentence. Also, the length of the licence period was divorced from the expiry of the sentence and increased to two years for the general prison population (though brought down to five years for lifers). Licences were suspended if, within two years following the expiry of the licence period (or within five years in the case of lifers), licensees committed a further offence for which they were sentenced to imprisonment for a term longer than three months. In 1950, decision-making responsibility shifted back to the judiciary and Local Misdemeanours Courts in particular, the required minimum length of stay in prison increased further to 12 months, while the length of the licence period rose to three years for the general prison population and to ten years for lifers. Licences were suspended if, during the licence period, the licensee committed a premeditated offence for which the court imposed an unappealable sentence of imprisonment for a term longer than three months.

Disappointments were still in the future. Inconsistent decision-making practices by local courts, on the one hand, and their limited use of conditional release, on the other, were combining with the inhumane conditions of overcrowded captivity to enhance frustration and anger among prisoners (and undermine the very function of the scheme as a mechanism of prisoner control, for that matter). With a view to pre-empting the impending crisis, a law was passed in 1957 to convey the message that individual prison establishments were by no means involved in the granting of parole. But this was to no avail. If with some delay, caused in part by the ascendancy of the military junta and its seven-year stay in power (1967–74), prisoner riots and hunger strikes started becoming a commonplace occurrence in the early 1980s, the prime demand being the expansion of opportunities for early release. The Greek state first responded by forming inquiry committees of 'specialists', some of whom spoke as such while others merely parroted provisions from jurisdictions elsewhere. One way or another, a string of reforms was produced in the 1990s, giving rise eventually to the parole system which is in place today.

We shall shortly turn to those reforms and the current era. First, however, it is important to put the discussion into context by reference to statistical trends in the use of imprisonment and conditional release in Greece over the last three decades or so.

2. Data on the use of imprisonment and conditional release in contemporary Greece: 1980s to the present

Although not themselves devoid of substantive gaps and methodological pitfalls, the yearbooks compiled and published by the National Statistical Service of Greece (NSSG) constitute the most comprehensive and reliable source of information about past and current imprisonment trends in the country. Secondary works, however, fall far short of exhausting NSSG data and reading them with accuracy.[4] For instance, secondary literature usually relies on one-day snapshots alone (at times also on rather irregular snapshots), to the exclusion of annual caseloads[5] of prisoners and annual totals of admissions to the prison. Evidently, this leaves one in the dark as to the number of offenders held in custody over the course of a year, the number of offenders sent to prison by the Courts over that year and the length of their stay in prison. Likewise, what is read as total prisoner population typically refers to the convict population only, despite explicit or implicit claims that the analysis concerns both convicted and remand prisoners. This is no small error, as remand prisoners in Greece comprise one third to one quarter of the total prison population (see Table 9.1) and the vast majority of them are kept in the same facilities as convicted prisoners. What is more, the average length of remand detention (that is, 365 days) far exceeds the minimum custodial sentence and is the highest in the EU (Commission of the European Communities 2006). Whether by relying solely on one-day snapshots or by missing out the prison population on remand, secondary works understate the overall scale and severity of imprisonment. Precisely because it is judged in proportion to such understated measurements of imprisonment, the extent to which non-custodial alternatives are implemented in practice is exaggerated. With a view to helping remedy the problem, this

[4]Space limitations do not allow exploration of the individual reasons lying behind such failures, nor of the attending socio-political consequences, only to note that many – though not all – of those works bear the names of the darlings of the sitting parties: those among academic criminologists whose self-professed expertise is called for to legitimate policy decisions that have already been made by government officials (see, further, Cheliotis forthcoming).

[5]The term 'caseload' refers to the total number of cases of offenders (whether convicts or pre-trial detainees) held in custody during a given year. To put it differently, the caseload of offenders held in custody during a given year is the sum total of the number of prisoners remaining in custody at the end of the previous year and the number of prisoners admitted to the prison system during the year at issue. On occasion, multiple cases may regard single individuals who were, for example, discharged, readmitted and discharged again within the same year. Precisely due to the possibility of duplication or multiple counts (a possibility that remains small due to the ever-increasing length of stay in prison), the terms 'caseload' and 'cases of offenders held in custody' are preferred here to 'yearly totals of *individual* prisoners held in custody', which is the description employed erroneously by the NSSG and others (see, further, Cheliotis forthcoming).

Table 9.1 Caseload of convicted and remand prisoners in Greece, 1980–2006

Year	Total caseload of prisoners	Caseload of convicted prisoners		Caseload of remand prisoners	
	(n)	(n)	(%)	(n)	(%)
1980	11,455	8,186	71.4	3,269	28.5
1989	10,763	6,748	62.6	4,015	37.3
1990	11,835	7,588	64.1	4,247	35.8
1991	12,595	7,992	63.4	4,603	36.5
1992	14,242	8,649	60.7	5,593	39.2
1993	14,847	9,866	66.4	4,981	33.5
1994	14,390	9,883	68.6	4,507	31.3
1995	13,944	9,377	67.2	4,567	32.7
1996	13,281	8,786	66.1	4,495	33.8
1997	13,344	8,997	67.4	4,347	32.5
1998	13,912	10,130	72.8	3,782	27.1
1999	13,409	9,910	73.9	3,499	26.0
2000	14,708	11,555	78.5	3,153	21.4
2001	16,446	12,687	77.1	3,759	22.8
2002	16,444	12,684	77.1	3,760	22.8
2003	17,191	12,889	74.9	4,302	25.0
2004	17,227	12,634	73.3	4,593	26.6
2005	17,869	13,082	73.2	4,787	26.7
2006	18,070	13,170	72.8	4,900	27.1

Sources of primary data: NSSG, *Statistical Yearbook* and *Justice Statistics*. The data were compiled and analysed by the author.
Note: Data for the years 2002, 2003 and 2004 are based on NSSG estimates, as they were published originally. The latest (2007) statistical yearbook of the NSSG provides slightly different estimates that hardly affect the analysis.

section offers a summary of basic findings from a broader reanalysis of NSSG data (see, further, Cheliotis forthcoming).

Imprisonment in Greece has grown explosively over the last two decades. Following a modest decline during the 1980s, the annual total caseload of prisoners (including pre-trial detainees) rose by 52.6 per cent between 1990 and 2006, from 11,835 to 18,070. This is not so much due to the rise in the caseload of pre-trial detainees as in that of convicted prisoners. Whereas the caseload of pre-trial detainees increased by 15.3 per cent between 1990 and 2006, from 4,247 to 4,900, the proportion of cases of pre-trial detainees among the total prisoner caseload fell, from 35.8 to 27.1 per cent. By contrast, the caseload of convicted prisoners rose by a massive 73.5 per cent, from 7,588 in 1990 to 13,170 in 2006. Correspondingly, the share of cases of convicted prisoners among the total prisoner caseload increased from 64.1 to 72.8 per cent (see, further, Table 9.1). As one would expect, prison admissions have also been on the rise. Following an important decline of 22.4 per cent, from 8,490 in 1980 to 6,585 in 1989, the annual total of admissions grew by 13.2 per cent between 1990 and 2006, from 7,242 to 8,199. The rise, in this case, is modest and relates to convicted prisoners only. Unlike what is commonly assumed, the total of admissions of pre-trial detainees is on the decline. Between 1990 and 2006, it fell by 32.1 per cent, from 2,690 to 1,824, while the proportion of prison admissions of pre-trial detainees among the total of admissions of all prisoners dropped from 37.1 to 22.2 per cent. The total of admissions of convicted prisoners, on the other hand, rose by an impressive 40 per cent, from 4,552 in 1990 to 6,375 in 2006, while the share of admissions of convicted prisoners among the total of prisoner admissions increased from 62.8 to 77.7 per cent (see Table 9.2).

In and of themselves, then, prison admissions do not suffice to account for the growth in the caseload of prisoners. In the same vein, the rise in prison admissions under conviction cannot alone adequately explain the increased caseload of convicted prisoners. Most notably, the drop in prison admissions on remand appears to contradict the rise in the caseload of pre-trial detainees. The key variable here is length of sentence. From 1990 to 2006, for example, there was a fall in the caseload of prisoners sentenced to terms of less than a month (by 76.6 per cent, from 476 to 111), between six and 12 months (by 17.4 per cent, from 1,201 to 991) and between one to three years (by 31.5 per cent, from 2,788 to 1,909). But there was a huge expansion in the caseload of prisoners sentenced to terms of one to six months (by 122.4 per cent, from 616 to 1,370), three to five years (by 323.3 per cent, from 616 to 2,608), five to 20 years (by 332.7 per cent, from 1,246 to 5,392) and life imprisonment (by 155.1 per cent, from 270 to 689). The caseload of prisoners sentenced to a term of five to 20 years was by far the highest (40.9 per cent) in 2006. Turning to the annual caseloads of offenders admitted to the prison during the period 1990–2006, there was a fall for terms of less than a month (by 77.7 per cent, from 462 to 103), between six and 12 months (by 19.8 per cent, from 947 to 759) and between one to three years (by 35.6 per cent, from 2,003 to 1,289). But again, there was a huge expansion in the caseload of offenders admitted to the prison for a term of one to six months (by 127.1 per cent, from 535 to 1,215), three to five years

Table 9.2 Prison admissions of convicted and remand prisoners in Greece, 1980–2006

Year	Total number of admissions	Admissions of convicted prisoners		Admissions of remand prisoners	
	(*n*)	(*n*)	(%)	(*n*)	(%)
1980	8,490	5,846	68.8	2,644	31.1
1989	6,585	3,757	57.0	2,828	42.9
1990	7,242	4,552	62.8	2,690	37.1
1991	7,462	4,455	59.7	3,007	40.2
1992	8,880	5,250	59.1	3,630	40.8
1993	8,402	5,779	68.7	2,623	31.2
1994	7,580	5,099	67.2	2,481	32.7
1995	8,326	5,429	65.2	2,897	34.7
1996	7,524	5,015	66.6	2,509	33.3
1997	8,105	5,504	67.9	2,601	32.0
1998	7,819	6,035	77.1	1,784	22.8
1999	6,403	5,308	82.8	1,095	17.1
2000	8,563	7,142	83.4	1,421	16.5
2001	11,921	8,901	74.6	3,020	25.3
2002	8,473	6,610	78.0	1,863	21.9
2003	9,347	6,803	72.7	2,544	27.2
2004	9,057	6,485	71.6	2,572	28.3
2005	8,851	6,702	75.7	2,149	24.2
2006	8,199	6,375	77.7	1,824	22.2

Sources of primary data: NSSG, *Statistical Yearbook* and *Justice Statistics*. The data were compiled and analysed by the author.
Notes: Data for the years 2002, 2003 and 2004 are based on NSSG estimates, as they were published originally. The latest (2007) statistical yearbook of the NSSG provides slightly different estimates that hardly affect the analysis. Data for the year 2001 should be treated with caution: the calculations on which they are based use data for the year 2000 that do not include 2,036 cases of convicted prisoners and 777 cases of remand prisoners about whom no information was provided by the authorities in charge.

(by 699.4 per cent, from 186 to 1,478) and five to 20 years (by 305.3 per cent, from 374 to 1,516). Overall, admissions to prison for a term of life imprisonment remained stable. Of the caseloads of prisoners admitted to the prison in 2006, the highest were for terms of five to 20 years (23.7 per cent), three to five years (23.1 per cent), one to three years (20.2 per cent) and one to six months (19 per cent). Not, then, that the judiciary has become more liberal in recent years, but their traditionally punitive mentality manifests itself in the excessive use of long custodial sentences, more so than in the use of custodial sentences as such. This, as we shall see later, is the case especially with petty drug-related offences.

With insignificant variation over time, cases of convicted prisoners in Greece are overwhelmingly of male and adult individuals (for example, 93.4 and 99.2 per cent of the total prisoner caseload in 2006, respectively). As regards the nationality of convicted prisoners in the total caseload, however, the temporal variation is significant. Between 1996 and 2006, for example, the annual total caseload of non-Greek convicts rose by 140.5 per cent, from 2,253 to 5,420. Correspondingly, the proportion of non-Greeks among the total caseload of convicts increased from 25.3 to 41.1 per cent. This is four times higher than the estimated proportion of non-Greeks in the general population of the country, but the level and nature of their criminal involvement fail to justify the discrepancy (see, further, Cheliotis forthcoming; Karydis forthcoming). During the same period, the annual total caseload of Greek convicts increased by 16.8 per cent, from 6,632 to 7,750, yet fell in reference to the annual total of cases of convicted prisoners, from 74.6 to 58.8 per cent.

In parallel, the annual caseload of convicted and remand prisoners released for any reason increased by 16.9 per cent during the period 1990–2006, from 6,607 to 7,725, but fell in proportion to the annual caseload of convicted and remand prisoners, from 55.8 to 42.7 per cent. To differentiate between convicted and remand prisoners, the annual caseload of convicted prisoners discharged for any reason increased by 46.1 per cent during the period 1990–2006, from 4,021 to 5,876, but fell in proportion to the annual caseload of convicted prisoners, from 52.9 to 44.6 per cent. As concerns remand prisoners, the annual caseload of discharges for any reason during the same period fell by 28.4 per cent, from 2,586 to 1,849, and from 60.8 to 37.7 per cent in proportion to the annual caseload of remand prisoners. In conclusion, the rise in the rate of discharge for any reason has proved too low to put a halt to the increase in the caseload of prisoners.

The same could not but be true of the narrower category of release on parole (which is also the major reason for release from prison). For instance, the caseload of convicted and remand prisoners released on parole increased by 17.8 per cent between 1998 and 2006, from 3,035 to 3,578, but fell in proportion to the annual caseload of convicted and remand prisoners, from 21.8 to 19.8 per cent. During the same period, the caseload of convicted prisoners released on parole rose by 17.4 per cent, from 2,515 to 2,954, but dropped in proportion to the caseload of convicted prisoners, from 24.8 to 22.4 per cent. The caseload of remand prisoners released on parole increased by 20 per cent, from 520 to 624, but fell in proportion to the caseload of remand prisoners, from 14.2 to 12.7 per cent.[6] One might deduce that the judiciary still exhibits far greater propensity to pass custodial sentences than to grant release on parole, or that parole eligibility is delayed in good part due to the ever-increasing length of custodial sentences. Or, as Karydis and Koulouris (2002) go on to suggest, that lengthier sentences may well be the means by which Judges manage to control the release process even before offenders are put behind bars. Unfortunately, these themes have yet to be subjected to thorough and methodologically-reliable empirical scrutiny.

3. Conditional release in contemporary Greece: 1990s to the present

We are now in a position to address the reforms of the law on conditional release since the 1990s, as well as the practical effects, if any, that those reforms have generated in turn.[7] In November 1991, the maximum term required before parole eligibility was reduced to three fifths of the sentence for the general prison population and to half the sentence for prisoners aged over 70. Owing to conservative resistance on the part of the judiciary, however, the use of conditional release actually fell. The caseload of convicted prisoners released on licence, for example, decreased by 25.4 per cent, from 440 (or 6.1 per cent of the total annual caseload of convicted and remand prisoners released) in 1991 to 328 (or 4.2 per cent of the total annual caseload of convicted and remand prisoners released) in 1992. The corresponding rate *vis-à-vis* all reasons for release of convicted prisoners dropped from 9.6 per cent in 1991 to 7.2 per cent in 1992. What is worse, prison admissions of convicted and remand prisoners concurrently

[6]Data for earlier years are not available or calculable (see, further, Cheliotis forthcoming).

[7]In those cases where laws were ratified within the first half of the calendar year (January–June), statistical comparisons are between the preceding year and the year when the law at issue was ratified. In those cases where laws were ratified within the second half of the calendar year (July–December), statistical comparisons are between the year when the law at issue was ratified and the year that follows. The underlying principle is that the practical effects of legislative reforms will become clearer if examined over sufficient time (i.e., at least six months subsequent to their ratification).

rose by a significant 16.1 per cent, from 7,462 (or 73 per 100,000 inhabitants) in 1991 to 8,880 (or 86 per 100,000 inhabitants) in 1992, thereby feeding a 13 per cent rise in the caseload of convicted and remand prisoners, from 12,595 (or 123 per 100,000 inhabitants) in 1991 to 14,242 (or 137 per 100,000 inhabitants) in 1992 (see Tables 9.1 and 2). Further outbreaks of prison unrest were on their way.

In response, December 1993 witnessed the introduction of automatic early release for prisoners fulfilling the pertinent criteria, particularly that of orderly custodial behaviour. Certainly, this provision reinvigorated the control powers of prison officials, as they now appeared to hold the fate of prisoners tightly in their hands. At the same time, the judiciary was seemingly relegated to a mere 'approving body'. A great many Judges vocalized their opposition and many even actively resisted compliance with the law, continuing to process cases at will (Massouri 2006: 287–8).

As this caused further rioting in prisons, a new law was ratified in March 1994 whereby parole eligibility was extended to prisoners serving appealable sentences. The maximum term required before parole eligibility was reduced to two fifths of the sentence for prisoners aged over 70, and to 18 years for lifers of the same age group. More importantly, the required minimum of stay in prison was brought down to two fifths of the sentence for prisoners earning 'good-time' credits for participation in either educational and vocational training programmes or prison work. But, in practice, opportunities for placement onto 'good-time' schemes were so few that their function changed quickly from a means by which prisoners could expedite release to a powerful mechanism of prisoner control in the hands of allocating authorities in prison. Because the problem of overcrowding was thus bound to persist, the law also introduced a new, one-off, 'exceptional' type of automatic release, whereby short-term prisoners could be released at the one-quarter point of their sentence. As an immediate result, the caseload of convicted prisoners released on licence shot up by 382 per cent, from 338 (or 4.2 per cent of the total annual caseload of convicted and remand prisoners released) in 1993 to 1,630 (or 18.9 per cent of the total annual caseload of convicted and remand prisoners released) in 1994. The corresponding rate *vis-à-vis* all reasons for release of convicted prisoners rose from 6.7 per cent in 1993 to 28.1 per cent in 1994. Meanwhile, however, judicial use of custody remained excessively high, which meant that imprisonment rates could only be slightly affected by the rise in the use of conditional release. More specifically, prison admissions of convicted and remand prisoners fell by 9.8 per cent, from 8,402 (or 80 per 100,000 inhabitants) in 1993 to 7,580 (or 72 per 100,000 inhabitants) in 1994, yet remained high enough to confine the drop in the corresponding annual caseload to a mere 3 per cent, from 14,847 (or 142 per 100,000 inhabitants) in 1993 to 14,390 (or 136 per 100,000 inhabitants) in 1994 (see Tables 9.1 and 9.2). The eruption of further prison unrest came as a logical consequence.

As if to undercut disparity in decision-making, a law ratified in March 1995 introduced two innovations. Firstly, parole assessments were entrusted to three-member prison-based boards consisting of governors and specialist staff with a 'welfarist' mentality (for example, social workers, psychologists, criminologists). And, secondly, prosecutors were assigned to individual prison establishments to supervise the internal operations thereof. But the very lack of specialist professionals, coupled with the punitive outlook predictably brought to the process by prosecutors, afforded prison governors abundant leeway to continue deploying parole as a tool of prisoner control. Judges, all the while, persisted in imposing their own preferences on the granting of early release, even as they were threatened with disciplinary proceedings (Massouri 2006: 298–9). It comes as no surprise that the caseload of convicted prisoners released on licence dropped by 27.4 per cent, from 1,630 (or 18.9 per cent of the total annual caseload of convicted and remand prisoners released) in 1994 to 1,182 (or 14.7 per cent of the total annual caseload of convicted and remand prisoners released) in 1995. The corresponding rate *vis-à-vis* all reasons for release of convicted prisoners fell from 28.1 per cent in 1994 to 21.7 per cent in 1995. Prison admissions of convicted and remand prisoners rose by 9.8 per cent, from 7,580 (or 72 per 100,000 inhabitants) in 1994 to 8,326 (or 78 per 100,000 inhabitants) in 1995. An insignificant 3 per cent drop can be observed in the corresponding annual caseload, from 14,390 (or 136 per 100,000 inhabitants) in 1994 to 13,944 (or 131 per 100,000 inhabitants) in 1995.

Further laws were ratified in June 1996 and September 2001, whereby parole eligibility was redefined according to length of sentence and seriousness of offence, respectively. With variation only in particulars, the provisions of these laws are still in force today. The most radical change in the law of 1996 was the abolition of a minimum term required of prisoners serving five years or less, while the maximum term required before eligibility was reduced to two fifths of the sentence. For prisoners serving between five and 20 years, the minimum term required before eligibility was set at a third of the sentence, and the maximum term at three fifths. The minimum term for lifers was set at 16 years and the maximum remained 20.

Maximum terms were lowered to two fifths of the sentence for prisoners serving between five and 20 years, and to 16 years for lifers, in the case of prisoners over 70 years of age. Provisions were also made that prisoners aged over 65 earn double credit for each day spent in actual custody, and that juveniles (that is, persons aged between 13 and 18) be eligible for conditional release at the one-third point of their sentence.[8]

In 2001, the minimum and maximum terms before eligibility were, respectively, raised to two thirds and four fifths of the sentence for drug-related offenders serving between five and 20 years. The minimum term before eligibility was set at 25 years for prisoners serving a life sentence for a drug-dealing offence. A law passed in 2002 provided that foreigners subject to deportation orders following imprisonment are eligible for conditional release, but are to be deported immediately after conditional release is granted. When deportation is not possible, foreigners may stay in the country under conditional release. The latest legislation (see below) mandated that the minimum term before eligibility for those convicted of terrorist acts be 25 years (Kaiafa-Gbandi *et al.* 2008: 491), but it set no minimum for prisoners convicted of high treason. At the same time, automatic release for reasons of ill-health was extended to include prisoners diagnosed with one of the following: AIDS; long-term kidney failure which requires regular dialysis; resistant tuberculosis; quadriplegia; cirrhosis of the liver with a degree of disability that exceeds 67 per cent; dementia at the age of 80 or over; or final-stage malignant neoplasms (cancer). But the list was drafted in such a way as to disqualify controversial cases: from a half-blind and nearly deaf amputee, Savvas Xiros, a captive member of the terrorist group November 17, to elderly and terminally ill junta officers still alive in prison (see, for example, Ministry of Justice 26 November 2008).

At the time of writing, applications for conditional release are submitted by prison governors to Local Misdemeanours Councils one month prior to the eligibility date.[9] If the applicant is deemed unsuitable for release, prison governors may also submit to the Council a pertinent account, along with a report drafted by the social services authorities of the establishment. At least ten days prior to the hearing, prisoners are invited to attend, whether in person or via their chosen legal representative. Despite expressing concerns over what they

[8]Irrespective of age, each day of work in prison counts as one and a half days towards the sentence.
[9]Juvenile cases are dealt with in three-member juvenile tribunals.

depict as their declining role in the decision-making process (Karydis and Koulouris 2002), Judges enjoy as wide discretion as ever. On the one hand, the law provides for the grant of conditional release as a general rule and stipulates that negative decisions can be only an exceptional means by which to prevent further re-offending, in which case the burden of proof rests with the judiciary. On the other, risk of reoffending is to be assessed by resort to subjective court rulings. This is why risk assessments remain tightly and exclusively tied to such a slippery criterion as that of 'custodial behaviour', even though it bears a tenuous link with recidivism. It is indicative that, while most Judges equate good custodial behaviour with the absence of prior disciplinary record, there is no consensus as to whether past failure to comply with the conditions of home leave should count against the applicant (Massouri 2006: 340–1; Papacharalambous 1999).

In the event of conditional release being granted, conditions may be imposed upon the parolee regarding his 'lifestyle and especially his place of residence'. These conditions may be revoked or modified upon the request of the parolee. As concerns adult prisoners, if the remainder of the sentence to be served is three years or less, the licence stays in force for three years. If the remainder of the sentence to be served exceeds three years, the licence stays in force until the entire sentence has expired. In the case of lifers, the licence stays in force for ten years. As concerns juvenile prisoners, the licence stays in force until the entire sentence has expired. Responsible for the supervision of parolees is the newly-established body of probation officers (see below). The law draws a technical distinction between recall and suspension of conditional release. Licences are *recalled* by the Local Misdemeanours Council following the recommendation of the supervising authorities when parolees fail to abide by the conditions imposed. In such cases, the time spent on licence does not count towards the sentence. Licences are *suspended* when parolees commit premeditated offences punishable by imprisonment for a term longer than six months. In such cases, parolees are returned to prison to serve both the new sentence and the whole of the period between release on licence and the expiry of the original sentence.

Thanks to the law of 1996, the caseload of convicted prisoners released on licence rose by an impressive 47.6 per cent within a single year, from 1,182 (or 14.7 per cent of the total annual caseload of convicted and remand prisoners released) in 1995 to 1,745 (or 22 per cent of the total annual caseload of convicted and remand prisoners released) in 1996. The corresponding rate *vis-à-vis* all reasons for release of convicted prisoners increased from 21.7 per cent in 1995 to

33.6 per cent in 1996. Meanwhile, prison admissions of convicted and remand prisoners fell by 9.6 per cent, from 8,326 (or 78 per 100,000 inhabitants) in 1995 to 7,524 (or 70 per 100,000 inhabitants) in 1996. The corresponding annual caseload dropped by 4.7 per cent, from 13,944 (or 131 per 100,000 inhabitants) in 1995 to 13,281 (or 124 per 100,000 inhabitants) in 1996. To assess the impact of the 1996 reform on a longer-term basis, the caseload of convicted prisoners released on licence rose by 116.5 per cent, from 1,182 (or 14.7 per cent of the total annual caseload of convicted and remand prisoners released) in 1995 to 2,560 (or 35 per cent of the total annual caseload of convicted and remand prisoners released) in 2000. The corresponding rate *vis-à-vis* all reasons for release of convicted prisoners increased from 21.7 per cent in 1995 to 45.1 per cent in 2000. All the while, prison admissions of convicted and remand prisoners saw a slight increase of 2.8 per cent, from 8,326 (or 78 per 100,000 inhabitants) in 1995 to 8,563 (or 78 per 100,000 inhabitants) in 2000. The corresponding annual caseload rose by 5.4 per cent, from 13,944 (or 131 per 100,000 inhabitants) in 1995 to 14,708 (or 109 per 100,000 inhabitants) in 2000 (see Tables 9.1 and 2). It is reasonable to conclude that the rather modest increase in the use of custodial sentences, on the one hand, and the significant rise in the use of conditional release, on the other, helped minimize the growth of the prisoner caseload during 1995–2000.

Turning to the impact of the law of 2001, the caseload of convicted prisoners released on licence fell by 5.4 per cent, from 2,639 (or 31 per cent of the total annual caseload of convicted and remand prisoners released) in 2001 to 2,497 (or 30.5 per cent of the total annual caseload of convicted and remand prisoners released. The corresponding rate *vis-à-vis* all reasons for release of convicted prisoners fell from 40.2 per cent in 2001 to 38.1 per cent in 2002. All the while, the annual total caseload of convicted and remand prisoners remained essentially static (falling from 16,446 (or 150 per 100,000 inhabitants) in 2001 to 16,444 (or 150 per 100,000 inhabitants) in 2002.[10] On a longer-term basis, the caseload of convicted prisoners released on licence rose by 11.9 per cent, from 2,639 (or 31 per cent of the total annual caseload of convicted and remand prisoners released) in 2001 to 2,954 (or 38 per cent of the total annual caseload of convicted and remand prisoners released) in 2006. The corresponding rate *vis-à-vis* all reasons for release of convicted prisoners increased from 40.2 per cent in 2001

[10]For reasons relating to the accuracy of the data for the year 2001, reference is not made to admissions data in this case (see, further, Table 9.2).

to 50.3 per cent in 2006. At the same time, the annual caseload of convicted and remand prisoners rose by 9.8 per cent, from 16,446 (or 50 per 100,000 inhabitants) in 2001 to 18,070 (or 162 per 100,000 inhabitants) in 2006 (see Tables 9.1 and 2). In stark contrast, then, with the previous six years, the rise in the use of conditional release proved insufficient to prevent a significant growth in the prisoner caseload, even as prison admissions fell.

4. Concluding remarks

The prison system of Greece was shaken to its roots in November 2008. For 18 consecutive days, some 6,000 prisoners, or half the prison population at the time, either abstained from prison food or, as became increasingly the case, went on complete hunger strike. During this time, two prisoner deaths were reported and there was one attempted suicide, while tens of others sewed their lips together. It was a desperate mass protest directed against the underuse and unfair administration of parole and temporary release, overcrowded and degrading conditions, inadequate medical provision and abusive prison staff, to name but a few of the grievances. A significant minority among the Greek public sympathized with the protesters. With marches and motorbike rallies through city centres, demonstrations outside prisons, open-air concerts featuring well-known Greek artists and internet blogging, supporters joined prisoners in calling not only for reforms but also for the eventual abolition of prisons (Cheliotis and Xenakis 2008). Opposition extended outside the country's borders, as the then Minister of Finance, Yorgos Alogoskoufis, discovered at the London School of Economics, where he came under sustained egg-pelting from Greek anti-prison agitators.

The government responded spasmodically. A new law was passed within less than a month, introducing various measures of a one-off character.[11] Most notably, the maximum term before eligibility for discretionary conditional release was lowered from four fifths to three fifths of the sentence for prisoners serving drug-related sentences

---

[11] The sole exception were the aforementioned provisions for early release on the grounds of ill-health, which were given a permanent character.

between five and 20 years.[12] Prisoners convicted of serious, organized drug dealing were exempted, but the authorities declared emphatically that the remaining two thirds (or 4,900) of drug convicts would still benefit from the new law (Ministry of Justice 19 November 2008). Further provisions included the automatic conditional release of misdemeanour offenders (after serving a fifth of sentences up to two years or a third of sentences over two years) and the discretionary conversion of sentences up to five years into monetary penalties at a minimum rate of 3 euros per day. Eligible prisoners lacking the necessary financial resources were given the alternative to opt for early release on a community-work order.

Following what was described as a thorough examination of the records of all 12,315 offenders held in prison at the time, the Minister of Justice, Sotiris Hadjigakis, announced that 5,500 were to be released by April 2009 at the latest (*Kathimerini* 2009). Of those, 3,720 were to be released imminently so that they could 'spend Christmas and New Year's with their significant others'. All this, Hadjigakis asserted in a speech he gave to Parliament, was a gesture of '[Aristotelian] leniency', 'sin-forgiving' and 'benefaction', a 'second chance [to petty offenders] to start their lives afresh' (Ministry of Justice 25 November 2008). Official predictions were made concurrently that the overall capacity of the prison estate would quickly overtake the number of prisoners behind bars (8,243 *vs.* 6,815, respectively, by April 2009; Ministry of Justice 26 November 2008).

But it was only by way of heuristic analogy that state authorities compared the promised reduction of the prison population by half with 'closing down three large prison establishments' (*Kathimerini* 2009). Prison population forecasts were based on the two-fold assumption that the courts would suddenly cease passing custodial sentences (for releases and releases alone could hardly ever suffice to bring the prison population down to 6,815), and that the use of early release would expand according to plan. If the former

[12]As recently as December 2009 (while this chapter was already at the proof stage), and largely in response to prisoner protests in eight establishments one month earlier, the newly elected centre-left government of PASOK passed a number of permanent amendments to the legal provisions concerning conditional release. Crucially, the amendments included lowering the maximum term before eligibility for discretionary conditional release to three fifths of the sentence for prisoners serving drug-related sentences between five and 20 years. The applicability of the amendments, however, is likely to be plagued by the same problems encountered with the 2008 law (on which more in a moment).

was false by definition, the latter was bound to be disproved very soon. Anticipating the obvious, Hadjigakis coupled his discourse of generosity and open-heartedness with stern assurances that four new prison establishments (or an additional 1,290 places) would be ready to operate before the end of 2009 (*Kathimerini* 2009).

Indeed, the new law was replete with self-defeating features. Though referred to as the major 'beneficiaries' of the new law, petty drug-possession offenders could only rarely fall under the provisions for conditional release at the three-fifth point of sentence. The reason was that most had been penalized so harshly by sentencing Courts as to be convicted of serious, organized drug dealing (a phenomenon on which see, further, Lambropoulou 2003). Not dissimilarly, the conversion of prison sentences into monetary penalties was a real possibility solely for the tiny minority of prisoners who could find the financial means required (Aloskofis 2005). For want of a permit to stay in the country, the majority of foreign prisoners were not even entitled to a tax number (similar to a UK Schedule D number), the latter being a necessary prerequisite for the conversion of their prison sentence into a monetary penalty. The alternative to opt for community work was essentially a non-option, given that opportunities for work of this kind were few and far between. To top it all off, with its discretionary powers untouched, the judiciary could in any case ensure that 'front-door' entries would not be offset by 'back-door' conversions of sentences into monetary penalties or community-work orders.[13]

Further difficulties were to be found beyond the narrow confines of the law. Leaving aside the pockets of public sympathy to prisoners and their struggles, the broader socio-political climate could not have been less conducive to the application of decarcerative reforms on the shopfloor. Before the new law was even ratified formally, the fatal shooting of unsuspecting 15-year-old Alexandros Grigoropoulos by a police officer sparked three weeks of violent civil unrest across Greece. Unwilling to address the root causes of the crisis (that is, a mixture of police brutality and impunity, political corruption, unemployment and precarious labour under conditions of neoliberalism, and degraded education), the Greek government spoke of 'acts of blind violence' resulting from 'the exploitation of the anxieties of the youth by extreme elements' (Athens News Agency 2008). Pledges to exhibit

[13]This is not to negate the possibility of professional resistance (on which, see further Cheliotis 2006b), only to doubt the degree of its applicability in the case at issue.

'zero-tolerance' and restore 'law and order' followed suit (see, for example, *The Sunday Times* 2008; see, further, Cheliotis forthcoming). The cacophony of warring voices must have sounded like music in the ears of judges, for they were now more able than ever to legitimate and enhance their long-standing punitive stance.

It comes as no surprise that a mere 370 prisoners were released under the new law by the end of 2008 (Ministry of Justice 29 December 2008), and only 968 by 10 April 2009 (*Eleftherotypia* 2009), not to mention that most of them would have been released under previous law anyway. Nikos Dendias, who took over as Minister of Justice in the meantime, was forced to admit to what he termed a 'partial failure'. Of which, however, he also absolved himself and his predecessor by blaming the missed target on a 'tragic mistake in the calculations owing to the lack of a dedicated statistical service at the ministry' (*Eleftherotypia* 2009). Explaining away failures is deeply ingrained in everyday practice throughout contemporary Greece. As Herzfeld says of Greek bureaucrats, for instance, 'the buck-passing is consistent: clerk to supervisors, registrar to superiors, deputy mayor to mayor, mayor to prefect and minister' (1992: 92). And minister to no one, we may now add.

At first sight, more constructive steps seem to have been taken towards helping parolees in the transition between imprisonment and discharge. Following a 13-year period of gestation, for example, the establishment of a nationwide probation agency entrusted with responsibilities for aftercare supervision was finally brought into effect in 2004. Ever since, however, street-level practice has been fraught with difficulties, from ill-defined duties for practitioners and their lack of training to understaffing and disproportionately high caseloads (see, further, Giovanoglou 2006: 204–13; Pitsela forthcoming). It is plausible to suggest that the small but growing body of probation officers is mainly preoccupied with running routine checks on parolees for technical infractions, more so than with the demanding tasks of a welfarist, aftercare orientation (for example, assistance in securing employment, housing or placement onto professional training schemes).

The emerging gap is said to have been filled by a private-law, state-supervised organization named EPANODOS, meaning 're-entry', which was inaugurated amid great fanfare in 2007. In this case, too, however, there is a yawning abyss between theory and practice. It is not so much that EPANODOS suffers from insufficient resources (certainly human and possibly financial), nor the flawed presumption underlying its rhetoric (and reflected in its very name) that prisoners were once included in mainstream society. It is principally that the organization itself lacks conviction in the possibility of rehabilitation for the vast majority of prisoners. In a paper presented at the retraining programme of the National School of Judges in 2005, for example, the academician later appointed head of EPANODOS declared that the problems faced by young prisoners in seeking employment after discharge 'appear insurmountable'. In good part, he went on to explain by reference to a self-exonerative conventional wisdom, this is due to chronic drug addiction and the attribute of 'laziness' instilled into the youth as a result of their incarceration, to such an extent that they would rather choose prison over life on the outside. If there is any rehabilitative hope for young prisoners, he concluded, it is to be placed mainly with the youngest of them, 'there where the branch is not yet crooked' (Courakis 2005: 11).[14] Were all this to be true, then riots and hunger strikes would merely be games by which 'lost causes' break their monotony, rather than generalized struggles for dignity and freedom.

But there is more. While high fear of crime among Greeks remains stubbornly disproportionate to the objective risk of victimization (Tseloni and Zarafonitou 2008; Zarafonitou forthcoming), the head of EPANODOS led the publication of a state-funded manual instructing 'active citizens' as to the 'best practices' of minimizing vulnerability: from installing bolt-type locks on home doors and avoiding riding in lifts with strangers, to parking cars tightly adjacent to pavement edges lest thieves plan to tow vehicles away (see Courakis 2006: 21–42). It requires quite a stretch of the imagination to believe that such an organization can actually help prisoners find their way back into a community that never wished to incorporate them anyway. It is, instead, more likely that the function of EPANODOS is to provide an evermore punitive system with a veneer of humanism – a 'human face', as the suggestive buzzword of the day has it. Ostensibly in opposition to the beautification of penality, a group of self-dubbed anarchists went so far as to violently interrupt a conference organized by EPANODOS in central Athens in February 2009.

There is no inherent contradiction to the fact that legal and practical restrictions on parole fuel unrest in prisons and beyond, or that mixing increased surveillance of parolees with inadequate provision to them is destined to push recall and suspension rates higher, or that rises in the use of imprisonment may well be causally

[14]For a multifaceted analysis of the relationship between youth and crime in contemporary Greece, see Papageorgiou and Cheliotis forthcoming.

related to recidivism (Cheliotis 2008). The buck, in this case, is passed to the victims. Cohen puts the point astutely when he writes that, in the same way as the health industry attributes iatrogenic illness to purported faults of patients, so crime-control ideologues blame systemic failure on offenders, be they captive or otherwise: 'A special group of offenders is particularly to blame: the incorrigibles, the hard cores, the career criminals who so ungratefully persist in keeping recidivism rates so high. If only they would cooperate!' (1985: 169). Ultimately, and utterly paradoxically, the misfires of penality legitimate its own existence, aggrandizement and harshening at the expense of decarceration.

Acknowledgements

Ioannis Papageorgiou's contribution to this chapter consisted in helping the author locate official data on the use of conditional release in Greece as well as pertinent legislation. Thanks are due to Effie Lambropoulou, Charis Papacharalambous and Garyfallia Massouri also for helping locate official data on the use of conditional release in Greece; to Loïc Wacquant and Sappho Xenakis, for their constructively critical comments on earlier versions of this chapter; and to the editors of this book, for their patience and suggestions.

References

Aloskofis, W. (2005) *Social and Penal Situation of Prisoners in the Judicial Prison of Korydallos: Differences between Natives and Foreigners* (report submitted to the Ministry of Justice) (in Greek).

Athens News Agency (2008) 'Greek Prime Minister calls for an end to "acts of blind violence" ', 12 December.

Cheliotis, L.K. (2005) 'The prison furlough programme in Greece: findings from a research project in the male prison of Korydallos', *Punishment and Society*, 7: 201–15.

Cheliotis, L.K. (2006a) 'Demystifying risk management: a process evaluation of the prisoners' home leave scheme in Greece', *Criminology and Criminal Justice*, 6: 163–95.

Cheliotis, L.K. (2006b) 'How iron is the iron cage of new penology? The role of human agency in the implementation of criminal justice policy', *Punishment and Society: The International Journal of Penology*, 8: 313–40.

Cheliotis, L.K. (2008) 'Reconsidering the effectiveness of temporary release: a systematic review', *Aggression and Violent Behavior*, 13: 153–68.

Cheliotis, L.K. (2009) 'Before the next storm: some evidence-based reminders about temporary release', *International Journal of Offender Therapy and Comparative Criminology*, 53: 420–32.

Cheliotis, L.K. (forthcoming) 'The psychopolitics of law and order in neoliberal Greece', in L.K. Cheliotis and S. Xenakis (eds) *Crime and Punishment in Contemporary Greece: International Comparative Perspectives*. Oxford: Peter Lang.

Cheliotis, L.K. (under review) 'The great decarceration that never was: understanding the scale and nature of parole in contemporary Greece.'

Cheliotis, L.K. and Xenakis, S. (2008) 'Public support for prison protests: Greece in the spotlight', *Statewatch: Monitoring the State and Civil Liberties in Europe* (available online at: http://www.statewatch.org/news/2008/nov/greece-prison-protests.pdf).

Cohen, S. (1985) *Visions of Social Control*. Cambridge: Polity Press.

Commission of the European Communities (2006) *Commission Staff Working Document, Accompanying Document to the Proposal for a Council Framework Decision on the European Supervision Order in Pre-trial Procedures between Member States of the European Union: Impact Assessment* (available online at: http://ec.europa.eu/justice_home/doc_centre/criminal/recognition/docs/sec_2006_1079_en.pdf9).

Courakis, N.E. (2005) 'Recidivism problems of young prisoners: findings from a follow-up study.' Paper presented at the 12th Re-training Programme of the National School of Judges, Komotini, 11–14 October (in Greek) (available online at: http://www.law.uoa.gr/crime-research/nearoiapofylakizomenoi.pdf).

Courakis, N.E. (ed.) (2006) *In Order for us to Feel Safe in a Society of Active Citizens: A Practical Manual for the Lawful Protection of Citizens from Everyday Lawbreaking* (in Greek). Athens-Komotini: Ant. N. Sakkoulas Publications.

Eleftherotypia (2009) 'Dendias: the project of releases failed', 10 April (in Greek).

Giovanoglou, S. (2006) *Institutional Problems of Social Reintegration of Released Prisoners* (in Greek). Athens-Thessaloniki: Sakkoulas Publications.

Herzfeld, M. (1992) *The Social Production of Indifference: Exploring the Symbolic Roots of Western Bureaucracy*. Chicago, IL and London: University of Chicago Press.

Kaiafa-Gbandi, M., Symeonidou-Kastanidou, E. and Mpitzilekis, N. (2008) *The Law of Penal Measures* (in Greek). Athens: Nomiki Vivliothiki.

Karydis, V. (forthcoming) 'Immigration, crime and criminal justice in contemporary Greece', in L.K. Cheliotis and S. Xenakis (eds) *Crime and Punishment in Contemporary Greece: International Comparative Perspectives*. Oxford: Peter Lang.

Karydis, V. and Koulouris, N. (2002) 'Conditional release: a ship without governor and destination?' (in Greek), *Poiniki Dikaiosyni*, 49: 504–6.

Kathimerini (2009) '"Ticket of leave" for hundreds of prisoners', 1 January (in Greek).

Kokolakis, E. (1994) *Conditional Release of Prisoners* (in Greek). Athens-Komotini: Ant. N. Sakkoulas Publications.

Lambropoulou, E. (2003) 'Drug policy in Greece: a balance between enforcement and persuasion', *European Journal of Crime, Criminal Law and Criminal Justice*, 11: 18–39.

Massouri, G.S. (2006) *The Introduction and Development of Conditional Release for Adults in Greece as Idiosyncratic Pardon* (in Greek). Athens-Komotini: Ant. A. Sakkoulas Publications.

Ministry of Justice (2008) 'Final provisions for a modern correctional system', 19 November (press release in Greek).

Ministry of Justice (2008) 'The goal of the Ministry of Justice is that 3,720 prisoners released under the beneficiary provisions spend holidays with their families', 25 November (press release in Greek).

Ministry of Justice (2008) 'The social programme for the correctional system was ratified unanimously by the governmental committee', 26 November (press release in Greek).

Ministry of Justice (2008) 'Prisoner discharges', 29 December (press release in Greek).

Panourgiá, N. (2008) 'Desert islands: ransom of humanity', *Public Culture*, 2: 395–421.

Papacharalambous, C. (1999) 'The article 106 PC [Penal Code] between the good behaviour of the prisoner and the "bad" behaviour of the legislator' (in Greek), *Poinika Chronika*, 49: 501–15.

Papageorgiou, I. and Cheliotis, L.K. (forthcoming) 'Youth and crime in contemporary Greece', in L.K. Cheliotis and S. Xenakis (eds) *Crime and Punishment in Contemporary Greece: International Comparative Perspectives*. Oxford: Peter Lang.

Pitsela, A. (forthcoming) 'Youth justice and probation in contemporary Greece', in L.K. Cheliotis and S. Xenakis (eds) *Crime and Punishment in Contemporary Greece: International Comparative Perspectives*. Oxford: Peter Lang.

Rothman, D.J. (1980/2002) *Conscience and Convenience: The Asylum and its Alternatives in Progressive America*. New York: Aldine de Gruyter.

Sunday Times (2008) 'Greek riots spark fear of Europe in flames', 14 December.

Tseloni, A. and Zarafonitou, C. (2008) 'Fear of crime and victimisation: a multivariate multilevel analysis of competing measurements', *European Journal of Criminology*, 5: 387–409.

Voglis, P. (2002) *Becoming a Subject: Political Prisoners during the Greek Civil War*. New York and London: Berghahn Books.

Zarafonitou, C. (forthcoming) 'Fear of crime in contemporary Greece', in L.K. Cheliotis and S. Xenakis (eds) *Crime and Punishment in Contemporary Greece: International Comparative Perspectives*. Oxford: Peter Lang.

Chapter 10

Ireland

Thomas O'Malley

Summary

By virtue of the constitutional separation of powers, the selection of sentence in Ireland is exclusively a judicial function. Most prisoners serving determinate sentences are entitled to one-quarter remission of sentence, although in certain circumstances this may increase to one third of the overall sentence. Additionally, the executive branch of government is empowered to grant early or temporary release to most prisoners. This is treated as a privilege rather than a right which means that the courts are reluctant to grant review of executive decisions relating to early release. The courts do, however, insist that certain standards of procedural fairness be observed when temporary release is being revoked prior to its intended expiry date. Ireland has had a non-statutory Parole Board since 2001 but its sole function is to advise the Minister for Justice, Equality and Law Reform on the early release of long-term prisoners.

1. Introduction

In a country committed to proportionality as the overarching principle of sentencing, as Ireland claims to be, the early release of prisoners represents something of a triumph for pragmatism over principle. Ireland retains a highly discretionary system of sentencing and, unlike some other common-law jurisdictions, has so far refrained from introducing any form of guidelines or tariff to structure judicial sentencing decisions. Apart from murder, which carries a mandatory life sentence, and a small number of drug-trafficking and firearms offences, which attract presumptive or mandatory minimum sentences (as described later in this chapter), all other serious offences are governed by maximum sentences expressed in terms of imprisonment, fine or both. Certain judicially developed principles do, however, exist, and failure on the part of a trial judge to apply those principles may amount to an appealable error. A century ago, the English Court of Criminal Appeal held that it would not ordinarily interfere with a sentence unless it disclosed an error of principle.[1] The Irish Court of Criminal Appeal, established in 1924, quickly adopted the same principle and has applied it ever since. For present purposes, it will be sufficient to note two fundamental sentencing principles. The first is that the selection of sentence, when there is a selection to be made, is exclusively a judicial task which may not be assigned to another branch of government. It was so held by the Supreme Court in *Deaton* v. *Attorney General and Revenue Commissioners* (1963)[2] which happens to be one of the few Irish cases that have 'travelled' in the sense of being occasionally quoted with approval elsewhere (and particularly by the Privy Council when interpreting constitutional provisions of certain Commonwealth jurisdictions).[3] The *Deaton* principle is of constitutional as opposed to common-law origin in Ireland. It was derived by the Supreme Court from those provisions of the Irish Constitution dealing with the separation of powers and the administration of justice.

The second fundamental principle is that a sentence must be proportionate to the gravity of the offence and the personal circumstances of the offender.[4] This, too, has occasionally been described as a constitutional principle, though the courts have yet to specify the exact rationale for that conclusion. In any event, it is now well embedded as the fundamental distributive principle of criminal punishment in Ireland. One practical consequence of this principle is that, because account must be taken of offender as well as offence

---

[1]*R* v. *Sidlow* (1908) 1 Cr. App. R. 28.
[2][1963] I.R. 170, 98 I.L.T.R. 99.
[3]Examples include *Browne* v. *The Queen* [2000] A.C. 45; *Hinds* v. *The Queen* [1977] A.C. 195; *DPP of Jamaica* v. *Mollison* [2003] 2 W.L.R. 1160. See also *Wynbyne* v. *Marshall* (1997) 117 N.T.R. 11.
[4]Leading authorities include *People (DPP)* v. *M* [1994] 3 I.R. 306; *People (DPP)* v. *Kelly* [2005] 2 I.R. 321, [2005] 1 I.L.R.M. 19.

circumstances, the courts are obliged, in principle at least, to adopt a two-tier approach towards the selection of sentence. A court must begin by locating the particular offence on the overall scale of gravity in order to identify an appropriate starting point. It must then make any further reduction to reflect the presence of any mitigating factors connected with the circumstances of the offender which, for this purpose, would include matters such as a guilty plea. The superior courts have stressed that mitigation, where it exists, must be applied to the otherwise proportionate sentence (the initial starting point) as opposed to the maximum sentence. Thus, theft carries a maximum sentence of ten years' imprisonment. In a given case, the court might be satisfied that the offence was about half-way up the scale of gravity which would suggest a five-year starting point. However, allowance must then be made for any mitigating factors, and that might result in a final sentence of two or three years. A similar commitment to proportionality exists in Australia (among other jurisdictions) but there, a strong difference of opinion has arisen as to whether a so-called instinctive or intuitive synthesis approach should be adopted in preference to the two-tier approach (Edney and Bagaric 2007: ch. 2). On paper at least, Ireland seems firmly committed to the two-tier approach.

It may seem contradictory, therefore, to permit the executive reduction of a sentence which has been chosen in accordance with the proportionality principle. The reality, of course, is that each of the three branches of government has an important role in the sentencing process. The legislature must decide upon the mandatory or maximum sentence to attach to each offence and also decide upon the range of sentencing options to be available to the courts. The judiciary is responsible for the selection of sentence, when there is a selection to be made, and the executive is responsible for implementing sentences imposed by the courts. Most countries have some system in place, whether by way of pardon, commutation or some form of remission, to reduce or mitigate the effect of a sentence at some point during its currency (Sebba 1977; Moore 1997). As a general principle, however, courts, when selecting sentence, should not take account of any remission or early release to which the offender may later become entitled (O'Malley 2006: 135).

1.2 The use of imprisonment

By international standards, the Republic of Ireland, with an overall population of 4.2 million inhabitants, has a relatively low prison population and a moderate rate of imprisonment. Half a century ago, in 1958, the average daily prison population stood at 369, the lowest in the State's history (O'Malley 2000: ch. 2). Today, there are approximately 3,500 prisoners, one fifth of whom are in pre-trial detention or on some other form of remand. Women account for less than 4 per cent and foreign nationals for about 12 per cent of the total. The prison population also includes some illegal immigrants held pending deportation proceedings although they have not been charged or convicted in criminal proceedings. As of 2008, the imprisonment rate stood at 76 per 100,000 of the population which, according to the tables regularly published by King's College London, placed Ireland in 162nd place worldwide out of a total of 217 countries. England and Wales occupied 82nd place on the same table with an imprisonment rate of 152 per 100,000. While the number of prisoners has increased significantly in Ireland over the past half-century, the overall number of persons in state custody has declined even more dramatically. The prison population in 1958 may have been less than 400 but there were then more than 20,000 patients detained in psychiatric hospitals (mostly for want of more suitable accommodation) and approximately 5,000 children in industrial and reformatory schools. Similar patterns have emerged in other western countries. Harcourt (2006), in one of his pioneering studies of this phenomenon in the USA, has referred to the 'continuity of spatial exclusion and confinement between the asylum and the penitentiary'. This certainly holds true of Ireland as well. By 2007 the number of inpatients in psychiatric hospitals had declined to about 3,000, compared with almost 11,000 in 1987, and only a small number of children remained in residential care or detention (Mental Health Commission 2008).

The profile of sentenced prisoners is obviously relevant for present purposes. In early December 2007, there were 2,696 sentenced prisoners, 17 per cent of whom were serving sentences of less than 12 months and a further quarter sentences of one to three years (Irish Prison Service 2008). Almost 1,100 (about 40 per cent of the total) were serving sentences of five years or more, including life. On that date there were 239 life prisoners of whom 228 (including 5 women) were serving sentences for murder. Typically, therefore, life prisoners account for about 9 per cent of the average daily population. There are 15 different prison institutions in the State although two of these are women's prisons attached to predominantly male prisons (at Limerick and Mountjoy in Dublin). The average number of women prisoners is usually about 110, although the number of actual committals is much higher. In 2007, there were more than 1,000 female committals compared with 8,500 males.[5] By international standards, most of our prison institutions are quite small, the largest being Mountjoy Prison in Dublin which has just over 600 male and female inmates. Most of the others have fewer than 300 inmates, or so the most recently available official figures suggest.

2. Varieties of early release

Three distinct forms of early release exist in Ireland. The first is the power constitutionally vested in the executive branch of government (and equivalent to what would formerly have been a royal prerogative) to commute or remit any sentence including a custodial sentence. We may refer to this as special remission. The second is the entitlement of certain prisoners under the Prison Rules to earn remission of a portion of their sentences, the standard rate currently being 25 per cent. Thirdly, the executive branch of government is statutorily empowered to grant temporary release to prisoners at any time before they qualify for ordinary remission, and also to life prisoners who are ineligible for ordinary remission. The last-mentioned power is roughly equivalent to parole although it is governed by less formal procedures than those attaching to parole release elsewhere. Standard remission of sentence differs from temporary release in a number of respects (Cavadino and Dignan 2002: 265). Firstly remission is now treated as a right or an entitlement, though one which may be forfeit in whole or in part through misbehaviour while in prison. Temporary release, on the other hand, is a privilege within the gift of the government. Secondly, temporary release will, more or less by definition, be granted at an earlier point in the sentence than remission. Thirdly, temporary release is granted subject to conditions, and the person released may be subject to probationary supervision. Finally, a breach of temporary release conditions leaves the person liable to be returned to prison. Remission, if granted, is unconditional and any further offence which the released prisoner is alleged to have committed must be the subject of separate criminal proceedings.

2.1 Special remission

Ireland is a common-law jurisdiction with a written constitution

[5]These figures do not necessarily, or even probably, refer to different individuals. A person may be counted more than once if committed more than once.

which was enacted in 1937 and which may not be amended except by a majority of those voting in a popular referendum. The Constitution protects a reasonably wide range of personal rights and confers upon the High Court and Supreme Court the power to invalidate a law which conflicts with any of its provisions. Article 13.6 of the Constitution provides: 'The right of pardon and the power to commute or remit punishment imposed by any court exercising criminal jurisdiction are hereby vested in the President, but such power of commutation or remission may also be conferred by law on other authorities.'

The *Oireachtas* (the legislature) later took advantage of the final part of this provision to confer upon the executive branch of government the power to commute or remit, in whole or in part, any punishment imposed by a criminal court subject to such conditions as it may think proper.[6] Provision was also made for delegating this power to the Minister for Justice.[7] The use of the word 'remit' in this constitutional context is apt to cause some confusion in the light of its concurrent use to describe the statutory power to grant a standard period of remission to certain prisoners for good behaviour, a practice described further below. In 1937, however, the terms 'commutation' and 'remission' had reasonably well-settled meanings in the constitutional practice of most common-law countries. Commutation involved the substitution of one form of punishment for another (e.g. life imprisonment for the death penalty), whereas remission involved the reduction of a sentence without changing its character (Newsam 1954; Brett 1957; Smith 1983; Pattenden 1996). In 1933, the Supreme Court of Canada had held that a prisoner whose sentence is wholly or partly remitted is one whose term has expired, at least within the meaning of the statute at issue in that case – an Immigration Act which permitted deportation on the expiry of a sentence.[8] Remission, therefore clearly entailed the outright reduction of punishment with the result that the offender was no longer liable to serve any further portion of the sentence. Executive powers of commutation and remission were particularly important in Ireland, as in other countries, while murder remained a capital offence.

[6]Criminal Justice Act 1951 s. 23(1) as amended by the Criminal Justice Act 1990 s. 9.
[7]Criminal Justice Act 1951 s. 23(3) as substituted by the Criminal Justice (Miscellaneous Provisions) Act 1997 s. 17.
[8]*Re Royal Prerogative of Mercy upon Deportation Proceedings* [1933] S.C.R. 269, [1933] 2 D.L.R. 269; see also *R* v. *Veregin* [1933] 2 D.L.R. 362 and brief commentary in (1935) 1 Univ. of Toronto L.R. 183.

The modern history of capital punishment in Ireland may briefly be summarized as follows (O'Malley 1995). All murders were capital crimes until 1964[9] when the death penalty was abolished for all offences except certain aggravated murders, notably the murder of a member of the police or a prison officer acting in the course of their duty, and a small number of other offences, such as treason, piracy, and certain offences contrary to the Defence Act 1954 and the Offences against the State Act 1939. Capital murder was the only one of these offences ever prosecuted between 1964 and 1990 when the death penalty was completely abolished. In fact, the last execution had taken place as far back as 1954. A significant number of those who had been sentenced to death for murder between 1922 (when the State was founded) and 1964 had their sentences commuted to imprisonment, and records show that the terms served by some of them before being released were relatively short. Capital punishment was abolished entirely by the Criminal Justice Act 1990 and, then, following a referendum held in 2001, the Constitution was amended to include a prohibition on the reintroduction of the death penalty for any offence.

In the 1970s and 1980s, a number of police officers were murdered, mostly while trying to apprehend bank robbers, and those found guilty had to be sentenced to death in accordance with the terms of the Criminal Justice Act 1964. As it happened, however, each of those death sentences was commuted by the government to a term of 40 years' imprisonment. The Criminal Justice Act 1990 effectively placed this arrangement on a statutory footing by providing that a person convicted of what might be described as aggravated murder[10] had to be (1) sentenced to life imprisonment and (2) ordered to serve at least 40 years' imprisonment. Those sentenced under this provision may qualify for the standard one-quarter remission but not ordinarily for parole-type early release. The relevant provisions are discussed further below. Those convicted of an attempt at an aggravated murder are liable to a maximum sentence of life imprisonment, but must be ordered to serve at least 20 years' imprisonment. They too qualify for remission but not for parole-type early release.

[9]The Criminal Justice Act 1964 provided that everybody convicted of what might be termed 'ordinary' murder was to be sentenced to life imprisonment.
[10]The term 'aggravated murder' does not appear in any of the statutory provisions. It is used here purely for the sake of convenience to describe those murders which, until 1990, were capital and which now attract special sentencing arrangements.

With the abolition of capital punishment, the need to exercise the commutation power rarely arises. There is greater possibility of special remission being granted as it applies to all forms as criminal punishment, and not just to imprisonment. Until the mid-1990s offenders who had been fined following conviction in courts of summary jurisdiction frequently applied to the Minister for Justice, usually through their local political representatives, for remission of all or part of the fine, and it appears that many such applications were successful. However, in *Brennan* v. *Minister for Justice*,[11] the High Court held that this practice, although permitted by the Constitution, was not intended to operate as a parallel system of justice. The Court said that the power should be used sparingly and that it was only in the rarest of circumstances that the Minister should alter a fine on the basis of an opinion that the amount imposed was wrong.[12] The case was unusual in that the applicant was a District Court Judge whose fines had been reduced on a number of occasions by the then Minister. By the time the case was decided, the applicant had retired from the bench and, by a twist of political fate, the respondent Minister was no longer in office owing to a sudden change of government in late 1994. That may explain why the High Court decision was never appealed to the Supreme Court. As noted below, special remission may not be granted to prisoners convicted of certain offences which carry presumptive or mandatory minimum terms of imprisonment.

2.2   Standard remission

Very few prisoners actually serve the full sentences imposed upon them by the courts. This has been true since the present prison system took shape in the mid-nineteenth century following the introduction of penal servitude as a substitute for transportation. The modalities of early release have varied over time, but by the early twentieth century the principal method employed in all British and Irish jurisdictions took the form of standard periods of remission. Until 1948 in England[13] and 1997 in Ireland,[14] penal servitude and imprisonment co-existed as distinct legal forms of custody although, as time went by, there was little practical difference between the two. In England, those serving

---

[11] [1995] 1 I.R. 612, [1995] 2 I.L.R.M. 206.
[12] The Court was, however, careful to stress that it was concerned solely with the remission of fines as opposed to other punishments, such as prison sentences.
[13] Criminal Justice Act 1948.
[14] Criminal Law Act 1997.

determinate sentences of imprisonment were entitled to one third remission. Male convicts undergoing determinate sentences of penal servitude were entitled to one quarter remission while female convicts were entitled to one third. Following the abolition of the distinction between imprisonment and penal servitude in England in 1948, all prisoners, apart from those serving life sentences, became entitled to one third remission. In Ireland, meanwhile, everyone serving a determinate sentence of imprisonment of one month or longer was entitled to one quarter remission. Provision had been made in the Rules for the Government of Prisons 1947 for the application of remission to sentences of penal servitude but, for legal reasons, that provision was held by the Supreme Court to be *ultra vires* (because the government had purported to make the rule under the authority of an Act which applied to imprisonment only).[15] From then onwards, those sentenced to penal servitude were eligible for early release on licence at the discretion of the Minister but they were not entitled to standard remission. The abolition of penal servitude in 1997 meant that all prisoners, other than life prisoners and those serving one month or less, thenceforth qualified for remission which remained set at one quarter of the sentence.[16]

The power to grant remission has been preserved in new prison rules enacted in 2007.[17] A person serving a determinate prison sentence of one month or longer may, by good conduct, earn remission not exceeding one quarter of the sentence. The new rules do, however, have one novel feature in that they permit up to one third remission for prisoners who have shown further good conduct 'by engaging in authorised structured activity' to such an extent as to satisfy the Minister that, as a result of this engagement, they are less likely to reoffend and will be better able to reintegrate into the community. This innovation was probably a response to concerns expressed in recent years about low participation rates in the various treatment and training programmes provided for convicted prisoners, and sex offender treatment programmes in particular. The possibility of increased remission may now provide an incentive to prisoners to participate in such programmes. Neither the Prison Rules themselves nor the parent legislation offer any indication as to how the risk

---

[15]*State (Carney)* v. *Governor of Portlaoise Prison* [1957] I.R. 25.
[16]Rules for the Government of Prisons 1947 (S.I. 320 of 1947) r. 38(1).
[17]Prison Rules 2007 (S.I. 252 of 2007) r. 59. The Rules were made pursuant to a power granted by the Prisons Act 2007 s. 35 which specifically mentions remission as one of the matters in respect of which rules may be made.

of reoffending is to be assessed for this purpose. Remission is not available to a person serving a life sentence or to a person committed to prison for contempt of court or for failure to comply with a court order but, as noted below, life prisoners are eligible for temporary release.

The suspended sentence was judicially developed in Ireland, probably in the late nineteenth century (Osborough 1982). It was placed on a statutory basis by the Criminal Justice Act 2006 s. 99 as amended by s. 60 of the Criminal Justice Act 2007. Any sentence of imprisonment, other than a mandatory or mandatory minimum sentence, may be suspended in whole or in part. When a part-suspended prison sentence is imposed, remission is calculated by reference to the custodial portion as opposed to the entire sentence.[18] Thus, a person sentenced to six years' imprisonment with the last two years suspended can ordinarily expect to serve three years (i.e. three quarters of the custodial portion). During the 1980s and 1990s, some trial judges adopted the practice of imposing reviewable sentences whereby, for example, a six-year sentence would be imposed with a direction that the offender be brought back before court on a particular date, say three years from the date of sentence. If, at that point, he was shown to have been of good conduct while in prison or, better still, that he had taken some additional positive step such as participation in a drug treatment programme, the balance of the sentence would then be suspended. However, in 2001, the Supreme Court effectively banned the use of part-suspended sentences, largely because it ran counter to the executive power to grant remission.[19]

The effect of remission, once granted, is that the offender is no longer subject to any punishment for the offence in respect of which he was serving sentence. There is relatively little authority on the matter but the High Court did once say:

'Remit' in law usage has various meanings: the meaning to be ascribed depends on the particular context. In the present context [which involved standard remission under the Prison Rules 1947] it must mean to release or to forgive further punishment in that, on grant of remission, no further punishment remains to be suffered. That was, and is, the effect of remission in relation to sentences of imprisonment.[20]

[18]*Harris* v. *Delahunt* [2008] IEHC 152.
[19]*People (DPP)* v. *Finn* [2001] 2 I.R. 25, [2002] 2 I.L.R.M. 211.
[20]*State (Carney)* v. *Governor of Portlaoise Prison* [1957] I.R. 25 at 27.

This indeed was the clear intent of s. 1 of the Prisons (Ireland) Act 1907 which, until relatively recently, formed the statutory basis for prison regulations permitting standard remission. It provided that once a prisoner, having earned remission, was released, his sentence was deemed to have been discharged. The Prisons Act 2007 now simply includes remission among the matters in respect of which regulations may be made but there is nothing to suggest that the nature of remission itself was thereby intended to be altered. As already noted, this was also the effect of remission in the sense in which it is used in Art. 13.6 of the Constitution. However, remission in that constitutional sense, or special remission as we shall call it, may be granted at any time at the will of the executive, although the prisoner has no legal entitlement to it. It might be granted, for example, if a prisoner or a member of his immediate family became seriously ill (though nowadays the prisoner would be more likely to receive temporary release subject to conditions), or perhaps because the prisoner had performed some particularly heroic or creditable act while in custody, or for other exceptional reasons. Cross (1975), for example, refers to remission being granted in several cases in 1973 because of assistance rendered by prisoners to the authorities as well as releases granted on medical and humanitarian grounds. Standard remission, on the other hand, has crystallized into an entitlement, though one that may be forfeit in whole or in part through misbehaviour while in prison. Unless so forfeit, the prisoner is automatically entitled to release on having served three quarters of the judicially imposed sentence and, once released, he may not be required to serve any further portion of that sentence.

The Republic of Ireland now appears to be the only British or Irish jurisdiction retaining standard remission in the traditional sense. The precise rationale does not appear to have been articulated, in recent times at least, though it is clearly something that may be earned by good behaviour. In the mid-nineteenth century, Sir Joshua Jebb, the Director of Convict Prisons, said that sentences of penal servitude should be so structured as to maintain 'an invigorating hope and a salutary dread' at every stage of the prisoner's progress (McConville 1981; Livingstone and Owen 1993). Remission may well provide an invigorating hope though the same, of course, is true to an even greater extent of parole-type early release.

2.3 Parole-type release

The term 'parole' does not yet appear in modern Irish legislation, but there is a statute-based temporary release scheme which, in many respects, resembles the more formal parole arrangements in place elsewhere. In fact, as noted below, Ireland has had a non-statutory body called the Parole Board since 2001. While a formal parole system was introduced in England and Wales by the Criminal Justice Act 1967 (Carlisle 1988), Ireland has remained content with a much more discretionary system of temporary release first introduced in 1960 and used ever since to grant release to certain prisoners before they become eligible for standard remission, and also to life prisoners who are ineligible for such remission in any event. Formal provision for this type of release was first made in s. 2(1) of the Criminal Justice Act 1960 which simply provided: 'The Minister [for Justice] may make rules providing for the temporary release, subject to such conditions (if any) as may be imposed in each particular case, of persons serving a sentence of penal servitude or imprisonment, or of detention in St. Patrick's Institution.' (St Patrick's Institution was formerly Ireland's one and only Borstal and was, in fact, formally renamed St. Patrick's Institution by the Act of 1960 itself. It is used to detain young male offenders between the ages of 16 and 21 years and, rather unfortunately, it is part of the Mountjoy Prison complex in Dublin where it has been located since 1956.)

It is accepted that the system of early release established under the Act of 1960 is entirely separate and independent from the general power of commutation and remission conferred upon the government by art. 13.6 of the Constitution.[21] It may seem strange that parole in this informal sense was introduced in 1960 at a time when there were fewer than 400 prisoners and 60 per cent of them were serving sentences of three months or less. There was no obvious problem with either prison overcrowding or prison discipline. The reason, in fact, was rather more mundane. A short time earlier when the then Minister for Justice was first appointed, he received a request from a prisoner for temporary release to attend his mother's funeral. While the Minister granted the request, he was advised at the time that he had no formal authority to do so and that if the prisoner had not returned to prison at the appointed time (though in fact he did), there was nothing that could have been done about it (Senate Debates 1960). It was therefore decided to include the above provision in the Act of 1960 which was principally concerned with regulating what had hitherto been known as Borstal training. General regulations were later introduced governing the conditions to attach to grants of temporary

[21]*Kinahan* v. *Minister for Justice, Equality and Law Reform* [2001] 4 I.R. 454.

release and related matters.[22] It is clear from parliamentary debates on the Criminal Justice Bill, which were brief and uncontroversial, that the government envisaged temporary release being granted for short periods for compassionate reasons, or to allow some prisoners to return home for Christmas or 'the harvest' (we were then very much an agricultural country!), although the possibility of granting release to long-term prisoners to assist in their social reintegration was also mentioned (Dáil Debates 1960).

Needless to say, as the prison population expanded rapidly in the 1980s and early 1990s, temporary release was used in a manner which would scarcely have been envisaged in 1960. With the demand for prison places greatly exceeding supply, there were allegations, probably well founded, of a revolving-door policy whereby many prisoners were released early simply to accommodate the influx being committed by the courts. It is important to note that what the Criminal Justice Act 1960 permitted was the grant of 'temporary release' rather than 'early release'. The idea was, and remains, that a prisoner would be granted release for a defined period with the expectation that he would return to prison at the end of that period unless granted a further extension. In effect, however, the grant of temporary release came to function for all practical purposes as an early release or parole system because those serving life sentences, for example, were released after a certain number of years and, unless they committed further offences or were found in clear breach of their release conditions, they could expect to remain at large indefinitely. The same held true of others who were serving long sentences but granted temporary release.

In 2003, s. 2 of the Criminal Justice Act 1960 was replaced with a more elaborate provision authorizing the Minister to grant early release to prisoners.[23] The new provision sets out in some detail the many grounds on which release may be granted. These include assessing the person's ability to reintegrate into society, assisting in the detection of crime, humanitarian considerations, ensuring the good government of the prison concerned (which may safely be treated as a euphemism for relieving prison overcrowding) and various others. It also lists the matters to which the Minister must have regard before granting temporary release. As might be expected, these include considerations of public safety and any risk of reoffending posed by the prisoner. Essentially, however, the system remains unaltered, and

[22]Prisoners (Temporary Release) Rules 1960, S.I. no. 167 of 1960.
[23]Criminal Justice (Temporary Release of Prisoners) Act 2003.

the principal effect of the new statute was to render more explicit those factors and considerations which would probably have guided early release decisions in any case. One event which undoubtedly precipitated the introduction of new legislation was a High Court decision in 2000[24] holding that rules made in respect of one particular prison which permitted the Minister to distinguish between categories of prisoner when making temporary release decisions was *ultra vires* the Act of 1960. Not surprisingly, the Act of 2003 permits the making of category-based rules.

3. Statutory restrictions on early release

Ireland has been no more immune than other common-law countries to the pressure to introduce more mandatory and mandatory minimum sentences, and it has occasionally yielded to that pressure in recent years. As already mentioned, the complete abolition of capital punishment in 1990 was accompanied by the introduction of new sentencing arrangements for certain aggravated murders. A person convicted of such a murder must, in addition to being sentenced to life imprisonment, be ordered to serve at least 40 years in prison. An attempt at such a murder carries a mandatory minimum sentence of 20 years. Standard remission may be applied to the minimum term which means, in effect, that a person convicted of aggravated murder can ordinarily expect to serve at least 30 years. Special remission may not be granted before the prisoner becomes eligible for standard remission. Temporary release may be granted but only for 'grave reasons of a humanitarian nature' and then only such limited duration as is justified by those reasons.[25]

Similar provision has been made in respect of certain presumptive and mandatory minimum sentences for drug and firearms offences introduced in more recent times. It would, in the time-honoured phrase, be well beyond the scope of this chapter to describe those sentencing arrangements in any detail but the following brief summary will hopefully suffice. The Criminal Justice Act 1999 introduced a new offence, popularly known as a section 15A offence, which consists of having for the purpose of sale or supply a controlled drug with a street value of 13,000 euros or more.[26] This offence carries a maximum

[24]*Corish v. Minister for Justice, Equality and Law Reform* [2000] 3 I.R. 548.
[25]Criminal Justice Act 1990 s. 5.
[26]The minimum value was originally set at 10,000 Irish pounds but converted to 13,000 on the introduction of the euro.

sentence of life imprisonment[27] but the Act of 1999 also requires the Court to impose a sentence of least 10 years' imprisonment unless satisfied that there are exceptional circumstances which justify a lower sentence. In this sense, what the Act requires is more in the nature of a presumptive than a mandatory minimum sentence. However, the Criminal Justice Act 2006 now provides that a person convicted of a second or subsequent s. 15A offence must be ordered to serve at least 10 years' imprisonment, and the courts have no discretion to impose any lower sentence. Standard remission may be applied to any presumptive or mandatory minimum sentence imposed for these offences, but the government may not otherwise grant special remission prior to the date on which the prisoner becomes eligible for standard remission. Furthermore, a person sentenced to imprisonment for a first or subsequent s. 15A offence may not be granted temporary release 'unless for a grave reason of a humanitarian nature, and any release so granted shall be only for such limited duration as is justified by such reason'.[28]

The Criminal Justice Act 2006 also introduced presumptive sentencing arrangements for a range of firearms offences, the sentences in question ranging from five to ten years' imprisonment. The restrictions on the grant of special remission and early release applicable to section 15A drug offences also apply to prison sentences for the firearms offences in question.

4. The Parole Board

In 2001, a body entitled the Parole Board was established by the Minister for Justice, Equality and Law Reform and it has existed on a non-statutory basis ever since. Its purpose is to review the sentences of prisoners referred to it by the Minister. According to its annual reports, which appear to be the sole publicly-available source of information on the Board's operation, prisoners sentenced to a term

[27]The offence of possessing a controlled drug for sale or supply had carried a maximum sentence of life imprisonment since first introduced by the Misuse of Drugs Act 1977.
[28]Misuse of Drugs Act s. 27(3I) as substituted by the Criminal Justice Act 2007, s. 33 (which usefully consolidates the sentencing arrangements for s. 15A offences). The same arrangement applies to s. 15B offences which involve the importation of prohibited drugs. The language of the provision regarding temporary release was obviously adopted from the Criminal Justice Act 1990.

of eight years or more but less than 14 years are eligible to have their cases referred at the half-way mark. Those serving sentences of 14 years or more, including life-sentence prisoners, generally have their cases referred after serving seven years. Second and subsequent reviews generally take place on an annual basis in the case of prisoners serving less than ten years, and every three years in all other cases.

The Board makes recommendation to the Minister with whom the final decision as to release rests. A high proportion of the Board's recommendations are accepted. In 2007, for example, 90 per cent of recommendations were accepted in full and further 6 per cent accepted in part. The overall number of cases involved is relatively small. In 2007, 74 cases were referred to the Board but the overall number of cases at various stages of review is usually in the region of 200. Somewhat unfortunately, the Board's reports, while indicating the level of acceptance of its recommendations, fail to indicate what those recommendations were, with the result that we have no way of knowing how many prisoners, and in which sentence categories, have actually been released. While the release ultimately granted to prisoners following a Parole Board recommendation formally amounts to an exercise of power under the Criminal Justice Act 1960 which, as noted, deals with temporary release, it seems implicit that those granted renewable release from long sentences can expect to remain at liberty provided they abide by the applicable conditions. The Board currently consists of 11 members including the Chairperson (a solicitor), the Director of the Probation Service, a consultant psychiatrist, a representative of the Prison Service, an official of the Department of Justice, Equality and Law Reform and six others described as 'community representatives' (Parole Board 2008: 11). It is precluded from dealing with a few categories of prisoner, notably those serving extended sentences for aggravated murder as described in section 3 above.

The minimum term to which a prisoner must have been sentenced before being eligible for review places a clear limitation on the functions and powers of the Parole Board. Prisoners serving sentences of eight years or longer make up no more than a modest proportion of the prison population and this is reflected in the rather small number of cases referred to the Board since its establishment. Table 10.1 lists the numbers of new cases referred during the years 2002–7.

The total caseloads in those years, including cases which came up for second or subsequent review, varied from 141 to 226. The annual reports do list the factors which are taken into account when

Table 10.1 New cases referred, 2002–07

Year	No. of cases referred
2002	67
2003	72
2004	43
2005	109
2006	58
2007	74

formulating recommendations to the Minister. They include the gravity of the offence, length of time served, previous convictions, risks associated with granting release to the person in question, conduct while in custody and so forth. The absence of a statutory foundation for the Board is distinctly unfortunate in at least one respect – namely, that there is no clear legislative mandate as to the factors that should be taken into account in making recommendations or as to the priority to be accorded to the various individual and social interests involved. For instance, in his Foreword to the most recent report, the Chairperson states that 'first and foremost, there is the gravity of the crime and the circumstances under which it was perpetrated'. He then proceeds to list other factors, such as evidence of remorse and the presence of circumstances which might satisfy the Board that the prisoner would not pose a threat to the public if released. He then lists as a further issue: 'the abhorrence of the general public of the crime that was committed and the sufficient part of the prisoner's sentence which must be served in custody to allay this' (Parole Board 2008: 4). These are factors which can clearly point in different directions in terms of recommending release and it might be questioned if all of them, particularly the question of public abhorrence, however that is to be measured, should be a matter within the purview of a parole authority or, if so, the weight that should be attributed to them.

The operation of the Parole Board does not appear to have been subject to any empirical study as yet, but a few preliminary comments may be made about it. It continues to operate on a non-statutory basis despite occasional calls, mainly from opposition politicians, for its replacement with an equivalent statutory body. A statutory basis is not, of course, essential for the effective operation of the Board though, as already noted, it might provide greater clarity as to the criteria by which release applications should be evaluated. The Irish scheme differs from parole arrangements elsewhere in terms of eligibility. While some other countries with similar structures allow parole at a certain point (perhaps the half-way point) of the sentence, Ireland confines eligibility for parole consideration to those who are serving long sentences (eight years or more). As against this, it must be recalled that the government is in no way prohibited from granting early release to those sentenced to shorter terms of imprisonment by virtue of the general powers conferred upon it by the Criminal Justice Act 1960. The advantage, however, of having a case referred to the Parole Board is that it provides an opportunity for careful consideration of the prisoner's suitability for early release. This would surely be useful in the case of prisoners serving sentences in the four- to seven-year bracket. Again, of course, it must be recalled that all these prisoners have an entitlement to one-quarter remission in any event, and may perhaps qualify for one-third remission under the terms of the new Prison Rules of 2007. All the indications are that the Parole Board carries out its work carefully and conscientiously, though it would benefit from clearer official guidance on release eligibility criteria.

5. Lack of legal aid for proceedings before the Parole Board

Although Ireland has a remarkably generous state-funded criminal legal aid scheme, both the legislature and the courts have been reluctant to extend entitlement to legal aid, whether under the civil or criminal schemes, to persons appearing before tribunals other than the law courts.[29] The few judicial decisions to date on prisoners' entitlement to legal representation or legal aid when appearing before bodies charged with making release recommendations have been remarkably disappointing. The High Court has held that a prisoner does not even have a right to legal *representation* before a sentence review group which existed at the time and which was charged with advising the Minister on the release of long-term prisoners.[30] It was held that the introduction of full legal representation at the oral hearing would be 'disproportionate and would have the effect of changing the whole character of the procedure' involved.[31] For such

[29]*Corcoran* v. *Minister for Social Welfare* [1991] 2 I.R. 175; *McBrearty* v. *Morris*, unreported, High Court, 13 May 2003; *Grogan* v. *Parole Board* [2008] I.E.H.C. 204 (where the earlier authorities are reviewed).
[30]*Barry* v. *Sentence Review Group* [2001] 4 I.R. 167.
[31][2001] 4 I.R. 167 at 170.

a statement to be made at the beginning of the twenty-first century is quite extraordinary. A sentenced prisoner may not have a right to release but he has a strong liberty interest. In many countries decisions on early release are made either by parole authorities or by the executive following receipt of recommendations from a parole authority or a body such as the review group which existed in Ireland at that time. The proceedings before the board or review group in question are usually of vital importance to the prisoner seeking early or temporary release and should therefore warrant a right to legal representation, state-funded or otherwise.

The Sentence Review Group was the precursor of the present Parole Board and the High Court has more recently held that a prisoner is not entitled to legal aid for the purpose of preparing legal submissions to the Board. It seems accepted that prisoners may have legal advice for this purpose (the law could scarcely be otherwise) and, while the authorities do not supply relevant documents directly to solicitors, they apparently supply two copies to the prisoner on the understanding that he can forward one to his solicitor. In the case in question, *Grogan* v. *Parole Board* (2008),[32] the Court analysed the claim in detail, while noting the earlier decision that a person was not entitled to legal representation before the former sentence review group.[33] It also noted that the Minister may take account of factors other than the Parole Board recommendation and distinguished an earlier case in which a person detained in a psychiatric facility following a 'guilty but insane verdict' was said to be entitled to legal aid for the purpose of preparing a submission to a body charged with making release recommendations. A person found guilty but insane was in law an acquitted person and this, according to the Court in *Grogan*, was an important if not decisive distinction. Among the other factors taken into account were the fact that the applicant in *Grogan* had a law degree and should therefore have been in a position to make adequate representations to the Parole Board.

On the basis of existing precedents, it would have been difficult to come to a different conclusion. However, this entire area is ripe for review in an appropriate Supreme Court appeal. Legal representation, state-aided in some instances, is now an accepted feature of parole hearings in other jurisdictions including England and Wales and New Zealand. Furthermore, Parole Board recommendations do have a significant influence on executive release decisions. In *Grogan*, for

---

[32][2008] I.E.H.C. 204.
[33]*Barry* v. *Sentence Review Group* [2001] 4 I.R. 167 (see above).

example, it was noted that the Minister accepts about 90 per cent of the Parole Board's decisions and this, indeed, as noted earlier, is reflected in the Board's annual reports. One would, hope, for example, that courts would adopt a different approach to life prisoners when applying for early release, as in their case (unlike those such as the applicant in *Grogan* who are serving long sentences) there is no obvious release date to which they can look forward. In *Grogan* the High Court drew a distinction between an application for release and proceedings arising from the recall of a prisoner whose release was being terminated and rightly noted that the latter situation did not arise in that case. However, in the light of evolving international jurisprudence on the rights of prisoners, it is suggested that rights to legal representation and, in some cases at least, legal aid should be available when the liberty interest at stake in parole hearings is being addressed.

6. Fluctuations in the numbers of prisoners on temporary release

In some recent years there was a significant decline in the number of prisoners on temporary release. The so-called revolving-door situation which existed in the 1990s seemed to have disappeared, because of the growth in prison space. In fact, despite the significant increase in the numbers of prisoners over the past decade or so, the system was occasionally operating slightly below capacity. In October 1996 (when the average daily population was just over 2,000), there were 550 prisoners on temporary release. By 2001, this had declined to 200, representing a drop from 19 to 6 per cent of the prison population (National Economic and Social Forum 2002). It later declined even further. In 2007, the average number of sentenced prisoners on temporary release was 153, accounting for 4.4 per cent of the population (Irish Prison Service 2008), though this figure does not appear to include those on full temporary release from life sentences and lengthy determinate sentences. However, anecdotal evidence suggests that in more recent times, the numbers granted temporary release in order to relieve prison overcrowding have increased considerably. Up-to-date official statistics are often difficult to access, but according to the website of the Irish Penal Reform Trust in early July 2009 the current prison population stood at almost 3,900, although the total bed capacity is about 3,600. Despite present economic difficulties, the government is pressing ahead with plans to build a new prison to cater for up to 1,400 prisoners on the outskirts of Dublin. This will replace Mountjoy Prison which is currently the main prison in the capital.

7. The life sentence

Murder carries a mandatory sentence of life imprisonment (Criminal Justice Act 1990 s. 2). Several other offences, including manslaughter, robbery, serious sex offences and the possession of drugs for sale or supply, carry discretionary life sentences. Courts are entitled to impose the maximum sentence, even if it is a life sentence, where they consider it appropriate to do so, but in reality they seldom do. In *People (DPP) v. Conroy (No. 2)* (1989),[34] the Supreme Court held that the life sentence would quite legally be imposed for manslaughter, even in the case of a guilty plea although in that particular case, it imposed a total sentence of 17 years' imprisonment instead. The Criminal Justice Act 1999 s. 29(2) permits the imposition of the maximum sentence specified for any offence (which might, of course, be a life sentence) when there were exceptional circumstances to warrant it. Discretionary life sentences are, in fact, rarely imposed, but they have occasionally been imposed and upheld, as in the case of *People (DPP) v. McC* (2008)[35] where the Supreme Court refused to interfere with several concurrent life sentences imposed for offences of serial child abuse.

Although the death penalty for murder (other than aggravated murder) was abolished in Ireland at about the same time as it was abolished in England and Wales, the two jurisdictions differed in one significant respect in terms of the alternative sentencing arrangements put in place. In Ireland, murder was made punishable with a life sentence *simpliciter*, without any provision for a judicial recommendation as to the minimum length of time to be served. Nor was there anything equivalent to the English tariff. As a result, a person sentenced to life imprisonment in Ireland remains in prison until granted temporary release by the executive branch of government. Nowadays, a recommendation will have been received from the Parole Board before any release decision is taken. In formal terms, at least, there is no provision for release on licence in the sense of granting outright early release to persons serving life

[34][1989] I.R. 160, [1989] I.L.R.M. 139.
[35][2008] 2 I.R. 92.

sentences. In effect, however, it appears that they may be granted renewable temporary release which is, in many respects, equivalent to release on licence. The difficulty with this arrangement is that, since the decision on a life prisoner's release date rests exclusively with the executive branch of government, this could be regarded as tantamount to the exercise of a sentencing power which, in turn, one might argue, should rest exclusively with the judiciary. This is currently the subject of litigation before the Irish courts and, very recently, of an application to the European Court of Human Rights. The first case in which the matter was directly litigated recently failed before the High Court though it will be doubtless subject to an appeal to the Supreme Court.[36]

The point at which life prisoners are released has also been the subject of some public controversy though, more often than not, it has been a controversy fuelled by a misperception of the length of time typically served by life prisoners. The point at which life prisoners are released has varied over time and in accordance with the circumstances of individual cases, but the present government policy is that the length of time served should be 'in double figures'. In a statement made on 24 March 2006, the then Minister for Justice, Equality and Law Reform stated that even in optimum circumstances, a life prisoner cannot expect to be released before having served 12–14 years. He further said that those convicted of murders characterized by serious aggravating factors should serve 15 years.

8. Conditions of temporary release

As already noted, the Criminal Justice (Temporary Release of Prisoners) Act 2003 made more elaborate provision than had hitherto existed regarding the ministerial power to grant temporary release to prisoners. This was followed by a set of regulations[37] which provide that, in addition to any specific conditions imposed in any one case, the release of any prisoners shall be subject to the following general conditions:

(a) the person shall keep the peace and be of good behaviour during the release period;

[36]*Whelan and Lynch* v. *Minister for Justice, Equality and Law Reform* [2008] 2 I.R. 142.
[37]Prisoners (Temporary Release) Rules 2004 (S.I. 680/2004).

(b) he or she shall be of sober habits during that period;
(c) he or she shall return to prison on or before the expiration
of the release period.

All conditions must be communicated in writing to the prisoner at
the time of release (and there is a standard form for that purpose)
and the prisoner is under a statutory obligation to abide by the
specific conditions.[38] A prisoner who breaches a condition of release
is deemed to be unlawfully at large and this, in turn, has a number
of important consequences. Firstly, being unlawfully at large is in
itself a criminal offence carrying up to six months' imprisonment.[39]
Secondly, the currency of the sentence is suspended for such period
as the person is unlawfully at large. Thirdly, any member of the
gardai (the police) may arrest without warrant any person whom
they suspect of being unlawfully at large and return that person to
prison.[40]

It will be noted that the general conditions attachable to the grant
of temporary release are few in number though the second, being
of sober habits, is rather vague and certainly enhances the risk of
a person being found in breach of a release condition and therefore
being unlawfully at large. The authorities appear to have virtually
unbounded discretion in the imposition of additional conditions
in individual cases, and the courts are unlikely to intervene unless
convinced that the decision to impose a challenged condition was
irrational or capricious. In *Breathnach* v. *Minister for Justice, Equality
and Law Reform* (2004)[41] the applicant had provisionally been allowed
a short period of temporary release to visit an elderly parent on
condition that he remained handcuffed during the release period.
Applying the prevailing test of irrationality or unreasonableness which,
in Ireland, is very difficult to satisfy,[42] neither the High Court nor the
Supreme Court was willing to hold that a claim of irrationality had
been made out. An element of flexibility in the imposition of specific
conditions may, of course, be beneficial insofar as they might require,
for example, that the prisoner stayed away from a particular person
or locality. On the other hand, it is distinctly unfortunate that neither
the legislation nor the regulations provide any general guidance on
the nature and purpose of permissible conditions in specific cases.

[38]Criminal Justice Act 1960 s. 4(2).
[39]Criminal Justice Act 1960 s. 6.
[40]Criminal Justice Act 1960 s. 7.
[41][2004] 3 I.R. 336.
[42]*O'Keeffe* v. *An Bord Pleanála* [1993] 1 I.R. 39, [1992] 1 I.L.R.M. 237.

9. Revocation of temporary release

There is relatively little Irish case law on revocation decisions. This is doubtless due in large measure to release being treated as a privilege rather than a right and release decisions themselves being executive rather than judicial in nature. Judicial review or, more rarely, *habeas corpus* proceedings will be the usual form of legal challenge to revocation decisions. However, as set out in the paragraph immediately below, some important principles have developed in relation to revocation. First and foremost, a distinction must be drawn between a refusal to grant or renew release on the one hand and, on the other, a decision to terminate a release period before its due expiry date. Because early or temporary release is merely a privilege, a refusal to grant or renew release is not usually reviewable. In any event, the legislation now provides that the grant of a temporary release period shall not entitle the recipient to any further release.[43] However, a person whose temporary release is revoked, in the sense of being ended prematurely, has certain procedural rights. First and foremost, there must have been a breach of one or more conditions of release. The fact that a person has been questioned in connection with another offence or even charged with another offence will not in itself amount to a breach of condition warranting revocation.[44] Referring to this principle, the Supreme Court, *per* Murray J. (as he then was), has said:

> However, this does not mean that those who have responsibility for the possible termination of a prisoner's temporary release when a condition of that release has been breached must remain passive or do nothing when the fact of such an investigation, particularly in relation to a very serious offence, comes to their attention. They must be entitled to inquire into any circumstances which give rise to a concern that a prisoner may have breached a condition of his release. This may include obtaining information or material from the [police] authorities. If, having made such inquiries, they conclude, reasonably and on the basis of objective

[43]Criminal Justice Act 1960 s. 2(6) as inserted by the Criminal Justice (Temporary Release of Prisoners) Act 2003 s. 1. See also *Ryan* v. *Governor of Limerick Prison* [1988] I.R. 198 and *Dowling* v. *Minister for Justice, Equality and Law Reform* [2003] 2 I.R. 535.
[44]*State (Murphy)* v. *Kielt* [1984] I.R. 458, [1985] I.L.R.M. 141; *Dowling* v. *Minister for Justice, Equality and Law Reform* [2003] 2 I.R. 535.

material, that the prisoner has breached a condition of his release, then the prison governor or the respondent, as the case maybe, may be entitled to terminate the temporary release subject to an inquiry of the nature referred to by Griffin J. in *State (Murphy) v. Kielt* (1984) [45] before there is a definitive decision to terminate the temporary release.

As noted below, *State (Murphy) v. Kielt*, referred to in this passage, is a leading authority for the proposition that when the authorities have reason to suspect that a condition of release has been breached they should institute an inquiry, which may be reasonably informal in nature, and allow the released prisoner an opportunity to be heard. Thus far, there does not appear have to have been any significant litigation based on Art. 5 of the European Convention on Human Rights, though the Convention was incorporated after a fashion into Irish law in 2003.[46]

10. Judicial review of temporary release decisions

The courts have repeatedly insisted that the grant of temporary release is entirely within the discretion of the executive branch of government. In one of the leading authorities on the matter, the Supreme Court said:

> The length of time which a person sentenced to imprisonment for life spends in custody and as a necessary consequence the extent to which, if any, prior to final discharge, such a person obtains temporary release is a matter which under the constitutional doctrine of the separation of powers rests entirely with the executive...[47]

Although that particular case involved life imprisonment, the same principle applies to all prison sentences, as later Supreme Court

[45][1984] I.R. 458.
[46]European Convention on Human Rights Act 2003. See, in particular, *Engel v. The Netherlands (No. 1)* (1976) 1 E.H.R.R. 647, and *R (West) v. Parole Board* [2005] UKHL 1, [2005] 1 W.L.R. 350, [2005] 1 All E.R. 755 (HL).
[47]*Murray v. Ireland* [1991] I.L.R.M. 465 at 472, referring to *People (DPP) v. Tiernan* [1988] I.R. 250, [1989] I.L.R.M. 149.

decisions have affirmed.[48] Having said this, the same court has also held that powers of temporary release, no less than any other public power, must not be exercised in a capricious, arbitrary or unjust fashion. The courts may not, however, intervene merely because they might have reached a different decision themselves in any particular case.[49] Revocation decisions are also subject to the requirements of natural justice. When the prison authorities have reason to suspect that a person on temporary release has been in breach of a condition, they should first of all investigate the matter and then, if of the opinion that a breach has occurred, inform the person of the reason why it is intended to revoke grant of release. The person should also be given an opportunity to respond. The courts have, however, indicated that a relatively informal reason will suffice provided the elements of natural justice are observed[50] though it is natural to expect that, with the passage of time, they might insist on more rigorous procedures in this regard. The mere fact that the person has been arrested or charged in connection with another offence is in itself an insufficient reason for revocation.[51] It will be apparent therefore that the courts are concerned with the procedural fairness as opposed to the merits of the particular case; this, of course, is the hallmark of judicial review proceedings within common-law jurisdictions generally. Whether fair procedures always produce fair outcomes is an entirely different matter, though procedural fairness undoubtedly adds to the legitimacy and acceptability of the process (Tyler 2003, 2004).

II. Special release provisions for political prisoners

In April 1998, two agreements, collectively known as the Good Friday Agreement, were reached between the Irish and British governments and the main political parties in Northern Ireland with the aim of bringing about a political settlement and the restoration of democratic

[48]*Kinahan* v. *Minister for Justice, Equality and Law Reform* [2001] 4 I.R. 454; *Doherty* v. *Governor of Portlaoise Prison* [2002] 2 I.R. 252.
[49]*Dowling* v. *Minister for Justice Equality and Law Reform* [2003] 2 I.R. 535.
[50]*State (Murphy)* v. *Kielt* [1984] I.R. 458, [1985] I.L.R.M. 141; *Cunningham* v. *Governor of Mountjoy Prison* [1987] I.L.R.M. 33; *Sherlock* v. *Governor of Mountjoy Prison* [1991] 1 I.R. 451; *Dowling* v. *Minister for Justice, Equality and Law Reform* [2003] 2 I.R. 535.
[51]*State (Murphy)* v. *Kielt* [1984] I.R. 458, [1985] I.L.R.M. 141; *Dowling* v. *Minister for Justice, Equality and Law Reform* [2003] 2 I.R. 535.

institutions in Northern Ireland. As part of this agreement, both governments agreed to put in place mechanisms to provide for the accelerated release of certain prisoners. This provision was to apply only to certain offences and could not be taken advantage of by any prisoner affiliated to any organization which had not established or was not maintaining a complete and unequivocal ceasefire. In the Republic of Ireland, a special commission was established by statute to advise the Minister for Justice, Equality and Law Reform on the release of prisoners in accordance with the terms of the Good Friday Agreement.[52] It did not, however, confer any additional powers of release. Instead, prisoners would be released, where appropriate, by the Minister using existing statutory powers of temporary release, commutation or remission and the exercise of ministerial power for this purpose remained, as always, discretionary.[53] Many prisoners were released under this arrangement, and it is now, we hope, largely of historical interest. However, it is mentioned here as an indication of the variety of circumstances in which remission and other forms of early release may be granted. This would not, of course, have been the first time that such powers were used in a political context. There are recorded instances of so-called spy swaps in which a spy imprisoned in Great Britain was released in order to secure the release of a British subject imprisoned elsewhere (Smith 1983). However, the release of prisoners in the wake of the Good Friday agreement would probably have been the most extensive programme of politically-motivated prisoner release in recent times.

12. Early release provisions for transferred prisoners

Ireland is party to the Convention on the Transfer of Sentenced Prisoners which was concluded under the aegis of the Council of Europe and given domestic legislative effect by the Transfer of Sentenced Persons Act 1995 (as amended in 1997). In 2007, eight prisoners were transferred into the State, six of them from the UK. One difficulty to which the arrangement gives rise in the present context is that once transferred into Ireland they become liable to the remission arrangements in force there. Right now, persons serving prison sentences of any appreciable length in England and Wales

[52]Criminal Justice (Release of Prisoners) Act 1998.
[53]*Doherty* v. *Governor of Portlaoise Prison* [2002] 2 I.R. 252, esp. judgment of Murray J. (as he then was) at 261 ff.

in particular are likely to qualify for early release sooner than they will qualify for ordinary remission in Ireland. However, such persons are usually informed in advance and in fairly clear terms of the consequences of obtaining a transfer to an Irish prison. Some prisoners in this situation have expressed a strong sense of grievance at what they perceive to be a heavy penalty for having taken advantage of the transfer arrangement. They are unlikely to receive much comfort from the courts, particularly in the light of certain *dicta* in *Grogan* v. *Parole Board*[54] where, as it happened, the applicant had earlier been transferred from the UK to Ireland. However, this is a factor which the Parole Board and, ultimately, the Minister might take into account when considering applications for early release.

References

Brett, P. (1957) 'Conditional pardons and the commutation of the death penalty', *Modern Law Review*, 20: 131–47.

Carlisle, M. (1988) *The Parole System in England and Wales: Report of the Review Committee* (Cm 532). London. HMSO.

Cavadino, M. and Dignan, J. (2002) *The Penal System: An Introduction.* London: Sage Publications.

Cross, R. (1975) *The English Sentencing System* (2nd edn). London: Butterworths.

Dáil Debates (Ireland) (1960) Debate on Criminal Justice Bill 1960 (Vol. 183, cols. 559–60).

Edney, R. and Bagaric, M. (2007) *Australian Sentencing.* Cambridge: Cambridge University Press.

Harcourt, B.E. (2006) 'From the asylum to the prison: rethinking the incarceration revolution', *Texas Law Review*, 84: 1751–86.

Irish Prison Service (2008) *Annual Report 2007.* Dublin: Stationery Office.

Livingstone, S. and Owen, T. (1993) *Prison Law: Text and Materials.* Oxford: Clarendon Press.

McConville, S. (1981) *A History of English Prison Administration.* London: Routledge & Kegan Paul.

Mental Health Commission (2008) *Annual Report (Book 1).* Dublin: Stationery Office.

Moore, K.D. (1997) *Pardons: Justice, Mercy and the Public Interest.* Oxford: Oxford University Press.

National Economic and Social Forum (2002) *Re-intergration of Prisoners (Report 22).* Dublin: NESF.

Newsam, F. (1954) *The Home Office.* London: Allen & Unwin.

[54][2008] I.E.H.C. 204.

O'Malley, T. (1995) 'Sentencing murderers: the case for relocating discretion', *Irish Criminal Law Journal*, 5: 31–66.

O'Malley, T. (2000) *Sentencing Law and Practice*. Dublin: Round Hall.

O'Malley, T. (2006) *Sentencing Law and Practice* (2nd edn). Dublin: Thomson/Round Hall.

Osborough, N. (1982) 'A Damocles' sword guaranteed Irish: the suspended sentence in the Republic of Ireland', *Irish Jurist*, 17: 221–56.

Parole Board (2008) *Annual Report 2007*. Dublin: Parole Board.

Pattenden, R. (1996) *English Criminal Appeals 1844–1994*. Oxford: Oxford University Press.

Sebba, L. (1977) 'The pardoning power – a world survey', *Journal of Criminal Law and Criminology*, 68: 83–121.

Senate Debates (Ireland) (1960) Debate on Criminal Justice Bill 1960 (Vol. 52, col. 1999).

Smith, A.T.H. (1983) 'The prerogative of mercy, the power of pardon and criminal justice', *Public Law*, Autumn, 398–439.

Tyler, T. (2003) 'Procedural justice, legitimacy and the effective rule of law', in M. Tonry (ed.), *Crime and Justice: A Review of Research. Vol. 30*. Chicago, IL: University of Chicago Press.

Tyler, T. (2004) 'Procedural justice', in A. Sarat (ed.) *The Blackwell Companion to Law and Society*. Oxford: Blackwell Publishing.

Chapter 11

Italy

Alessandra Gualazzi and Chiara Mancuso

Summary

Article 27(3) of the Italian Constitution provides that punishments must aim at resocializing the convicted. This is reflected in the wide number of alternative measures which allow a prisoner to serve some or all of his sentence in the community (such as the most commonly used 'probation period under social services supervision' – *affidamento in prova*). Conditional release, or *liberazione condizionale*, is used less than these alternative measures. The chapter describes the different schemes, identifying the limited (and often inconsistent) role of the Supervision Tribunal and Supervision Judges. It concludes with a plea for greater clarity and a proper allocation of financial and human resources.

1. Introduction and historical overview

The Italian justice system lays down different types of early release schemes. Parole (*liberazione condizionale*), regulated by the Criminal Code, is awarded to a prisoner who has already served part of his custodial penalty and who has shown remorse for the crime committed. However, parole is the least-used form of release from prison. Much more common are the types of early release regulated by Law 354/1975 – the 'Law on the Penitentiary System' (PL). The PL provides five legal schemes (and a few sub-schemes) that allow prisoners to leave, permanently or temporarily, prison before the end of their sentence. These schemes are called 'alternative measures to detention' and aim at the re-education and resocialization of inmates, according to the principle of the flexibility of the penalty, which is recognized by the Constitutional Court as a founding unwritten principle of the Italian prison system.[1]

The term 'measure' (instead of the term 'penalty') is used with a specific meaning. In Italian law, alternative measures are not penalties[2] and, therefore, they are not imposed by the Trial Judge. Rather, this expression refers to a 'way of executing the penalty' and to the prisoner's possibility of leaving prison after having served only a part of his custodial sentence. Other forms of exceptional early release are parliamentary pardon (indulto),[3] amnesty (amnistia)[4] – which is usually used as a tool to tackle prison overcrowding – and mercy (grazia),[5] a prerogative of the Italian President to grant an act of individual clemency.

In Italy, during the Fascist period (1922–45), punishment was deemed to be merely retributive and afflictive, an approach that was consistent with the authoritarian policy pursued by the regime. The postwar years, after the fall of the regime (1945–6), were characterized by high rates of criminality, mainly political, which led to serious disorder in the prisons. Imprisonment became a political instrument to punish Fascist criminals. Moreover, the militarization of prison staff in 1945 (and their subjection to the provisions of the Military Criminal Code) contributed to widening the gap between guards and inmates.[6] With the enactment of the republican Constitution in 1948, the sanction system provided by the 1930 Criminal Code was partially revised. Article 27(3) of the new Constitution clearly states that 'punishments may not contradict humanity and must aim at re-educating the convicted'.

In the new political climate, Parliament ordered inquires into the state of the country's prisons and on the methods adopted by

[1]Corte Cost. 343/1987; Corte Cost. 282/1989; Corte Cost. 125/1992 (see Margara 1995).
[2]Alternative measures should not be confused with 'alternative penalties' which, in Italian law, are special penalties imposed exclusively by lay judges.
[3]Articles 75 and 79 of the Italian Constitution and Arts. 174 and 184 of the Criminal Code (CP).
[4]Articles 75 and 79 of the Constitution and Arts. 151 and 184 CP.
[5]Article 87 of the Constitution and Arts. 174 and 184 CP.
[6]The penitentiary police were demilitarized only in 1990, by Law 395/1990.

prison staff. Between the mid-1950s and the beginning of the 1970s, and following the UN Standard Minimum Rules for the Treatment of Prisoners (adopted by the First United Nations Congress on the Prevention of Crime and the Treatment of Offenders in 1955), a new concept of penalty and of the forms of its execution was adopted: penitentiary staff should not be just 'guards' but should also play an important social role in the rehabilitation of prisoners.

The comprehensive penitentiary law finally enacted in July 1975 stressed that all penalties should be directed at resocializing offenders and that the period of the execution of the punishment should provide the necessary material and psychological resources to facilitate the prisoner's return to society. These objectives cannot be achieved in the trial because the Trial Judge does not have any power to make or consider criminological or psychological evaluations of offenders. The observation and treatment of offenders are, therefore, assigned to the penitentiary staff (social services, etc.), while the Supervision Judge is called upon to approve the rehabilitation programme, which is generally formalized within three months of the offender's imprisonment.

In particular, the law sets down different roles for those involved in the prisoner's resocialization programme and in the application of the various forms of early release. The Prison Director is in charge of the prison's administration and of the team conducting scientific observations of the prisoner. The educators, working closely with the social services, collect information on the prisoner's personality and life to be used in drafting the rehabilitation programme. The social services[7] which are independent of both the prison management and the supervision judiciary, conduct a social investigation into the convict's situation and background. The results are used, once again, to draft the rehabilitation programme. The social services can also provide the supervision judiciary with information about the application of, changes in or recall of an alternative measure. Finally, psychologists and criminologists carry out a three-monthly psychological-criminological assessment of the prisoner.

The years following 1975 were marked by political and social tensions provoked by the terrorist events which severely shocked the public and encouraged governments to adopt severe measures to punish the terrorists. Only in the second half of the 1980s, when the terrorist emergency was over, was new legislation enacted. Law 663/1986 was aimed at increasing prisoners' chances of leaving prison through the introduction of new early release schemes, among

[7]Social services are organized into *Uffici di Esecuzione Penale Esterna* (UEPE), set up by Law 154/2005.

which there were some forms of probation, home detention curfews and good behaviour licences. But the main effect of the new schemes was the overloading of the supervision judiciary with massive numbers of applications. This led the Judges in practice to pay more attention to prisoners' behaviour than to their personalities. Hence the Judges' evaluations focused less on the person and more on his actions.

The law did not provide clear or specific criteria for the application of the new procedures. Instead it laid down only generic provisions, which have gradually increased the Judges' discretionary power and have been applied very differently in different territorial courts. In 1990 violent crimes committed by the mafia resulted once again in limited access – at least to certain categories of prisoners – to early release schemes.

This situation did not last long. The considerable increase in the prison population and the difficulties encountered by the supervision judiciary in managing the high number of applications presented by prisoners were at the centre of a big political debate, which led to the passing of Law 156/1998. This law attempted to tackle these problems by extending prisoners' access to early release measures and by introducing a mechanism for the automatic suspension of penalties, which allows offenders to be awarded an alternative measure to imprisonment *before* the beginning of the penalty's execution. Offenders, therefore, can be released from prison without ever having entered it! Under this provision, which is regulated by Art. 656 of the Code of Criminal Procedure (CPP), custodial sentences of less than three years (or six years in some specific cases related to drug offences) are suspended automatically. Exceptions apply for some categories of offences (such as terrorism, organized crime[8], some types of theft and others[9]), for repeat offenders[10] and for those held in pre-trial custody who cannot benefit from the provision.[11]

[8]Moreover, offenders who commit the crimes listed in Art. 4(a) PL can obtain an early release measure or another benefit only if they co-operate with the justice authorities and do not have any links with organized crime.
[9]See Law 125/2008.
[10]In particular, Law 251/2005 has reduced access to a wide range of benefits for repeat offenders.
[11]It should also be mentioned that, according to Arts. 163 ff. CP, the Trial Judge has the power to impose a suspended sentence (*sospensione condizionale della pena*) for a period of five years or less (according to the different categories of offences) when the defendant is sentenced to a term of imprisonment of less than two years or to pay a fine, and when he is unlikely to commit other offences. Suspended sentences cannot be granted to repeat offenders.

The Public Prosecutor serves notice on the convicted person, informing him of his right to apply, within the following 30 days, for an alternative measure to detention. If the offender does not apply within the prescribed period, his custodial penalty, already suspended, reacquires its legal force and must be executed without delay. This means, in practice, that the offender will be brought to prison by the police, on an order issued by the Public Prosecutor, to serve his penalty. The law was aimed at avoiding the negative effects of imprisonment on petty offenders who, once in prison, could quickly obtain a form of early release. Also in this case, however, the Judges were not provided with clear and consistent guidance.

More recent proposals on the reform of the CP (and, in particular, of the penalty system)[12] and of the prison system, which have been presented to Parliament, have not gone forward owing to lack of political consensus. A wide-ranging legislative proposal directed at an incisive modification and revision of the PL and, therefore, at modifying the actual legal framework for regulating early release schemes, was presented by the left-wing party in November 2005.[13] This Bill's main aim was a reduction of the number of prisoners (and an improvement in prison conditions), the strengthening of the constitutional provision relating to the re-education of criminals and the enforcement of the principle of the penalty's flexibility. As the report accompanying the proposal stated: 'the granting of an alternative measure (*and therefore access to an early release scheme*) is not to be seen as an exceptional fact, but it should be regarded as the ordinary conclusion of the execution of the penalties.'[14]

According to the authors of the Bill, the public needs to be educated to understand that the mechanisms of early release are not shortcuts to escape punishment but are a way of serving the punishment. The proposal addressed serious organizational deficiencies and the

[12]Such as the work carried out by the Commissions for the Reform of the Criminal Code appointed in 1988 (chaired by Prof. A. Pagliaro), in 1998 (chaired by Prof. C.F. Grosso); in 2001 (chaired by Judge C. Nordio) and in 2006 (guided by Lawyer G. Pisapia). In particular, the Commission Grosso proposed the abolition of the life sentence and its replacement with a new 'special' custodial penalty (up to 30 years); a reduction of the maximum period of imprisonment (up to 18 years); the introduction of home detention curfew as a new principal penalty; the abolition of imprisonment for minor offences; and the introduction of community penalties. For comments on these proposals, see Dolcini (2001); Niro (2008).
[13]Bill 6164/2005; see Deriu and Morgante (2008), Niro (2008).
[14]Report to Bill 6164/2005, p. 26.

shortage of resources affecting the supervision judiciary, the prison system and social services. It also called for the introduction of clear criteria to help Judges and a reduction in the inconsistencies in the judicial positions adopted by Supervision Judges in the application of the various alternatives. Following the election of the right-wing Silvio Berlusconi government in 2008, the Bill was not passed. The new government, pressed by a series of criminal events which have spread fear and tension among the public, has so far adopted a partial legislative approach. Early release has been addressed in a new Bill laid before Parliament in April 2008.[15] In line with the executive programme, this Bill introduces severe limits to early release. In particular, the proposal increases the length of the penalty which must be served by prisoners before applying for early release schemes. It also abolishes automatic remission and reduces from three years to one the maximum penalty which is suspended automatically, as described in Art. 656 CPP. However, this proposal is not yet in force.

2. Early release in practice

As we have seen, the Italian system provides for different early release schemes for custodial sentences: parole (regulated by criminal law) and the so-called 'alternative measures to detention' set down by the PL (probation under social services' supervision, home detention curfew and automatic remission). Other, anomalous, forms of release include day release and good behaviour licences.[16] These are anomalous in the sense that the prisoner does not leave the prison permanently but does so only for part of a day, or for some days, and then returns.

Prisoners can apply to leave prison before the completion of their sentence when they meet the requirements laid down by the law and pass the risk assessment process or another type of evaluation by the supervision judiciary. Despite not being 'penalties' but simply ways of executing the penalty, alternative measures must be granted by a judicial body following a judicial proceeding. Therefore, an early

[15]Bill C 158 (2008). See also Bill C 1864 (2008), presented before Parliament in November 2008, which proposes to reduce the penalty limit provided by Art. 656 CPP from three years to just six months.
[16]Mercy and amnesty are not covered in the chapter. Some brief information, however, is provided on pardon. *Grazia* (which we translate as 'mercy') can be granted only by the President and is an 'individual' act of clemency. *Indulto* (pardon) is granted by Parliament by law and is a 'general' act involving all prisoners (exceptions can apply for serious offenders).

release measure cannot be awarded by the prison's management or by other administrative bodies. This is a rule set down in Art. 13 of the Constitution, which states that 'no form of detention ... or any other restriction on personal freedom is permitted, except by order of the Judiciary stating a reason and only in such cases and in such manner as provided by law'.

Early release proceedings are conducted by the Supervision Tribunal (*tribunale di sorveglianza*) and by the Supervision Judge (*magistrato di sorveglianza*), who initiates proceedings before the Court. Every district of the Court of Appeal has a Supervision Tribunal. Its decisions are taken by a panel of four: the President of the Court, the Supervision Judge under whose jurisdiction the prisoner is placed and two experts in social and psychological matters. The tribunal has the jurisdiction, in the first instance, to grant (or revoke) parole, probation under social services, home detention and day release. Its pronouncements can be challenged before the Court of Cassation.

The Supervision Judge is competent to supervise the execution of penalties within those prisons under their territorial jurisdiction; to approve the prisoner's rehabilitation programme; and to grant the prisoner automatic remission or a good behaviour licence. The Judge's decisions can be appealed to the Supervision Tribunal. The Supervision Judge follows the convicted person's case from the final judgment to the execution of the penalty and performs the delicate task of collecting information on the prisoner's personality, social and family life, and other circumstances in order to provide the Supervision Tribunal with all the necessary elements for an early release decision.

The decision should be communicated to the applicant within two or three months of the first hearing. During this period the Supervision Judge will gather relevant information on the prisoner's personality, the improvements he has achieved, his chances of a job after release and his commitment to return to society. If the Court declares the application admissible, it informs the Public Prosecutor, the prisoner and his Counsel within ten days of the date of the hearing. The presence of both the Public Prosecutor and the defence lawyer is a legal requirement, but the applicant is not required to attend the hearing (but may do so if he wishes). If the applicant does not have a defence lawyer, the tribunal will nominate one for him. However, in practice, the role of the defence lawyer in supervision proceedings is marginal.

Supervision proceedings have an inquisitorial nature, mainly because the Court which adopts the decision has wide discretionary powers in calling evidence and acquiring documents and information. The main characteristics of the proceedings are as follows:

- The hearing where the parties present their case is not held in public.

- The object of the proceedings is not a decision on a fact; rather, it is a positive or negative judgment on the prisoner's personality and an assessment of the likelihood of his being reintegrated into society.

- The proceedings can be instituted *ex officio*.

- The Tribunal can order the competent authorities to disclose all the documents and information it may need for its decision (such as a social services' report, a police report or a prison report).

- The Tribunal may grant the applicant a different (and less favourable) measure from the one requested by the applicant.

Once released, offenders are supervised by the Social Services which have the task of helping and supporting them in their return to the community.

3. Statistics

From the annual data published by the Department of Penitentiary Administration of the Ministry of Justice[17] it is possible to compare the total numbers of prisoners in Italian prisons every year with the numbers of offenders who are awarded early release.[18] On 31 December 2008, the total number of prisoners in Italy was 58,127, of which 2,526 were women (accounting for 4.3 per cent of the total).

[17]Data available online at http://www.giustizia.it/statistiche/statistiche_dap/dap_indice.htm

[18]Note, though, that the data provided by the Ministry of Justice do not refer to all types of release. No information is provided for automatic remission or for good behaviour licences (apart from the years 2007 and 2008). No information is available on the recalling of parole regulated by Art. 174 CP. No data are directly provided for the type/length of penalty imposed or served by offenders who apply for or are granted early release or on the crimes they have committed.

Table 11.1   Italian prison population, 2001–08

Year	Total prisoners	Women	%	Non-Italian prisoners	%
2001	55,275	2,369	4.28	16,294	29.40
2002	55,670	2,469	4.44	16,788	30.16
2003	54,237	2,493	4.60	17,007	31.36
2004	56,068	2,589	4.62	17,819	31.78
2005	59,523	2,804	4.71	19,836	33.32
2006	39,005	1,670	4.28	13,152	33.72
2007	48,693	2,175	4.47	18,252	37.48
2008	58,127	2,526	4.30	21,562	37.09

There were 21,562 foreign prisoners (accounting for 37.09 per cent of the total). As Table 11.1 shows, the Italian prison population has grown steadily in the last decade. The lower rates in 2006 (39,005 prisoners) and in 2007 (48,693 prisoners) are due to the general pardon (*indulto*) granted by Parliament in July 2006 in order to address the problem of prison overcrowding. In consequence of the pardon, nearly half the prisoners serving a final custodial sentence were released.[19] However, by the end of 2007 the number of prisoners had risen quickly and to a significant extent again, mainly because of the recall of many of those who had been granted the pardon and because of an increase in the number of foreign prisoners in the system.

The percentage of women prisoners has not varied considerably in recent years, whereas the numbers of non-Italian prisoners have constantly increased. The number of prisoners on 31 March 2009 was 61,057 – 18,000 more than the certified accommodation capacity of the country's prisons.[20]

With regard to prisoners' legal status (see Table 11.2), on 31 December 2008 there were 26,587 prisoners serving final sentences, less than half (45.74 per cent) of the entire prison population; 14,671 prisoners were awaiting trial; and 13,420 had appealed or had challenged a previous decision before the Court of Cassation. At the end of 2007, after the

[19]*Statistical Data on the Prison Population. The effects of the Pardon: Prisoners before and after Law 241/2006* (June 2007) (Department of Penitentiary Administration)   See   http://www.giustizia.it/statistiche/statistiche_dap/det/2007/efffetti_indulto_giugno2007.pdf.

[20]Source: http://www.ilsole24ore.com/art/SoleOnLine4/Italia/2009/04/carcere-piu-detenuti-prima-indulto.shtml?uuid=96520c6c-21e3-11de-b61d-701d01a38a99&DocRulesView=Libero.

Table 11.2 Legal status of prisoners, 2001–08

Year	Untried prisoners	Sentenced prisoners who have appealed or challenged their judgment before the Court of Cassation	Sentenced prisoners (final sentence)	Internees or to be determined	Total
15 January 2002 (referring to 2001)	12,481	10,924	31,024	1,322	55,751
2002	11,957	9,725	32,854	1,134	55,670
2003	11,570	8,655	32,865	1,147	54,237
2004	11,541	8,495	35,033	999	56,068
2005	12,204	9,458	36,676	1,185	59,523
2006	13,495	8,650	15,468	1,392	39,005
2007	15,417	12,771	19,029	1,476	48,693
2008	14,671	13,420	26,587	3,449	58,127

Table 11.3 Length of penalty served by finally sentenced prisoners, 2001–08

Year	Up to 1 year	1–3 years	3–6 years	6–10 years	10–20 years	More than 20 years	Life sentence	Total
15 January 2002 (referring to 2001)	2,970	6,491	9,178	5,028	4,471	2,018	868	31,024
2002	2,846	6,958	9,790	5,473	4,709	2,088	990	32,854
2003	3,006	6,661	9,704	5,455	4,816	2,155	1,068	32,865
2004	3,143	7,580	10,505	5,565	4,863	2,216	1,161	35,033
2005	3,356	7,917	11,209	5,640	5,026	2,304	1,224	36,676
2006	1,069	1,770	3,194	2,830	3,455	1,913	1,237	15,468
2007	2,061	4,009	4,058	2,724	3,206	1,614	1,357	19,029
2008	2,919	6,977	7,012	3,312	3,332	1,627	1,408	26,587

enactment of the general pardon, 19,029 prisoners were serving a final sentence – a slightly higher percentage than those awaiting trial (15,417) and than those waiting for a pronouncement from the Court of Appeal or the Court of Cassation (12,771).

Table 11.3 shows that in 2008 there were 2,919 prisoners serving a

Table 11.4 Remaining penalty period to be served by finally sentenced prisoners, 2001–08

Year	Up to 1 year	1–3 years	3–6 years	6–10 years	10–20 years	More than 20 years	Life sentence	Total
15 January 2002 (referring to 2001)	9,195	9,912	6,068	2,486	2,026	469	868	31,024
2002	9,304	10,582	6,654	2,726	2,142	456	990	32,854
2003	8,657	10,635	6,967	2,826	2,268	444	1,068	32,865
2004	9,447	11,652	7,130	2,922	2,271	450	1,161	35,033
2005	10,193	12,271	7,227	2,951	2,311	499	1,224	36,676
2006	2,724	3,838	3,338	2,101	1,821	409	1,237	15,468
2007	5,510	5,298	3,396	1,771	1,399	298	1,357	19,029
2008	8,526	8,466	4,435	2,048	1,411	293	1,408	26,587

final sentence of imprisonment of up to one year, while 6,977 were serving a sentence of up to three years. All these prisoners were, in principle, eligible to apply for one or more alternative forms of release. With the exceptions of 2006 and 2007 (in consequence of the pardon), similar numbers can be seen for previous years.

Table 11.4 shows the length of the remaining penalty period to be served by finally sentenced prisoners from 2001 to June 2008. In 2008 the majority of prisoners (a total number of 16,992 out of 26,587) were serving a remaining penalty period of less than three years and could have, therefore, applied for an early release scheme. The same was true of the other periods considered, with the exception of 2006 when, as a consequence of a pardon, the majority of prisoners who were serving a custodial penalty of less than three years were released.

As already mentioned,the available official data refer only to probation under Social Services, home detention curfew, day release (despite this being an 'anomalous' early release mechanism) and parole. No information is provided for automatic remission or good behaviour licences.[21]

Despite the fact that parole, automatic remission, probation, home detention curfew and day release are all forms of release from prison, they result in important differences in relation to the juridical status of the offenders subject to them. Offenders subject to home detention curfews and day release are still considered to be prisoners. Thus, if they do not respect the terms imposed upon them by the Supervision

[21]See footnote 18 above.

Table 11.5 Numbers of prisoners on probation under Social Services and on parole, 2001–08

Year	Cases per year (total)	Probation under Social Services (after serving part of the sentence in prison)		Parole	
		Subtotal	%	Subtotal	%
2001	5,315	5,154	96.97	161	3.02
2002	5,674	5,540	97.63	134	2.36
2003	5,750	5,628	97.87	125	2.17
2004	5,829	5,730	98.30	99	1.69
2005	6,056	5,955	98.33	101	1.66
2006	6,029	5,928	98.32	101	1.67
2007	2,300	2,299	99.95	1	0.04
January–June 2008	N/A	2,076		N/A	N/A

Table 11.6 Numbers of prisoners on home detention curfew and day release, 2001–08

Year	Cases per year (total	Home detention curfew (after serving part of the sentence in prison)		Day release (after serving part of the sentence in prison)	
		Subtotal	%	Subtotal	%
2001	6,416	3,286	51.21	3,130	48.78
2002	6,905	3,577	51.80	3,328	48.19
2003	6,656	3,502	52.61	3,154	47.38
2004	6,189	3,348	54.09	2,841	45.90
2005	6,245	3,471	55.58	2,774	44.41
2006	5,599	3,116	56.05	2,483	44.66
2007	2,761	1,432	51.86	1,329	48.13
January–June 2008	2,201	1,189	54.02	1,012	45.97

Judge, they might commit the criminal offence of escape (*evasione*). However, if a person under probation or parole breaches the terms of his licence, he would 'simply' be recalled to prison. This is why the figures relating to parole and probation are presented in a different table from than those relating to the other release schemes (see Tables 11.5–11.7). Moreover, it should be stressed that probation,

Table 11.7 Numbers of prisoners applying for alternative measures to imprisonment, 2001–08

Year	Cases per year (total)	Probation under Social Services (Art. 656 CPP)		Home detention curfew (Art. 656 CPP)		Day release (Art. 656 CPP)	
		Subtotal	%	Subtotal	%	Subtotal	%
2001	28,060	20,998	74.83	6,590	23.48	472	1.68
2002	30,646	22,625	73.82	7,377	24.07	644	2.10
2003	33,156	24,676	74.42	7,820	23.58	660	1.99
2004	35,127	26,238	74.69	8,241	23.46	648	1.84
2005	34,583	25,826	74.67	8,073	23.34	684	1.97
2006	28,685	21,561	75.16	6,583	22.94	541	1.88
2007	4,470	2,825	63.19	1,576	35.25	69	1.54
January–June 2008	4,453	2,966	66.60	1,393	31.28	94	2.11

home detention curfew and day release, apart from being types of release from prison, are also alternative measures to imprisonment and can be granted, by virtue of Art. 656 CPP, immediately after the offender has been served a final prison sentence. In particular, as one can see from Table 11.7, the number of convicts applying for an alternative measure in terms of Art. 656 CPP (i.e. before entering prison) is considerable higher than the number of offenders who are awarded the same measures as forms of early release (see Tables 11.5 and 11.6). Because they are not a 'proper' form of release, no further comment will be made on the related statistics.

The figures clearly show that probation under Social Services is the most common release scheme, followed by home detention curfew, day release and parole. In particular, as is shown by Tables 11.5 and 11.6, out of total of 5,061 cases in 2007,[22] 2,299 prisoners were awarded probation. This was followed by one prisoner who was awarded parole; 1,432 prisoners who obtained home detention; and 1,329 prisoners who had been granted day release.

The number of prisoners using early release schemes declined significantly in 2006 and 2007 as a result of the 2006 pardon. This

[22]This number has been calculated by adding the number of cases of probation and parole shown in Table 11.5 (2,300) to the number of cases of home detention curfew and day release reported in Table 11.6 (2,761).

data can be matched with the decline in the rate of prisoners serving a final sentence in the same period, from 36,676 in 2005 to 15,468 in 2006, and to 19,029 in 2007 (as seen in Table 11.2). Another reason for the lower number of successful applications is the increase in the number of foreign prisoners who are in the country illegally (Table 11.1). Indeed, illegal immigrants are often not able to obtain early release because they do not meet the requirements set down by the law (for example, stable accommodation or a job). Moreover, as is shown later, the use of early release for merely practical reasons (that is, to cut down the excessive number of prisoners) rather than for re-educative purposes has recently led the supervision judiciary to adopt a stricter approach in the award of those benefits, in line with public demands for severe punishments.

Finally, Tables 11.8–11.13 show the number of recalls from probation under Social Services, home detention and day release in 2006, 2007 and in the first six months of 2008. A distinction has been made, again, to show when the benefits were awarded as a form of early release (Tables 11.8, 11.10, 11.12) or as an immediate alternative to imprisonment (Tables 11.9, 11.11, 11.13). No official information is available about the recall of parolees or about those granted automatic remission.

With regard to offenders who were granted early release (Tables 11.8, 11.10 and 11.12), in the first six months of 2008, 259 offenders were recalled to prison, accounting for 5.75 per cent of a total of

Table 11.8 Recalls of offenders having been granted probation after serving part of their sentence in prison, 2006–08

Year	Total cases per year	Failure to comply with terms of licence		Commission of an offence during the licence period		Other reasons		Total recalls per year	
		Nos.	%	Nos.	%	Nos.	%	Nos.	%
2006	5,928	330	5.56	14	0.23	57	0.96	401	6.76
2007	2,299	113	4.91	7	0.30	25	1.08	145	6.30
January–June 2008	2,298	105	4.56	12	0.52	13	0.56	130	5.65

Table 11.9 Recalls of offenders having been granted probation under Art. 656 CPP, 2006–08

Year	Total cases per year	Failure to comply with terms of licence		Commission of an offence during the licence period		Other reasons		Total recalls per year	
		Nos.	%	Nos.	%	Nos.	%	Nos.	%
2006	21,562	602	2.79	20	0.09	139	0.64	761	3.52
2007	2,825	80	2.83	6	0.21	9	0.31	95	3.36
January–June 2008	2,966	59	1.98	13	0.43	12	0.40	84	2.83

Table 11.10 Recalls of offenders having been granted home detention curfew after serving part of their sentence in prison, 2006–08

Year	Total cases per year	Failure to comply with terms of licence		Commission of an offence during the licence period		Other reasons		Total recalls per year	
		Nos.	%	Nos.	%	Nos.	%	Nos.	%
2006	3,116	168	5.39	4	0.12	101	3.24	273	8.76
2007	1,432	62	4.32	5	0.34	48	3.35	115	8.03
January–June 2008	1,189	42	3.53	4	0.33	23	1.93	69	5.80

4,499 early release cases.[23] The greatest number of recalls was caused, in all cases, by a failure to comply with the terms of the licence.

With specific reference to probation (Table 11.8), out of a total of 2,298 cases awarded, 105 offenders (4.56 per cent) did not respect the terms of their licences; 12 offenders (0.52 per cent) were recalled for committing an offences while outside prison; and 13 offenders (0.56 per cent) were recalled on other grounds (for example, on the basis of a change in juridical status because of the imposition of a new

[23]This figure has been calculated by combining the data related to the total number of early release cases indicated in the second columns of Tables 11.8, 11.10 and 11.12 with the data referring to the number of recalls reported in the last columns of the same tables.

Table 11.11 Recalls of offenders having been granted home detention curfew under Art. 656 CPP, 2006–08

Year	Total cases per year	Failure to comply with terms of licence		Commission of an offence during the licence period		Other reasons		Total recalls per year	
		Nos.	%	Nos.	%	Nos.	%	Nos.	%
2006	6,583	291	4.42	18	0.27	184	2.79	493	7.48
2007	1,576	54	3.42	9	0.57	35	2.22	98	6.21
January–June 2008	1,393	52	3.73	5	0.35	21	1.50	78	5.59

Table 11.12 Recalls of offenders having been granted day release after serving part of their sentence in prison, 2006–08

Year	Total cases per year	Failure to comply with terms of licence		Commission of an offence during the licence period		Other reasons		Total recalls per year	
		Nos.	%	Nos.	%	Nos.	%	Nos.	%
2006	2,483	144	5.79	4	0.16	174	7.00	322	12.96
2007	1,329	78	5.86	5	0.37	79	5.94	162	12.18
January–June 2008	1,012	33	3.26	6	0.59	21	2.07	60	5.92

Table 11.13 Recalls of offenders having been granted day release under Art. 656 CPP, 2006–08

Year	Total cases per year	Failure to comply with terms of licence		Commission of an offence during the licence period		Other reasons		Total recalls per year	
		Nos.	%	Nos.	%	Nos.	%	Nos.	%
2006	541	34	6.28	3	0.55	32	5.91	69	12.75
2007	69	6	8.69	0	0.00	2	2.89	8	11.59
January–June 2008	94	4	4.25	0	0.00	1	1.06	5	5.31

sentence for offences committed before the award of the measure and, in consequence of which, the penalty limit requirement stated for the type of release is no longer met; on the grounds of monitoring failure; or for other unspecified reasons). The same patterns can, generally, be observed for 2007 and 2006.

4. Content and legal criteria

4.1 Conditional release (parole)

Conditional release or parole (*liberazione condizionale*) is regulated by Arts. 176 and 177 of the Italian Criminal Code[24] and is granted by the Supervision Tribunal on the basis of an evaluation of progress made by the prisoner during his time in custody. *Liberazione condizionale* 'extinguishes' the penalty,[25] which is deemed to be completely executed if no other offences are committed in its residual period or within five years in the case of life imprisonment. Prisoners can obtain parole after having served at least 30 months or after having reached the halfway point of their sentence if the residual penalty is no longer than five years. Repeat offenders[26] can apply for the measure after having served at least four years and not less than three quarters of their sentence.

Life-sentence prisoners can be released after having served at least 26 years or 21 years if they have been awarded the penalty discounts provided by automatic remission.[27] The Supervision Tribunal awards the prisoner parole only after having verified his certain repentance (*sicuro ravvedimento*).[28] The assessment of the prisoner's rehabilitation and the contrition is based on the following factors:

[24]As modified by Law 663/1986.

[25]Unlike the events which extinguish the offence (for instance, the offender's death before the conviction), events which extinguish only the penalty interrupt the execution of the punishment, while all other eventual 'penal effects' remain (e.g. the conviction will be on the offender's criminal record; the offender could be banned from some activities or kinds of employment, such as working with children or opening a business).

[26]The different categories of repeat offender are listed in Art. 99 CP.

[27]See section above.

[28]According to Art. 682(2) CPP, if conditional release is not granted because of the absence of a clear expression of remorse by the offender, a further application can be presented not earlier than six months from the date when the applicant's request had been refused by the Court.

- The seriousness of the crime committed.
- The evolution of the prisoner's personality.[29]
- His attitude towards the victim of the offence.
- The prisoner's health.
- Victim compensation, which is seen as evidence of the prisoner's resolve to change and to abandon his criminal lifestyle.[30]

In principle, good conduct (*buona condotta*) alone does not constitute a sufficient condition for conditional release. The Supervision Tribunal also takes into account the prison's report (which should contain information relating not only to the prisoner's disciplinary profile but also to his general behaviour in prison, and to his relationships with other prisoners and with prison staff), the prisoner's criminal records, the police report and all other useful information.[31]

Once granted parole by the Supervision Tribunal, the prisoner is placed under police supervision (*libertà vigilata*) until the end of the licence period and must be recalled to prison either when he perpetrates a further offence (similar to the one for which he had been granted the release)[32] or when he fails to comply with the positive and negative conditions imposed by the Court.

---

[29]It is necessary to assess whether there have been improvements in the prisoner's behaviour after the commission of the offence.

[30]In this respect, the impossibility of compensating victims is not deemed an impediment to granting early release. However, the offender should at least show a sincere sign of human solidarity towards the victim, as stated by Trib. Sorveglianza Turin, 20 March 2007. See also Trib. Sorveglianza Milan, 10 October 2006, (2007) (1) *Foro ambrosiano*, p. 1, with the comment of Giannangeli.

[31]See Trib. Sorveglianza Turin, 19 February 2008, unpublished; Trib. Sorveglianza Turin, 31 January 2006, unpublished; Trib. Sorveglianza Turin, 1 February 2005, unpublished; Trib. Sorveglianza Milan, 17 October 2002, in (2002) *Foro ambrosiano*, p. 527; Trib. Sorveglianza Turin, 15 November 1991, (1993) *Giurisprudenza di merito*, p. 144.

[32]According to the ruling of the Constitutional Court (Corte Cost. 418/1998), the commission of another offence or the violation of parole conditions should not automatically lead to the offender's recall to prison. In these cases the Supervision Tribunal should carry out an investigation to check if the offender's conduct, in relation to the crime perpetrated or the gravity of the conditions infringed, is still compatible with the continuation of the probation period.

According to Art. 177 CP, if returned to prison, the offender should serve all the remaining sentence. However, this provision has been invalidated by the Italian Constitutional Court (*Corte Costituzionale*; Corte Cost.), which has stated that the probation period must be calculated as a portion of the penalty.[33]

4.2 Forms of early release regulated by special legislation: the 'alternative' measures to imprisonment

The forms of early release regulated by the PL and its further modifications are, as mentioned above, probation under the supervision of the Social Services (*affidamento in prova al servizio sociale*); home detention (*detenzione domiciliare*); and automatic remission (*liberazione anticipata*). The PL refers to two remaining measures – day release (*semilibertà*) and a good behaviour licence or temporary release (*permessi premio*) – that, despite not having the effect of completely dismissing the convict from prison, do tend to have the same objectives of the other early release schemes insofar as they are aimed at containing the negative effects of imprisonment and facilitating the convict's return to the community.

4.2.1 Probation period under Social Services' supervision (affidamento in prova)

Probation under the supervision of the Social Services (Art. 47 PL) is the most common scheme of early release. It allows the offender to serve his custodial sentence (in whole or in part) outside prison and under the supervision of the social services. An offender sentenced to a term of imprisonment of no more than three years (or those whose remaining sentence does not exceed this period) can be released and placed under this form of probation for an equivalent period to the penalty to be executed. It can even be granted to those who have committed a serious crime, given the large reduction of penalty (up to a third) that can be obtained by choosing one of the several forms of plea-bargaining (or, literally, special summary proceedings) available in Italian criminal procedure. However, some restrictions apply to particular types of offences (for example, organized crime, terrorism and sex offences).[34] Special cases of probation are regulated by Art. 47(a) PL (drug and alcohol addicts who are willing to start or continue a therapeutic programme) and Art. 47(c) PL (prisoners

[33]See Corte Cost. 28/1989 and 161/1997.
[34]See Art. 4(a) PL.

suffering from Aids or other particularly serious illnesses who are following or about to undergo medical treatment).

The main legal criteria for the awarding of this form of probation are the availability of stable accommodation or a stable place where the offender can be regularly contacted by the Social Services,[35] and a positive assessment of the prisoner's re-education (*prognosi di rieducabilità*). The prisoner is observed for at least four weeks[36] within the prison as is, on a more general level, his personal conduct during the custodial period (for example, his disciplinary record and his contacts with other detainees; Art. 47(2) PL). The Supervision Tribunal gives its decision only when satisfied that there is a good chance of the offender's resocialization outside prison. This assessment is inferred from the following:

- The means and circumstances of the offence, the type of injury and harm suffered by the victim, the degree of intention and the reason for the criminal behaviour.[37]
- Pending proceedings and previous convictions.
- The offender's behaviour since the commission of the offence.
- Information contained in the police and Social Services' reports for offenders who have not yet been imprisoned or who are under home arrest.
- Reports and observations supplied by the prison.

The Supervision Tribunal is not bound by the positive or negative opinions of the social services, prisons and police. Often the tribunal's decision does not follow the indication provided in the reports, especially those drafted by the Social Services, whose evaluations of the convicted person's situation and personality tend to be excessively

[35]Despite the Court of Cassation's ruling (Cass. pen., sez. I, 7 February 2007, n. 16697) that the existence of accommodation should not be regarded as a *conditio sine qua non* for the approval of the offender's application, the availability of a fixed residential address is, in practice, considered a fundamental requirement by the Supervision Tribunal in order to award the measure and/or to release a prisoner early.
[36]Probation can be awarded without the observation period when, according to his post-offence behaviour, the convict is classified as a low-risk offender (art. 47(3) PL).
[37]All these aspects are deducted by the Supervision Tribunal from the information provided by the Sentencing Judge.

positive or too general.[38] Given its inquisitorial nature, and in order to deliver its judgment, the Supervision Tribunal can always obtain *ex officio* further opinions and information related to the prisoner's character and social dangerousness (*pericolosità sociale*) by requiring a criminological assessment (*perizia criminologica*). Such an assessment is produced by criminologists appointed (and paid) by the Tribunal. This assessment, which is mainly focused on understanding the motives which led the person to commit the offence, would not be admissible at the trial and is only rarely ordered by the Court, since it is more interested in the offender's conduct in the aftermath of the crime.

When the Supervision Tribunal decides that the prisoner is eligible to apply for an alternative measure, it must specify a list of conditions that must be accepted by the convicted person, who is required to sign a document of acceptance in front of the Prison Director.[39] These conditions have the dual function of encouraging the offender's rehabilitation (for example, the obligation to report periodically to a social worker and the duty to attend an educational programme or to undergo therapeutic treatment) and of limiting risk situations which might push him to commit further offences (for example, a limitation on personal freedoms – i.e. prohibitions on meeting specific people, being in specific places or possessing specific objects, such as weapons). During the period of the measure's execution, the offender is supervised by the Social Services which, at least in theory, should also provide him with the necessary support to help him deal with the difficulties of reintegration into society.

At least every three months the Social Services submit periodical reports on the person's behaviour to the Supervision Tribunal. The Supervision Judge can also modify the Tribunal's conditions according to the offender's changing needs, on the basis of the Social Services' reports; or the Judge can obtain information on the state of execution of the measure, can order the measure's temporary suspension (until the Tribunal has reached a definitive decision); and, lastly, can start proceedings before the Supervision Tribunal to recall the offender to prison. Probation can be suspended by the Supervision Judge and, eventually, revoked by the Tribunal when the offender infringes the

[38]For case law on the evaluation criteria for the application of the measure, see Trib. Sorveglianza Turin, 7 May 2008; Trib. Sorveglianza Bari, 27 March 2008; Cass. pen., sez. I, 20 February 2008, n. 1838; Trib. Sorveglianza Turin, 27 November 2007; Trib. Sorveglianza Turin, 19 September 2007, unreported; Trib. Sorveglianza Turin, 19 June 2007; Trib. Sorveglianza Turin, 11 April 2007; Trib. Sorveglianza Turin, 21 February 2007.

[39]Or in front of the Social Services' Director, if the offender is not in prison.

Court's conditions, commits a further offence or receives another definitive sentence, or when his behaviour appears to be incompatible with the prosecution of the probation period.

In the first six months of 2008 only 130 out of 2,298 cases of probation under the Social Services were revoked, accounting for 5.65 per cent of all recalls (Table 11.8). The most common cause for recall (105) was a failure to comply with the terms of the licence. It is interesting to note that in just 12 cases offenders were returned to prison for the commission of an offence while on probation. Finally, 13 offenders were recalled for other unspecified reasons.

Research carried out in 2005 by the Department of Penitentiary Administration of the Ministry of Justice[40] aimed at assessing the rate of repeat offending among those who had been placed under Social Services' probation. The study took a sample of 8,800 offenders who had successfully completed probation in 1998 and attempted to find out how many offenders had committed one or more offences after the end of their probation period (and not during it). It was discovered that, after seven years (1998–2005), only 19 per cent of those who had been granted probation had committed another crime.[41] However, among offenders who had been serving their overall sentence in prison (and who had served their penalty fully in 1998), the percentage of repeat offenders in the research period (equivalent to 81 months) was 69 per cent. According to the authors of the research, these data – considered along with the small number of recalls of probation under Social Services cases due to the commission of an offence during the probation period – show that early release schemes in general (and probation under the Social Services in particular, being the most common early measure), despite not often being an effective tool to tackle prison overcrowding, represent an essential channel for criminals' resocialization. Despite the criticism that probation is awarded to a selected number of (low risk) offenders who have already passed a risk assessment process, the report provides interesting information on the evaluation of this type of early release.[42]

[40]See Leonardi (2007).
[41]As the research shows, the majority of offenders who committed a further crime while on probation were drug- or alcohol-dependent.
[42]It is worth noting that the rate of repeat offenders was lower among those who had been granted probation by virtue of the mechanism provided by Art. 656 CPP (and who had not entered prison at all) than among offenders who were awarded the benefit after having served part of their sentence in prison.

4.2.2 Home detention curfew (detenzione domiciliare)

Home detention curfew was introduced by Law 663/1986, which added a new Article 47(b) to the PL.[43] Offenders who are granted home detention serve part or all of their custodial sentence either in their home or in any other private accommodation or public place of assistance and treatment. Despite its original re-educative intent, the alternative measure of home detention is, in practice, a useful and effective way of reducing the prison population. It can be granted when the offender has been sentenced to imprisonment of no more than two years (or when less than two years remains of a longer sentence) and when he is not eligible for probation and not socially dangerous.[44] Home detention may also be granted to someone serving a custodial sentence of up to four years (even when this is the residual portion of a longer sentence) when he belongs to one of the following categories:

* Pregnant mothers or mothers with children younger than ten years old living with them.
* Fathers with children younger than ten years old living with them because of the death or serious illness of the mother.
* Seriously ill offenders who need regular medical treatment.
* Older people (more than 60 years old) when not fully able.
* People younger than 21 years old with health, educational, working and family needs.

[43]Article 47(b) was then modified by Law 165/1998, which extended the types of offender eligible to home detention.
[44]There are no clear rules (apart from the prescribed law requirements relating to the length of penalty, etc.) to evaluate when the offender is not eligible for probation but can be awarded home detention. The lack of uniformity and consistency between the different territorial supervision courts in awarding alternative measures in general is also an issue of debate among Italian practitioners. Home detention is a more restrictive measure than probation under the Social Services because it considerably limits the offender's social relationships and contacts with the external world. However, the general home detention curfew (not caused by a particular state or personal condition of the offender, such as age, pregnancy, etc.) is awarded instead of probation to those offenders who did not show collaborative and constructive behaviour towards the Social Services during the risk assessment process; or to offenders who have not demonstrated a minimum critical revision of their crime that is often regarded as a key factor in granting probation (see Degl'Innocenti and Faldi 2005).

As described above, the prisoner applies to the Supervision Tribunal which, after the presentation of the case by the Supervision Judge, decides on his eligibility for the alternative measure. When granting the measure, the Tribunal fixes conditions with which the prisoner must comply and which can be modified only by the competent Supervision Judge. Unlike in some other countries, Italian prison authorities do not have the power to release prisoners or to modify the conditions of an early release measure. Those under home detention are managed by the police.

Offenders can be recalled to prison if their behaviour is incompatible with the prosecution of the measure; if they infringe the list of prescriptions imposed by the Court; if their legal status is changed; or, finally, if they leave their accommodation for a period longer than the one set up by the Court (in this case they can be charged with the criminal offence of escape (*evasione*), regulated by Art. 385 CP). As shown in Table 11.10 above, the rate of recalls for home detention is higher than probation. The most common reason for recall in the first six months of 2008, which accounted for 3.53 per cent of all recalls, was breaching home detention curfew conditions. Only 0.33 per cent of recalls were on the grounds of being charged with a new offence.

4.2.3 Anticipated release/automatic remission (liberazione anticipata)

Another form of early release is *liberazione anticipata*, or automatic remission. This measure is regulated by Art. 54 PL (and further modifications) and is a sentence reduction aimed at promoting the participation and involvement of prisoners in the resocialization process. It can be requested by any offender who is serving a custodial sentence, including a life sentence, either in prison or under home detention. Law 277/2002 has also extended this mechanism to those who are serving their sentence on probation.

Automatic remission awards a discount of 45 days for every six months of the penalty served to prisoners who have demonstrated active participation in reintegration treatment. It is a reward for the prisoner[45] and is applied automatically by the Supervision Judge, without the intervention of defence lawyers,[46] when the applicant meets the requirements laid down by the law. In particular, according to Art. 103(2) of the implementing regulation (230/2000), the general

[45]See Fiandaca (1987).
[46]The offender can always challenge the Judge's decision before the Supervision Tribunal.

parameter which ought to be met in order to obtain the six months' sentence reduction is the offender's willing 'commitment to taking advantage of the opportunities offered during the treatment programme and the maintenance of good and constructive relationships with staff, inmates, family and [when available] the external world'.

The offender's participation in an re-educational programme is usually evaluated[47] with particular reference to his diligence in following prison rules and/or in complying fully with the provisions imposed by the Supervision Judge; his behaviour and relational skills inside and outside prison (for example, if under home detention); and the progress achieved in his work or study. Due to the broad terms used by the law, the prisoner's involvement in the treatment programme is mainly verified through prison reports, the police (if the offender is under home detention) or the Social Services.[48]

In practice, an automatic remission is granted to every prisoner who behaves well and who has not committed disciplinary infractions. That is why this measure has been regarded by the Court of Cassation as a useful and effective tool to keep order in prisons.[49] According to Art. 54 PL, the discount of penalty obtained by the offender is regarded as fully served penalty in order to meet the length requirement laid down by the law to apply for parole, day release or temporary release. This means, for instance, in case of lifers, that instead of serving the required 26 years, prisoners can apply for parole after having served only 21 years. The same can be said for day release (16 years instead of 20) and temporary release (8 years instead of 10).

Each inmate has a personal dossier containing all the prison authorities' opinions and comments. The file's content is revised and updated every six months and is the main document upon which the decision on automatic remission is based. Unlike other alternative measures, after the enactment of Law 277/2002 the competence to grant the benefit (but *not* to revoke it) lies with the Supervision Judge, and not with the Tribunal. The judicial assessment is referred to each six-months period of served penalty, including any pre-trial or home detention the offender has served. As noted above, the judicial proceeding does not require the presence of the applicant and his Counsel. The Judge's pronouncement can be appealed within 10 days

[47]Corte Cost. 276/1990.
[48]See Cass. Pen., sez. I, 8 November 2007, n. 7117; Cass. pen., sez. I, 5 April 2006, n. 16748.
[49]Cass. Pen., 11 May 1995, with comment by Ianni G. (1996) *Cassazione penale*, p. 2373.

before the tribunal and, ultimately, it can be challenged before the Court of Cassation.

As prescribed by Art. 54(3) PL, the offender can be recalled to prison by the tribunal when he commits (or is convicted for) an intentional crime (*delitto non colposo*). However, after a famous ruling delivered by the Constitutional Court in 1989,[50] the recalling mechanism does not operate automatically and the automatic remission can be revoked only if the subject's general behaviour and his personality, in relation to the crime committed, appear to be incompatible with the measure's use. Finally, the offender can also be recalled after having served his penalty. In this case he should be rearrested and conducted to prison for an equivalent period to the discount of penalty already enjoyed (up to 45 days).

No statistical data are available on the number of offenders who receive the penalty discount granted by automatic remission. Nevertheless, as the former President of the Constitutional Court has pointed out,[51] the number of proceedings related to the *liberazione anticipata* is particularly high and can be estimated as thousands of applications per year, the large majority of which are successful. This situation has led to an overload of the supervision judiciary and to considerable delays (of months but also years) in the reviews of applications, with substantial infringements to the offenders' rights to a fair hearing within a reasonable time, as stated by Art. 111 Corte Cost., implementing Art. 6 of the European Convention on Human Rights. That is why there is currently an ongoing debate on the reform of automatic remission which, accordingly to the opinion of many, should be awarded automatically to all offenders and eventually revoked if offenders do not show any interest or do not take part in re-educational programmes.

5. Anomalous forms of release: day release and temporary release

The Italian penitentiary system includes two other forms of release: day release and temporary release. Unlike the other schemes already described which allow the offender to serve part (or all) of his custodial penalty outside prison, the following forms of release lead to a partial release: the inmate is permitted to leave prison for a few

[50]Corte Cost. n. 282/1989.
[51]See Onida (2005).

days or for a few hours each day. These measures have the same rationale as the other release schemes, being directed at the offender's resocialization and rehabilitation.

5.1 Day release (semilibertà)

Day release, regulated by Arts. 48–51 PL, allows the prisoner to spend part of the day outside the prison to take part in all kinds of activities (work, study, education), which may help his re-entry into mainstream society. The benefit can be granted to those who have received a sentence of up to six months' imprisonment when not placed under (or not eligible for) Social Services probation. In all other cases prisoners can be awarded day release after having served at least half (or two thirds for repeat offenders and three quarters for some serious offences)[52] of the sentence. Those who have been sentenced to life imprisonment have to have served at least 20 years before being considered for day release. The number of prisoners granted day release is significantly smaller than the number of those who are awarded probation under Social Services or a home detention curfew (see Table 11.5).

There is no fixed list of activities in which the prisoner can participate in order to benefit from *libertà controllata*. The only compulsory requirement is that these activities are aimed at reintegrating the prisoner into society. In principle, the decision on day release should follow a serious assessment on the offender's progress in his rehabilitation. In practice, though, due to the lack of staff and resources, the decision is taken simply on the basis of the prisoner's good behaviour in prison. As Art. 51 PL states, offenders are recalled to prison if they are not suitable for the programme. Prisoners who remain outside prison for more than 12 hours, without a valid justification, receive a disciplinary penalty and can be recalled to prison. If they leave for a longer period, they can be charged with the offence of escape (Art. 385 CP). (For the statistics on recalls in 2006–8, see above.)

5.2 Good behaviour licence (permessi premio)

Good behaviour licences[53] are a form of temporary release which can be granted for no more than 15 days (for a total of 45 days in a year) to foster affective, cultural or working interests. *Permessi premio*

[52]New Art. 50(a) PL, introduced by Law 251/2005.
[53]*Ibid.*, Art. 30(b).

are awarded to prisoners who are not socially dangerous and who have maintained a constant sense of responsibility and rectitude in their personal behaviour, in the activities organized by the prison and in the working or cultural activities they have taken part in. Offenders who have received a custodial sentence of up to three years; offenders who have been given a sentence of more than three years after having served at least one quarter of the sentence; serious offenders who have committed crimes listed in Art. 4(a) PL (e.g. terrorism, organized crime, sex offences, etc.) after the halfway point of their sentences (but no more than 10 years); and prisoners serving life sentences are all eligible after having served at least 10 years.

The measure is granted by the Supervision Judge and not by the Supervision Tribunal, after having heard the (not binding) opinion of the Prison Director. Prisoners can challenge the Judge's decision before the Tribunal. These licences are different from *permessi di necessitá* (necessity licenses)[54] which can be obtained by prisoners when a member of their family or their partner's life is in danger or in other serious events. The competence in the matter belongs, once again, to the Supervision Judge. The prison authorities have no power in the matter. The only requirements are the prisoner's good behaviour in prison and a positive risk assessment on social dangerousness. In line with the provision in new Art 30(c) (introduced by Law 251/2005), good behaviour licences can be awarded to repeat offenders after serving a longer penalty period.

The only official data available on the awarding of the benefit refer to 2007 (7,439 good behaviour licences awarded) and to the first six months of 2008 (6,973 awarded).[55]

5. Concluding remarks

Article 27(3) of the Italian Constitution provides that punishments must aim at re-socializing the convicted. The specific Italian Penitentiary Law 354/1975, which introduced the so-called 'alternative' measures to prison sentences, aimed at enforcing this constitutional principle of the correctional and re-educative function of the implementation of a sentence. Thus, the prison sentence imposed by the Trial Judge

[54]*Ibid.*, Art. 30.
[55]Source: http://www.giustizia.it/statistiche/statistiche_dap/det/detg00_organigramma.htm It is worth noting that the low number of good behaviour licences awarded in 2007 is, once again, a consequence of the general pardon granted by the Italian parliament in 2006.

(*giudice di cognizione*) becomes the *maximum penalty* to be served. Its length and forms of application can be adjusted to the offender's individual rehabilitation programme, at the end of a further judicial process conducted by a specialized judge.[56] The different functions and powers given to the various judicial authorities make clear the distinction between the trial phase and the later judicial proceedings devoted to the actual execution of the penalty. While the Trial Judge does not make a real assessment of the offender's criminological attitudes, the Supervision Tribunal can, as a specialized Court, obtain information on the convict's personality through the Social Services' reports, or it can order a criminological examination to assess whether the offender is likely to attain a crime-free lifestyle.[57]

With a view to re-education, the Italian legislature has developed in prisons, as well as outside, different ways to assist the prisoner's rehabilitation and to improve his chances of a successful return and, once released, reintegration into society. However, even though – unlike in some countries, such as the USA and the UK – all prisons are entirely state run, there are considerable regional variations. In particular, the wide economic gap between the north and south of Italy often affects prisoners' opportunities and conditions.

As has been stressed, the Italian prison population has increased greatly in recent years. The two main reasons for this growth are the rise in illegal immigration and the increase in the pre-trial/remand population (including those who are still awaiting sentence). Those detained as illegal immigrants find it particularly difficult to obtain an alternative measure since they find it hard to secure either stable accommodation or a lawful job, both of which are normal requirements. However, the widespread use (and abuse) of pre-trial custody is one of the causes of prison overcrowding. This is closely linked to the legal status of Italian prisoners. The sentence imposed by the first-instance Judge is not immediately effective as the convict has the right to challenge the decision before the Court of Appeal or the Court of Cassation. The penalty becomes effective (and must be promptly executed) only when the definitive sentence is confirmed. The excessive duration of ordinary proceedings in the

---

[56]See Della Casa (2002).

[57]Article 220 CPP states that, apart from what is provided in relation to the finalities of the execution of the penalty or the security measure, criminological evaluations to determine if the defendant is a habitual or professional offender or to investigate the defendant's character, personality, and in general, any psychological characteristics not related to pathological causes, are not admissible.

Italian criminal justice system[58] must also be taken into account when considering the vast numbers held in custody pending trial. In order to tackle the urgent problem of overcrowding, at the end of July 2006 the former left-wing government enacted Law 241 which granted a general pardon (*indulto*) and remitted the penalty of all offenders[59] who had received a prison sentence of less than three years for one or more offences committed before 2 May 2006. The pardon applied not only to offenders who were serving a definitive sentence but also to defendants who had been convicted by a first-instance Court or an Appeal Judge for offences perpetrated before 2 May 2006 whose penalty had not yet been executed.

The immediate effect of the *indulto* has been a significant reduction in the number of prisoners serving a final custodial sentence: from 38,193 out of 61,264 prisoners in June 2006, to 17,042 out of 43,957 prisoners in June 2007. However, considering that the certified normal accommodation capacity of Italian prisons is only 43,177 units, it is clear that the emergency is not yet over. Moreover, since 2007 the number of prisoners has shot up largely due to the recall of those who have committed further offences after having been granted pardon.[60] According to data released by the Ministry of Justice on 31 March 2009, 61,057 prisoners were detained in the country's prisons. The 2006 general pardon offered only a short-term solution to the problem of overcrowding, without providing a stable legal framework able to address the question of the effective rehabilitation of the released prisoner. This is mainly because pardon is a general

[58]Italy has repeatedly been found in breach of Art. 6 of the European Convention on Human Rights for the excessive length of criminal proceedings. Between mid-October and mid-November 2008, for example, 13 rulings were pronounced against Italy (ECrHR, 14 October, *Belperio* v. *Italy*; ECrHR, 14 October, *Abate* v. *Italy*; ECrHR, 14 October, *D'Alessio* v. *Italy*; ECrHR, 15 October, *Di Brita* v. *Italy*; ECrHR, 21 October, *Faella* v. *Italy*; ECrHR, 21 October, *Iannotta* v. *Italy*; ECrHR, 13 November, *Di Vico* v. *Italy*; ECrHR, 13 November, *Fontana* v. *Italy*; ECrHR, 13 November, *La Frazia* v. *Italy*; ECrHR, 13 November, *Di Maria* v. *Italy*; ECrHR, 13 November, *Rubortone* v. *Italy*; ECrHR, 13 November, *Buffolino* v. *Italy*; ECrHR, 13 November, *Morone* v. *Italy*.
[59]Article 2 of Law 241/2006 lists the offences excluded from pardon (among which are terrorism, organized crime, the trafficking of human beings and child pornography).
[60]Pardon is revoked if offenders commit an intentional crime (and receive a custodial penalty of no less than two years) within five years from the enactment of the law (Art. 3 of Law 241/2006).

and generalized measure and, unlike other forms of release, it does not entail a personalized risk assessment of the offender.

Since the maximum penalty of up to three years to which the pardon applied was the same as that applicable for the main alternative measure (probation under Social Services), those prisoners who left prison having been pardoned might in many cases have been given an alternative measure. That option, though, was not chosen because of the partial inability of the system of early release measures to achieve the desired results. This was largely because it was more complex and related to an evaluation of the individual offender. Although some early release schemes seem to work, as the low rate of repeat offenders among those who had been awarded probation under Social Services would seem to show,[61] the ineffectiveness of the early release measures is indicated by the continuous rise in the number of prison entries every year. Even if the phenomenon of immigration (legal and illegal) represents one of the main reasons for the excessive number of prisoners, it can be said that, since 1975, the progressive extension of types of early release (and of their possible users) has often been aimed merely at a reduction in the prison population rather than at accomplishing the more difficult goal of a true social reintegration of sentenced persons.[62]

The Italian government's policy is clearly evident if one observes that the widening of benefits has not been followed by a proper allocation of financial and human resources directed to prisoner resocialization. Besides, non-judicial actors (such as psychologists or social workers) and administrative bodies (such as the police or prison authorities), despite often having a better understanding of the prisoner's condition, play a very limited role in the awarding of early release. Moreover, the lack of clear rules on the application of releases has produced very diverse judicial practices and has generated uncertainty among offenders and practitioners. It is, indeed, difficult to foresee what the immediate future of early release will be in Italy. One can only hope that the new law – if and when it is approved – will be able to achieve a more satisfactory balance between the complementary principles of certainty and flexibility of the penalty and, ultimately, between offenders' social recovery and society's safety.

[61]See section 3.
[62]See Della Casa (2002).

References

Bandini, T. (2004) *Criminologia. Il contributo della ricerca alla conoscenza del crimine e della reazione sociale. Vol. II.* Milan: Giuffrè Press.

Bishop, N. and Schneider, U. (2001) 'Improving the implementation of the European Rules on Community Sanctions and Measures: introduction to a new Council of Europe Recommendation', *European Journal of Crime, Criminal Law and Criminal Justice*, 9(3): 180–192.

Bortolotto, T. (2002) *L'educatore penitenziario. Compiti, competenze e iter formativo. Proposta per un'innovazione.* Milan: Franco Angeli Press.

Bricola, F. (1977) *Le misure alternative alla pena nel quadro di una 'nuova' politica criminale, in Pene e misure alternative nell'attuale momento storico.* Milan: Giuffrè Press.

Canepa, M. and Merlo, S. (2004) *Manuale di diritto penitenziario.* Milan: Giuffrè Press.

Cesaris, L. (2001) 'Dal *panopticon* alla sorveglianza elettronica', in M. Bargis (ed.) *Il decreto 'antiscarcerazioni'.* Turin: Utet Press.

Degl' Innocenti, L. and Faldi, F. (2005) *Misure alternative alla detenzione e procedimento di sorveglianza.* Milan: Milan Press.

Della Casa, F. (2001) 'Misure alternative ed effettività della pena tra realtà e prospettive', *Giustizia penale*, (2): 75.

Della Casa, F. (2002) 'La crisi d'identità della misure alternative tra sbandamenti legislativi, esperimenti di "diritto pretorio" e irrisolte carenze organizzative', *Cassazione penale*, 1: 3278.

Deriu, A. and Morgante, L. (2008) 'Le misure alternative e il trattamento rieducativo nelle nuove proposte di riforma dell'ordinamento penitenziario', *Rivista penitenziaria e criminologica*, 1: 119.

Dolcini, E. (2001) 'Riforma della parte generale del codice e rifondazione del sistema sanzionatorio penale', *Rivista italiana di diritto e procedura penale*, (3): 835.

D'Onofrio M. and Sartori, M. (2004) *Le misure alternative alla detenzione.* Milan: Giuffrè Press.

Fassone, E. (1987) *La riforma penitenziaria.* Naples: Jovene Press.

Favara, F. (2002) *Relazione sull'amministrazione della giustizia nell'anno 2001* (available online at www.giustizia.it/studierapporti2002).

Fiandaca, G. (1987) 'Commento all'art. 18 L. 10 ottobre 1986 n. 663', *Legislazione penale*, 203.

Filippi, L. and Spangher, G. (2003) *Manuale di esecuzione penitenziaria.* Milan: Giuffrè Press.

Fiorentin, F. and Marcheselli, A. (2005) *L'ordinamento penitenziario.* Turin: Utet Press.

Fiorentin, F. and Sandrelli, G.G. (2007) *L'esecuzione dei provvedimenti giurisdizionali.* Padova: Cedam Press.

Frudà, L. (2006) *Alternative al carcere. Percorsi, attori e reti sociali nell'esecuzione penale esterna: un approfondimento della ricerca applicata*. Milan: Franco Angeli Press.

Gaito, A. and Ranaldi G. (2005) *Esecuzione penale*. Milan: Giuffrè Press.

Giambruno, S. (2001) *Lineamenti di diritto dell'esecuzione penale*. Milan: Giuffrè Press.

Giostra, G. (1983) *Il procedimento di sorveglianza nel sistema processuale penale*. Milan: Giuffrè Press.

Giuffrida, M.P. (1999) *I centri di servizio sociale dell'amministrazione penitenziaria. Operatori e competenze nel contesto dell'esecuzione della pena*. Rome: Laurus Robuffo Press.

Grevi, V. (1994) *L'ordinamento penitenziario tra riforme ed emergenza*. Padova: Cedam Press.

Klein, A.R. (1997) *Alternative Sentencing, Intermediate Sanctions and Probation*. Cincinnati, OH: Anderson Publishing.

Leonardi, F. (2007) 'Le misure alternative alla detenzione tra reinserimento sociale e abbattimento della recidiva', *Rassegna penitenziaria e criminologica*, 2: 7.

Maccora, E. (2001) 'L'esecuzione: ovvero la certezza della pena?', *Questione giustizia*, 1187.

Margara, A. (1995) 'L'evoluzione della normativa e la situazione penitenziaria dopo la riforma del 1986', *Quaderni del CSM*, 8: 94.

Marinucci, G. (1991) 'Politica criminale e riforma del diritto penale', in Marinucci-Dolcini (ed.) *Studi di diritto penale*. Milan: Giuffrè Press.

McGuire, J. (1995) *What Works: Reducing Reoffending*. Chichester: Wiley.

Morris, M. and Tonry, N. (1990) *Between Prison and Probation*. New York: Oxford University Press.

Mosconi, G. (2002) 'La crisi postmoderna del diritto penale e i suoi effetti sull'istituzione penitenziaria', in U. Curi and G. Palombarini (eds) *Diritto penale minimo*. Rome: Rome Press.

Neppi Modona, G. (1976) 'Appunti per una storia parlamentare della riforma penitenziaria', *Questione criminale*, (2/3): 322.

Niro, M. (2008) 'Misure alternative tra deflazione carceraria e revisione del sistema sanzionatorio penale', *Rassegna penitenziaria e criminologica*, 1: 113–7.

Onida, V. (2005) 'Sulle procedure relative alla liberazione anticipata (art. 54 dell'ordinamento penitenziario)', *ATRID-Rassegna*, 14 (available online at http://www.astrid-online.it/rassegna/Rassegna-2/15-09-2005/ONIDA-Liberazione-anticipata-08_08_0.pdf).

Petersilia, J. (2001) 'When prisoners return to communities: political, economic and social consequences', *Federal Probation*, 3.

Stella, F. (1999) 'Something works: realtà e prospettive del principio di rieducazione del condannato', *Indice penale*, 141.

Travis, J. (2000) 'But they all come back: rethinking prisoner reentry', in *Research in Brief – Sentencing and Corrections, Issues for the 21st Century*. Washington, DC: US Department of Justice, National Institute of Justice.

Tuttini Vita, R. (2005) 'Riflessioni sul future dell'esecuzione penale', *Rassegna penitenziaria e criminologica*, (2): 55–67.

Vitello, F. and Stefanizzi, S. (1996) 'Genere e criminalità: alcune considerazioni sui dati delle statistiche giudiziarie italiane', in L. De Cataldo Neuburger (ed.) *La criminalità femminile tra stereotipi e malintese realtà*. Padova: Cedam Press.

Chapter 12

The Netherlands

Martin Moerings

Summary

In 2008 conditional release was reintroduced in the Netherlands. The aim of conditional release is to reduce repeat offending by stipulating general and specific conditions for the probation period and, ultimately, to make society safer. This has not been consistently expressed in the new arrangement of the law. Granting early release is not only a matter of looking forward but it is also a matter of looking back: how did someone behave in prison?

By making conditional release the key to a safer society, the Justice Department is creating a dilemma for itself: early release can be granted to reduce repeat offending via interventions but early release can also be denied to reduce repeat offending. Risk assessment is an essential part of the early release decision-making process, but this is done by people, and people sometimes make mistakes. How this will be addressed depends on the image of society in the decision-makers' minds.

1. Returning to society

The Dutch Criminal Code, enacted in 1886 and still in use today, first introduced the system of early conditional release. After serving two thirds of their sentences, prisoners could be released under certain conditions. In the beginning, early release was granted at the discretion of the Minister of Justice. During a period of probation, the prisoners who had been released early would have to act in accordance with certain conditions. Initially, this conditional release was granted only sporadically. As a result, in part, of the policy of the Penal Law Chamber at the Court of Appeal in Arnhem, to which prisoners could appeal if they were refused early release by the Minister of Justice, in the course of the twentieth century early release was granted more and more frequently (Vegter 2005: 515–25). This Chamber felt that, since prisoners were going to return to society at some point in the future anyway, there was all the more reason to be lenient in its decisions. This did not fail to affect the Minister of Justice's policy, who could not have been happy at constantly being second guessed.

Granting early release became more and more automatic, and prisoners gradually came to view it as something to which they had a right. This had an effect in turn on the legislation passed exactly a century later. Only in very exceptional cases could early release now be denied; for example, if a prisoner misbehaved seriously or attempted to escape from prison. No further conditions were stipulated for early release, so conditional release could not be denied. The terminology was altered accordingly and conditional early release became early release without further conditions.

In the mid-1980s, what was viewed as the obvious logic of this change disappeared almost as rapidly as it had emerged. By 1994 a bill had been proposed to eliminate the automatic granting of early release. Instead, a prisoner's early release was to depend on his conduct while incarcerated. Good conduct should be rewarded by granting early release and misconduct punished by not doing so. This proposed bill disappeared from view but without resolving the social and political debate. On the contrary. The public at large found it hard to accept that, for example, a prison sentence of 15 years meant the prisoner would be released after only ten years. And people wondered whether the judge passing the sentence was not already anticipating that early release would be automatically granted so that, basically, the whole arrangement was a bit of a sham. The fact that approximately 70 per cent of ex-prisoners later became repeat offenders was another point in the debate, which was certainly no less important. At a time when thinking was so adamantly focused on safety, this was an unbearable idea. The longer prisoners were kept in prison, the longer society would be protected from them. When prisoners were released, there should be some way to keep them under control by attaching certain conditions to their release.

The Dutch Parliament also perceived it as problematic that, once early release had been granted, it could not be rescinded.[1]

2. Conditional release: looking forward

The upshot of this discussion is clear from the early release arrangement that came into force on 1 July 2008: prisoners should be eligible for conditional release after serving two thirds of their sentence. The term 'early release' was replaced once again by 'conditional early release', with the crucial assumption that repeat offending would be reduced by a return to society under certain conditions and that this would ultimately serve the safety of society.

In the proposal formulated in the mid-1990s, early release was still viewed as a reward for good behaviour. In other words, it was retrospective, whereas in the new legislation the focus is more on the future. The aim of the probation period is to contribute towards a life without crime (for example, through all kinds of interventions). This is clearly a different perspective. Prisoners are eligible for early release after serving two thirds of their sentence of at least one year unless society's safety would be better served by having them complete the sentence in prison, since early release does entail a sizeable risk of

[1]This chapter does not consider another form of early release – the pardon. Being pardoned is possible for all the prisoners in the Netherlands. This means the government may intervene in the consequences of an irrevocable conviction to reduce the sentence, discontinue it or commute a life sentence to a fixed-term sentence. There is also the possibility of granting a conditional pardon. Currently, a pardon is the only way in which a sentence of life imprisonment can be converted into a fixed-term sentence. In recent decades a pardon has only once been granted to a prisoner serving a life sentence. The very limited possibilities for a lifer to be pardoned are much debated in some juridical circles in the Netherlands, which it is one of the few countries in Europe that does not permit a periodic review of life sentences by an independent board. The Council for the Application of the Criminal Law and Child Protection has recommended the introduction of a periodic review after 15 years to evaluate what risk there is of a lifer committing further offences. The consequence of this review could be that a prisoner is transferred to another, less protected, regime or the sentence could 'set in years' instead of life. However, the State Secretary of Justice, supported by rulings of the Dutch Supreme Court, does not regard the introduction of a periodic review as a necessity because of the possibility prisoners have of requesting a pardon.

something going wrong during the probation period. This can be a reason to postpone early release or to deny it altogether. If there is a sizeable risk of repeat offending and prisoners do not take part in programmes to reduce this risk while incarcerated, the decision can be made not to release them conditionally, or to do so only at a later stage. This also holds true if a prisoner is unwilling to adhere to the conditions. Conditional release can also be postponed or denied if a prisoner seriously misbehaves or does so repeatedly, or commits a criminal act while incarcerated. If a prisoner who would otherwise be a prospect for early release has made an attempt to escape from prison or has escaped, conditional release can also be postponed or denied. These are the criteria that were also valid in the old arrangement and that refer back to the prisoner's behaviour while incarcerated, but that were rarely applied.

From now on, anyone sentenced to more than one year in prison or anyone serving a number of short consecutive sentences that total at least one year can be released only under certain conditions. This means a probation period is also stipulated. Persons who are released early and who violate the conditions of early release during the probationary period will have to serve the rest of the sentence or part of it.

Under the old law, if a person who had already been released committed another crime, the release could not be denied. Making the release conditional means that it is now the offenders who are released early who themselves are responsible for their own future. This is why fewer persons who are released early are now expected to commit another crime after they are released. The aim is to make a contribution towards society's safety. Making early release conditional is one of the numerous measures the Cabinet has taken to reduce repeat offending. An individual approach is of central importance.

3. General and specific conditions

Whenever prisoners are released early, there is always the general condition that they must not commit another offence during the probation period. The probation period starts the day they leave prison and is precisely as long as the remainder of the sentence, with a minimum duration of one year. For the rest, the Public Prosecutor can stipulate specific conditions that require participation in programmes and restrictions on certain forms of conduct. This is stipulated by law (s. 15a of the Criminal Code) in these general terms;

the conditions are not formulated in detail. This gives a great deal of freedom to the Public Prosecutor, who arrives at a decision based on the recommendations made by the prison and probation authorities. But this has not satisfied the legislature. From the perspective of legal certainty for the prisoner, and to give the Public Prosecutor and the Adult Probation and Early Release Department (who not only make recommendations but also supervise the probation arrangements) more guidance, the specific conditions will soon be stipulated by law. Since the conditions referred to above can already be enforced on the basis of the existing legislation, in itself the list of conditions is not very innovative. It is more of a codification of the conditions to be enforced by the Public Prosecutor or the Court.

The conditions can entail various kinds of restrictions – for example, refraining from association with certain individuals or organizations or from being in the vicinity of a certain location. The person who is granted early release can also be required to report to a certain place at a certain time, to report to a certain agency, to abstain from alcohol or drugs and to take blood or urine tests in order to monitor whether these requirements are being adhered to.

The conditions that influence behaviour can also be stipulated. The person who is released early can be required to register at a certain care facility and to receive intramural or extramural treatment, to take part in a behavioural intervention programme or to live in a supervised residential facility or shelter.

Lastly, there is a safety-net stipulation that subjects prisoners who are released early to other conditions in respect of their behaviour. I feel this is inherently positive since it creates an opportunity to adjust the conditions as much as possible to the individual in question. What is more, it makes it possible to experiment with new developments and forms of interventions. There is a probation period for all these specific conditions but, unlike the case with the general condition, they can never be imposed for longer than the rest of the sentence's duration. The prisoner who is released early has to state his willingness to adhere to the conditions; otherwise he will forfeit an early release. The stipulation of the specific conditions cannot be appealed. Another specific condition, which is important for foreign prisoners, is discussed in section 5 below.

The formulation of the conditions in the legislation is in keeping with the trend towards consistency in the legal system. Specific conditions related to suspended sentences are also included in the legislation. As a result of the unique nature of conditional release (where the conditions are part-and-parcel of a supervised return to society), the conditions only partially coincide with those of the suspended sentence. In the case of the suspended sentence, which is in itself an alternative to imprisonment, the conditions are linked far more closely to the notion of punishment. Specific conditions (for example, paying damages, financial restitution and transferring an amount of money to a damages fund) are more appropriate to the suspended sentence than to conditional release. However, as a result of the safety-net stipulation, it is possible to impose conditions such as these on prisoners who are released early, if only because European legislation on the international enforcement of penal sentences can require the Netherlands to collect damages charged by other countries from prisoners who are released early in the Netherlands.

4. Granting early release: the jurisdiction of the Public Prosecutor and the Court

In the first instance, a decision to grant early release is within the jurisdiction of the Public Prosecutor. The Public Prosecutor is advised in this connection by the Adult Probation and Early Release Department and by the prison authorities, who use risk assessment scales to estimate the chances of repeat offending. If the Public Prosecutor's decision is affirmative, this also determines whether, in addition to the automatically enforced general obligation not to commit a repeat offence during the probation period, specific conditions are to be linked to the conditional release. The Public Prosecutor can also be of the opinion that early release should be postponed or denied. The Public Prosecutor does not make this decision themselves; they issue a request for the Court's opinion. If a prisoner is conditionally released and does not adhere to the stipulated conditions during the probation period, this will call for a rapid response. Depending on the severity of the infringement, early release can be terminated, the specific conditions can be altered or, if it is only a very slight infringement, a warning will suffice. This decision is also within the mandate of the Court.

The police and probation authorities play an important role in overseeing adherence to the conditions. It is the Probation Officer who monitors the prisoner and supervises adherence to the conditions. Supervision consists of activities that help motivate the prisoner to meet the specific conditions. Monitoring consists of regular personal contact with the prisoner and with key people and institutions in his surroundings (for example, the school, his employer or the mental healthcare facility where treatment is given). If necessary, the prisoner is kept under electronic supervision. If the Probation Officer observes that such a person is not adhering to the stipulated conditions, they report this to the Public Prosecutor.

The police pay particular attention to whether a suspect apprehended for a punishable act is a prisoner who has been released early. If this is the case, the prisoner has violated the general condition and the conditional release can be rescinded.

5. Foreign prisoners and the early release system

In principle, foreign prisoners are eligible for early release but, unlike Dutch national prisoners, there are specific conditions linked to their release that can or cannot be enforced. In this connection, distinctions should be drawn between various categories of foreign prisoners.

First are foreign prisoners who have been categorized by the Minister of Alien Affairs or, if they have appealed their case, by the Administrative Court as 'undesirable aliens'. These prisoners are unlawful residents of the Netherlands who have repeatedly committed punishable acts or lawful residents of the Netherlands who have been convicted of an offence punishable by a sentence of three or more years (s. 67 of the Aliens Act). Following their conditional release, they are to leave the country of their own volition or, otherwise, to be deported. Since they have to leave the country, no specific conditions are linked to their release.

If an undesirable alien nonetheless remains in the Netherlands, these are grounds to rescind the conditional release. For this category of foreign prisoners, remaining in the Netherlands is a punishable act (s. 197 of the Criminal Code). By committing this punishable act, they violate the general condition that pertains to every person who is released early – that is, not to commit any punishable act in the probation period. It should be noted that, as such, the executive order declaring a person an undesirable alien is not a decision of the Public Prosecutor or the Criminal Court.

The second category of foreign prisoners are those who cannot be classified as undesirable aliens (for example, because the offence they have been convicted of is not serious enough). The Minister of Alien Affairs or the Administrative Court has, however, decided that they are illegal aliens and that they should leave the Netherlands. If they are granted early release, the Public Prosecutor or the Criminal Court can incorporate this decision into a specific condition. Since they have to leave the country, this is the only specific condition to which they are subject. This decision thus derives from the one made by the Minister or the Administrative Court. It is not the mandate of the Public Prosecutor or the Criminal Court to make a decision about a foreign prisoner's right to remain in the country. In the first instance, this is the responsibility of the Minister of Alien Affairs and, after an appeal, of the Administrative Court. If either decides not to allow the prisoner to remain in the Netherlands, and the Public Prosecutor then translates this decision into a specific condition, then early release is rescinded if it is violated.

In such cases early release is rescinded because the prisoner has violated the specific condition and not because he has committed a punishable act, as has, for example, an undesirable alien who has remained in the Netherlands and thus violated the general condition. The undesirable alien can be punished twice (that is, he can been convicted for the punishable act cited in s. 197) and has to serve the suspended part of the sentence from which he had been conditionally released.

Lastly, there are those foreign prisoners who do not lose their existing rights to reside in the Netherlands when they are granted early release and can thus remain in the country. Such prisoners are eligible for the same specific conditions as Dutch national prisoners.

It appears as if an effort has been made to find an instrument to compel the first two categories of foreign prisoners to leave the country. Should the options offered by the Aliens Act not suffice, the authorities turn to the criminal law. The obligations cited by the Aliens Act are sanctioned in the criminal law system via the conditional modality (Council for the Application of Criminal Law and the Protection of Juveniles 2009).

6. Transitional law

The new legislation on conditional release makes provision for a transitional period of five years. For people convicted before 1 July 2008, the old early release regulation will continue to be valid for the next five years. After 1 July 2013, the new conditional release regulation will be valid in all cases. Convictions dating back to before 1 July 2008 but still in effect on 1 July 2013 are thus subject to the new regulation. This means there is in effect a retrospective extension of punishment for those serving lengthy sentences. In the summer of

2009, the first conditional releases were granted according to the new regulation so that, at the moment, no information is as yet available in this regard.

7. Critical comments

7.1 Looking forward by looking back

When conditional release is granted, the focus is on the future. This is an important point of departure in the new early release legislation. On closer examination, though, this is not quite as unambiguous as it would seem.

In addition to cases where there is a sizeable chance of repeat offending, early release can also be denied in a number of other instances. The reason for so doing may go back to some past event, such as a serious infringement during imprisonment. It may also relate to a conviction for a new offence or to repeated acts of misconduct in prison leading to disciplinary measures. It may similarly relate to a fight with fellow prisoners, drug use or to a successful or unsuccessful attempt to escape. It would seem as if a predictive value is thus attributed to negative acts during incarceration – in other words in the past, if one takes the early release system's central point of departure into consideration.

This is all the more striking because the notion of rewarding good conduct with an earlier release has been whole-heartedly abandoned since it has no predictive significance. Just as it may be the cleverest, seemingly most well-adjusted prisoners who manage to evade the law after their release, it may also be the more troublesome prisoners who resist because of their dissatisfaction with the penitentiary system but who manage to adjust well once they have returned to society. There is very little empirical research to support either of these suppositions. It is striking in any case that counter-indications for early release are linked to conduct during incarceration without their predictive value having been demonstrated. What is more, this is conduct prisoners have already been punished for in prison. Denying early release in these cases is viewed as double punishment, certainly by the prisoners themselves. And rightly so. I cannot help but feel that, in these counter-indications, the legislation has been influenced in part by the popular belief that a prisoner who does not behave properly should not go home early: as many people say, 'They are already pampered too much while they are inside.' These considerations are not mentioned in the Explanatory Memorandum.

In the end, however, troublesome prisoners are also released and without any effort being made to reduce their risk of repeat offending through targeted interventions. Does this serve the interests of a safe society?

7.2. Risk of repeat offending: the authorities' dilemma

The aim of the early release system is to enhance safety in society by addressing the risk of repeat offending in the probation period through targeted interventions. A drug addict needs supervision if they are to kick the habit that led them to become a thief or a burglar. The same can hold true for alcoholics. What is more, in the prison population addiction is often accompanied by psychological problems (co-morbidity) so that mental health care is called for.

At the same time, apart from the question of whether misconduct during imprisonment is a reason to deny early release, a strong risk of repeat offending can be a reason so to do. In practice, this leads in turn to a significant dilemma, in which political viewpoints play an important role, even though the point of departure for the new arrangement is grant early release unless... And then what risks are still acceptable and what risks are not? These are policy decisions shaped by safety-thinking in a risk society.

The dilemma seems to be, therefore, when to take a risk and to grant a prisoner early release, imposing binding interventions and stipulating strict supervision by the Adult Probation and Early Release Department. After all, if the conditions are not adhered to, the remaining part of the prison sentence can still be put into effect. The dilemma continues: when should the Public Prosecutor refrain from releasing a prisoner under supervision?

7.3. Risk assessment: a helpful tool and a pitfall when granting early release[2]

The Adult Probation Department will play an important role in resolving this dilemma. It will make recommendations to the Public Prosecutor based on Repeat Offending Assessment Scales scores. In the Netherlands, these scales have been the primary diagnostic tool for some years to help the Adult Probation Department assess the risk of repeat offending.

[2]See also Moerings (2003).

Risk assessment already plays an important role in the present-day administration of justice when deciding whether pre-trial incarceration should be terminated and in enforcing sanctions as regards the length of the sentence as well as the type of sanction. This is particularly the case where incarceration under a hospital order is involved. The hospital order is a penal measure that can be issued for perpetrators who were suffering from a psychological disorder at the time of committing a serious offence or who have retarded mental development. Lastly, risk assessments are used in the framework of sanction enforcement (for example, in decisions on granting early release).

The Repeat Offending Assessment Scales (which are closely related to ones used elsewhere – for example, OASys and OGRS in the UK) estimate the risk an individual presents on the basis of certain static or dynamic factors. Since they are fixed, static factors (not to be confused with statistical factors) are also referred to as historical factors. Examples include the perpetrator's age when he committed the most recent offence and the first one, a lack of adjustment at a young age, a prior history of drug use or repeat offending, the perpetrator's sex and his country of origin (ethnic background). It is these last few factors in particular that are good predictors, although they do not provide any opportunities for interventions to influence future behaviour. By definition, they are fixed.

The dynamic risk factors can, however, be influenced. These can be divided into environmental and clinical factors. Environmental factors include, for example, little or no support from the social network, drug addiction or a poor educational level. Examples of clinical factors include an inability to control impulses, rage and hostility, or a negative attitude to treatment.

The Repeat Offending Assessment Scales are a diagnostic tool for the early release officer. The Adult Probation Department incorporates the answers to questions on the scales into the report it draws up that leads to recommendations on granting parole and to the formulation of a plan of approach. This is not a mechanical process, as Antoine Mooy has emphasized on many occasions as regards reports on suspects' accountability and the decision whether or not to issue a hospital order. But his observations are similarly valid as regards the reports by the Adult Probation Department on whether or not early release should be granted. As Mooy (2004: 209) notes:

A certain kind of offence has a certain chance of being repeated, just as an individual's ethnic background, educational level and prior offences imply a statistical chance of a certain type of behaviour being repeated. Probability calculations on this kind of chance cannot however replace the required risk assessment. Firstly, a statement on the individual as a member of one or more classes still does not justify a statement about this concrete individual (see also Koenraadt and Mooy 2007: 176).

Repeat Offending Assessment Scales are widely used and the Justice Department has high expectations of them, but their value has yet to be demonstrated. It is frankly acknowledged that research is called for into the predictive value (validity) of these instruments. Do the scales really measure the chance of repeat offending? Probation officers have the impression that, in the case of a number of specific target groups, the scales lead to a lower estimate of the risk of repeat offending than they feel is plausible in actual practice (van der Knaap *et al.* 2007). The more dangerous the behaviour, the harder it is to predict. Reoffending by a paedophile who has molested a young child is far more difficult to predict than that of a drug-addicted repeat offender who breaks into cars.

Even if the scales are further refined and their validity is improved, predicting is accompanied – by definition – by uncertainties and errors. In sentencing on the basis of risk assessment, two types of errors can be made. Offenders who are assessed as presenting a low risk of reoffending can nonetheless, commit another offence. These are the false negatives. Offenders are also released who then prove to be a danger to society.

The opposite kind of errors can also be made. Offenders can be wrongly assessed as presenting a danger. After all, not everyone who took part in criminal behaviour in the past is going to do so again. These are the false positives.

Regardless of the assessment results, it is the Public Prosecutor or the Judge who decides what to do with the information. They deal with the chance of false positives in various ways. They can do so, for example, by concentrating on the severity of the offence. The more serious the offence, the more likely they will be to keep the prisoner incarcerated. The more safety-oriented a society, the less acceptable the risks inherent in granting early release. The degree to which a society is safety-oriented has nothing to do with the scores on a measuring instrument, but it does depend on the willingness of the early release system and the Court to meet society's demands for greater safety.

There are no empirical scientific research results to demonstrate the consequences of early release: personal convictions, the desire to alleviate a sense that society is not safe or an acknowledgement of the significance of this lack of safety can all play a decisive role.

Another danger with this type of risk assessment has more to do with legal ethics. Instruments such as the Repeat Offending Assessment Scales show that certain features greatly increase the chances of repeat offending. Because of this strong predictive aspect, these features can be a reason to hold certain prisoners in prison for longer.

It is a fact that, in combination with several other factors (for example, prior repeat offending and addiction), being a member of an ethnic minority is a strong indicator of future criminal behaviour (Netherlands Criminology Association study afternoon, 17 November 2006). Purely on the basis of this statistical correlation, it is tempting to take ethnic background into account as a risk factor when granting early release in court. As a historical, unchanging factor, ethnic background is incorporated into risk predictions even though it is not an explanatory factor. The fact that suspects are of Moroccan descent does not mean they are going to commit a criminal offence, but it can help to explain why they have a poor educational level, are torn between two cultures or seem to be outside the Dutch social control system. It is these aspects, and not necessarily ethnic background in itself, that can be a cause of future danger.

7.4. Starting inside

The probation period should be used to stimulate changes in individuals' personal and social lives. It is not wise to wait until they are out of prison – important steps need to be taken while they are still in prison. During their incarceration, prisoners should also be prepared for their return to society (s. 2 of the Penitentiary Principles Act).

In recent years, however, there have been sharp budget cuts in the prison system. These cuts were not inspired as much by the recession as by a no-nonsense policy focused on keeping people locked up to ensure society's safety. In addition to the introduction of two prisoners to a cell, there is now a streamlined daily programme – in other words, a reduced number of hours prisoners can spend out of their cells. In a regime of total communality, where prisoners spend their days in common rooms and communal work premises, the minimum daily programme has been reduced from 78 to 59 hours a week. There is now only a minimum of 18 rather than the former 48 hours of activities and visiting hours. For partial communality, where prisoners are given the opportunity to take part in communal activities, the minimum duration of the daily programme is no longer stipulated and only a minimum of 18 hours of activities is offered. For the prisoners, this means they can be outside their cells only from 8.00 am to 5.00 pm, and the evening programme has been discontinued at all the prisons. This is certainly not a regime seriously equipped to prepare prisoners for a return to society.

A new trend, however, seems to be in the offing. If the intentions that the Minister and State Secretary of Justice recently announced to the Lower Chamber of the Dutch Parliament are put into effect, we are heading in a new direction (Letter to the Lower Chamber of Parliament 29 August 2008). A prisoner's return to society requires continuity – life before, during and after imprisonment is a continuum. There has to be one basic approach for all prisoners, with attention devoted to housing, income, care and identity papers. The risk of repeat offending has a great deal to do with how people cope with these primary areas of life. A prisoner's transition from a long prison sentence to freedom – and, in principle, this is the category of prisoner eligible for early release – needs to be gradual and monitored carefully. For such people, a basic approach will not suffice. They need an individual approach. This holds especially true in the case of prisoners with a psychological disorder, addiction or mental disability, either separately or in combination.

At the moment, there are more than 40 different types of prison. There are maximum-security, normal, semi-open and open prisons, and within these there are the different regimes, ranging from total or limited communality to individual confinement. In addition, there are numerous facilities or wards that provide special care for prisoners with psychological or addiction-related problems.

This diversity will be reduced to facilities for six target groups: prisoners in pre-trial detention; prisoners serving short sentences or sentence remainders of up to four months; prisoners serving long sentences; special groups with extra care or management needs, such as prisoners with psychological disorders; foreign prisoners; and women. In addition to standard activities such as getting a breath of fresh air, engaging in sports, recreation and visits, every prisoner is to be given an opportunity to work. Prisoners with long sentences are eligible for vocational training or primary school courses, such as a literacy scheme. On the basis of screening (for example, using the Repeat Offending Assessment Scales), interventions in keeping with their individual criminogenic shortcomings will be offered to prisoners serving long prison sentences. Most of the plan should be put into effect in the course of 2010, or so politicians state in a very different tone from the one their predecessors used in recent years.

On paper, there seems to be a serious intention to launch the reintegration process during the period of imprisonment, certainly for future early-release prisoners. For the time being, we will have to wait to see whether financial limitations will allow these ambitions to be put into effect.

7.5 Challenge for the early release system

The introduction of conditional release is a new challenge for the Adult Probation Department. In recent years, its responsibilities have been increasingly reduced to writing informative reports, implementing the Repeat Offending Assessment Scales and monitoring how public service sentences are carried out. The options for actual assistance, which had been the trademark of the early release system for decades, were increasingly restricted by the obligation to produce – which was then how the system was judged. With the launching of the new conditional release, there will hopefully once again be more of an opportunity for Probation Officers to motivate ex-prisoners and to counsel them on their return to society.

8. Conclusion

It is a good thing conditional release has been reintroduced. However, the aim of conditional release – which is to reduce repeat offending by stipulating general and specific conditions and, ultimately, to make society safer – has not been consistently expressed in the new arrangement. Granting early release is not only a matter of looking ahead but is also a matter of looking back.

By making conditional release the key to a safer society, the Justice Department is creating a dilemma for itself. Early release can be granted to reduce repeat offending through interventions, and early release can also be denied to reduce repeat offending. Risk assessment, which is such an essential part of the early release decision-making process, is done by people, and people sometimes make mistakes. How this will be addressed depends on the image of society of the decision-makers have in their minds.

References

Brief aan de Tweede Kamer (2008) Maatregelen recidivereductie: nadruk op nazorg (29 augustus) (Letter to the Lower Chamber of Parliament, 'Measure to reduce repeat offending: emphasis on after-care', 29 August 2008).
Brief aan de Tweede Kamer (2008) Modernisering Gevangeniswezen (9 december) (Letter to the Lower Chamber of Parliament, 'Modernization of the prison system', 9 December 2008).
Koenraadt, F. and Mooy, A. (2007) 'Mentally ill offenders', in M. Boone and M. Moerings (eds) *Dutch Prisons*. The Hague: Boom Legal Publishers.
Moerings, M. (2003) 'Straffen met het oog op veiligheid; een onderneming vol risico's.' Inauguration speech, University of Leiden, 23 September.
Mooy, A.W.M. (2004) 'De ruimte van oordeelsvorming binnen de rapportage pro Justitia', in M. Boone, R.S.B. Kool, C.M. Pelser and T. Boekhout van Solinge (eds) *Discretie in het strafrecht*. The Hague: Boom Legal Publishers.
Raad voor Strafrechtstoepassing en Jeugdbescherming (2009) Advies Wetsvoorstel voorwaardelijke veroordeling (April). (Recommendation made by the Council for the Application of Criminal Law and the Protection of Juveniles. Conditional Conviction Bill. The Hague, April 2009.)
van der Knaap, L.M., Leenarts, L.E.W. and Nijssen, L.T.J. (2007) *Psychometrische kwaliteiten van de Recidive Inschattingsschalen (RISc). Interbeoordelaarsbetrouwbaarheid, interne consistentie en congruente validiteit.* The Hague: Research and Documentation Centre of the Ministry of Justice.
Vegter, P.C. (2005) 'Wie beslist over V.I.?', in A. Harteveld, D.H. de Jong and E. Stamhuis (eds) *Systeem in ontwikkeling, Liber Amicorum G. Knigge*. Nijmegen: Wolf Legal Publishers.
Verslag NVK-studiemiddag (17 november 2006) (Report, Netherlands Criminology Association study afternoon, 17 November 2006). 'Risicotaxatie van recidive van volwassenen: statische en dynamische factoren' by Gijs Wijters is available online at <http://www.criminologie.nl/nvk/Verslag_NvK_studiemiddag_Risicotaxatie_080107.doc>.

Chapter 13

Scotland

Douglas Thomson

Summary

The present system for the early release of prisoners has its genesis in the Criminal Justice Act 1967, an Act of the UK Parliament which first introduced a statutory right to release at a fixed stage of sentence and created the Parole Boards for Scotland and for England and Wales. Since 1993, and in particular since criminal justice and criminal sentencing became the responsibility of the Scottish Parliament following the coming into force of the Scotland Act 1998, Scotland has developed its own practices in respect of parole and early release, which now differ significantly from those of England and Wales. Long-term prisoners, who are defined as those serving four years or more, are eligible for release at the halfway point of the custodial part of their sentences, and if not so released must be released on licence at the two-thirds point of the custodial sentence. If the sentence is an 'extended sentence', with an additional fixed period of licence supervision, then they may be returned to custody at any time up to the conclusion of the sentence. The release or otherwise of life prisoners is solely the responsibility of the Parole Board, whose decisions are binding upon ministers.

1. History

In common with the rest of the UK, the release of prisoners prior to the conclusion of their custodial sentences, or the release on licence of a life-sentence prisoner, began as a somewhat *ad hoc* method of rewarding good conduct in prison, originating from the 'ticket' system in which prison governors rewarded deserving prisoners, and developing into a more organized system subject to political approval, in that any decision to release was made by, or on behalf of, a government minister.

The parole system in something approaching its present form was first introduced throughout the UK by the Criminal Justice Act 1967; and the Prisoners and Criminal Proceedings (Scotland) Act 1993, which came into force on 1 October 1993, introduced substantial changes into the previous system. While the Act has been substantially amended since it came into force, in its current form it remains the primary legislation in respect of the release and recall of sentenced prisoners.

Following a referendum in 1997, the Scotland Act 1998 created the Scottish Parliament which has powers devolved from the UK Parliament. Some legislative areas are 'reserved' to the Parliament of the UK: but all matters that are not explicitly reserved are automatically the responsibility of the Scottish Parliament, and these matters include criminal justice. Scotland and England retained their own separate legal and court systems after the union of the two countries' Parliaments in 1707. Between then and devolution, matters relating to criminal law and sentencing in Scotland were usually dealt with by separate Acts of the UK Parliament applying only to Scotland. Since 1999, imprisonment and conditional release policy in Scotland has not gone hand-in-hand with that in the rest of the UK. In terms of the Scotland Act, the ministers of the Scottish government, with the exception of the First Minister, have no defined statutory roles or duties, and they are thus known collectively simply as the 'Scottish Ministers'.

Those prisoners sentenced before the 1993 Act came into force were considered under the pre-existing system. There are no longer any determinate sentence prisoners in Scotland sentenced prior to 1 October 1993. Parole in Scotland permits the Scottish Ministers to order that a prisoner serve part of his sentence under licence in the community, during which time the prisoner is subject to recall if he fails to comply with licence conditions. The Criminal Justice Act 1967 established the Parole Boards for England and Wales and for Scotland, the latter's function being initially to advise Ministers on any matter connected with the early release or recall of prisoners in any cases referred to the Board by the Secretary of State. Since June 2003, with the exception of prisoners liable to removal from the UK, where the Scottish Ministers are not bound to accept the recommendations of the Board, the Parole Board's powers in respect of the release of prisoners they consider to present an acceptable risk are directive; where they recommend release on parole, the Scottish Ministers must grant such release. The Parole Board (Scotland) Rules 2001 set out a list of matters which may, without prejudice to the Board's powers to consider other matters, be taken into account by the Board in making its decisions.

Membership of the Board is set at a minimum of five and must include a Lord Commissioner of Justiciary (High Court judge), a consultant psychiatrist, a person with an academic interest in crime and its treatment, and a person experienced in the after-care of offenders. In future, once the Custodial Sentences and Weapons (Scotland) Act 2007 comes into force, currently not expected to be before late 2010, the Board will also be required to include among its number a person with knowledge of, and experience in, risk assessment, and a person with knowledge of the effect of crime on victims. At present, the membership of the Board is between 22 and 25 members, the majority of whom are not legally qualified in Scotland. In addition to the members whose expertise is specified by statute, the Board will generally include social workers, psychologists, former members of the police and Prison Service, lay magistrates, practising or retired lawyers from the prosecution and defence sides, and current or retired sheriffs (judges with the power to sentence up to five years). The Scottish Ministers may make rules authorizing cases to be dealt with by a prescribed number of members of the Board. When appointing a member of the Board, the Scottish Ministers must comply with such requirements as to procedure and consultation as may be provided for in regulations. Members must be appointed for a period of between six and seven years and their appointment must come to an end at the age of 75. The conditions under which they are appointed, and the circumstances in which a specially-appointed tribunal may be convened to determine whether a member should be removed from office, are now specified by statutory provisions.

2. Legal criteria

2.1 Short-term prisoners

In terms of s. 27(1) of the Prisoners and Criminal Proceedings (Scotland) Act 1993, 'short-term prisoner' means a person serving a sentence of imprisonment for a term of less than four years. In terms of s. 1(1) of the 1993 Act, and subject to exceptions in respect of sex offenders and offenders serving extended sentences, 'as soon as a short-term prisoner has served one-half of his sentence, the Secretary of State [now the Justice Minister] shall, without prejudice to any supervised release order to which the prisoner is subject, release him unconditionally'. Since July 2006, Ministers have had the power, in terms of s. 3AA of the Prisoners and Criminal Proceedings (Scotland) Act 1993, to release certain short-term prisoners assessed as presenting a low risk of reoffending, on Home Detention Curfew, for up to one quarter of the total sentence or 166 days, whichever is the lesser. With effect from 12 January 2006, the Management of Offenders (Scotland) Act 2005 provides that anyone sentenced to a period of between six months and four years imprisonment for a sexual offence, as defined in the Sex Offenders Act 1997, is no longer released unconditionally. Instead, he is released subject to such licence conditions as Scottish Ministers consider necessary for the protection of the public, and are therefore liable to be recalled to custody in respect of non-compliance with licence conditions. These conditions are not negotiable and remain valid whether the offender elects to 'accept' them or not. It is not necessary for the offender to reoffend for his licence to be revoked.

2.2 Long-term prisoners

Any prisoner serving a custodial sentence, or combination of sentences, amounting in total to a calendar period of four years or more is defined by s. 27(5) of the 1993 Act as a 'long-term prisoner'. In terms of s. 1 as now amended:

(2) As soon as a long-term prisoner has served two-thirds of his sentence, the Secretary of State [since 1999, this function has been exercised by Scottish Ministers] shall release him on licence unless he has before that time been so released, in relation to that sentence, under any provision of this Act

(3) After a long-term prisoner has served one-half of his sentence, the Secretary of State shall, if recommended to do so by the Parole Board under this section, release him on licence.

Release on parole is therefore discretionary at any time between the halfway and two-thirds point of the offender's sentence, and all release, whether on parole or not, is subject to the imposition of licence conditions, breach of which can result in recall to custody at any point up to the offender's sentence end date. With effect from 1 April 1995, s. 1 of the Prisoners and Criminal Proceedings (Scotland) Act 1993 was amended to the effect that, where a prisoner was serving less than ten years' imprisonment and the Parole Board recommended his release on licence, the Secretary of State releases him on licence, and with effect from 27 June 2003 the Act was further amended to provide that Scottish Ministers release on licence any long-term offender whose release is recommended by the Parole Board, except where the prisoner is liable to removal from the UK, in which case Scottish Ministers may release the prisoner on licence. It should perhaps be noted that the former power held by a prison governor to award additional days in custody for certain breaches of prison discipline has not been in operation since 2001, and the most recent version of the Prison Rules for Scotland, published in 2006, does not permit such a punishment.

2.3 Extended sentences

With effect from 30 September 1998, the Crime and Disorder Act 1998 inserted a new s. 210A into the Criminal Procedure (Scotland) Act 1995, providing that, where a person is convicted on indictment of a sexual or violent offence, and the Court intends to pass a determinate sentence of imprisonment in relation to a sexual offence, or a sentence of four years' imprisonment or more for a violent offence, and the Court considers that the period (if any) for which the offender would be subject to licence would not be adequate for the purpose of protecting the public from serious harm from the offender, the Court may pass an extended sentence on the offender. If the sentencing Judge considers that protection of the public from serious harm makes such a sentence necessary, they must impose a sentence consisting of two parts – the 'custodial term' which the Court would otherwise have passed, and the 'extension period' for which the offender is to be subject to a licence, of such length as the Court considers necessary. The extension period is not taken into account in determining whether a prisoner is a long-term or short-term prisoner as defined above. The maximum extension period competent in the High Court is ten years for both sexual and violent offences. In the Sheriff Court, the maximum extended sentence is the aggregate of a custodial term not exceeding the maximum term the Sheriff may impose (currently five years) and an extension period not exceeding five years. Where the custodial term exceeds four years, parole may be granted at the halfway stage of that part of the sentence and release on licence is mandatory at the two-thirds stage, which in practice often means that the period to be served under supervision in the community is considerably longer than the term spent in custody (for example, a ten-year extended sentence comprising a six-year custodial term plus a four-year extension will generally require an offender to spend close to four years in custody by virtue of the original sentence, and at least six years in the community subject to supervision on licence and at risk of recall for non-compliance).

2.4   The powers and practices of the Parole Board

In dealing with a case, the Board may take into account any matter that it considers relevant, including any of the following:

- The nature and circumstances of any offence of which the person has been convicted or found guilty by a court.
- The person's conduct since the date of the present sentence.
- The likelihood of the person committing any offence or causing any harm to any other person.
- The person's intentions on release and the likelihood of them being realized.
- Any written information sent to the Board or otherwise obtained by the Board.

Any information in connection with proceedings before the Board (including a tribunal dealing with a case) about any application, document, written or oral information given to the Board or tribunal, or about the name of any person concerned in the proceedings is confidential, and is not be disclosed to the public or any person not involved in the proceedings, except where either the Chairperson of the Board or tribunal, as the case may be, otherwise directs, or in connection with any court proceedings. It follows, therefore, that any information volunteered by a prisoner (for example, in respect of drug supply or use or about the facts of an outstanding case yet to be tried) can competently be reported to the prosecution authorities.

There are no statutory criteria governing the grant or refusal of parole, nor is the system based upon any actuarial point-scoring system. Each case is considered wholly on the participating members' individual assessments of the prisoner's level of risk and whether, in their view, he presents an acceptable risk to the public. The Board must balance the prisoner's interests in regaining his liberty against the wider public interest in the prevention of further offending, and must release only those who are felt objectively to present an acceptable risk. It is not necessary for a prisoner to have pleaded guilty or to accept his guilt before parole can be granted. While those who deny their guilt may decline to engage in offence-focused coursework, and who express certain misgivings over supervision in the community – factors that may militate against the grant of parole – there is no hard-and-fast practice to state that only those who accept guilt and show remorse should be granted parole. The Board is not merely concerned with 'good behaviour' in prison. While an absence of misconduct reports and drug test failures, combined with swift progression to low supervision status and thence to open conditions, may seem encouraging, this may merely prove that an experienced inmate is 'jail-wise' and knows how to work his way through the prison system. This in itself would not be enough to guarantee early release on parole licence. The Board seeks objective evidence of a reduced level of risk. Each individual case is presented at a meeting by a particular member of the Board, and all the other members of the Board (save the interviewing member, who is the only person present who has met the prisoner) may comment upon the recommendation and may agree or disagree. The paper review system was challenged with some success in *Campbell, Petr* ([2008] CSOH 16, 2008 SLT 231): the failure to afford the prisoner an oral hearing was unfair, even though no request for an oral hearing had been made, where there were disputed allegations of non-compliance with licence conditions. A prisoner unhappy either with the refusal of parole or with the licence conditions imposed may seek judicial review of the Board's decision (see the two unreported cases of *Gallagher* v. *Parole Board* (2005 CSOH 126) and *Baker* v. *Parole Board* (2006 CSOH 31)).

In determining a case when it first comes before it at a casework meeting, the Board effectively has four options. To:

- allow parole with effect from the earliest date available – namely, the halfway point of the sentence;

- allow parole, but to grant it from a date between the Parole Qualifying Date (halfway point) and the Earliest Date of Liberation ('EDL' – two-thirds point) – this is known as a 'forward date';

- decline parole, but order that the case be returned to the Board for an earlier review than would normally be the case; or

- decline parole and direct that the prisoner remain in custody until his EDL.

The licence in terms of which a long-term, extended sentence or life prisoner is released, whether on parole or not, may include such conditions as the Scottish Ministers, upon the advice of the Parole Board, may decide. In present-day practice, while the licence issued to the prisoner on release proceeds in the name of the Scottish Ministers, the conditions contained therein are selected by the Parole Board, which forwards them to Ministers as recommended licence conditions. The standard conditions in a licence require the offender to report to a specified social work office, to be under supervision by a nominated social worker, to comply with any requirements specified and keep in touch, to inform a supervising officer of any change of place of residence or employment, to be of good behaviour and keep the peace, and not to travel outside Great Britain without prior approval.

Other conditions (for example, in relation to place of residence, co-operation with an agency experienced in the field of job search, alcohol or drug counselling or restricting the places to which a convicted sex offender may attend, persons with whom they may associate or access to Internet-enabled equipment), may be imposed as considered appropriate. The licence, which may be varied by the Secretary of State at any time, continues in force, unless revoked, until:

- in the case of a determinate sentence prisoners paroled under provisions of the Prisons (Scotland) Act 1989, the expiry of the sentence, subject to such remission as would have been available to him;

- in the case of a determinate sentence prisoner paroled under the Prisoners and Criminal Proceedings (Scotland) Act 1993, the expiry of the whole sentence imposed on him;

- in the case of prisoners serving an indeterminate sentence, for life.

In the case of prisoners given extended sentences in terms of s. 210A of the Criminal Procedure (Scotland) Act 1995, they remain subject to licence conditions until the expiry of the total sentence.

In common with England, there has been some criticism of the perceived lack of co-operation between prisons and the outside agencies responsible for community supervision. The provision of a mechanism by which the various components of the criminal justice system were enabled to work together – and become a system in the proper meaning of the word – in the form of the setting up of Community Justice Authorities in terms of the Management of Offenders (Scotland) Act 2005 is still in its infancy, and its long-term effects will not be known for some years yet.

2.5   Life-sentence prisoners

Life imprisonment is mandatory in Scotland following a conviction for murder and may be imposed in the High Court on a discretionary basis for several other offences. In practice, discretionary life sentences or orders for lifelong restriction are sometimes imposed for second or subsequent offences of rape, serious violence against the person, serious sexual offending, culpable homicide or wilful fireraising The procedure for the release of offenders serving indeterminate sentences – that is life, detention without limit of time, detention during Her Majesty's Pleasure after conviction for murder and, in due course, for those sentenced since 2006 to an Order for Lifelong Restriction in terms of the Criminal Justice (Scotland) Act 2003 (still a rarely-used form of discretionary life sentence, imposed on average around ten times per year), none of whom are eligible for consideration of release for some years yet – is different from that for prisoners serving determinate sentences. The Convention Rights (Compliance) (Scotland) Act 2001 imposes a new scheme for the sentencing and release of all life prisoners, in respect of which the power to direct whether or not they are released rests not with the Scottish Ministers but with the Parole Board for Scotland. With effect from the coming into force of that Act, there is no longer any distinction in law between the procedures for deciding upon the release or continued detention of those serving mandatory indeterminate sentences and discretionary life-sentence prisoners.

Following the passing of the 2001 Act, all courts imposing life imprisonment are required to make an order declaring the 'punishment part', regardless of the date upon which the offender was convicted. In determining the period, the requirements of retribution and deterrence should be borne in mind, while any period of confinement which might be necessary for the protection of the public should be ignored. While the matter was due to be considered again by a Full Bench of the High Court in late 2009, the current law governing the selection of the appropriate punishment parts is as stated in *Flynn* v.

HM Advocate (no. 1) (2004 SC (PC) 1, 2004 SCCR 281), in which it was held that in determining what part of the sentence is appropriate to satisfy the requirements for retribution and deterrence in the case of prisoners sentenced before 2001, the Court may have regard to various matters that would not have existed at the date of the sentence, and the prisoner's human rights are not thereby breached.

Reasons must now be given when the Parole Board for Scotland declines to direct that a prisoner be released, and a date must be fixed for the Parole Board next to consider the prisoner's case, being a date not later than two years after the date of its decision to decline to direct the prisoner's release. Provision is made to cover the situation where a reference has been made to the Parole Board and the prisoner receives another sentence of imprisonment, either before a date has been fixed for considering his case or after such a date has been fixed but before the date on which his case will be considered.

Where a prisoner has been sentenced to life imprisonment, and the punishment part of that sentence has been served in full (including any days during that period when the prisoner was unlawfully at large), then Scottish Ministers refer his case to the Parole Board, which must then convene a tribunal to consider the prisoner's case. Scottish Ministers must, if directed to do so by the Parole Board, release a life prisoner on licence. The Parole Board does not give a direction to release a prisoner unless Scottish Ministers have referred the prisoner's case to the Board and the Board is satisfied that it is no longer necessary for the protection of the public that the prisoner should be confined.

2.6 Life-prisoner tribunals

Where, on the disposal of any reference of a life prisoner's case, the Parole Board declines to direct that the prisoner be released on licence, it gives the prisoner reasons in writing for the decision not to direct his release on licence and fixes the date when it will next consider the prisoner's case, being a date not later than two years after the date of its decision to decline to direct the release of the prisoner.

Where the Parole Board has declined to direct that the prisoner be released on licence and has fixed a further date for a hearing, the Scottish Ministers refer the case to the Parole Board to enable it to consider the case on the date fixed by the Board. The Parole Board may, however, at the request of a life prisoner in respect of whom it has fixed the date for the next consideration of his case, direct Scottish Ministers to refer the case to the Board before that date.

The rules governing tribunals are set out in Part IV of the Parole Board (Scotland) Rules 2001. Any case may be dealt with, in whole, by three members of the Board appointed by the Chairperson of the Board to form a tribunal for the purpose of dealing with that case. No member of the Board who took part in making a recommendation for the recall of a prisoner to custody can be appointed by the Chairperson to take part in a tribunal where that prisoner's re-release is to be considered. The members of the tribunal appointed must include either a person who holds or has held judicial office, or is a solicitor or advocate of not less than ten years' standing, and the Chairperson of the Board appoints that person to be Chairperson of the tribunal. Unless both parties and the tribunal otherwise agree, there is an oral hearing of the prisoner's case. In practice, Scottish Ministers are always represented either by a civil servant and a member of Scottish Prison Service staff although, occasionally (usually where release is not opposed), only by a member of prison staff, and the overwhelming majority of prisoners elect to be present at the hearing of their case, usually with legal representation. Each party may be represented by any person whom they have authorized for the purpose, and parties must intimate in advance of the hearing the name, address and occupation of any authorized representative. If satisfied that there are good and sufficient reasons for doing so, the tribunal may refuse to permit a person to represent a party. Where a prisoner wishes to be legally represented, 'assistance by way of representation' is available for the conduct of parole hearings through the Scottish Legal Aid Board. Other accompaniment in addition to representation by a legal adviser (for example, where the life prisoner is a patient in a hospital and wishes the attendance of a mental health advocate) may be permitted at the discretion of the Chairperson of the tribunal, upon written application.

All hearings take place in private. The parties are heard in such order as the tribunal may determine. In practice, the representative of the Scottish Ministers addresses the tribunal first, and on conclusion of their presentation it falls to the prisoner to lead such evidence or make such submissions as he or his representatives see fit. Parties are entitled at the hearing to be heard either in person or through their representative, to hear each other's evidence and to put questions to each other (or, in the case of the Scottish Ministers, their official or officials attending the hearing) and to any person called by the other party, to call any person whom the tribunal has authorized to give evidence or to produce any document, and to make submissions to the tribunal. The tribunal may consider any evidence it considers relevant, including hearsay (see *Birrell, Petr* (2007 SLT 440)). Any member of the tribunal may put questions to any party or representative or any person giving evidence.

The decision of the tribunal may be taken by a majority and the decision must record whether it was unanimous or taken by a majority, provided that, where the tribunal is constituted by two members, following death, incapacity or unavailability of a member, the Chairperson has a second or casting vote. The tribunal's decision must be recorded in a document which contains a statement of the reasons for the decision, is signed and dated by the Chairperson and sent to the parties not later than 14 days after the end of the hearing. In practice, a decision letter setting out in detail the issues addressed at the hearing and the final view taken by the tribunal on the question of whether it is no longer necessary for the protection of the public that the prisoner continue to be detained, drafted by the Chairperson and approved by the members of the tribunal, is issued to the prisoner, his legal representative (if appropriate) and to Scottish Ministers. Any such decision is binding upon Ministers and upon the prisoner, although it may be subject to judicial review by either party in the Court of Session.

3. Statistics

Since its inception in 1967, the Parole Board for Scotland has presented an annual report to the Secretary of State for Scotland and (since 1999) Scottish Ministers. Until 2006 the report covered a calendar year, but the most recent annual report covers the 15-month period from 1 January 2007 to 31 March 2008, and future reports will be issued covering the year from April to March. In 2007–8, out of 721 determinate sentence prisoners whose cases were considered (some at second or later review), 241 people were recommended for parole and 89 had their cases deferred for further consideration. Of the 197 prisoners serving extended sentences whose case were considered, 9 were recommended for parole and 18 deferred for further consideration. Some 325 life-prisoner cases were referred, of which release was directed in 75 cases, 52 were adjourned or postponed, 62 tribunals had not yet convened and one died while his case was under referral. Some 98 determinate sentence and 100 life sentence and extended sentence prisoners were recalled to custody by the Board, although a considerable number of other offenders were recalled by Scottish Ministers in terms of their statutory powers, without reference to the Board. Of the determinate sentence prisoners recalled to custody, 16 had their cases determined by an oral hearing, the relatively-new form of procedure introduced in order to comply with the recent English Appeal Court decisions referred to below (Parole Board for Scotland 2008).

In considering Scottish parole statistics, it is important to recognize that the Board's function was purely recommendatory until 2001, in that the Secretary of State had an unfettered right to reject any recommendation the Board made in favour of parole. Thus, any analysis of present-day practice should commence in October 2001, when the Convention Rights (Compliance) (Scotland) Act 2001 came into force. The period since 2001 has seen a marked decline in the percentage of prisoners being granted parole each year, from over 55 per cent to below 40 per cent, with a significant increase in the number of offenders (generally those not granted parole on the basis of their perceived level of risk but released at the two-thirds stage as required by statute) returned to custody (Scottish Prisons Commission 2008: Part 3).

It should be noted that reconviction rates, in respect of the percentage reconvicted within two years, for those sentenced to imprisonment in Scotland have remained virtually static, at around 65 per cent, between 1995–6 and 2003–4, although in the same period the reconviction rate for those given community service declined from around 50 per cent to 40 per cent. The number of recorded crimes in Scotland peaked at close to 575,000 in 1991 and has since declined steadily, falling to 420,000 in 2006–7. Over the same 16 years, though, the average daily prison population increased from 6,000 to 7,200 (Scottish Prisons Commission 2008: Part 2).

Given that less than 10 per cent of the average daily population of prisoners in Scotland are eligible for parole, even a statistically significant variation in the grant or refusal of parole of the order of 15 per cent has, in practical terms, a minimal effect on the cost of the Scottish prison system. In practice, political interference with the Board's decision-making process is unknown, and the Board is under no statutory or other duty to consider prisoner numbers in reaching its decisions. In present practice, a considerably greater number of offenders are released from custody early in terms of the Home Detention Curfew Provisions introduced, with effect from 3 July 2006, to many prisoners serving three months or more, whose level of risk is considered manageable in the community and who have a fixed address. A curfew condition is one which requires the released person to remain, for periods for the time being specified in the condition, at a place for the time being so specified, and may require him not to be in a place, or class of place, so specified at a time or during a period so specified. The curfew condition may specify different places, or different periods, for different days, but a condition may not specify periods which amount to less than nine hours in any one day, excluding the first and last days of the period for which the condition is in force. At present there are around 350–80 such short-term prisoners in the community each day.

4. Recall procedures

Throughout the currency of a licence, including a life licence (which remains in force until the prisoner's death), the person on parole remains liable to variation of licence terms and to revocation of the licence. There are two separate and distinct provisions in respect of which a prisoner may be returned to custody following release. Where a released prisoner has committed a further offence punishable by imprisonment between his liberation date and the date upon which his custodial sentence would have come to an end, he may, in addition to any penalty imposed for the new offence, be returned to custody to serve all or part of the unexpired portion. An order in these terms may be made even when the conviction itself post-dates the expiry of the sentence, providing the offence date was within the set period.

Where a prisoner is released on licence of any sort, breach of any of the conditions of that licence, whether involving to commission of a fresh offence or not, may give rise to him being recalled to custody. The statutory provisions governing recall for prisoners sentenced before 1 October 1993 are found in the Prisons (Scotland) Act 1989, and the modern power of recall is set out in s. 17 of the Prisoners and Criminal Proceedings (Scotland) Act 1993. Where a long-term or life prisoner has been released on licence and is not detained in custody by virtue of any other legal provision, Scottish Ministers, if recommended to do so by the Parole Board, or may, if revocation and recall are, in their opinion, expedient in the public interest and it is not practicable to await such a recommendation, revoke the licence and recall the prisoner to custody. Where a long-term or life prisoner has been released on licence and subsequently legally detained, then the Ministers, if recommended to do so by the Board, or may, if revocation is, in their opinion, expedient in the public interest and it is not practicable to await such a recommendation, revoke the licence *simpliciter*. Where any licence is revoked, a warrant is immediately granted by Scottish Ministers for the apprehension of the prisoner. During the period between the recall warrant being issued and the prisoner's apprehension, he is unlawfully at large and any such period spent in the community is disregarded in respect of sentence calculation. Recalled prisoners must be informed immediately upon revocation of their licence of the reasons for their recall, and may make written representations in respect of such recall. The Board and Ministers are granted a very wide discretion in determining when they may recommend recall to custody. In considering the question of recall, they are not obliged to have regard to whether the prisoner has been granted bail by any Court before which he has appeared on new charges. It is not necessary for a prisoner on licence to be convicted of, or charged with, a new offence before he may be recalled, provided information is provided that the prisoner is not complying with one or more conditions of his licence, and his level of risk is therefore considered to be unacceptable. The Courts recognize that the freedom enjoyed by a life prisoner is more circumscribed by law and more precarious than the freedom enjoyed by the ordinary citizen.

There is some evidence that many of the problems giving rise to the recent increase in the number of prisoners recalled to custody, at a time when the proportion of prisoners being granted parole is declining, are a result, direct or indirect, of a lack of government funding for post-release supervision. The provision of state funds for the aftercare of released prisoners has never been politically popular, despite it being fairly well established that those who are released with stable homes and employment prospects have a lower risk of reconviction within two years of release. Many criminal justice social workers are expected to supervise several prisoners on licence in addition to their other duties in respect of writing reports for Court and supervising offenders on probation. It remains to be seen whether the more 'joined-up' system proposed under the Management of Offenders (Scotland) Act 2005 will assist in bridging this funding gap.

4.1 Re-release procedure

Where a prisoner elects to make representations against recall, the manner in which further determination of his case takes place is governed by whether he is a determinate sentence prisoner, an extended sentence prisoner or a life prisoner. Re-release must in all cases be by decision of the Parole Board; even where Ministers have directed recall, the question of re-release must be determined by a quasi-judicial body. This may be contrasted with the system operating in England and Wales. Prior to 2006, the cases of determinate sentence prisoners were considered by a quorum of three members of the Board, based on a paper review only. This system of paper review only was challenged unsuccessfully in *Dempsey* v. *Parole Board for Scotland* (2004 SLT 1107). The legal position in Scotland has, however, changed, following the decision of the House of Lords in *R* v. *Parole Board ex p Smith and R* v. *Parole Board ex p West* ([2005] UKHL 1). Both appeals related to the question of whether it was appropriate in some circumstances for a prisoner's representations in favour of re-release following recall to be determined by an oral hearing rather than a paper review. In finding in the prisoners' favour, the Court held that Art. 5.4 of the Convention was breached by the failure to offer an oral hearing.

Following this decision, the Board altered its procedures for consideration of the re-release of recalled prisoners. The initial paper review by three members now requires to be chaired by a legally-qualified member of the Board, with authority to act as a tribunal Chairperson. On consideration of the dossier, it is minuted whether the prisoner has requested an oral hearing and whether, regardless of a request being made, in the view of the Board the interests of fairness require that there be such a hearing. Where the Parole Board directs that an oral hearing takes place, it takes place in the establishment where the prisoner is situated. The procedure adopted in the hearing is entirely at the discretion of the Board members, save that it must be recorded whether the the hearing's decision is unanimous or by a majority. When considering a case by way of a paper review, and where an oral hearing is not considered necessary to determine the issues at stake, the Board may either direct re-release or decline to direct re-release.

If the Board recommends immediate release of any such person, Scottish Ministers must give immediate effect to the recommendation. In such a situation, the Board may recommend that Scottish Ministers insert, vary or cancel conditions in the prisoner's licence. Where the Board declines to direct re-release and the prisoner has less than a year to serve until his sentence expiry date, then, unless the Board directs an early review of his case, he will remain in custody until the expiry of the sentence. The increase in the number of extended sentence tribunals and oral hearings in the past decade has materially increased the workload and expense of the Parole Board, whose annual budget is fixed by Scottish Ministers

Where the recalled prisoner is subject either to an extended sentence or a life licence, and the prisoner is not at the time serving a further sentence, then his case must be considered by a tribunal of the Board. The hearing will almost always take place in the prison where the offender is situated. The procedure at tribunal hearings is governed by the Parole Board (Scotland) Rules 2001, which are specifically designed to allow a degree of flexibility in the conduct of tribunals and to ensure that the hearing is carried out in such a way as to clarify the issues before it, and be conducted in a manner consistent with the requirements of common-law procedural fairness.

The tribunal has a duty to conduct the hearing in such manner as it considers most suitable to the clarification of the issues, and to avoid formality in the proceedings. At the beginning of the hearing, the Chairperson of the tribunal explains the order of proceeding which the tribunal proposes to adopt at the hearing. The parties are heard in such order as the tribunal may determine; in practice, Scottish Ministers address the tribunal first, and on conclusion of their presentation it falls to the prisoner to lead such evidence or make such submissions as he or his representatives see fit. The parties are entitled to be heard either in person or through their representative, to hear each other's evidence and to put questions to each other (or, in the case of the Scottish Ministers, their official or officials attending the hearing) and to any person called by the other party, to call any person whom the tribunal has authorized to give evidence or to produce any document, and to make submissions to the tribunal. Any member of the tribunal may put questions to any party or representative or any person giving evidence.

Unlike the cases of determinate sentence prisoners, where the parole Board is considering granting parole on some future date, the question for the tribunal is whether, as at the date of the hearing, it is no longer necessary for the protection of the public that the prisoner should be confined. If the Board finds that confinement is no longer necessary, then it must direct release, in which situation the prisoner will be released into the community within 24 hours of receiving the Board's decision. The decision rests with the Board alone. It may direct release where it is opposed and may decline so to direct even where both parties move it to direct release.

In respect of life-sentence prisoners, the legal test to be applied is specified in s. 2 (5) of the 1993 Act as 'The Parole Board shall not give a direction to release a prisoner under Subsection (4) above (i.e. on life licence) unless Scottish Ministers have referred the prisoner's case to the Board; and the Board is satisfied that it is no longer necessary for the protection of the public that the prisoner should be confined'. The test for extended sentence prisoners is not identical. Where such a case is referred to the Board, it will, if it is satisfied that it is no longer necessary for the protection of the public from serious harm that the prisoner should be confined (but not otherwise), direct that he should be released. The higher 'serious harm' test in respect of extended sentence prisoners has its genesis in an English appellate decision (*R (Sim)* v. *Parole Board* [2004] QB 1288), applying the principles of the European Convention on Human Rights (ECHR) in *Stafford* v. *United Kingdom* ([2002] 35 EHRR 32), in which it was held that where an offender had been recalled for breaching the conditions of his extended sentence licence, the nature of the breach had to be referable to the risk elements that gave rise to the imposition of the extended sentence. Such a direction is also binding upon Ministers. Unlike the cases of life-sentence prisoners, where the tribunal fixes the date of the next review (which may be six to nine months after the instant review), there is no power whereby the tribunal may order that the case be considered earlier than the statutory period of not less than one year.

5. The future for parole and licence

Parole and early release have been the subject of two recent government-sponsored reviews. First, the Scottish Executive set up a 'Sentencing Commission for Scotland', an independent, judicially-led (by High Court judge, Lord Macfadyen) body, under its policy statement 'A partnership for a better Scotland'. The Commission, which was launched in 2003, was given the remit to review and make recommendations to the Scottish Executive on:

- the use of bail and remand;
- the basis on which fines are determined;
- the effectiveness of sentences in reducing reoffending;
- the scope to improve the consistency of sentencing; and
- the arrangements for early release from prison and the supervision of prisoners on their release.

Its report on 'early release' was published in 2005, and the Commission was dissolved in November 2006. It is currently proposed that

Scotland sets up a Sentencing Council, with statutory powers to set guidelines in respect of many types of sentence. These proposals, which go beyond the recommendations of the Commission, remain controversial and opposed by most sentencers. At the time of going to press, it is not clear whether such a Council will be set up in Scotland.

As we shall see, this has been followed by a very different 'Scottish Prisons Commission', devised by the victorious Scottish National Party administration after the 2007 Scottish parliamentary elections to analyse the impact for courts, prisons and community justice services of early release provisions contained in the Custodial Sentences and Weapons (Scotland) Act 2007, and its report was published in July 2008.

Shortly before the 2007 Scottish parliamentary elections, the outgoing administration had secured the passage into law of the Custodial Sentences and Weapons (Scotland) Act 2007. Effectively, this Act seeks to sweep away the terminology of the 1993 Act. Those behind the Act proposed that, in future, sentences of 15 days and over are to be based on a 'combined structure' model, with the Court imposing a 'custodial part' and a 'community part' in all sentences. The minimum 'custodial part' is proposed to be 50 per cent of the length of the whole sentence, although the Court will have a discretion to increase this up to a maximum of three quarters (and Ministers will retain the right to vary or amend these statutory maxima and minima). The Act provides that risk assessment be carried out in respect of all prisoners serving sentences in excess of 14 days, although it should be noted that the Sentencing Commission's proposed threshold for this had been 12 months. The Act places assessment of risk at the forefront of the entire custodial system, and obliges prison staff to be engaged in a constant assessment of harm throughout any custody and community prisoner's sentence. A written risk assessment is expected to be available not only before the halfway point of such a sentence but (at least in theory) also to be available in time for Ministers to assess it, determine whether the prisoner is to be released at the halfway point and, if not, to refer the case to the Board for it to direct release or not.

The Act further empowered Scottish Ministers to take back certain powers currently in the hands of the Parole Board for Scotland, although the existence of the Board itself remained guaranteed. The decision as to whether to recommend certain offenders for release on supervision into the community, jealously guarded by Ministers in the past, and gradually eroded by European jurisprudence and

UK case law, reverted to their control, thus on the face of it restoring a political element to the sentencing process. In order to meet any anticipated challenges that the proposed new system is not ECHR compliant, the Parole Board, which will be transformed into something of an appellate body under this system, will have the right to direct Ministers to release prisoners, even when release is not proposed, and likewise, where Ministers elect to revoke a prisoner's licence (that power also being removed from the Parole Board), review of that decision will fall within the remit of the Board. Thus, instead of being the body at first instance that decides whether to recommend parole, the Board is proposed to have an appellate function, effectively reviewing the information considered by Ministers and determining whether the Ministers' recommendation was the correct one in respect of public protection. Periodic reviews of this decision are provided. In addition, the Act provides that the Board has referred to it high-risk cases, where the Ministers recommend that the offender should be detained beyond the minimum custodial part fixed by the Court. These cases, in respect of all custody and community prisoners, will be considered by the Board, whose statutory function is now to be defined as 'advising Scottish Ministers in relation to any matter referred to it in relation to the release of prisoners'.

Many of the provisions of the 2007 Act were unpopular with prison staff, prisoners, sentencers and other criminal justice professionals and, following the election of an administration of a different political hue in May 2007, there was an absence of impetus to bring the Act into force as enacted. Instead, the incoming administration set up the Scottish Prisons Commission, whose report 'Scotland's Choice', which made several recommendations aimed at reducing the Scottish prison population from over 8,000 to a figure of around 5,000, was published in July 2008. Its central conclusions were that Scottish Courts overused both remands in custody and custodial sentences, often sending persons who had not committed serious crimes, and who did not present a danger to the public, into custody for short periods, to no great public or economic benefit. It observed that the reliance on prisons to hold people for short periods only increased the chances of them coming back repeatedly, noting that the nearly 7,000 offenders who had received custodial sentences in 2006–7 had accrued between them around 47,500 prior spells in prison.

The Commission noted the absence of evidence that short custodial sentences of less than six months operated in any retributive, deterrent or rehabilitative manner, and recommended that the government pursue a target of reducing the use of such sentences, by requiring a sentencing judge who would otherwise have imposed a sentence of six months or less to impose a Community Supervision Sentence instead, unless the sentencer is satisfied, having regard to one or more of six specified circumstances, that a custodial sentence should be imposed. Scottish Ministers have not, however, been wholly in favour of the effective abolition of short-term custodial sentences of less than six months, and their current proposals offer a greater degree of judicial discretion in favour of short custodial sentences than that proposed by the Commission. Any changes in the law, including the enactment in amended form of the Custodial Sentences and Weapons (Scotland) Act, cannot at this time be predicted with any confidence, and are in any event unlikely to come into force until 2011. All decisions regarding the release and re-release of long-term and life prisoners, and the majority of decisions in respect of their recall, remain the responsibility of the Parole Board for Scotland.

References

Parole Board for Scotland (2008) *Annual Report, 2007–08*. Edinburgh: HMSO.

Scottish Prisons Commission (2008) *Scotland's Choice*. Edinburgh: Scottish Prisons Commission.

Sentencing Commission for Scotland (2006) *Early Release from Prison and Supervision of Prisoners on their Release* (available online at www.scottishsentencingcommission.gov.uk/publications.asp).

Thomson, D. (2007) *Prisons, Prisoners and Parole*. Edinburgh: W. Green & Son.

Thomson, D. (2009) 'Penal institutions', in *The Stair Memorial Encyclopedia*. Edinburgh: Law Society of Scotland/Butterworths.

Chapter 14

Slovenia

Katja Šugman Stubbs and Matjaž Ambrož

Summary

The legal regime of parole in Slovenia has remained practically unchanged since the 1950s, and so some of its provisions are clearly not in accordance with present-day demands. Despite the fact that Slovenia has one of the lowest prison rates in Europe, prison rates have increased in recent years, and so Slovenia faces the imminent problem of prison overcrowding. In consequence it is to be feared that the prison system's physical capacity to hold prisoners may become a factor – by design or otherwise – in future decisions on parole. This state of affairs does not accord with the aims and purposes of parole as it is viewed in Slovenia. This chapter presents an overview of the legal framework of parole in Slovenia, provides some statistical data regarding the early release system and discusses the legal nature of parole and its purpose. It also examines the possibilities for reforming the parole system so that it becomes more transparent, efficient and fit for the purpose of rehabilitation. With regard to such an improvement, several questions are raised. Firstly, the composition of the Parole Commission needs some reappraisal: the judicial impact on parole decisions and the input of penological and criminological experts should be increased. Secondly, the procedure for deciding on parole should be made more explicit and the parolee's rights defined more clearly. The third weakness of the system is an inadequate elaboration of the criteria for parole.

I. History

In Slovenian law, general guidelines on the early release rules are provided in the Criminal Code,[1] but more specific provisions are set down in the Enforcement of Penal Sentences Act,[2] the Pardon Act[3] and in the Rules on the Implementation of the Sentence of Imprisonment.[4]

The Republic of Slovenia adopted a new Criminal Code in May 2008, which came into force on 1 November 2008. The most important change insofar as release is concerned is the change made to the penalty system. From 1994, when the first Slovenian Criminal Code was adopted, the longest custodial sentence was 20 years' imprisonment. An amendment in 1999 raised the possible length to 30 years' imprisonment. Unfortunately, the life sentence has now been adopted in the new Criminal Code.

Before the introduction of the life sentence, an intense, often fierce, debate took place in both academic journals and the popular press. Almost all the experts disagreed with the proposal that it was necessary to make provision for a sentence of life imprisonment (Kmet 2007; Penko 2007; Petrovec 2007a, 2007b; Bavcon 2007, 2008; Zakonjšek 2008). The new Criminal Code was written by just three lawyers in less than one year (something one would not believe possible).

Various arguments in support of life imprisonment were advanced by those in favour of the new Code. First, it was claimed that the life sentence was needed to implement the Rome Statute of the International Criminal Court (Deisinger 2007). When it was demonstrated that this argument was inaccurate (Novak 2007, 2008a, 2008b), it was claimed that the life sentence was necessary for Slovenia despite the fact that

[1] *Official Journal of the Republic of Slovenia* (OJ), 63/94, 23/99, 40/04.
[2] OJ 22/00, 59/92, 70/06. The Rules on the implementation of the sentence of imprisonment are elaborated by the Minister of Justice, based on authorization derived from Arts. 17, 56, 72, 87 and 206 of the Enforcement of Penal Sentences Act. Generally speaking, rules are a lower level of legislation compared with codes. Codes are always adopted by Parliament while rules can be adopted by different institutions, including Ministries. Rules have to have a legal basis in one of the codes and they cannot regulate (especially restrict) the rights of citizens beyond the scope provided by the code on which they are based. They are usually a means by which a general authorization given by a code is elaborated in more detail.
[3] OJ 45/05, 86/04.
[4] OJ 102/00, 127/06, 112/07.

violent and other serious crimes had not increased in the recent, or indeed the distant, past (Bele 2007). Strongly supported by the right-wing government then in power, the new Criminal Code introduced substantial changes in many areas of substantive law, most of them without due consideration or even necessity, and despite extremely forceful opposition from academics, judges, advocates, Parliament's legislation service and even the Governmental Office for Legislation. All the opponents of the new Code made three basic observations: the changes were unnecessary, rushed and, for the most part, badly designed. But the parliamentary 'voting machine' ensured that the law was adopted.[5]

The new Minister of Justice (a new government having been elected in November 2008) has recently established an Advisory Council for the Criminal Law. This Minister has already announced essential changes that will be adopted in the next four years in the field of criminal law, including sentencing.[6] Until now, none of the Acts passed in Slovenia has adopted any EU or Council of Europe instruments on sentencing, but it is expected that the forthcoming amendments to the legislation will encompass European instruments.[7]

2. Statistical data

Slovenia has a very low prison population in comparison with most other European countries (63 per 100,000 of the overall population in 2008),[8] but the rate of both imprisonment and the number of prisoners are increasing rapidly. Data from 2005 show that there were (on average)[9] 1,137 prisoners in Slovenian prisons, while the figures for 2006 and 2007 show the average prison population rising to 1,267 and 1,339 respectively. The average number of prisoners convicted of criminal offences in 2006 was 890 and, in 2007, was 935. On 31 December 2005 there were 802 convicted prisoners in Slovenian

[5]After being adopted by the National Assembly, it was rejected by the second chamber (the National Council) of Parliament but was subsequently narrowly reenacted in the National Assembly.
[6]See http://www.dnevnik.si/novice/slovenija/1042241671
[7]To date Slovenia has not been found by the European Court of Human Rights to have breached any prisoners' rights.
[8]Slovenia has approximately 2,000,000 inhabitants.
[9]'Average' means the daily average of imprisoned people in the Republic of Slovenia during a given calendar year.

prisons; on 31 December 2006, 869, and on 31 December 2007, 958.[10] There has, therefore, been a substantial annual increase in the prison population.

Table 14.1 shows that the percentage of prisoners released on parole has been fairly constant but began to decline in 2004 (by 10 per cent by 2007). Table 14.2 shows that 861 prisoners were released from prison in 2000, of whom 398 were released on parole. Table 14.3,

Table 14.1 Prisoners released on parole, 2000–07

	2000	2001	2002	2003	2004	2005	2006	2007
Number	398	489	385	410	395	374	356	297
Per cent	46.2	51	43.5	43.6	43.7	41.7	36.2	32.2

Table 14.2 Types of release from prison in 2000, by sex for both first offenders and recidivists

		Served the full sentence	Parole	Released on the Governor's decision	Par- don	Total	Per cent released on parole
Male	First offenders	74	277	155	1	507	54.6
	Recidivists	91	105	123	0	319	32.9
Total		165	382	278	1	826	46.2
Female	First offenders	3	12	11	0	26	46.1
	Recidivists	2	4	3	0	9	44.4
Total		5	16	14	0	35	45.7
Total	First offenders	77	289	166	1	533	54.2
	Recidivists	82	109	137	0	328	33.2
Total		**159**	**398**	**303**	**1**	**861**	**46.2**

Source: Prison Administration of the Republic of Slovenia (2001: 25).

[10]Prison Administration of the Republic of Slovenia, (2007: 17; 2008: 17, 18–21).

Table 14.3 Types of release from prison in 2007, by sex for first offenders and recidivists

		Served the full sentence	Parole	Released on the Governor's decision	Par-don	Other	Total	Per cent released on parole
Male	First offenders	104	203	143	0	15	465	43.6
	Recidivists	181	80	142	0	8	411	19.5
Total		285	283	285	0	23	876	32.3
Female	First offenders	8	13	12	0	1	34	38.2
	Recidivists	7	1	4	0	0	12	8.3
Total		15	14	16	0	1	46	30.4
Total	First offenders	112	216	155	0	16	499	43.3
	Recidivists	188	81	146	0	8	423	19.1
Total		**300**	**297**	**301**	**0**	**24**	**922**	**32.2**

Note: As the *Annual Report* (Prison Administration of the Republic of Slovenia 2008: 21) states, the percentage of prisoners released on parole decreased by 4.2 per cent compared with 2006 and by 9.5 per cent compared with 2005.

however, shows that, of 922 prisoners released in 2007, only 297 were released on parole. Unfortunately there are no data on how many prisoners requested parole and how many were granted it, only data on the general numbers of prisoners released on parole and on those released on the basis of other orders.

Tables 14.4 and 14.5 classify prisoners released on parole in 2000 and 2007 according to their sex and whether they were first offenders or recidivists. Most prisoners are granted parole in the last one to three months (38.1 per cent in 2000 and 31.6 per cent in 2007 of all parole granted) or the last three to six months (29.5 per cent in 2000 and 33.7 per cent in 2007) of their sentence. Again there are no data comparing the length of the original sentence and the period of parole granted. Therefore periods of parole granted to the whole prison population in one year can only be detected, not the sentence a prisoner granted parole was serving in the first place.

Table 14.4 Period of parole 2000

Category of prisoner	Up to 30 days	1 month to 3 months	3 months to 6 months	6 months to 1 year	1 year to 2 years	2 years to 3 years	3 years to 5 years	Over 5 years	Total
Male									
First offenders	11	131	76	41	14	2	2	0	277
Recidivists	2	39	32	22	10	0	0	0	105
Total	13	170	108	63	24	2	2	0	382
Female									
First offenders	0	4	3	4	1	0	0	0	12
Recidivists	0	2	1	1	0	0	0	0	4
Total	0	6	4	5	1	0	0	0	16
Total	13	176	112	68	25	2	2	0	398
Percentage	3.3	44.2	28.1	17.1	6.3	0.5	0.5	0.0	100.00

Source: Prison Administratio of the Republic of Slovenia (2001: 78).

Table 14.5 Period of parole 2007

Category of prisoner	Period of parole								
	Up to 30 days	1 month to 3 months	3 months to 6 months	6 months to 1 year	1 year to 2 years	2 years to 3 years	3 years to 5 years	Over 5 years	Total
Male									
First offenders	2	60	60	45	27	6	3	0	203
Recidivists	1	29	36	5	3	4	2	0	80
Total	3	89	96	50	30	10	5	0	283
Female									
First offenders	0	4	3	4	1	0	0	0	13
Recidivists	0	2	1	1	0	0	0	0	1
Total	0	6	4	5	1	0	0	0	14
Total	3	95	100	55	31	10	5	0	299
Percentage	1.0	31.7	23.4	18.4	10.4	3.00	1.7	0.00	100.00

Source: Prison Administratio of the Republic of Slovenia (2008: 65).

3. Release on parole

3.1 Legal aspects

As a general rule, two conditions must be met in order for parole to be granted:

- A formal condition – that is, that a certain period of time has already been served in prison.
- A substantive condition – whether it is reasonable to expect that the prisoner will not offend again.

The formal condition varies according to the severity of the custodial sentence and according to the circumstances, but the substantive one must be satisfied each time parole is granted. A general rule regarding the formal condition is that release on parole *may* be granted to a prisoner who has served at least half of his sentence. There is, therefore, no mandatory early release system in the Republic of Slovenia. Since all sentences (except, now, life imprisonment) are determinate, the time spent in prison before a prisoner is allowed to request parole depends on the length of the sentence imposed by the sentencing Court.

The second essential parole condition is that the prisoner does not commit another offence before the initial sentence of imprisonment has elapsed (Art. 88(1) of the Criminal Code). Generally, this is the most important factor the Commission takes into account, since Art. 109(5) of the Criminal Code provides that a prisoner can be released on parole when it is reasonable to expect he will not reoffend.

A person sentenced to more than 15 years' imprisonment may be released on parole after serving only three quarters of the sentence (Art. 88(2)). The new legislation provides that offenders who have been sentenced to life imprisonment may be released on parole after they have served 25 years' imprisonment (Art. 88(3)). This period appears to be very long in comparison with other legal systems the Slovenian legislator commonly uses for comparative purposes.[11]

In exceptional cases a prisoner may be released on parole after serving only one third of the sentence if special circumstances regarding the prisoner's personality indicate that he will not reoffend

[11]The Austrian, German and Swiss Criminal Codes, for example, require that the offender has served at least 15 years (See Art. 57a of the German Criminal Code, Art. 46(5) of the Austrian Criminal Code, and Art. 86(5) of the Swiss Criminal Code).

(Art. 88(6) of the Criminal Code). This exception also applies to those who have been sentenced to more than 15 years' imprisonment. The following are examples of such considerable circumstances: the decline in a prisoner's health, disability and a well-founded expectation that the sentence will be lowered in a renewed procedure (Bele 2001: 588). Thus, the common interpretation of the provision transcends the literal meaning of 'circumstances regarding the prisoner's personality'.

The new Criminal Code has introduced a provision that enables the Court to put the parolee under so-called 'custodial supervision'. According to Art. 106(6) of the Enforcement of Penal Sentences Act (EPSA), this decision has to be made by the Court of first instance which has imposed the sentence. The Court decides whether to put the parolee under custodial supervision on the proposal of the Commission that decides on the parole (Art. 88(7)). Custodial supervision involves assistance, supervision and custody and is exercised by a guardian appointed by the Court. The guardian is under obligation, *inter alia*, to maintain relations with the parolee and, to offer him aid and supervision, as well to give him practical advice to prevent him from reoffending. The Court of first instance can also set certain requirements the parolee must meet once parole is granted (Art. 88(8)). The Commission deciding on parole may require that a person released on parole:

- undergoes therapy and rehabilitation in a specified medical institution and, where appropriate and with the released person's consent, undergoes treatment for addiction;
- attends appropriate centres for professional, psychological or other forms of counselling;
- accepts a job which suits his health, abilities and inclinations, or attends appropriate job training;
- uses his income to pay any family support required of him;
- does not socialize with certain person(s);
- obeys any restraining order issued to protect the victims of his crimes or other persons; and
- obeys any restraining order prohibiting him from visiting certain specified places.[12]

[12]It is not possible to present an overview of how these conditions will work in practice or how they will be monitored, since the new legislation has been in force for only a few months. According to the available data, no court decisions regarding the custodial supervision of parolees have as yet been made.

The system of custodial supervision is not new in the Slovenian legal system, but it was previously limited to cases of suspended sentences and even then was not applied very often by the Courts, most probably due to a lack of specific implementation regulations.

3.2 The legal nature of parole and the purpose of parole

It has been suggested that the legal nature of parole in the Slovenian system[13] should be regarded as 'a ground for the extinction of a sentence' or as 'a legal hindrance for the execution of a sentence' (Kurtović 1995: 314). This can be challenged, however. Technically, parole does not 'extinguish' the sentence since the sentence can always be resumed if parole is revoked. Indeed, parole is meaningless without this deterrent message. Treating parole as a legal instrument that disables the execution of a sentence, however, makes more sense but is not completely convincing because certain elements that belong to the execution of the sentence (such as custodial supervision) can still be maintained and required even during the period of parole (Novoselec 2007: 397). A solution that has won relatively-widespread support is thus that parole should be regarded as a special way of executing a sentence. This consensus has probably been achieved by a similar view found in the German academic literature, which largely influences Slovenian and ex-Yugoslavian academics in this respect (Jescheck and Weigend 1996: 849). Nevertheless, if we say that, during the period of parole, the sentence is 'being executed', we might also ask why this period should not count as time served if parole is later revoked (Stojanović 1984: 191; Kurtović 1995: 313).

Putting the disputes about the legal nature of parole aside, one thing remains clear. Parole in the Slovenian legal system – at least technically – does not mean a modification of a court judgment. It is a discretionary administrative act of a committee by which the regime of the execution of a penal sentence is changed. This accords fully with the Slovenian criminal justice system, in which the execution of penal sanctions is primarily an administrative matter. Nevertheless, a question can be raised as to whether Slovenia should, *de lege ferenda*, retain this administrative system or whether it should gradually

---

[13]When speaking about the legal nature of parole in the Slovenian legal system, we refer also to academic literature from other ex-Yugoslav republics. The systems of parole in these republics emanate from common roots and are, therefore, to a great extent comparable.

implement a more judicially oriented system for the execution of penal sanctions (Ambrož 2007: 288).[14]

There has been relatively little debate regarding the purpose of parole in the Slovenian legal system. Taking as a starting point the conditions that must be met for parole to be granted (a certain period having been served in prison and the existence of a reasonable expectation that the prisoner will not reoffend), one can assume that parole in the first place serves the goal of 'resocialization' – that is, reintegrating the prisoner into the community. An additional argument can be found in the provision that enables the Court to put the parolee under custodial supervision, which is in fact a further measure for the prisoner's resocialization. Some authors go further, claiming that resocialization should be the sole purpose of parole (Novoselec 2007: 398), rejecting the idea that the institution of parole should serve any other purpose (such as mitigating the problem of prison overcrowding, furthering the goals of justice or providing clemency).

Considering the resocialization of prisoners to be the main purpose of parole may be a clear and preferable standpoint,[15] but the reality of parole decision-making may not always reflect this. Due to the increasing problem of prison overcrowding, the prison system's capacity has probably become an important factor in parole decisions.[16]

4. Procedure for deciding on parole

4.1 Parole Commission

The procedure for deciding on parole is provided by the Enforcement of Penal Sentences Act (EPSA). The body responsible for parole is a special Commission appointed by the Minster of Justice. It consists of

[14]The proposed judicialization of the system of the execution of penal sanctions rests on the idea that the judiciary offers a potentially better standard of protection of human rights and freedoms than the administration. In Croatia (Slovenia's neighbouring country) such a reform has already been implemented with the introduction of 'Judges of Execution' in 1999 (see Ambrož 2007: 283–8).

[15]Again, it should be noted that a similar view in German academic literature (Jescheck and Weigend 1996: 849; Meier 2006: 129) has been influential in the countries of the former Yugoslavia.

[16]See also section 7 below.

three members, of whom one must be a Supreme Court Judge, one a Supreme State Prosecutor and one a civil servant from the Ministry of Justice (from the Prison Administration Unit) (Art. 105 EPSA). In practice, there is only one permanent member of the Commission, from the Ministry of Justice. The Commission's composition therefore varies.

The Commission decides on a motion filed by the prisoner, his family or the Prison Governor (Art. 106 EPSA). The prison's team of counsellors[17] must present a report each time an application for parole is filed. The report must contain the following:

- Personal information on the prisoner requesting parole.
- Information on the criminal offence and the penalty.
- Information on the prisoner's attitude towards the victim of his offence and the harm committed.
- An account of the prisoner's behaviour in prison and possible behavioural or personal changes the prisoner underwent while serving the sentence
- Information on the prisoner's health.
- Information on the prisoner's family's situation and social circumstances.
- Information on the conditions under which the prisoner would be living and the opportunities he would have if released on parole.

The report must also contain information about other possible criminal charges against the prisoner. The team must suggest whether it supports the prisoner's request for parole. In cases where the team suggests that parole should be granted, its report should also set out the reasons why it is reasonable to expect that the prisoner will not reoffend (Art. 127(1) of the Rules on the Implementation of the Sentence of Imprisonment (RISI)).

The Commission meets regularly every two or three months. These meetings take place where the prisoner requesting parole is imprisoned and are held in the presence of the Prison Governor and the team of counsellors who prepared the report (Art. 127(3) RISI). The counsellors are then able to give any further explanation the Commission may need. In the last few years it has become common for prisoners requesting parole also to be present at these meetings

[17]Each prison has a team of counsellors. Depending on the prison's policy and requirements, this team usually consists of psychologists, educational workers, social workers, etc.

so that they can hear what the counsellors say about them and to allow members of the Commission to ask them questions.

The Commission can also hold extraordinary meetings when the President of the Commission deems it necessary. These usually take place in Ljubljana, and it is common for them to decide on more urgent cases, especially those concerning short-term sentences where it would be inappropriate to leave a decision pending until the next scheduled meeting (Art. 127(4) RISI).

When the Commission considers its assessment, all other participants at the meeting must withdraw. Generally the main factor the Commission will take into account is the likelihood of the prisoner reoffending. The Criminal Code sets out specific criteria which the Commission must consider (Art. 109(4)):

- Whether the prisoner is a recidivist.
- Whether there are any unfinished criminal proceedings against the prisoner for criminal offences committed before his sentence began.
- The prisoner's current attitude towards the criminal offence committed and/or towards the victim of that offence.
- His conduct while serving the sentence.
- His efforts and progress in the treatment of addiction.
- His personal abilities and other considerations suggesting how capable he will be to rejoin society.

The Commission's decisions are reached by majority vote. The Commission then issues a decision along with a supporting argument in cases where the application is rejected (Art. 107(2) EPSA). In practice, however, the Commission discusses the application until a unanimous decision has been reached.

There is no appeal against the decision. There is, however, the possibility of initiating an administrative dispute (the possibility of demanding a judicial review of an administrative act) since the decision is considered to be an act of administration. According to the Administrative Dispute Act (ADA), everybody is entitled to demand the judicial protection of his rights and legal benefits against administrative decisions made by state bodies and against which no other legal remedies pertain (Arts. 1, 2 ADA). There are no specific statistical data concerning the number of prisoners who have not been granted parole and who have therefore initiated an administrative dispute. However, a Supreme Court Judge who has sat on the Commission for many years and whom we interviewed when preparing this chapter (see below) has indicated that an awareness of this course of action is growing among the prison population. He reported that some parole seekers who were not successful initiated administrative disputes and lodged constitutional complaints as well. According to the available data, none of them succeeded.

All the Commission's decisions must be officially recorded (Art. 128 RISI). A positive decision on parole must contain personal information about the parolee, information on the final judgment by which he was convicted and given a custodial sentence, and the date on which the parolee is to be released. A decision rejecting an application must also give the reasons why parole was denied (Art. 129 RISI).

The decision on parole can be temporarily revoked if new or previously unknown circumstances suggesting that parole should not be granted come to light before the prisoner's release date (Art. 130 RISI).[18] In such cases the Commission meets again to reconsider the application.

4.2 The Prison Governor's powers

Independently of the Commission deciding on parole, a Prison Governor has the power to decide on preliminary release from prison. In cases where the Governor receives a positive report from the prison's counselling staff, he may grant prisoners preliminary release if they are behaving appropriately, showing eagerness to work and involving themselves actively in other prison rehabilitation activities. Preliminary release can be authorized in cases where at least three quarters of the penalty has been served and less than one month remains before the end of the sentence. There is no appeal against this decision (Art. 108 EPSA). An important difference between preliminary release from prison and parole is that preliminary release cannot be revoked.

4.3 Pardon

A prisoner may also apply for a pardon. A pardon is an act of clemency granted by the President of the Republic (Art. 1 of the Pardon Act). By means of a pardon, a person designated by name can be granted immunity to prosecution, a partial remission of sentence, mitigation of the imposed sentence and the substitution of the imposed sentence

[18]Typically, a prisoner commits a new offence while in prison or his personal circumstances change substantially.

by a suspended sentence. In addition, the removal of the conviction from the prisoner's criminal record may be granted as well as a cessation or reduction of the legal consequences of the conviction.[19]

Even though it may not be directly connected to the question of early release, the fact that the President's right to grant pardon encompasses the possibility of granting immunity to prosecution merits further attention. One could argue that the Pardon Act goes too far in giving such power to the President: the institution of pardon can be accepted as a *corrigendum* of judicial decisions, but surely not as a means of thwarting them? It should be noted, however, that the procedure of pardoning somebody by ceasing criminal proceedings against him can be triggered only *ex officio* (by the Minister of Justice) and not at the defendant's request. There has been no case recently to suggest that this kind of pardon would be granted.

In 2006, when the former President of the Republic of Slovenia, Janez Drnovšek, pardoned a well-known businessman who had been convicted of a serious economic crime, a broad public debate took place about this particular decision as well as about the institution of pardon in general. Pardons were criticized *inter alia*, for infringing the condition of equality before the law, for leaving the door wide open to arbitrariness and for violating the principle of the division of powers. However, even in modern legal systems, there is a need for a certain meta-juridical tool that can correct judicial mistakes, redress injustices and mitigate the unjustified severity of punishment in cases where no other legal remedies exist. When applied restrictively and reasonably, pardon as defined in the Pardon Act most probably does not represent a serious threat to the rule of law.

When comparing the institutions of pardon and parole in the Slovenian legal system, certain parallels should be pointed out. There is a similarity, for example, between a remission of a sentence or a mitigation of the imposed sentence as granted by pardon, and an early release from prison as granted through parole. A vital difference between these two legal institutions is that, in the case of pardons, the decision cannot be revoked if the beneficiary of the pardon should reoffend.

However, one of the possibilities in the pardon procedure is that the prison sentence in question may be substituted by a suspended prison sentence. In such cases the pardoned person takes on a position

[19]Similar effects can be reached by means of an amnesty (Art. 96 of the Criminal Code), but an amnesty is granted to a group and is not individualized. Parliament must pass a special law to grant an amnesty.

very similar to that of a parolee (who faces the possibility of the suspension of his prison sentence being revoked should he reoffend). The technical difference between this kind of pardon and parole is that pardon amends the judicial decision on the penal sanction, while parole does not interfere with the judicial decision and is understood to be 'only a special way of executing the prison sentence'.[20] Another important difference distinguishes between the conditions to be met: while in the case of parole part of the sentence (in most cases, half) must be served, pardon can, in principle, be granted even before the execution of sentence has begun.

When granting a pardon, the rules of the general part of the Criminal Code apply. In principle, there are no other limitations on pardon, such as that a part of the sentence should have been served. The new Criminal Code has made one exception: in the case of life sentences an act of pardon is limited to substituting the life sentence with a sentence of between 25 and 30 years' imprisonment.

5. Revoking parole

Release on parole can be revoked. The Court must revoke parole if the parolee commits one or more criminal offences for which a prison sentence of more than one year may be imposed (Art. 89(1) of the Criminal Code). However, the Court may revoke parole – that is, has the option of doing so – if the parolee commits at least one criminal offence for which a sentence of up to one year only may be imposed. The Court may also revoke parole if the parolee does not obey the rules and additional conditions stipulated in the decision to grant parole (as a result of the newly added Art. 88(8) – see section 3.1 above). The competent Court in such cases is the one that tries the parolee for a newly committed criminal offence. When deciding on whether to revoke parole, the Court must consider in particular the similarity of the offences committed, their seriousness, the motives for which they were committed and other circumstances that may indicate whether it is reasonable to revoke the parole (Art. 89(2)). According to the new Criminal Code, which has introduced the possibility of imposing certain requirements the parolee must meet once parole is granted (Art. 88(8)), the Court may (but is not obliged to) revoke the parole when the parolee does not meet these requirements (Art. 89(2)). Unfortunately there are no other, more specific provisions regarding the revoking of parole in such cases.

[20]As regards the legal nature of parole, see also section 3.2 above.

When revoking parole, the suspended part of the sentence comes back into force because the condition of not committing another offence has not been met. In cases where parole is revoked because another offence has been committed, the Court decides on a new combined sentence. First, the part of the original sentence remaining must be served, which the Court takes as determined (Art. 89(3)). The Court then passes a sentence for the newly committed offence, according to the rules of the Criminal Code. A combined sentence is ultimately determined according to rules set in Arts. 53 and 55.

The same rules apply when the parolee is convicted of another offence committed before being released on parole (Art. 89(4)). If the parolee is newly sentenced to imprisonment for a term not exceeding one year and the Court decides not to revoke parole, the remaining period of parole is suspended until the end of this further sentence (Art. 89(5)). If the parolee commits an offence that violates the terms of his release while still serving parole but the Court does not pass judgment until that term has already expired, the parole may still be revoked, retrospectively, but only within one year after the expiry of the term of parole (Art. 89(6)).

6. Practical challenges

The major problems Slovenian prisons face at the present time are overcrowding[21] and a shortage of staff. Unfortunately, the number of counsellors and other staff has substantially decreased in recent years, which resulted in calls for strikes.[22] Staff claim that the system needs around 200 new employees, of whom about 70 should be professionals: psychologists, social workers and health workers. They suggest that the resocialization of prisoners is seriously threatened by a lack of professional treatment. As a result, the Minister of Justice has promised higher salaries and new jobs.[23]

Another problem connected to early release is the system's weakness when it comes to managing prisoners after release. All newly released prisoners have a special post-prison plan (devised in collaboration

[21]Slovenian Prisons are 25 per cent overcrowded, according to the required standards (7–9 m^2 per prisoner) (Prison Administration of the Republic of Slovenia, 2008: 96).
[22]See http://www.dnevnik.si/novice/kronika/1042220643
[23]See http://www.delo.si/clanek/75485   http://www.dnevnik.si/novice/slovenija/1042241933

with social work centres, the health services, social security services, schools etc.) that provides advice on common social problems, and on ways of obtaining education or employment, treatment for addictions, etc. Slovenia does not have specific parole officers but a similar type of counselling is supplied by specialists in social work centres. Due to the increasing prison population these workers have also reported a shortage of staff and other difficulties.[24]

Since the only condition for parole until 1 November 2008 was that a prisoner must not reoffend, we cannot report here on other conditions commonly attached to parole (for example, undergoing therapy or obeying a restraining order). The Slovenian system does not impose physical restraints on a parolee's movements (for example, electronic monitoring).

7. Conclusion

In the course of preparing this chapter we interviewed a Supreme Court Judge who has sat on the Parole Commission for many years. While he did not report any gross deficiencies in the parole system, he did hint at issues that are perhaps worth rethinking. Like many other European states, Slovenia has for some time been facing the problem of prison overcrowding. In consequence it is feared that the system's physical capacity to hold prisoners may become a factor, (by design or not) in future decisions on parole – a state of affairs that does not accord with the aims and purposes of parole as it is viewed in Slovenia.

As regards the composition of a Parole Commission, several questions can be raised. The first concerns the role of Judge in the Commission. At the moment one of the Commission's members must be a Judge of the Supreme Court of the Republic of Slovenia. Our interviewee, as a Supreme Court Judge himself, raised doubts as to whether a representative of the Supreme Court is the best choice for the judicial member of the Commission. A better solution might be to have first instance Judges on the Parole Commission, since courts of first instance are more directly involved in questions of sanctioning and their implications. Academic studies have also suggested that parole decisions should be taken only by a judicial body, because, in effect, such decisions change a Court decision (Jakulin 1989: 544).

[24]Prison Administration of the Republic of Slovenia (2008: 96, 49–50).

Some critics have pointed out that it is unsatisfactory that no criminological and penological experts are involved in parole decision-making (Krstanovski 1991: 50). One has to agree with this – there is a danger that the system will become over-dependent on the experience and commitment of one or two of the most senior officials working in parole. In a country the size of Slovenia it is possible for the chairman of the Parole Commission, for example, to be aware of the details of every long-term prisoner in the country. The means, therefore, should be developed both for disseminating and updating such experience and expertise.

The parole procedure also needs revising, although progress is clearly being made. As mentioned above, parolees can now be present while the Commission and expert team are discussing their applications. This has proved a positive experience because prisoners now hear what the team says about them, and this builds trust between the prisoner and the panel. The law also requires that negative decisions on parole applications must be clearly explained. This contributes to the transparency of the procedure. This explanation is especially important to trust and transparency since there is no possibility of appeal.

The criteria for parole should also be more clearly elaborated: they are enumerated in (Art. 109(4) of the Criminal Code, but no prognostic criteria are required by law and so a decision is made even more arbitrary because different experts have very different professional backgrounds and, thus, very different levels of expertise. Some authors have made a case for criteria based on prognostic instruments, which would guarantee greater equality among prisoners (Brinc 1990: 43). Currently, prognostic instruments are used by psychologists and other members of the counsellor team in each prison for assessment purposes only. There is no legal requirement to use statistical reconviction tools or prognostic instruments, and so practice differs among Slovenian prisons.

There is still the question about the kind and scope of the rights to which prisoners applying for parole are entitled. Do they have a right to have a lawyer present at the hearing? Do they have the right to inspect the file prepared by the prison team and to object to certain assertions? Are they merely passive listeners at those meetings or can they present their cases, including producing evidence? These questions touch on issues other than those concerning protocol. Accordingly, there is still much legal and ethical thinking to be done in refining Slovenia's rules on early release.

Acknowledgements

The authors would like to thank Marko Šorli, Supreme Court Judge and Vice-President of the Supreme Court of Republic of Slovenia, and Miha Wohinz, of the Ministry of Justice, for their kind help in preparing this chapter.

References

Ambrož, M. (2007) 'Izvrševanje kazni zapora in sodni nadzor (Enforcement of penal sentences and judicial control)', in L. Bavcon (ed.) *Sodobne usmeritve kazenskega materialnega prava*. Ljubljana: Inštitut za kriminologijo.

Bavcon, L. (2007) 'Ali bi Slovenija zmogla brez kazni dosmrtnega zapora? (Could Slovenia be without life sentence?)', *Pravna praksa*, 26: 23–5.

Bavcon, L. (2008) 'Še en traktat o novi smeri kazenskega prava (Another tract on the new direction of criminal law)', *Pravna praksa*, 27: 14–16.

Bavcon, L. and Šelih, A. (2003) *Kazensko pravo: splošni del (Criminal Law: General Part)*. Ljubljana: Uradni list RS.

Bele, I. (2001) *Kazenski zakonik s komentarjem, splošni del (Commentary on the General Part of Criminal Code)*. Ljubljana: GV.

Bele, I. (2007) 'Kdo posluša vox populi? (Who listens to vox populi?)', *Dnevnikov Objektiv*, 17 November: 14.

Brinc, F. (1990) *Pravice zapornikov in njihovo varstvo v Republiki Sloveniji (Rights of the Convicted Persons and their Protection in the Republic of Slovenia)*. Ljubljana: Inštitut za kriminologijo.

Brinc, F. (2004) 'Kriminalna prognoza – iluzija ali resničnost? (Crime prognosis – illusion or reality?)', *Revija za kriminalistiko in kriminologijo*, 54: 341–55.

Damjanović, I., Kokić-Puce, Z. and Klarić-Baranović, S. (2004) 'Uvjetni otpust s izdržavanja kazne zatvora (od 1998 do 2002) (Early release from prison on parole (from 1998 to 2002)', *Hrvatski ljetopis za kazneno pravo i praksu*, 11: 2, 867–92.

Deisinger, M. (2007) 'Zaznane težnje po spremembah v posebnem delu Kazenskega zakonika (Detected tendencies for change in the special part of the Criminal Code)', *Podjetje in delo*, 33: 1640–51.

Jackson, J. (2007) 'Evidence and proof in parole hearings: meeting a triangulation of interests', *Criminal Law Review*, 54: 417–40.

Jakulin, V. (1989) 'Pogojni odpust in preklic pogojnega odpusta (Parole and revoking of parole)', *Pravnik*, 44: 533–52.

Jakulin, V. (2008) 'S spremembami moralne zavesti se spreminja tudi kazensko pravo (With changes of moral consciousness criminal law also changes)', *Dnevnikov Objektiv*, 19 April: 15.

Jescheck, H. and Weigend, T. (1996) *Lehrbuch des Strafrechts, Allgemeiner Teil (Textbook on the General Part of the Criminal Law)*. Berlin: Duncker & Humblot.

Kmet, S. (2007) 'Dosmrtni zapor – družba prezira? (Life sentence – society of contempt?)', *Pravna praksa*, 26: X–XI.

Krstanovski, M. (1991) 'Uslovni otpust kao penološka mera (Parole as a penological measure)', *Forum*, 67: 46–50.

Kurtović, A. (1995) 'Ustrojstvo i pravna priroda uvjetnog odpusta (The structure and the legal nature of parole)', *Zbornik Pravnog fakulteta sveučilišta na Rijeci*, 16: 309–22.

Meier, B.-D. (2006) *Strafrechtliche Sanktionen (Penal Sanctions)*. Berlin: Springer.

Novak, A. (2007) 'Dosmrtni zapor na trhlih temeljih (Life sentence on weak grounds)', *Pravna praksa*, 26: VI–VIII.

Novak, A. (2008a) 'Nepotrebnost usklajevanja kazenskih sankcij z Rimskim statutom (No necessity to adapt criminal sanctions to Rome Statute)', *Pravna praksa*, 27: 17–18.

Novak, A. (2008b) 'O ustavno skladni implementaciji Rimskega statute in vrednotah (On the implementation of the Rome Statute in accordance with the Constitution and on values)', *Pravna praksa*, 27: 19–20.

Novoselec, P. (2007) *Opći dio kaznenog prava (The General Part of the Criminal Law)*. Zagreb: Sveučilište u Zagrebu.

Penko, B. (2007), 'Prosim za besedo, gospod minister' ('Minister, May I Have a Word Please'), *Dnevnikov objektiv*, 27. October: 14–15.

Petrovec, D. (2007a) 'Dosmrtni zapor in javno mnenje (Life sentence and public opinion)', *Večer*, 18 October: 8.

Petrovec, D. (2007b) 'Smrt v zaporu (Death in prison)', *Dnevnik*, 25 August: 7.

Prison Administration of the Republic of Slovenia (2001) *Annual Report, 2000*. Ljubljana: PARS (available online at http://www.mp.gov.si/fileadmin/ mp.gov.si/pageuploads/2005/PDF/uiks/porocilo_uiks2000.pdf)

Prison Administration of the Republic of Slovenia (2007) *Annual Report, 2006*. Ljubljana: PARS (available online at http://www.mp.gov.si/fileadmin/ mp.gov.si/pageuploads/2005/PDF/uiks/Letno_porocilo_07_web.pdf)

Prison Administration of the Republic of Slovenia (2008) *Annual Report, 2007*. Ljubljana: PARS (available online at http://www.mp.gov.si/fileadmin/ mp.gov.si/pageuploads/2005/PDF/uiks/LP2006.pdf)

Ristić, S. (1980) *Uslovni otpust* (Parole). Niš: PF u Nišu.

Stojanović, Z. (1984) 'Uslovni otpust: problemi i predpostavke (Parole: problems and suppositions)', *Zbornik pravnog fakulteta u Zagrebu*, 35: 185–200.

Šugman, K., Jager, M., Peršak, N. and Filipčič, K. (2004) *Slovenia: Criminal Justice Systems in Europe and North America*. Helsinki: HEUNI (European Institute for Crime Prevention and Control) affiliated with the United Nations.

Zakonjšek, E. (2008) 'Javna objava kaznivega dejanja (Public announcement of a criminal offence)', *Dnevnikov Objektiv*, 16 February: 14.

Chapter 15

Spain

José Cid and Beatriz Tébar

Summary

Spanish law provides three mechanisms for early release from imprisonment: pardon, release on home detention curfew and parole, although pardons are used only very rarely. It is also important to consider the former generous 'good time' credit system for all prison sentences (which was abolished with the 1995 Criminal Code), since this shortened the time to be served before a prisoner was eligible for parole. Home detention curfew and parole are discretionary early release mechanisms included in the penitentiary law as a means of managing the transition from imprisonment to unconditional release. In order to be eligible for these early release mechanisms, prisoners must be assessed as having a good prognosis, which normally requires them to have benefited from home leave and to have spent a period of time in an open prison. In this sense, open prisons should be considered as a pre-early release mechanism.

Overall, the Spanish system of early release faces three main problems: the disparity in the implementation of early release mechanisms; the long time that a prisoner must statutorily serve before being granted parole in comparison with most other European countries; and the restrictive use of early release as a way of ending a sentence.

358

I. Introduction

Spanish penal law provides the following mechanisms for early release from prison: pardon, release on home detention curfew and parole.[1] Given that pardon is used very rarely, this chapter is devoted mainly to home detention curfew and parole. It is, however, important to remember that, until the adoption of the 1995 Criminal Code, there was a generous 'good time' credit system for all prison sentences.

Home detention curfew and parole are discretionary early release mechanisms included in the penitentiary law as a means of managing the transition from imprisonment to unconditional release. In order to be eligible for these early release mechanisms, prisoners must be assessed as having a good prognosis, which normally requires them to have benefited from home leave and to have spent a period of time in an open prison. In this sense, open prison should be considered as a pre-early release mechanism.

Overall, the Spanish system of early release faces three main problems: the disparity in the implementation of early release mechanisms; the long time that must statutorily be served before being granted parole in comparison with most other European countries; and the restrictive use of early release as a way of ending a sentence.

This chapter is structured as follows. The following section gives a general history of early release mechanisms that is needed in order to understand the present Spanish system. Next, the chapter deals with the main aspects of home detention curfew and parole. The following section focuses on the statistical data that can be used to understand the practical problems underlined in the ensuing section. Finally, as a conclusion, there is a theoretical discussion about the Spanish model of early release. (Figure 15.1 provides a summary of the Spanish early release system).

[1]Throughout this chapter the terms 'parole', 'conditional early release' and 'conditional liberty' are used interchangeably. When employing them, we have the following broad definition in mind: a penal measure whereby a convicted person is released into the community before the end of a custodial sentence, subject (whether or not under supervision and until the sentence expiry date) to the observance of certain rules or conditions, among which the duty not to reoffend is always included. The distinction between 'parole' and 'conditional early release' is mainly associated with the type of release procedure, but in Spain there is no such distinction since all types of early conditional release measures follow the same procedure.

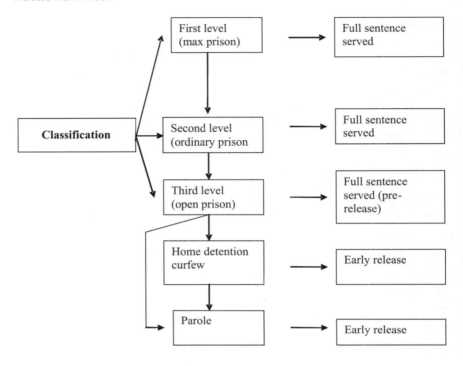

Figure 15.1 Prison classification and release systems in Spain

Before advancing into the text, it may be useful for the reader to view the diagram above that summarises the Spanish system of early release.

2. History

The history of early release procedures in Spain can be divided into three main stages. The first period is from the emergence of the prison sentence up to the nineteenth century when pardons (mainly a royal prerogative) were still the only way to be released from prison before the sentence expiry date. The second period begins when new ideas about penal and penitentiary reform began to emerge in Spain. These reforms were reflected in such measures as 'good-time' credits and parole. Finally, the third phase commenced in 1995 when a new

Criminal Code heralded an era of reforms based on the ideal of truth in sentencing[2] and punitiveness.

2.1 Pardons

The use of mercy as an early release mechanism has its origins in ancient Spanish law. Three measures can be distinguished under the concept of mercy: general pardons (these cancel the whole or part of the sentence for a general category of prisoners), particular pardons (these cancel the whole or part of the sentence for an individual prisoner) and amnesties (these cancel not only the sentence but also the conviction, leaving a category of prisoners or an individual prisoner free of any criminal record). All these institutions are an instrument of the absolute power of the Sovereign (Linde 1976). At the same time, they played a role in tempering the severity of criminal laws, in particular during the Ancient Regime (Tomás y Valiente 1969).

Both the classical school (Becccaria and Bentham) and the positivist and Spanish correctionalist school (Garofalo, Ferri, Arenal and Dorado) expressed negative opinions about the idea of mercy. Classical thinkers considered that mercy was in opposition to the separation of powers and the supremacy of the law and the judiciary. Positivist and correctionalist scholars believed that, in an indeterminate sentencing system based on the idea of rehabilitation, the institution of mercy lost ground (Antón 1960).

In spite of the influence of both the classical and positivist schools on Spanish legislation and sentencing practice since the eighteenth century, all the mechanisms of mercy not only survived but – in particular, general pardons – were also granted very frequently (Linde 1976). This wide use of pardons explains the low rates of imprisonment in Spain until 1978, when the Spanish Constitution prohibited general pardons.[3]

---

[2] We use the term 'truth in sentencing' to capture the reforms introduced in several jurisdictions to reduce discretion, requiring that every convicted prisoner serves a relevant part of the sentence passed by the Judge before being released. Possible examples of these reforms in American jurisdictions are the abolition of discretionary parole or the laws requiring that 85 per cent of the sentence should have expired before release (Petersilia 2003).

[3] Under the general Spanish regulation of reprieves (s. 62.I of the Spanish Constitution and Pardon Act 1870, as modified by 1/88 Act), the government, on the prior proposal of the Minister of Justice, can grant pardons after conviction. Pardons can commute the whole or part of the sentence imposed. In this latter sense, partial pardons are the only measure in the Spanish

2.2. Reform and individualization

The introduction of more sophisticated early release procedures into the Spanish penal system owes much to the general prison reform that took place in the Western world during the last quarter of the eighteenth century and throughout the nineteenth century.[4] The humanitarian intentions of this reform movement brought about the implementation and development of modern prison systems,[5] which eventually resulted in progressive prison regimes. Based on the idea of gradually eliminating the physical constraints in the enforcement of a prison sanction, progressive regimes usually included an early release mechanism at the end of the sentence.

An outstanding precedent of the progressive prison regime is to be found in the practice adopted by Coronel Montesinos in the San Agustin Prison, in the city of Valencia (1835–55). Montesinos implemented a prison regime with three stages, where the last one involved working outside prison. Offenders could progress through the stages as a reward for their good conduct and work. Montesinos' ideas inspired other influential progressive regimes. These included the regimes implemented by Alexander Maconochie in the English colonies in Australia (1840) and Sir Walter Crofton in Ireland (1853),[6] whose prison regime was later adopted in some Spanish prisons during the late eighteenth century and for the whole of Spain in 1901.

penal system that can remit part of a custodial sentence. No public official statistics are available, but it appears that pardons are rarely applied as an early release procedure. Thus, according to data provided by the Ministry of Justice and published by the national newspaper, El País (27 February 2006), 453 pardons where granted in 2005 (cited in Sánchez-Vera 2008: 11).

[4]The origins of this movement have been traced to the publication of The State of the Prisons in England and Wales (1777), the famous work of the English penal reformer, John Howard (Lastres 1875 113–14; Wines 1910: 122; Neuman 1984: 53). It has been pointed out that this work did not introduce new ideas but popularized the humanitarian prison movement and the idea that prisons should reform the offender (McGowen 1995: 87).

[5]Thus the Philadelphian and Auburn systems (see, generally, Beaumont and de Tocqueville 1833).

[6]Sir Walter Crofton acknowledged Montesinos for his pioneering progressive system at the International Penitentiary Congress held in London in 1872 (Bernaldo de Quirós 1940: 210).

Moreover, at the end of the nineteenth century, rehabilitation found acceptance as a justification for punishment. In this context, in 1914 legal provision was made for a system of parole. This system allowed the discretionary conditional release of offenders serving a prison sentence of more than one year, once the three-quarter point of the sentence had been reached and provided they had been classified as suitable for the most open prison regime. In addition, evidence was required of a prisoner's 'irreproachable' behaviour in prison, as well as some proof of a future 'honest life'.

Prisoners released conditionally remained on licence until the expiry date of their sentences. Two situations could lead to the revocation of the licence: committing a new offence and behaving in a way that could be regarded as 'bad conduct'.[7] As a cause of revocation, a new offence implied the loss of the time spent on licence. The decision to grant and to revoke parole rested ultimately with the Minister of Justice.

The introduction of a parole system in Spain was based on the idea that an individualized penal intervention could lead to the offender desisting from crime. The key concept that underlay this idea was reform or correction. Pragmatic concerns also played some role in the introduction of a conditional release system. On the one hand, it has been pointed out that the introduction of a conditional release system in Spain was just a restructuring of the old government pardon prerogatives and that this was done to diminish the prison population, which started to concern the Spanish government in the late nineteenth century (Roldán 1988: 168–75). On the other, it has been noted that the closing in 1911 of the Spanish prisons in the North African colonies hastened the introduction of a conditional release system (Castejón 1915). A progressive system with a period of conditional release had been implemented in the colonies of Ceuta and Melilla since the last quarter of the nineteenth century.[8] When these

[7]This ground for revocation was vaguely defined by the Conditional Liberty Act 1914, which states only that 'bad conduct' implies but is not limited to the breach of the conditions and duties imposed on the parolee.

[8]This system evolved as a result of a shortage of workers in the colonies (Fraile 1987: 116–17). The system divided a prison sentence into four periods. Each period entailed less restraint on the movement of the prisoners, who progressed according to their good behaviour (that is, compliance with prison discipline). During the third period prisoners were allocated different tasks in the city and they only stayed overnight in prison. After having completed three quarters of their sentences, prisoners could serve the remainder outside prison but under the supervision of a master. Prisoners in this period were

territories ceased being used as prison colonies, many prisoners were transferred to the Peninsula. This movement not only increased the prison population density but also created tension among prisoners who required a general implementation of the progressive system.[9]

The basic structure of the parole system laid down by the 1914 Act has remained almost unchanged until the present day. Most changes in the system throughout the twentieth century were in terms of implementation, which was shaped by the ideologies of the different political regimes that were established in Spain during that period.[10]

A quite generous remission scheme was introduced under Franco's regime after the Civil War (1936–9) as a way of dealing with the enormous mass of political prisoners. Initially, good-time credits were to be given to prisoners who worked during their sentence. However, due to a lack of prison work, good-time credits came to be granted automatically on the basis of good behaviour in prison – that is, an absence of breaches of prison discipline. Ordinarily, good-time credits allowed a remission of one third of the sentence. Additionally, an extraordinary remission was introduced by the 1956 Prison Rules, whereby the sentence could be reduced by up to one half, provided that work or treatment activities were undertaken. This remission scheme, which was abolished in 1995, was compatible with the system of discretionary parole, because sentence reductions on the basis of good-time credits counted towards the minimum time required to access parole.

The ideas of reform and individualization were influential throughout the twentieth century, in different forms and degrees of

said to be 'on conditions'. They had to work for their master during the day and the master had to provide them with a place to sleep (Salillas 1888: 254–5).

[9]The prisoners who were transferred lost their chance to be released 'on conditions', while the ones already in the Peninsula did not find the pre-existing inequality of the systems fair.

[10]Under the Liberal government of the Spanish 2nd Republic (1931–6), a humanitarian type of conditional release was established in 1932 for prisoners aged 70 years or more, who could be paroled at any time during their prison sentence. During the Spanish Civil War (1936–9) and the postwar period, modifications of the operation of the conditional release system were driven, on the one hand, by the need to reduce the inflated prison population, due to the massive imprisonment of the so-called 'Marxist rebels'. On the other hand, parole was used as another means to control political activities against General Franco's dictatorship. Specific legislation was enacted for political prisoners, and part of this was eventually extended to all prisoners.

intensity. Thus, as Bottoms points out for the English case, in 'the post-war period, "reform" became "rehabilitation" – that is religious and moral impulses in reformation became secularised, psychologised, scientised' (1980: 1). The notion of rehabilitation was introduced in the 1978 Constitution, which proposed a change in the whole penal system to the extent that sanctions must be governed by principles and rights suitable to a modern democratic and social state guided by the rule of law. Regarding the penitentiary system, the Spanish Constitution prescribes specifically that the enforcement of custody sentences is to be oriented towards the goals of 'social reintegration' and 're-education' (s. 25.2).[11]

The General Penitentiary Act 1979 established a new prison system based on individualization that allowed prisoners to be allocated to the third level of the regime – that is, open imprisonment – from the beginning of their custody sentence.[12] The General Penitentiary Act also introduced important safeguards by creating the office of Prison Judge – the authority who grants and revokes parole and decides on the conditions of the licence, on the basis of a prior report from the Prison Administration.

2.3 Truth in sentencing measures and punitiveness

The 1995 Criminal Code introduced an era of truth in sentencing measures that substantially modified early release mechanisms in the following years. In this sense, a major change introduced by the new Criminal Code was the abolition of the good-time credit system. This 'truth in sentencing' reform had a significant impact on the early conditional release system since, although the minimum time to be served in order to qualify for conditional early release remained at the three quarters' point of the sentence, the actual time served was extended as a consequence of the elimination of remission. A further change was the power granted to the trial Judge to decide, in the

[11]The meaning and scope of this section are controversial. Generally, the Spanish Constitutional Court has ruled that s. 25.2 does not contain a subjective right but a principle that must be followed in the regulation and enforcement of custodial sentences. For a discussion about the effects that s. 25.2 should have on the regulation and implementation of parole, see Tébar (2006a: 88–96).
[12]Unlike the former progressive penitentiary system, which required serving a minimum time in each period or category in order to be moved forward. The change from a progressive system to an individualized system was initiated by the 1968 penitentiary reform.

case of dangerous offenders and very long terms of imprisonment, that the sentence should be served without parole at all (s. 78). This measure seems not to have gained much acceptance among Spanish trial Judges as they have used this discretionary power on only a few occasions.

Nevertheless, the 1995 Criminal Code introduced some measures of a different kind which aimed to enhance the use of early release with supervision. Thus, the scope of implementation of early conditional release was extended to prisoners serving less than one year. Provision was also made for conditional release at the two thirds' point of the sentence. One of the most significant reforms referred to the possibility of attaching formal obligations to the liberty period, the breach of which could result in parole revocation. This new provision, however, improved certainty regarding revocation, as well as clarifying the powers of the Prison Administration to propose conditions during the parole period. As for reoffending, it continued to be a ground for revocation. However, the 1995 Criminal Code eliminated the loss of the time spent on parole, with the result that the period served during parole counted as time served in any case. Finally, the 1995 Criminal Code also improved the standard of the legislative drafting of the parole provisions, removing, at the same time, their moralistic connotations.[13]

A second stage in the truth-in-sentence era can be identified in 2003 when a series of rather opportunistic penal reforms was launched that had the effect of increasing the overall degree of punitiveness of the Spanish criminal system (Cid and Larrauri, 2009).[14] Regarding release mechanisms, significant changes were introduced by Act 7 of 30 June 2003,[15] although its major impact was on the sentences

[13]Thus, as for the criteria to be eligible to be released on parole, 'irreproachable' behaviour was phrased as 'good' behaviour, which in practice meant an absence of serious breaches of prison discipline. At the same time, 'a positive prediction of social reintegration' replaced the inappropriate presumption of an 'honest' future life. Classification in the third level of the prison regime was kept as an objective criterion.

[14]For instance, the maximum period that someone can serve in prison, following a prison sentence, has been extended from 30 to 40 years.

[15]Many of its provisions raise constitutional doubts, the analysis of which is beyond the scope of this chapter. The Act is particularly problematic in relation to ss. 25.2 and 117 of the Constitution, which embody, respectively, the rehabilitation and the judicial power principles.

of prisoners convicted for certain offences related to terrorism and criminal organizations.[16]

Regarding ordinary offences, the most significant changes were as follows:

- The introduction of a minimum mandatory period for sentences longer than five years in order to be classified in the third level of the prison regime.

- The widening of the legal provision for excluding prison sentences of any kind of pre-release and early release measures.

- Compensation to the victim, which was added as a requirement to be eligible for classification in third level and for conditional release.

As in the case of the 1995 truth-in-sentencing reform, the 2003 changes also included measures not guided by punitiveness. Thus the 2003 Act introduced an additional early conditional release scheme which allows the date of release to be advanced by up to 90 days for every year of the sentence that has been served in prison.

Finally, in respect of the process for deciding on conditional liberty, a further change should be highlighted that could limit the discretion of the prison Judge and grant more power to the Prison Administration. Thus, in terms of the letter of the legal provisions for parole set by Act 7 of 2003, only this latter body is now authorized to report on the prediction of future criminal behaviour.

Today, the trend towards populist punitiveness seems even greater. On the one hand, in some instances where prisoners sentenced for serious crimes have been released after the expiration of their sentences, both the media and politicians have asked for extended sentences on the grounds that they have not been rehabilitated. The government has presented a draft Bill that would make extension of

[16]Indeed, the enactment of the Act 7 of 2003 was mainly sparked off by the polemic, mainly fed by the media, caused by the conditional release in October 2002 of a member of the Basque separatist terrorist organization, ETA. This person had been sentenced to a nominal prison sentence of 298 years, which actually could mean up to a maximum of 30 years' imprisonment. As he met all the legal criteria to be eligible for parole, he was released after having served 13 years of his sentence. One month later the government announced the reform of the penal system in order to increase the actual time served in prison by offenders categorized as terrorists.

their sentences possible. On the other hand, after two serious murders of young people, the families of the victims have started a campaign to introduce life sentences in Spain. However, the latest news at the time of writing (February 2009) is that the judiciary do not seem to support the proposals for extended sentences (Consejo General del Poder Judicial 2009).

3. The Spanish early release schemes

3.1 The Spanish prison system: context and grounds for early release

The basic structure of the Spanish prison system was established by the General Penitentiary Act 1979. This Act introduced a progressive system based on an individualization of the prison regime, which provides four main levels of classification. The main features of the Spanish prison system and of the third level of classification are as follows.

There are four general levels of classification for convicted prisoners, the last being the conditional release period. So the higher the level, the more open the regime implemented:

- First level – closed or maximum security prison.
- Second level – ordinary prison.
- Third level – open prison.
- Fourth level – parole.

The third level implies a regime of semi-detention where, from Mondays to Thursdays, prisoners spend part of the time outside prison (usually working) and have to return to prison only at night. There are two legal possibilities for being classified as a third-level prisoner. Firstly, prisoners may be classified directly as belonging in the third level if they have a good risk prognosis. This is only possible for sentences of up to five years and, in practice, it is used only for first offenders with short sentences and very good risk prognoses (Capdevila *et al.* 2006). Secondly, the third level may be reached as a progression from the second level for convicted prisoners who have served at least a quarter of their sentences and are considered ready to be resettled. In practice, however, the following additional criteria must be met for allocation to this level: having served half of the sentence; having previously been granted temporary leave from prison; and having a remaining sentence that would make them eligible for ordinary parole in no more than two or three years (López i Ferrer 2004; Cid 2005). Both as a primary classification and as a progression from the second level, the third level requires prisoners to pay compensation or at least to give guarantees of payment, inasfar as they are able to do so.

For sentences longer than five years a minimum mandatory period of half the sentence is required before classification in the third level. This minimum mandatory period can be lifted by the prison Judge, provided that a low risk of reoffending is predicted.

Stricter criteria are required for those convicted of terrorism or organized crime offences. To be allocated to the third level they have to meet further criteria, such as demonstrating that they have disowned their past criminal activities and have apologized to the victims of their crimes. Additionally, for these prisoners there is no possibility of lifting the minimum mandatory time required for sentences longer than five years.

The power to decide on classification lies with the General Director of the Prison Administration in the case of the first, second and third levels, following prior assessment by qualified prison staff. Parole is granted by a prison Judge. The decision of the Prison Administration on initial classification cannot be delayed for more than two months. Subsequent classifications must be reviewed every six months. Both the prisoner and the Prosecutor are entitled to appeal against the classification to the prison Judge, with a possible further judicial review.

Although this open-prison regime might be regarded as a semi-parole system, and although it shares origins with the Spanish parole system, it is not a full early-release mechanism because prisoners have to spend some time in prison. In this way, the open regime has been configured as an intermediate stage between ordinary imprisonment and release on parole, since only third-level prisoners are eligible for parole.

3.2   Home detention curfew

Prisoners allocated to the third level (who work or who undergo treatment programmes outside the establishment) are eligible to be released on home detention curfew during the night. The 1996 Prison Rules established this special regime which allows third-level prisoners to replace the nightly return to prison with a home detention curfew so that they have to visit prison only for arranged interviews with their supervision agent. Generally, the home detention period, which normally lasts from 11 pm to 7 am, is monitored by electronic tagging or by police officers. Non-compliance with the electronic monitoring licence can result in being recalled to prison.

It should be noted that there is a contradiction between the 1995 Criminal Code, which is mainly based on a truth-in-sentencing philosophy (the abolition of good-time credits), and the 1996 Prison Rules, which introduced this early release scheme which allows the time requirement to be circumvented.[17] A possible explanation for this contradiction can be found in the different appeals of the Criminal Code and the Prison Rules. The former is geared more closely to punitiveness, whereas the latter are more sensitive to the demands of the prison authorities for a means to release low-risk prisoners.

3.3 Parole

3.3.1 Legal criteria for parole

Parole in Spain can be defined as a penal measure whereby a convicted person is released into the community before the end of a prison sentence, whether under supervision or not. Such a person is required to observe certain rules or conditions, among which is always included a duty not to reoffend. Parole remains in force until the sentence expiry date, unless it is revoked earlier and the offender is recalled to prison. As explained below, different modalities of parole can be distinguished according to the criteria for release. Mention also should be made of some cases where the type of prisoner, the number of offences committed and the length of the prison terms involved can lead to a prison sentence without parole.

Ordinary parole Ordinary parole can be granted from the three quarters' point of the sentence, provided the offender meets the requirements of a third-level classification, good behaviour and a good prognosis, which include the duty to comply with any of the civil liabilities resulting from the offence. In this latter sense, full restitution is not required but a willingness to compensate the victim to the extent that the offender has the means to do so.

Early parole The time for release on parole can be advanced to two thirds or even half of the sentence if additional requirements relating to participation in treatment and continuous labour activities

[17]For this reason, some Spanish authors have considered this system to be 'hidden parole' because release is granted without meeting all the parole procedures and criteria, especially the minimum time served requirement (Vega 2001; Renart 2003; Gonzalez-Baqué 2008).

are met. There are no clear legal or judicial criteria to distinguish between the use of ordinary and early parole.

Humanitarian parole A special parole regime is provided for humanitarian reasons for those who are 70 or more years old and for those who suffer from a serious and incurable illness. In these cases parole can be granted at any stage of the sentence, provided that the other criteria are met. The Spanish Constitutional Court has considered[18] that this type of parole is premised on the fundamental right of life and human dignity so it can be denied only on the basis of a high risk to public safety.

Parole for prisoners convicted of terrorism and of offences related to organized crime There are stricter parole rules for prisoners convicted of terrorism and offences related to organized crime. Such offenders are additionally required to repudiate their criminal activities and to apologize to their victims. They can be paroled only after they have served three quarters of their sentences, since they are legally excluded from any advanced form of parole. In addition, if at the time of the conviction they are banned from parole, or if the minimum time required to be conditionally released is extended in terms of s. 78 of the Criminal Code, and the prison Judge subsequently decides to allow such a measure, they can be granted parole only during the last eighth part of their sentence. Finally, in the case of terrorist offenders, revocation of parole implies the loss of the time spent on licence.

Sentences without parole The Spanish Criminal Code makes legal provision for excluding from parole lengthy prison sentences imposed for various offences (s. 78). This mechanism operates by calculating the date of release by adding together all the prison terms imposed in the same procedure and not basing this on the real sentence to be served. Prison sentences resulting from convictions for more than one offence are statutorily limited in two ways. On the one hand there is a relative limit whereby any prison sentence cannot exceed three times the length of the most serious prison sanction imposed. On the other, there is an absolute limit for prison sentences, which is ordinarily set at 20 years and can be raised to 25, 30 or 40 years, depending on the seriousness of the offences involved. The implementation of these limits results in a new prison sentence since the remaining prison terms are effectively cancelled. However, if the final prison term that must be served is shorter than half the sum of all the prison sentences imposed, the trial Judge may decide to work out the date for release

[18]Decision 48/1996, 25 March 1996.

mechanisms, including parole, by taking into account the original prison sentences imposed and not the one statutorily limited. This measure is optional in the case of prison sentences of up to 20 years and mandatory for longer sentences, but this discretionary power is scarcely ever used. The implementation of s. 78 of the Spanish Criminal Code normally results in a prison sentence without parole. In any case, during the prison sentence this restriction can be lifted by the prison Judge on the basis of a good prognosis.[19]

Foreign prisoners without legal residence Convicted foreign prisoners without legal residence do not have access to parole since legal provision is made for substituting their prison sentence by expulsion from the country. There are two types of scheme for the expulsion of foreign prisoners, depending on whether their prison sentence is under or over six years. In the case of sentences under six years, the Spanish Criminal Code establishes the mandatory substitution of the penalty for expulsion, which exceptionally may not be imposed by the sentencing Judge, after having heard the Public Prosecutor, on the basis of the type of the offence. Thus expulsion is generally not imposed on foreigners who enter the country in order to commit serious drug offences or offences related to human trafficking, since expelling them would effectively mean that they would not be punished for a first offence of this kind. In the case of sentences of six years or longer, there is statutory provision for expulsion, on request of the Public Prosecutor, once the third level of prison classification has been reached or three quarters of the sentence has been served. Again, exceptionally, the sentencing Judge may not impose such a removal measure on the basis of the nature of the offence committed. However, the legal provisions on the expulsion of foreign prisoners without lawful residence are not automatically applied, since the Spanish High Court generally construes such provisions in the light of the Spanish Constitution and the decisions of the European Court

[19]For example, if a person is convicted of four aggravated rapes and sentenced to 12 years for each, then the addition or the four penalties (48 years in prison) is more than double the maximum sentence that must be served in respect of mandatory limits (20 years). In this case the Judge has the discretion to decide whether the date of parole is to be worked out on the maximum sentence (20 years) or on the addition of the four individual penalties (48 years). Given that parole may be granted only at three quarters of the sentence (or, exceptionally, at two thirds or even half), the decision to take the addition of the four individual sentences (48 years) as a term of reference for parole would imply that the 20-year prison sentence will be served without parole.

of Human Rights. To this extent expulsion is not automatically applied by taking into account only the nature of the offence. The personal circumstances of the offender, such as settlement and family situation, are also considered before deciding on expulsion.[1]

3.3.2 Revocation

There are two main grounds on which parole can be revoked: reoffending and any breach of the licence conditions. Reoffending in this context is generally interpreted as committing a crime but not a misdemeanour. As for conditions that can be attached to the licence, these can relate to such restrictions as not frequenting certain places, not participating in certain activities or nor having any contact with the prisoner's victims and their relatives. Or they may impose an obligation to undergo treatment or to participate in training or educational programmes. The time spent in liberty before revocation counts towards the sentence, except in the case of terrorists and offenders convicted of organized crime.

3.3.3 Parole procedure

As pointed out above, the prison Judge is the authority who grants and revokes parole and who decides on the conditions of the licence. However, the Prison Administration has an important role in all parole procedures and has a strong influence on the final outcome.

The Prison Administration is in charge of preparing the parole file that will be sent to the prison Judge. The release procedure normally takes an average of six months, from the Prison Administration opening the parole file until the prison Judge's decision. According to the existing legal framework the Prison Administration must start the parole procedure with enough time before the three quarters' point of the sentence is reached. However, in practice this is generally not the case (Tébar 2006b). The prison Judge decides on parole based on the proposal of the Prison Administration made through the parole file, which includes a risk assessment of the likelihood of reoffending. The Prison Administration's proposal can be positive or negative: to grant or to refuse parole. If parole is proposed, specific licence rules can be suggested. A wide interpretation of the legal provisions leads to the conclusion that the prison Judge can dissent from a proposal of the Prison Administration. However, it should be noted that, in practice, the Prison Administration generally determines the outcome of the decision, since prison Judges tend to follow the Prison Administration's recommendation in almost all cases. (Tébar 2006a: 235–6).

[1]Spanish High Court decisions 901/2004, 8 July 2004; 906/2005; 8 July 2005 or 166/2007, 14 February 2007.

During the procedure, prisoners have the right to present statements at any stage and the decision taken by the prison Judge is open to further judicial review but no oral hearing is granted.

4. Statistical data

4.1 General data on the classification of prisoners

As stated above, the two early released mechanisms that exist in the Spanish system – home detention curfew and parole – can be granted only to convicted prisoners who are classified as being on the third level; that is, who are serving their sentence in an open prison. As explained below, some of the problems of the Spanish early release system arise from a very restrictive use of the open regime. Table 15.1 shows the evolution of the classification of prisoners from 1996 to 2008.

In order to have a clear picture of the implications of these figures it is useful to compare them with what might be an ideal progressive system, in which all the convicted prisoners would spend one third of their sentences in an ordinary prison, the second third in an open prison and the final third in an early release mechanism (home curfew and parole). Taking into account that, as shown in Table 15.2, in Spain approximately a quarter of the inmates are remand prisoners, the ideal figure should be similar to that represented in Figure 15.2. This figure should be compared with the real distribution of the Spanish prisoners and early release prisoners at the end of 2008 as shown in Figure 15.3.

4.2 Home detention curfew (HDC)

Table 15.3 shows data on the application of this special regime after the approval of the 1995 Criminal Code and the 1996 Prison Rules. From these data it is possible to draw two conclusions. On the one hand, although the number of curfews is not very high, this number cannot be considered insignificant, since, in 2008, it represented approximately 3 per cent of people who were submitted to a correctional intervention (prison and post-prison) (76,000). On the other, it seems that the Prison Administration intends to increase the use of curfew through electronic monitoring, given the low cost of the devices and the low rates of recall (González-Baqué 2008: 129–52).

Table 15.1 Classification of convicted prisoners, 1996–2008

Year	Total classified			Max. prison (first level %)			Ordinary prison (second level %)			Open prison and home detention curfew (third level %)		
	GAE	CAT	Total	GAE	CAT	Total	GAE	CAT	Total	GAE	CAT	Total
1996	22,599	4,112	26,711	3.0	2.2	2.9	81.7	75.2	80.5	15.3	23.3	16.6
1997	22,699	4,066	26,765	2.9	3.1	2.9	82.8	73.7	81.4	14.3	23.2	15.7
1998	24,250	4,079	28,329	3.1	2.6	2.8	83.8	72.0	82.2	13.5	24.5	15.0
1999	25,017	4,125	29,232	3.1	2.5	3.0	82.9	72.4	81.4	14.0	25.1	15.6
2000	26,466	4,417	30,838	3.0	3.0	3.0	83.7	71.9	82.0	13.3	25.1	15.0
2001	28,033	4,459	32,492	2.8	3.3	2.9	83.7	72.7	82.2	13.5	24.0	14.9
2002	29,939	4,896	34,835	2.9	3.5	3.0	83.5	70.4	81.7	13.6	26.1	15.3
2003	32,780	5,420	38,200	2.9	2.5	2.9	85.7	72.2	83.8	11.4	25.3	13.3
2004	35,017	5,792	40,809	2.5	2.4	2.9	85.6	70.0	83.4	11.4	27.5	13.7
2005	35,504	6,055	41559	2.7	2.5	2.6	84.3	71.2	82.5	13.0	26.2	14.9
2006	36,099	6,372	42,471	2.5	2.3	2.5	83.0	70.6	81.1	14.4	27.0	16.4
2007	37,366	6,350	43,716	2.3	2.2	2.3	81.3	73.1	80.1	16.4	24.7	17.6
2008	40,961	7006	47,961	2.1	2.4	2.1	82.0	71.9	80.5	15.9	25.7	17.3
Average				2.7	2.7	2.8	83.4	72.1	81.8	13.8	25.2	15.5

Source: Spain (General Administration of the State, GAE), Secretaríade General de Instituciones Penitenciarias, Estadística General de población reclusa. Evolución mensual. Catalonia (CAT), Secretaría de Servicios Penitenciarios, Rehabilitación y Justicia Juvenil, Estadísticas semanales de población reclusa. Data on 31 December of each year.

Table 15.2 Distribution of prisoners and early release prisoners, 2008

	Number	Percentage
Remand prison	17,598	22
Max-security prison	1,014	1
Ordinary prison	45,483	57
Open prison	6,162	8
Home detention curfew	2,159	3
Parole	7,059	9
Total	79,475	100

Source: Spain (General Administration of the State); Secretaría General de Instituciones Penitenciarias, Estadística General de población reclusa. Evolución mensual. Catalonia: Secretaría Servicios Penitenciarios, Rehabilitación y Justicia Juvenil, Estadísticas semanales de población reclusa. Data on 31 December 2008.

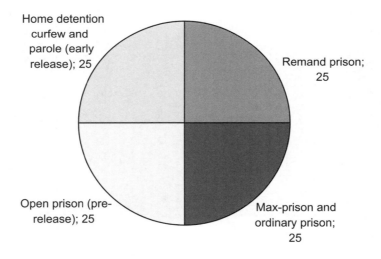

Figure 15.2 Ideal distribution of prisoners in a progressive system

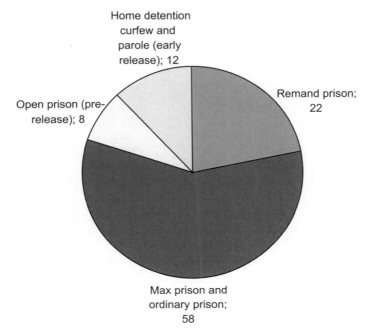

Figure 15.3 Real distribution of prison and early release population, 2008 (data on 31 December 2008)

In practice, home detention curfew has been used by the Prison Administration as a way of releasing prisoners with good prognoses, who were serving their sentences in an open prison until they reached parole (Capdevila *et al.* 2006). Therefore, this new way of releasing prisoners has not had an impact on the percentage of prisoners who have benefited from pre-release and early release mechanisms. As shown in Figure 15.4, the increase in the use of home detention curfew has brought about a reduction in the percentage of prisoners in an open-prison regime.

4.3 Parole

The practice of parole in Spain reveals three important trends. Firstly, there has been an important reduction in the number of parolees after the implementation of the 1995 Criminal Code. Secondly, only a minority of prisoners end their sentences on parole. Thirdly, most parolees were released on parole after having served three quarters of their nominal sentences. These trends can be explained as follows.

Table 15.3 Release on home detention curfew (HDC), 1996–2008

Year	GSA (N)	CAT (N)	Spain	Average prison and early-release population	Percentage of prisoners released on HDC over average prison and early release population
1996	0	0	0	52,996	0,0
1997	0	0	0	51,149	0,0
1998	0	0	0	50,962	0,0
1999	0	0	0	51,456	0,0
2000	0	0	0	50,937	0,0
2001	0	87	87	52,047	0,2
2002	550	134	684	55,551	1,2
2003	550	158	708	59,527	1,2
2004	625	209	834	64,154	1,3
2005	725	243	968	65,785	1,5
2006	963	277	1240	68,965	1,8
2007	1844	260	2104	72,038	2,9
2008	1892	267	2159	76,712	2,8

Source: Unpublished data provided by Secretaría General de Servicios Penitenciarios (General State Administration) and Secretaria de Serveis Penitenciaris, Rehabilitació i Justícia Juvenil (Catalonia) Prisoners released in HDC at 31 December of each year.

4.3.1 Numbers of cases of parole granted

The evolution of the use of parole shows that the introduction of the 1995 Criminal Code was coupled with a great reduction in the number of prisoners granted parole per year (see Table 15.4 and Figure 15.5). The explanation for this important fall in parole numbers after 1995 lies in the increase of penalties and in the abolition of good-time credits introduced by the new Criminal Code of 1995. Since good time was compatible with parole, most prisoners were generally eligible for early conditional release after having served between a third and a half of their sentences. As a consequence of establishing harsher penalties and of abolishing good time, there has been a progressive reduction in the number of convicted prisoners eligible for parole because now only prisoners who have effectively served three quarters of their sentences (or, exceptionally, two thirds or half) can benefit from parole (Tébar 2006b).

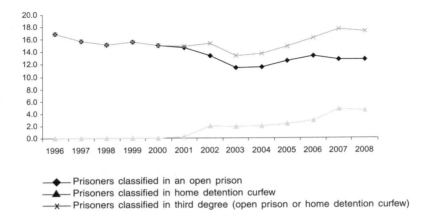

Figure 15.4 Evolution of the open prison regime and home detention curfew, 1996–2008

Table 15.4 Parole granted, 1990–2006

Year	Parole granted	Average convicted prisoners	Parole granted per 100 convicted prisoners
1996	8,684	33,724	25.8
1997	6,696	33,370	20.1
1998	6,215	33,475	18.6
1999	6,050	34,830	17.4
2000	5,628	35,580	15.8
2001	5,453	36,588	14.9
2002	5,442	38,796	14.0
2003	5,062	42,082	12.0
2004	5,499	45,661	12.0
2005	5,078	46,881	10.8
2006	5,703	48,668	11.7
2007	6,193	50,115	12.4
2008	6,303	53,003	11.9

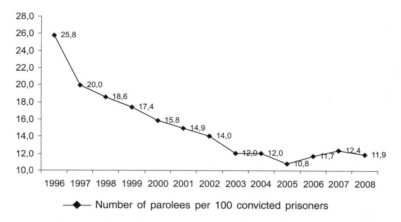

Figure 15.5 Parole granted, 1980–2006
Source: Anuario estadístico de España; Catalan Government, Conselleria de Justícia, Memoria anual

Alternative explanations for the reduction in the number of prisoners granted parole point to, on the one hand, a more restrictive policy on granting parole to eligible prisoners, due to the new requirements of the reform of 2003 (Tamarit 2007). On the other hand, the increasing number of foreign prisoners may have had an impact on the drop in parole figures because they are granted parole less frequently than nationals (Tébar 2006b).

4.3.2 How prisoners end their sentences

The only general data available in respect of the way prisoners end their sentences come from the Catalan Administration. According to these data, only a quarter of prisoners are released on parole (see Table 15.5 and Figure 15.6). Data from the Spanish General Administration, available only for 1999, reveal that, in the rest of Spain, the proportion of prisoners who end their sentence on parole is higher, approaching one third (Tubex and Tournier 2003).

One of the authors of this chapter conducted research in order to understand the limited use of parole by the administrative and judicial authorities that have the discretion to grant parole (Tébar 2006b). The research compared two representative samples of the Catalan population of convicted offenders who, on a given day, met the temporal criterion for being eligible for parole: one of prisoners and the other of parolees. The two samples were compared taking into account some factors that might be relevant to the decision to

Table 15.5 Ending of the sentence, Catalonia, 1996–2008

Year	Releases	Releases without parole	Releases on parole	Percentage releases on parole
1996	4,433	3,544	889	20.1
1997	4,014	3,124	890	22.2
1998	3,464	2,715	749	21.6
1999	2,710	2,055	655	24.2
2000	2,573	1,943	630	24.5
2001	2,441	1,855	586	24.0
2002	2,218	1,730	488	22.0
2003	2,194	1,719	475	21.6
2004	2,230	1,778	452	20.3
2005	2,248	1,755	493	21.9
2006	2,360	1,835	525	22.2
2007	2,574	2,041	533	20.7
2008	2,201	1,679	522	23.2
Average				22.2

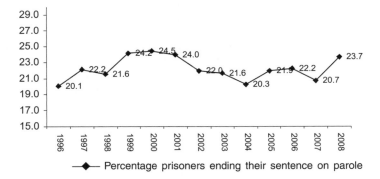

Figure 15.6 Convicted prisoners ending their sentence in parole, Catalonia, 1996–2008

grant parole (age, gender, nationality, family status, education, crime, criminal record, punishment, prison behaviour, participation in education, training and treatment programmes, prison leave and open regime). The data were submitted to bivariable and multivariable analysis in order to point out which factors would predict the decision on granting parole more strongly.

The research showed that the factors most relevant to being paroled are 1) not having an extended criminal record; 2) not having entering prison as a remand prisoner; 3) good behaviour in prison; and 4) having benefited from a high number of prison leaves while serving the sentence. The relationship between these factors and the restricted use of parole can be explained in the following way.

A significant proportion of convicts who enter prison have an extended criminal record (that is, 42 per cent of the population in the sample of the research; Tébar 2006b). As shown in Table 15.6, in Spain most prisoners begin their prison term as remand prisoners. While prisoners are on remand they cannot be classified and they are not eligible for leave and open prison. Although the time spent on remand is computed as time served, the longer the period spent as a remand prisoner, the less are the chances of benefiting from pre-release mechanisms such as leave and open prison regimes. These pre-release mechanisms allow prisoners to demonstrate elements of rehabilitation. As a consequence, convicted prisoners who entered

Table 15.6 Entries into prison, 1996–2008

Year	Entries into prison	Entries into prison as a remand prisoner	Percentage entries of remand prisoners	Entries of convicted offenders	Percentage entries of convicted offenders
1996	52,655	36,627	69.6	16,028	30.4
1997	55,742	34,978	62.7	20,764	37.3
1998	53,464	31,724	59.3	21,740	40.7
1999	49,013	30,217	61.7	18,796	38.3
2000	41,564	27,185	65.4	14,379	34.6
2001	41,359	27,421	66.3	13,938	33.7
2002	41,720	28,793	69.0	12,927	31.0
2003	40.465	27,327	67.5	13,138	32.5
2004	41,725	28,412	68.1	13,313	31.9
2005	39,774	28,631	72.0	11,143	28.0
2006	44,222	31,004	70.1	13,218	29.9
2007	47,441	34,415	72.5	13,026	27.5
2008	50,177	34,823	69.4	15,354	30.6
Average			67.2		32.8

Sources: Dirección General de Instituciones Penitenciarias, *Estadística General de Población Reclusa. Evolución mensual*. Cataluña, Conselleria de Justícia. *Memòria anual* y Secretaría General de Servicios Penitenciarios, Rehabilitación y Justicia Juvenil, *Estadístiques setmanals de població reclusa*

prison as remand prisoners tend to be less likely to be released on parole than prisoners who entered prison after their conviction.

Most prisoners find it difficult to avoid disciplinary infringements in prison. Even those offenders who benefited from parole had a significant number of disciplinary infractions in their records (Tébar 2006b). Possibly, the use of punitive methods to promote discipline in prisons has increased after the abolition of good-time credits by the Criminal Code of 1995.

Finally, the fact that prisoners have benefited from leave several times is strongly related to their classification. Third-level prisoners have most opportunities to be granted leave (weekend leave is the rule for this kind of prisoner). Given that only prisoners in the third level are eligible for parole, the extent to which this regime is used by the prison authorities is a significant factor. Figure 15.7 illustrates the small number of convicted prisoners classified in the third level in the period 1996–2008.

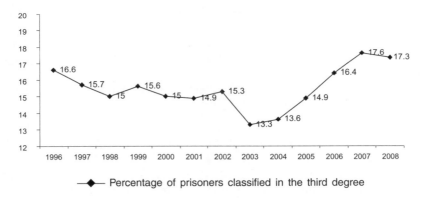

—◆— Percentage of prisoners classified in the third degree

Figure 15.7 Classification in the third level, 1996–2008
Source: Secretaría General de Instituciones Penitenciarias. Estadística General de Población Reclusa. Evolución mensual; Cataluña, Conselleria de Justícia. Memòria anual y Secretaria de Serveis Penitenciaris, Rehabilitació i Justícia Juvenil, Estadístiques setmanals de població reclusa. Data on 31 December (the percentage refers to the convicted prisoners classified)

4.3.3 How much time do parolees serve?

As stated above, three modalities of parole can be distinguished, according to the minimum time served requirement: three quarters, two thirds and half the sentence. Additionally, there is the possibility

Table 15.7 Parole, time served, General Administration, 1996–2007

	Total paroles	Parole three quarters		Parole two thirds		Parole one half		Other parole	
		n	%	*n*	%	*n*	%	*n*	%
1996	6,852	6,041	88.2	0.0	0.0	0.0	0.0	811	11.8
1997	6,684	5,836	87.3	0.0	0.0	0.0	0.0	848	12.7
1999	6,204	5,052	81.4	410	6.9	0.0	0.0	742	12.0
2000	5,925	4,241	71.6	883	16.3	0.0	0.0	801	13.5
2001	5,412	3,482	64.3	1,090	18.9	0.0	0.0	840	15.5
2002	5,757	3,142	54.6	1,354	27.9	0.0	0.0	1,261	21.9
2003	4,859	2,600	53.5	1,549	30.6	0.0	0.0	710	14.6
2004	5,068	2,550	50.3	1,807	34.2	15	0.3	696	13.7
2005	5,283	2,603	49.3	2,009	36.2	25	0.5	646	12.2
2006	5,555	2,766	49.8	2,087	35.7	57	1.0	645	11.6
2007	5,846	3,127	53.5	2,020	34.6	74	1.3	625	10.7
Average			64.0		21.9		0.3		13.7

Source: Unpublished data (provided by Secretaría General Instituciones Penitenciarias)
Note: Data refer not to the number of concessions of parole but to parole at 31 December. Classified for the type of parole.

of granting parole without the limits of time served for humanitarian reasons (serious illness and old age).

As shown in Tables 15.7 and 15.8, parole authorities, both in Catalonia and in the rest of Spain, require most prisoners to serve three quarters of their sentences before being granted parole. The modality of two thirds is less often used, although it has increased in the last years. Finally, the modality of half the sentence is so rare as to exist almost only anecdotally.

To summarize, the 1995 Criminal Code, besides increasing penalties for some common crimes, abolished good-time credit. These steps resulted in an important increase in the time actually served. This in turn led to a reduction of the number of prisoners eligible for parole and, as a consequence, in the number of paroles granted. In addition, even when the temporal criterion for being eligible for parole is met, most prisoners are not considered for early release owing to one or more of the following reasons: a considerable part of the sentence

Table 15.8   Parole, time served, Catalonia, 1996–2008

	Total paroles	Parole three quarters		Parole two thirds		Parole one half		Other parole	
		n	%	n	%	n	%	n	%
1996	1,087	947	87.1	6	0.6	0	0.0	134	12.3
1997	919	867	94.3	9	1.0	0	0.0	43	4.7
1998	762	710	93.2	19	2.5	0	0.0	33	4.3
1999	710	642	90.4	33	4.6	0	0.0	35	4.9
2000	611	534	87.4	51	8.3	0	0.0	26	4.3
2001	584	501	85.8	49	8.4	0	0.0	34	5.8
2002	462	332	71.9	98	21.2	0	0.0	32	6.9
2003	482	333	69.1	112	23.2	0	0.0	37	7.7
2004	507	370	73.0	137	27.0	0	0.0	0	0.0
2005	563	347	61.6	163	29.0	21	3.7	32	5.7
2006	560	316	56.4	185	33.0	33	5.9	26	4.6
2007	632	393	62.2	184	29.1	34	5.4	21	3.3
2008	590	321	54.4	188	31.9	47	8.0	34	5.8
Average			77.7		15.7		1.3		5.4

Source: Unpublished data (provided by Secretaria de Serveis Penitenciaris, Rehabilitació i Justícia Juvenil)
Note: Data refer to the numbers of concessions of parole per year.

has been spent on remand; risk factors (criminal record); personal disciplinary breaches (bad behaviour); or for not having been granted the opportunity to demonstrate rehabilitation (through leave and an open prison). Finally, the majority of prisoners who are granted parole usually have to serve three quarters of their sentence before achieving it.

4.4   Overall vision of the use of pre-release and early release mechanisms

Figure 15.8 summarizes the use of pre-release and early release mechanisms in Catalonia for three categories of prisoners:[20] 1) prisoners who served their full sentences in an ordinary prison (without any kind of pre-release and early release mechanisms); 2) prisoners who spent part of their sentences in an open prison or

[20]Unfortunately, data for the whole of Spain are not available.

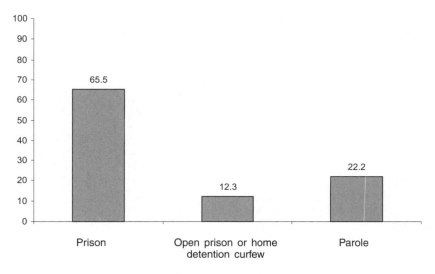

Figure 15.8 Use of re-release and early release mechanisms, Catalonia, 1996–2008 (average)

on home detention curfew but who were not released on parole; and 3) prisoners released on parole.

5. Practical Challenges

The most critical point in the Spanish early release system relates to the fact that only a minority of prisoners end their sentence with some type of pre-release mechanism (open prison) or with some kind of early release (home detention curfew or parole). As happens in other discretionary systems of early release (Piel and LoBuglio 2005; Shute 2007), offenders excluded from early release are those at higher risk of reoffending. Research done by Tébar (2006b) on the use of discretion by the administration and by Judges in the process of granting parole reveals that some relevant factors in predicting reoffending (criminal record, prediction of risk, breaches of prison rules and isolation from society) are decisive in order to know which offenders should be refused early release.

The fact that early release mechanisms are mainly used for low-risk offenders might be considered positive from some points of view. On the one hand, a consequence of targeting low-risk offenders is that the rate of recidivism of early release prisoners is considerably less than that of prisoners released at the end of their sentence (Luque *et al.* 2004; Capdevila *et al.* 2006),[21] although these different rates may not depend on the use of a transitional system of release but on the lower risk posed by prisoners who are released early. On the other hand, the supervision of early release prisoners (on home detention curfew or on parole) does not seem to be very problematic for the administration. A caseload of 60 parolees for a social worker, which is the usual ratio in Catalonia, could be considered unacceptable if the offenders to be managed were high risk.[22] However, it may be reasonable for offenders who, before being placed on parole, have spent time in pre-release mechanisms and who have given evidence of their rehabilitation.

Excluding medium- or high-risk prisoners from early release is problematic from the point of view of public protection. The following results from recent research may support the need to extend early conditional release for this kind of offender:

- Parole is moderately effective in reducing recidivism (Schlager and Robbins 2008).

- Parole is more effective with high-risk offenders (Ellis and Marshall 2000).

- Transitional release programmes (home leave, a halfway house, work and treatment outside prison) are effective in prisoner resettlement (Petersilia 2003; Seiter and Kadela 2003; Cheliotis 2008).

If it is accepted that this research evidence supports a policy based on a progressive release of offenders into the community, then the Spanish system of dealing with high-risk offenders through releasing them only at the end of their sentences may be criticized.

6. Conclusion

To conclude this analysis of the Spanish early release procedures, it must be stressed that both measures – release on home detention

---

[21]According to the four-year follow-up recidivism study of Luque *et al.* (2004), the rate of reincarceration of parolees for a new offence is 15.6 per cent and the rate of prisoners released at the end of their sentences is 34 per cent.
[22]Personal comunication from the Catalan Parole Service.

curfew and parole – are discretionary. As such, they are legitimately subject to the traditional criticisms about uncertainty and disparity in how they are granted (Von Hirsch and Hanrahan 1979).

With regard to the number of early releases, the instances of parole being granted have decreased considerably in the last decade, mainly as a consequence of the abolition of good time by the 1995 Criminal Code. Previously, parole could be granted from the one third point of the sentence, since good-time credits counted towards the calculation of the conditional release date, thus advancing parole eligibility. At present, ordinary parole can be granted only from the three quarters' point of the nominal sentence. In the European context, this is clearly a very strict time requirement, as parole in many European countries is normally granted at the halfway point of the sentence (Tubex and Tournier 2003). The home detention curfew release scheme allows the time of release to be advanced considerably, but this measure is still rarely used.

The most troubling issue, however, is that only a minority of prisoners end their sentences with some type of early release supervision – that is, most convicted prisoners are released at the expiration of their full sentences. The narrow existing legal framework, as well as its limited use, account for a minority of prisoners ending their sentences on early release. Thus, the criteria for being released on home detention curfew and parole target mainly low-risk offenders who would possibly not reoffend if they served their full sentences without any early conditional release mechanism.

Another point of criticism is the strong correlation that exists between compliance with prison discipline and being granted conditional release. To a large extent this correlation is determined directly by the legal framework, which establishes good prison behaviour as an eligibility criterion for parole. But it should be also noted that all the factors that affect the risk prognosis that can be determined by the Prison Administration (such as working within the prison, taking part in courses or treatment programmes or obtaining temporary leave) depend to a large extent on the prisoner's conformity to prison rules.

A final point to be made is that the Spanish early release scheme is well designed in terms of procedural safeguards. Prisoners have the right to present statements at any phase of the procedure, although no oral hearing is granted. As for parole, the decision is taken by a Judge and this can be further reviewed by another judicial authority. Prison allocation is also subject to judicial review. However, it should be highlighted that, in practice, the Prison Administration generally determines the outcome of the decision since prison Judges tend to follow the recommendation of the Prison Administration in almost all cases, although they can dissent from that recommendation.

Regarding our suggestions for change, we are of the opinion that the Spanish discretionary system of conditional early release mechanisms requires rethinking since it excludes most prisoners from them (in particular, those in more need of supervision). A debate about the advantages and disadvantages of a discretionary system, as opposed to an automatic model of early release, is unavoidable. Of course, neither the discretionary nor the automatic model is free of criticisms. As we have seen, the discretionary model fails to provide early release for high-risk offenders (Piel and LoBuglio 2005). The automatic model avoids disparity and does not exclude any group of offenders from early release. However, it may be criticized for not stimulating prisoners to work throughout their sentences for their resettlement. For this reason this model may be less effective in preventing recidivism than the discretionary one (Petersilia 2003).

A possible solution that could challenge criticisms of the two models of early release would be to opt for the automatic model of early release as a way of targeting all prisoners for supervision, but then to distinguish the conditions of supervision and the grounds for recall on the basis of risk and need assessment. Such an automatic model should be coupled with a discretionary advance of automatic early release for those prisoners who are more ready for resettlement.

This suggested model will possibly be more in compliance with s.4.a of the Recommendation of the Council of Europe on Conditional Release (Parole) (2003), according to which: 'In order to reduce the harmful effects of imprisonment and to promote the resettlement of prisoners under conditions that seek to guarantee safety of the outside community, the law should make conditional release available to all sentenced prisoners, including life-sentenced prisoners.'

Acknowledgements

This research has been funded by the Ministerio de Eduación y Ciencia (Spain) (Políticas de Reinserción en el ámbito penal, DER 2008–05041) and by the Catalan Government (AGAUR, 2005, Grupo de Investigación en Criminología aplicada a la Penología, SGR 00824). We would like to thank Lorena Antón, Patricia Martín and Anna Meléndez for their research assistance. Beatriz Tébar would like to thank the Catalan Government for the 'Batista i Roca' scholarship she was granted in 2003 to conduct comparative research on parole at the Institute of Criminology of the University of Cambridge.

References

Antón, J. (1944/1986) *Derecho penal* (2nd edn revised by J.J.H. Guijarro and L.B. Merino). Madrid: Akal.

Antón, J. (1960) 'La teoría de la pena en los correccionalistas españoles', in *Estudios Jurídicos-Sociales, Homenaje al Profesor Luis Legaz y Lacambra*. Santiago: Universidad de Santiago de Compostela.

Beaumont, G. and de Toqueville, A. (1833) *Système pénitentiaire aux États-Unis, et de son application en France suivi d'un appendice sur les colonies pénales et de notes statistique* (trans. into English by F. Lieber, *On the Penitentiary System in the United States and its Application in France with an Appendix on Penal Colonies and also Statistical Notes*). Philadelphia, PA: Carey, Lea & Blanchard.

Bernaldo de Quirós, C. (1940) *Cursillo de criminología y derecho penal*. Ciudad Trujillo: Montalvo.

Bottoms, A. (1980) 'An introduction to "the coming crisis"', in A.E. Bottoms and R.H. Preston (eds) *The Coming Penal Crisis: A Criminological and Theological Exploration*. Edinburgh: Scottish Academic Press.

Capdevila, M. *et al.* (2006) *La classificació inicial en règim obert dels condemnats a presó* (available online at http://www20.gencat.cat/docs/Justicia/Documents/ARXIUS/doc_47627964_1.pdf)

Castejón, F. (1914) *La legislación penitenciaria española*. Madrid: Hijos de Reus.

Castejón, F. (1915) *Libertad condicional*. Madrid: Hijos de Reus.

Cheliotis, L. (2008) 'Reconsidering the effectiveness of temporary release: a systematic review', *Aggression and Violent Behaviour*, 13: 154-68.

Cid, J. (2005) 'The penitentiary system in Spain: the use of imprisonment, living conditions and rehabilitation', *Punishment and Society*, 7: 147–66.

Cid, J. and Larrauri, E. (2009) 'National report: Spain', in F. Dünkel, T. Lapp-Sapälä, C. Morgenstern and D. van Zyl Smit (eds) *Development of Crime, Social Change, Mass Media, Crime Policy, Sanctioning Practice and their Impact on Prison Population Rates*.

Consejo General del Poder Judicial (2009) Informe del Anteproyecto de ley orgánica por la que se modifica la ley orgánica 10/1995, de 23 de noviembre, del código penal (available online at http://www.poderjudicial.es/eversuite/GetRecords?Template=cgpj/cgpj/principal.htm).

Council of Europe (2003) Recommendation Rec(2003) 22 of the Committee of Ministers to Member States on Conditional Release (Parole), adopted by the Committee of Ministers on 24 September 2003 at the 853rd Meeting of the Ministers' Deputies. Strasbourg: Council of Europe.

Dorado, P. (1915) *El derecho protector de los criminales*. Madrid: Librería General de Victoriano Suárez.

Ellis, T. and Marshall, P. (2000) 'Does parole work? A post-release comparison of reconviction rates for paroled and non-paroled prisoners', *Australian and New Zealand Journal of Criminology*, 33: 300–17.

Fraile, P. (1987) *Un espacio para castigar. La cárcel y la ciencia penitenciaria en España (siglos XVIII–XIX)*. Barcelona: Ediciones del Serbal.

González-Baqué, C. (2008) 'El control electrónico en el sistema penal.' Unpublished PhD dissertation, Universitat Autònoma de Barcelona.

Gurdiel, M. (1990) *Aproximación histórica a la progresión legislativa de la libertad condicional en España*. Madrid: Universidad Complutense de Madrid.

Howard, J. (1777) *The State of the Prisons in England and Wales with Preliminary Observations, and an Account of Some Foreign Prisons*. Warrington: William Eyres.

Lastres, F. (1875) *Estudios sobre sistemas penitenciarios*. Madrid: Librería de A. Durán.

Linde, E. (1976) *Amnistía e indulto en España*. Madrid: Túcar.

López i Ferrer, M. (2004) 'Cárceles abiertas'. Unpublished PhD dissertation, Universitat Autònoma Barcelona.

Luque, E., Ferrer, M. and Capdevila, M. (2004) *La reincidencia penitenciaria a Catalunya*. Barcelona: Centre d'Estudis Jurídics i Formació Especialitzada.

McGowen, R. (1995) 'The well-ordered prison: England, 1780–1865', in N. Morris and D. Rothman (eds) *The Oxford History of Prisons: The Practice of Punishment in Western Society*. New York: Oxford University Press.

Neuman, E. (1984) *Prisión abierta. Una nueva experiencia penológica* (2nd edn) Buenos Aires: Ediciones Depalma.

Petersilia, J. (2003) *When Prisoners Come Home: Parole and Prisoner Reentry*. Oxford: Oxford University Press.

Piel, A. and LoBuglio, S. (2005) 'Does supervision matter?', in J. Travis and C. Visher (eds) *Prisoner Reentry and Crime in America*. Cambridge: Cambridge University Press.

Renart, F. (2003) *La libertad condicional: Nuevo régimen jurídico*. Madrid: Edisofer.

Röder, K. (1876/2002) *Die herrschenden Grundlehren von Verbrechen und Straße in ihren inneren Widersprüchen* (trans. into Spanish by F. Giner, *Las doctrinas fundamentales reinantes sobre el delito y la pena en sus interiores contradicciones*). Madrid: Maxtor.

Roldán, H. (1988) *Historia de la prisión en España*. Barcelona: Promoción Publicaciones Universitarias.

Salillas, R. (1888) *La vida penal en España*. Madrid: Imprenta de la Revista de Legislación.

Sánchez-Vera (2008) 'Una lectura crítica de la Ley de Indulto'. (Available online at http://www.indret.com/es/derecho_penal/8/).

Schlager, M. and Robbins, K. (2008) 'Does parole work? Revisited: reframing the discussion of the impact of postprison supervision on offender outcome', *The Prison Journal*, 88: 234–51.

Seiter, R. and Kadela, K. (2003) 'Prisoner reentry: what works, what does not and what is promising', *Crime and Delinquency*, 49: 360–88.

Shute, S. (2007) 'Parole and risk assessment', in N. Padfield (ed.) *Who to Release: Parole, Fairness and Criminal Justice*. Cullompton: Willan Publishing.

Tamarit, J.M. (2007) 'Sistema de sanciones y política criminal', *Revista Española de Ciencia Penal y Criminología*, 09-06 (available online at http://criminet. ugr.es//recpc).

Tébar, B. (2006a) *El modelo de libertad condicional español*. Pamplona: Aranzadi.

Tébar, B. (2006b) 'La aplicación de la libertad condicional en España', *Revista de Derecho Penal y Criminología*, 19: 283–315.

Tomas y Valiente, F. (1969) *El derecho penal de la monarquía absoluta (Siglos XVI-XVII-XVIII)*. Madrid: Tecnos.

Tubex, H. and Tournier, P.V. (2003) *Etude sur la libération conditionnelle dans les Etats membres. Analyse des réponses au questionnaire général*. Council of Europe, Council for Penological Co-operation (PC-CP (2003) 4, Addendum).

Vega, M. (2001) *La libertad condicional en el derecho español*. Madrid: Cívitas.

Von Hirsch, A. and Hanrahan, K. (1979) *The Question of Parole: Retention, Reform or Abolition*. Cambridge, MA: Ballinger.

Wines, F. (1910) *Punishment and Reformation: A Study of the Penitentiary System* (2nd edn). New York: Thomas & Crowel & Co).

Part III

Converging themes

Chapter 16

Concluding thoughts

*Frieder Dünkel, Dirk van Zyl Smit
and Nicola Padfield*

Summary

This final chapter considers the extent to which a coherent and fair policy on release from prison is developing within the EU. It identifies the main challenges to successful comparative work on release from prison. One difficulty is that the fine line between imprisonment and liberty is not always clear. Definitional challenges abound when it comes to comparing different forms of release. Available statistics are limited.

Common themes include the need to clarify the purposes of conditional release, and the need to identify appropriate conditions and requirements. The chapter underlines the basic problems in predicting recidivism, and urges the use of early release to achieve the basic aims of punishment, especially the reintegration of offenders.

1. Introduction

The preceding chapters all tell differing stories about the release of sentenced prisoners before completion of the full sentences of imprisonment imposed on them, but these stories contain similar overarching themes. The most basic of these, which emerges piecemeal from the historical sections in the chapters in this collection, is that early release of prisoners has been a feature of penal practice for as long as sentences of imprisonment have been a primary form of punishment. However, what has characterized early release, in Europe

as elsewhere over the past century and a half, is the search for a
fair and justifiable form of early release, which does not depend on
the whims of a sovereign ruler but instead forms part of a coherent
penal policy.

The search has not always been successful. Indeed, some critics
have suggested that it has not always been conducted in good faith.
In this volume, for example, it is argued in the chapter on Greece,
which formally has a relatively developed scheme of conditional
release and sentence remission when compared with other European
countries, that the rhetoric of early release has been applied as a
mechanism to disguise a largely repressive penal practice. Even in
countries where this is not obviously the case, it is undoubtedly true
that the claims made about the practice of early release do not always
conform to the reality on the ground, both in terms of its practical
effects and in terms of meeting the (varying) justifications that have
been advanced for it. It is this sort of misinformation, deliberate or
otherwise, that the careful national studies presented in this book are
designed to combat.

2. Limits on comparison

We believe also that, in spite of the difficulties of getting and
comparing information, important lessons can be learnt from the
close study of how systems of early release have been developed in
the countries of Europe generally, and of the EU in particular. As
explained in the introductory chapter, the objective of this book was
to bring together accounts of the early release practices in various
countries of the EU in order to understand contextually how they
function. The underlying hope was that comparisons could be made,
and good practices identified, in a way that went beyond the facile
conclusions that can be drawn from mere statistical comparisons of
early release numbers and outcomes. That remains the objective but,
before doing so, it is necessary to identify some of the factors that
have emerged to make such comparisons highly complex.

2.1 Concepts

The first of these factors is conceptual clarity. While the precise
meaning of national legal terminology was an expected problem,
these chapters make clear that in twenty-first century Europe the
fluidity between imprisonment and liberty, presaged by some scholars

(Tulkens 1988; van Zyl Smit 1994; Boone 2000), can create definitional issues that may have a real impact on how national release systems are portrayed. In Belgium, for example, the current position is that prisoners sentenced to less than three years' imprisonment may be electronically tagged on the first day of their sentence and then allowed to remain in the community. Although they may never be detained within prison walls, they are formally regarded as prisoners. Similarly, in a number of jurisdictions (France and Scotland) for example, persons subject to home detention curfews may be regarded formally as *prisoners* in their own homes.[1] In other jurisdictions both electronic tagging and home detention may be recognized as restrictions on liberty, but those subject to them cease to be prisoners when they leave the prison. (We will return to the wider significance of these factors; for the moment they are raised simply to alert the reader to the danger of facile comparisons.)

Related to the complexity of the definition of prisoner are the differing approaches to who is regarded as a *sentenced* prisoner. A prisoner may be regarded as 'sentenced' once a sentence has been imposed by a court, which is normally the case in common-law countries. In other countries the prisoner is regarded as formally unsentenced until the appeal process has run its course. These differences not only distort comparisons of the ratio of sentenced to unsentenced prisoners in different prison systems, but may also have a real impact on when a prisoner fails to be considered for early release.

A further difficulty may be raised by sentences of imprisonment that are fully, but conditionally, suspended. In Germany, for example, as well as in other continental European penal systems, offenders are routinely sentenced to terms of imprisonment that are fully suspended on condition that they perform certain activities in the community. They do not become prisoners at all and therefore they are not physically 'released from prison'. The suspended sentences are the functional equivalent to directly-imposed community punishments or probation sentences in the common-law systems. As is so often the case, however, the common law/civil law distinction does not fully explain the range of possibilities. The Italian terminology is somewhat confusing for the outsider, as sentences of up to three, exceptionally

[1]This has an impact on the prison population rates as well as on statistics on overcrowding. French statistics, for example, count prisoners in home detention when determining prison population rates but exclude them when assessing the overcrowding of prison cells.

four years, which can be suspended immediately at the request of the offender, are dealt with as forms of early release. These sentences are not directly relevant to the present research as these offenders have not necessarily ever been in prison and therefore cannot be regarded as cases of early release from prison. In another sense, though, they are being released from the obligation initially imposed on them to serve a term of imprisonment.

The picture in civil law systems generally is also more complex, as some of those sentenced to a fully suspended sentence might have experienced pre-trial detention and at the time of their trial are released from there. Although this cannot be seen as a form of 'early release', similar problems arise: preparation for release, organizing accommodation, work, aftercare services, etc. Again this is not a problem restricted to common law systems. In Germany, about half of all sentenced offenders who were detained before conviction, are released after being sentenced to a fully suspended term of imprisonment. As in Germany, in many other countries in these cases pre-trial detention remains their only experience of deprivation of liberty,[2] and serious problems of preparing for release can be observed because of a lack of involvement of the probation and aftercare services.

The concept of *early* release raises similar difficulties. A simple model would be to imagine prisoners, serving fixed terms of imprisonment, who are released from the prison into the community before the end of their sentences. In the community they may be subject to varying restrictions on their liberty until the end of the period of their term, after which they will be free of all further restrictions related directly to their sentences.

In practice, the concept of early release is not nearly so clear cut. Prisoners may be granted various forms of temporary release from prison. At one end of the spectrum, it is easy enough to argue that this is not early release: a prisoner serving a long sentence who is allowed out briefly under escort to attend a family funeral or to undergo an emergency procedure in a hospital cannot be regarded as having been released early. At the other end, it is possible to imagine a situation where a person spends most of his time out of prison, working or even socializing in the community, and returns to the

[2]This is a problem often because the living conditions of pre-trial detainees are worse and offer fewer opportunities to participate in recreational and rehabilitative programmes than is the case for sentenced prisoners (Dünkel and Vagg 1994).

prison only at night to sleep. In most countries such a person is still regarded as a prisoner – such semi-liberty is what the Italian chapter calls an 'anomalous' form of release. However, one would do well to note that such a 'prisoner' may well be subject to fewer restrictions than someone who has been released early but on condition that he submits to a curfew in his home or stays in what is sometimes evocatively named a 'halfway house'. All early release in Ireland is temporary; and indeed the high number of prisoners recalled to prison during their period of release in some jurisdictions (notably England and Wales) may underline that all such releases may be in practice temporary. Indeed, we would encourage further research to explore in detail the practice of recall and revocation of licences in all jurisdictions. Is there any consistent practice, in relation to the revocation of grants of conditional release, whether provoked by further offending or breach of any other condition? Clearly, if someone commits an offence when on licence/conditional release, he is liable to be sentenced for the new offence. New sentencing issues arise: is this new sentence to be served consecutively or concurrently to the old sentence? Is it more severe in recognition of the aggravating factor that it was committed when on licence from the earlier offence?

A related question is raised by so-called combined sanctions. Is it early release if the sentencing judge immediately fixes a period to be served in prison and the remaining part as a suspended sentence, as is possible, for example, in Austria? The English legislature was attracted in 2003 to concepts of 'custody plus' and 'custody minus' for less serious offences, to enable a more seamless or 'joined-up' approach to the custodial and community parts of short sentences but, despite legislation, these changes have not been brought into effect. The traditional concept of early release means a fixed term of unconditional imprisonment, which after a certain period (half or two thirds of the sentence) can be the subject of a decision of another judicial authority (judge for the execution of sentences, parole board, etc.). Nevertheless, combined sanctions may be dealt with as early release, for the original determination of the unconditional and conditional part may be reviewed by the prison or other authorities in the light of good or bad behaviour in prison.

Although the focus of the book is on all forms of early release, the bulk of the attention is paid to what is called *conditional release*. In some chapters it is described, following national usage, as release on parole, or release on licence, but this is a terminological rather than a conceptual distinction. In the European context the term 'conditional release' raises conceptual problems of its own. The reason for this is that, as is explained in Chapter 2, the Council of Europe in its Recommendation concerning Conditional Release[3] has given the term a much narrower meaning than the literal interpretation that the offender is released on condition that for a set period he does not do anything that is forbidden, or meets some positive condition to do something during the period. Instead, the Recommendation limits the definition to 'early release of persons under individualised post-release conditions'.[4] This means that, if someone is released on the most common of all general conditions – that he does not commit a further offence during a set period – it may not be regarded as 'conditional' release, which clearly is an illogical use of the term, even though it may accurately portray the scope of this particular European recommendation.

The unsurprising result is that the term 'conditional release' is not used consistently across European jurisdictions, thus making comparisons that much harder to draw. Some authors have ameliorated the difficulty by interpreting their national practices very carefully in the light of the conceptions developed at the European level. In the Belgian chapter, for example, the authors are fully aware of this issue and distinguish between conditional release, defined in terms of the Council of Europe Recommendation, and 'provisional release', where someone is released simply on condition that they commit no further offence for a fixed period. In Spain, in contrast, the term 'conditional release' is used to cover both situations.

The same confusion can arise when the opposite term, 'unconditional release', which is undefined at the European level, is used. Literally, of course, it means that the person is in the same position as other people in free society as no conditions are attached to their freedom as a direct product of their sentences. In English the term 'remission of sentence' usually means a reduction of the sentence leading to an unconditional release. There is normally no provision for the revocation of this part of the sentence and therefore no conditions can be set. Yet it is sometimes suggested that even remission is subject to the condition that the person commits no further offence during the period for which it is granted. Such usage simply adds

[3]Recommendation (2003)22 of the Committee of Ministers to Member States on Conditional Release (Parole) adopted by the Committee of Ministers on 24 September 2003 at the 853rd meeting of the Ministers' Deputies.
[4]It also explicitly excludes all early releases resulting from amnesties and pardons, even though in some jurisdictions conditions may be attached to them.

to the confusion and should be avoided on linguistic grounds. More substantively, it may undermine legal certainty about what release means.

2.2 Statistics

The range of conceptual issues that we have outlined makes it clear how hard it is to produce meaningful statistics on early release. In this book, we nevertheless encouraged authors to produce useful quantitative data about national systems and to discuss the shortcomings of the available sources of information. Some authors have contributed an impressive amount of highly relevant and useful data, which both shed light on the operation of their national systems and raise important issues about how data can be presented in different ways to portray the relative 'success' of early release as a factor in national penal policy.

The quality of the available national data varies. In some instances it is fine-grained enough to be presented in a way which allows the reader to negotiate some of the conceptual difficulties noted above. In Italy, for example, statistics carefully distinguish between 'untried prisoners', 'sentenced prisoners who have appealed or challenged their judgment before the cassation' and 'sentenced prisoners (final sentence)'. This is useful in attempting to understand the relative importance of early release, as the number of prisoners in the middle category is almost as large as the untried prisoners in the first category, a factor that greatly increases the number of persons who do not qualify for early release.

In other countries the lack of good official data exacerbates underlying conceptual difficulties. In Germany there are no meaningful national statistical data available on the proportion of prisoners who are conditionally released compared with those who serve their prison sentences fully. In Austria valid data about (early) release from administrative detention are missing.[5]

Even where national statistics are available, one may reasonably differ about how best to present them to elucidate the practice of early release. In most chapters the choice was made to use the number of prisoners incarcerated on a given day or the daily average over a year as the point of departure in analysing the impact of early release on

---

[5]But this might be a unique case, as in most countries such administrative detention does not exist and, if it does, offenders are routinely included in the official statistics.

the system. Moreover, most attention has been focused on sentenced prisoners, although in some chapters, that on Spain for example, statistics of prisoners held prior to sentence are also analysed closely, as this may impact on their eventual release.

The Greek chapter adopts a different approach and bases its primary calculations on what the author calls the 'caseload' – that is, the number derived from reworking the official statistics to include all persons remaining in prison at the beginning of a given year plus the number of admissions to custody during the year. This inevitably, as the author recognizes, includes some double counting of individuals admitted more than once in a year. However, in his view, this risk is reduced by the increasing length of the time that individuals spend in prison. Moreover, he argues that this approach gives a clearer picture of the impact of the prison system, and in particular of release and readmission, as a form of social control than the more conventional data of average daily or specific day populations.

Double counting may take other forms. The French statistics, for example, include figures for temporary day release and work release which may be granted to an individual prisoner more than once in a sentence, as well as figures for conditional release, which may be permanent in the sense that the prisoner expects not to return to prison unless he breaches the conditions of his release. However, even conditional release may be granted more than once in a given statistical year, for a prisoner may return to prison as a result of a breach or may even be convicted, sentenced and released early more than once in a statistical year.

Given the limitations in availability of statistics on early release and the differences in presentation in this book – in the chapter on England and Wales the official statistics are simply taken at face value, for example – we have not been able to develop meaningful statistical comparisons. We should, however, point to the efforts that the Council of Europe has in made in this regard through its SPACE programme to develop a reliable source of comparative (official) penal statistics.[6] Of course, such statistics are only as reliable as the information presented to the authors, but the latest report on prison statistics shows widespread official co-operation[7] and careful cross-

[6]SPACE is the acronym for the Council of Europe Annual Penal Statistics project that was set up in 1983 (Aebi et al. 2007).
[7]In the most recent report, 37 of the 47 Council of Europe countries responded. Two major absentees were Greece and Russia but information about them was gained from other sources. Greece and Malta were the only EU members who did not respond.

tabulation and checking. The figures are sufficient to allow one to form an overall impression that imprisonment rates in Europe as a whole are largely stable and even declining slightly (Proband 2008)[8] but there are large variations between individual states. In this context states with significantly increasing prison populations, such as Greece, Spain and the UK, stand out. They should be considered closely to understand what role early release policies currently play, and could play in the future, in respect of their changing prison numbers.

The SPACE programme has another leg: the SPACE II statistics on community sanctions and measures. These statistics explicitly include conditional release, defined in the same way as in the Recommendation concerning conditional release, and might be expected to be of considerable interest as a comparative tool at the European level. In practice this is not the case: the last data under SPACE II were published in 2003 and referred to 2001. Moreover, although valiant attempts are made in this report to link the data on conditional release to sentences of imprisonment, there are so many gaps in it that one cannot draw general conclusions. SPACE II nevertheless has the potential to develop into a valuable statistical tool. The most recent information is that the Council of Europe has revived this aspect of its statistical programme, but new figures were not expected to be available until 2010 at the earliest.

3. Common themes

While there may be significant variations in practice, and even more significant difficulties in drawing meaningful comparisons, we wish to highlight some common themes which must be addressed if we are to move to fairer and more consistent practices across the EU.

3.1 Why release early?

First, it is important to understand why one wishes to release sentenced prisoners before the end of their sentences. The advantages of early release in general, and conditional release in particular, have been well explored: see the discussion of conditional release

---

[8]Proband's comments are based on SPACE I 2006 which was published in 2008. The same appear to be true of SPACE I 2007 published in 2009 but the absence of figures from Russia in particular makes overall conclusions more speculative.

in Chapter 2 as 'an effective and constructive means of preventing reoffending and promoting resettlement'. The penal justifications are, of course, tied to the purposes of punishment more generally. The emphasis that is placed on them may vary, depending on the stage of the penal process. One might imagine that those systems which put primary emphasis on proportionate sentences are likely to be more wary of flexible discretionary release processes, and seek to rely on a system of conditional release that will ensure that what it regards as minimum periods for the purposes of retribution and deterrence are met. Those whose aims are more clearly rehabilitative would be more likely to trust a more flexible and discretionary system. But we are struck on rereading the chapters of this book how difficult it is to identify the true purpose of what are often complex procedures.

Some constitutions stress the right of the prisoner to rehabilitation and reintegration. Thus, Italy's Art. 27(3) provides that punishments must aim at resocializing the convicted, while Spain's Art. 25(2) speaks of re-education and social rehabilitation. In Germany the principle of resocialization is developed as a 'constitutional principle' by the Federal Constitutional Court. The Court in this context stresses the necessity of regularly providing temporary and early release in order to improve the chances for social reintegration.

Other constitutional orders are silent on the subject of the purpose of the implementation of punishment. We note below how difficult it is to predict with accuracy successful rehabilitation, or even an individual prisoner's likelihood of reoffending. Another justification of flexibility is to provide an incentive on prisoners to behave well in prison. Parole can be a tool for institutional order: a danger highlighted in the Greek chapter, where the power of discretionary conditional release was given to the prison authorities with the unexpected result of a drop of early release numbers. Giving such powers to prison authorities in a system (such as England) where private companies run prisons is even more obviously risky. Our preferred option is to seek to reduce discretion within the system, and to develop better systems of public accountability where discretion is inevitable, without reducing the use of early release overall. Furthermore, it seems preferable to adjudicate the power to release to a judicial authority, either a sentencing judge or a parole board where lawyers or judges are represented and where an immediate access to appeal to a court is guaranteed. The German Constitution is very clear on this: any decision imposing or releasing from a sanction or measure of deprivation of liberty must be decided by a judge (Art. 104(2) *Grundgesetz*, GG).

There is a paradox identified in more than one chapter: in several countries (for example, England and Wales and Greece), as the rules on 'front door sentencing' become more punitive (Mucchielli 2008), the release rules apparently become more generous. In Spain there is a contradiction between the 1995 Criminal Code, which is mainly based on a truth-in-sentencing philosophy (and its abolition of good-time credits), and the 1996 Prison Rules, which introduced a flexible early release scheme. A rehabilitative release scheme grafted onto a largely retributive sentencing structure may be a common theme, and an appropriate policy position, but the chapters in this book suggest the need for vigilance in monitoring policy priorities at different stages in order to give coherence to the system as a whole.

Clearly there are real challenges to align theory and practice: if prisoners are to be rewarded for participating in rehabilitative programmes in prison, such programmes must be readily available and allocated fairly; if prisoners are to be supervised, monitored, controlled or assisted on release, there must be sufficient people to provide these services. In some jurisdictions, reducing disparities in sentences imposed by trial judges may be an objective. An important and basic question is: does discretionary release advance the goals of the sentencing system?[9]

Perhaps the simplest justification for early release is to reduce the prison population. Ultimately, the importance of this aspect cannot be overlooked. Even in England and Wales, where there has been a significant increase in the prison population as a whole, an increasing number of steps are being taken to release some categories of 'less serious' offenders early in order to make room for the burgeoning overall prison population. The result of this bifurcation is a growing distortion between the actual implementation of sentences for different types of offences, depending on whether those who commit them are regarded, as a category, as 'dangerous' or are otherwise in disfavour with the authorities. The same pattern seems to be playing itself out in practice in Belgium where the new law governing the release of prisoners serving sentences of under three years has not been brought into effect, *inter alia* because a system administered by the prison authorities is able to keep a cap on a growing prison population by releasing these relatively short-term prisoners earlier than a more formal process is likely to do.

[9]A question discussed in the American context by Reitz (2004).

405

3.2 How should release mechanisms be organized?

The traditional mechanism for releasing offenders early was the royal pardon or amnesty. In theory, an amnesty sets aside the conviction and sentence, while the pardon does not do so but merely allows immediate release of the prisoner or class of prisoners to whom it was granted. In practice, the distinction between the two is often blurred, particularly in the case of general pardons or amnesties (Lévy 2008). Notionally, they are often both granted to a class of prisoners to celebrate some anniversary or other great national occasion, but in fact they are used as devices to reduce the prison population to a more manageable level. General pardons and amnesties have long fallen into disuse in countries such as the UK and Germany. In France and Belgium they were used regularly until fairly recently but there, too, the state, more specifically the current president and king respectively, are reluctant to use them, because they are seen as an unjustifiable use of executive power. Only in Italy, where there is a much higher level of scepticism about the use of state power to punish than in most other European countries (Nelken 2009), are they still an important element of penal policy.

If one recognizes that the traditional forms of early release, that is, pardons and amnesties, have ceased to be the key mechanisms in this area, one can question what one can learn from a comparative survey of how early release, and particularly conditional release, are currently organized, legally and practically. In this regard we rely on evidence gleaned from the chapters in this book as well as further evidence compiled by one of us (Dünkel 2009) for comparative purposes.

While the constitutional objections against the use of pardons and amnesties may be well founded, the question remains whether other mechanisms for early release are performing the function of controlling the size of the prison population as effectively as they could or should. The evidence is mixed: the Finnish chapter suggests that a well-designed system can both meet the requirements of due process and be a key factor in reducing the prison population. The recent reform in Austria (2008) has also contributed to a decrease in the prison population and at the same time has emphasized rehabilitation more strongly by excluding general deterrence as a consideration when deciding on early release after having served two thirds of the sentence. On the other hand, policy changes can also go in the opposite direction, as in Spain where the abolition of 'good time' in 1996 has contributed to the increase of the prison population rate. In Germany, psychiatric hospitals experienced serious problems of overcrowding when, in 1998, the legal criteria for early release were formulated more restrictively.

The combination of information from various sources reveals that there is provision for early release in all European countries. It is, however, organized very differently in respect of who the decision-makers are; the minimum period to be served; the extent of the remainder of the sentence during which the offender remains subject to some form of restriction; the question of whether release is (predominantly) automatic or subject to an individual prognosis; the possibility of combining the decision on early release with a requirement specifying what the offender may or may not do during a period of conditional release; and finally the question relating to the recall of conditionally released offenders and the imposition of sanctions for infringements of the conditions on which the release may have been granted. Table 16.1 provides a synoptic overview of the legal requirements of early release.

3.2.1 Temporal requirements of conditional release

The features of the temporal requirements for conditional release are, on the one hand, the absolute minimum time that has to be served (see below) and the relative part of the sentence that has to be served, on the other. Most countries have very flexible requirements, which sometimes vary in respect of particular groups of offenders.

Thus, for example, in Belgium at least a third has to be served, in the case of recidivists at least two thirds; in France, Poland and the Czech Republic first offenders must serve half (also in Italy) and recidivists must serve two thirds (in Italy three quarters). In Estonia and Russia the minimum is half to two thirds, depending on the seriousness of the offence. In Finland prisoners are regularly released after half the sentence, and recidivists who have served a prison sentence during the preceeding three years after two thirds.

It is noteworthy that release after a third, which in Germany is only possible in juvenile criminal law, is possible routinely or at least by way of exception in Belgium, Denmark, Greece (one fifth or two fifths), Croatia, Lithuania and Slovenia. In the light of these international comparators, the practice in Germany, where first offenders serving up to two years may be released after half their sentences but those serving longer only if there are exceptional circumstances (see s. 57(2) of the Criminal Code), is relatively restrictive. Austria, Belgium, Croatia, England and Wales, Estonia, Finland (for those under the age of 21 years at the commission of the offence), France, Greece, Hungary (in the case of offences of more than three years), Italy, Lithuania, Poland, Russia, Scotland, Slovenia, the Czech Republic and Turkey all allow release after half the sentence to a greater extent. In as far as they are restricted to first offenders or those sentenced to imprisonment for the first time, there is no example of a requirement that restricts such release to short sentences in the same way as Germany does. The requirement of wider possibilities for release is apparent and predictable in countries with *a priori* harsher punishment and longer average sentences than Germany (for example, Russia; see Dünkel 2009).

Much rarer than the requirement that half be served is the requirement of two thirds of the sentence. It is the regular form of procedure in Denmark, Germany, Malta, the Netherlands (for more than two years of imprisonment), Romania, Scotland (this being the maximum term when release does not take place after half the sentence) and Switzerland (see Table 16.1).

Longer terms of three quarter or even four fifths that have to be served before release are found only exceptionally and then for particular groups of offenders in, for example, Armenia, Hungary (where a distinction is drawn between those serving sentences in prisons [three quarters], and penitentiaries [four fifths]), Romania, Slovenia and Turkey. In Spain, as a rule, three quarters have to be served, but exceptionally release is possible after two thirds or even half of the sentence.

In a few countries there is no provision for absolute minimum periods at all. Otherwise they are mostly, as in Germany, from two to six months. Exceptions are Finland with only 14 days, Sweden with one month and the Netherlands and Poland with – in certain cases – one year.

A special case is release from *life imprisonment*. Most countries that have life sentences provide a certain minimum term to be served: it is 10 years in Belgium (for recidivists 16 years), 12 years in Denmark and Finland, 15 years in Austria, Germany and Switzerland (exceptionally 10 years), 18 years in France (for recidivists 22 years), 20 years in the Czech Republic, Greece (with a possible remission to 16 years) and Romania, 25 years in Poland, Russia and Slovenia, 26 years in Italy and 30 years in Estonia and in certain cases in Hungary (Dünkel 2009: s. 38 notes 46 ff. with further references; van Zyl Smit 2008). In England and Wales, and in Scotland, the judge who sentences someone to life imprisonment, whether the sentence is discretionary or mandatory, may and usually does set a minimum

Table 16.1 Early release[1] from determinate sentences of imprisonment in Europe

Country	Legislative basis	Decision-making body	Range of determinate prison sentences	Period before release	Absolute minimum period before release	Prognosis/ automatic release	Additional grounds for early release (good time, etc.)	Conditions and period of community supervision
Austria	ss. 46 ff. Criminal Code	Senate of a regional court in the administrative district of the prison, ss. 152, 152a Prison Act	1 day–20 years	½, s. 46(1); exceptionally because of the seriousness of the offence and general preventive aspects ⅔, s. 46(2)	3 months; for offenders aged under 21 at the time of committing the crime: early release after min. 1 month	Good prognosis and evaluation, 'if the offender will be prevented from committing further crime by early release no less than by fully serving the sentence' General preventive reasons only in exceptional cases, see column 5	–	Directives/ supervision not obligatory for under 21-year-olds, however, regularly Period of probation: min. 1 year, max. 5 years; if remainder > 3 years: 5 years
Belgium	Act of 17 May 2006 on the External Legal Position of the Sentenced Prisoner and the Rights of the Victims Ministerial Circular 1771 of 17 January 2005	Prison authorities up to a max. of 3 years; otherwise: Sentence Implementation Court[2]	8 days–30 years	For sentences of up to 1 year ca. ⅙–¼[3] For sentences of over 1 year: ⅓ For recidivists sentenced to more than 3 years: ⅔	–	Automatic up to one year, otherwise requirement of absence of a negative prognosis	–	Community supervision compulsory for sentences of over one year, min. period 2 years; for serious crimes, min. 5 years up to 10 years

Table 16.1 continues overleaf

409

Table 16.1 continued

Country	Legislative basis	Decision-making body	Range of determinate prison sentences	Period before release	Absolute minimum period before release	Prognosis/ automatic release	Additional grounds for early release (good time, etc.)	Conditions and period of community supervision
Croatia	s. 55 Criminal Code; s. 159 Prison Act	Judge for the execution of sentences	30 days–15 years, exceptionally 20–40 years	½, exceptionally (good behaviour) ⅓	–	Consideration of personality, prior life, behaviour in prison and effects to be expected from early release	Release anticipated by max. 2 months before end of the sentence after having served ¾ of the sentence (decision of the Prison governor)	Not obligatory; Period is equivalent to the remainder of the sentence
Czech Republic	ss. 61 ff. Criminal Code; ss. 331 ff. Criminal Procedure Act	Court (individual judge)	1 day–15 years (exceptionally: 25 years)	½ for certain crimes; ⅔ for recidivists or certain very serious crimes	–	Good behaviour and prognosis or personal security (*Bürgschaft*) provided to the court	–	Not obligatory; 1–7 years
Denmark[5]	ss. 38–40 Criminal Code	Minister of Justice. Institutional authority: Section for Prisons and Probation	30 days–16 years (exceptionally 20 years)	⅔, exceptionally after ⅓	2 months	Requirements: absence of a negative prognosis; accommodation and income are guaranteed; undertaking to respect conditions of release	Placement of juveniles / elderly/ sick in homes and hospitals	Usually, conditions are set. Period max. 3 years; if balance of sentence is more, then max. 5 years
England/ Wales[6]	Criminal Justice Act (CJA) 1991; Crime	Parole Board for indeterminate and recalled prisoners (as far	1 day–whole life	Most determinate sentences: automatic release at ½ + discretionary	–	Automatic early release with supervision of the Probation Service	Max. 135 days before the date of release: placement on electronic	Conditions fixed by the Prison Governor for automatic + HDC

	and Disorder Act 1998; CJA 2003; Criminal Justice and Immigration Act 2008	as no automatic release is provided; see col. 7)		Home detention curfew up to 135 days earlier			monitoring (decision of Prison Administration); since 2007: end of custody licence: additional 18 days early release for sentences –4 years (with supervision)	Period of probation is identical with the suspended part of the sentence (i.e. the remaining term); but for dangerous offenders it can be up to lifelong
Estonia	ss. 76 ff. Criminal Code	Court of first instance	30 days–20 years (exceptionally 30 years); detention for minor offences: 1 day–30 days	½ or ⅔ (depending on the seriousness of the offence)	6 months	Good prognosis	–	Directives or obligations are obligatory (s. 76)
Finland	Criminal Code, ch. 2c, ss. 5 ff.	Prison Administration (automatic release); exclusion of early release can be imposed by the sentencing court for sentences of at least 3 years for dangerous recidivist (ch. 2c, s. 11)	14 days–12 years (exceptionally 15 years for cumulated sentences)	½ for (concerning the last 3 years) first-time incarcerated offenders, for others ⅔; for under 21-year-old young offenders: ⅓ or ½ depending on former incarcerations. If it is ordered to serve the sentence fully: release after ⅚ (see col. 3) (s. 12)	14 days	Automatic release (exceptionally it can be ordered to serve longer)	Max. 6 months before an early release: supervision by the Probation Service, possibly combined with electronic monitoring	Not obligatory. Period of probation is equivalent to the remainder of the sentence, max. 3 years; for offenders released from life imprisonment: 3 years

Table 16.1 continues overleaf

Table 16.1 continued

Country	Legislative basis	Decision-making body	Range of determinate prison sentences	Period before release	Absolute minimum period before release	Prognosis/ automatic release	Additional grounds for early release (good time, etc.)	Conditions and period of community supervision
France	Art. 729 ff. Code of Criminal Procedure	Judge for the execution of sentences In cases of sentences of more than 10 years or a remainder of more than 3 years: the district court for the execution of sentences	6 months–30 years	½ for recidivist offenders ²/₃; early release may be granted particularly in the case of sentences or the remainder of the sentence of up to 4 years, if the offender has to take care of children up to 10 years of age	In individual cases of sentences of more than 5 years a period of security (période de sûreté) of a max. of ²/₃ of the sentence may be fixed	Proof of 'considerable efforts to participate in rehabilitative activities'	Remission: good behaviour; max. 3 months per year (2 months for the 2nd and the following years) or 7 days per month;[7] electronic monitoring up to 1 year before ordinary release	Regularly directives and obligations and supervision by the Probation Service Period of supervision: remainder of sentence + max. 1 year (recidivist offenders: max. 15 years)
Germany	s. 57 Criminal Code (StGB)	Court for the execution of sentence at District Court, see ss. 454, 462a Criminal Procedure Act	1 month–15 years	²/₃, see s. 57(1) Criminal Code, ½ for first-time incarcerated with sentences of up to 2 years and exceptionally other sentences if special circumstances justify it, see s. 57(2) nos. 1 and 2 Criminal Code	2 months (s. 57(1)) 6 months (s. 57(2))	Good prognosis: if it can be justified with regards to the interests of public safety	6 days per year for working prisoners, see s. 43(9), (10) Prison Act	Directives and obligations not obligatory; after having served > 1 year regular supervision by the Probation Service should be ordered Probation period: 2–5 years, min. remaining term of the sentence
Greece	s. 105 ff Criminal Code	Local Misdemeanours Councils	10 days–20 years	²/₅ for sentences of less than 5 years; ³/₅	¹/₅ for sentences between 5 and 20 years (²/₅ for	Automatic release for reasons of ill-health; otherwise	Each day of work in prison counts as one	Under the supervision of probation

Country	Legal basis	Competent authority	Length of sentence	Proportion to be served	Minimum period	Conditions	Remission / good time	Probation
		(or Juvenile Tribunals for 13–18-year-old juveniles)		for sentences between 5 and 20 years (4/5 for drug offenders); (1/3 for 13–18-year-old juveniles)	drug offenders)	good risk prognosis based on custodial conduct	and a half days towards the sentence	officers; period contingent upon the remainder of the sentence (min. 3 years)
Hungary	ss. 47 ff. Criminal Code; ss. 8 ff. Prison Act	Judge for the execution of sentences decides on early release and recall; judge of first instance may exclude early release	2 months–15 years, exceptionally 20 years	Detention: 2/3; prison: 3/4; penitentiary (strict regime): 4/5; sentence < 3 years: exceptionally 1/2	2 months	Good prognosis and good behaviour; early release excluded for certain organized crimes[8]	–	Not obligatory; Period of probation equivalent to the remainder of the sentence, min. 1 year
Ireland	Criminal Justice Act 2006; Prison Act 2003	Prison authorities (remission); Minister of Justice on the recommendation of the Parole Board	1 day–life imprisonment	3/4; 2/3 (remission, see col. 8); Parole: prisoners serving 8 years up to 14 years	1 month	Good conduct; further good conduct, particularly participating in treatment programmes; Parole: good prognosis	Almost automatic regular remission of 1/4 of the sentence; in cases of further good conduct: 1/3 (see col. 6)	Remission is unconditional; Parole: different directives; supervision of the Probation Service
Italy	ss. 176, 177 Criminal Code	Supervision tribunal (tribunale di sorveglianza)[9]	5 days–24 years	1/2; for recidivist offenders 3/4 (the remainder must not exceed 5 years)[10]	30 months; for recidivist offenders 4 years	Good behaviour, which justifies the expectation of resocialization; obligations to compensate the victim are fulfilled or not fulfilled without being responsible for it	Liberazione anticipata (good time): up to 45 days per 6 months if the prisoner proves his participation in rehabilitative programmes	Obligatory; Period of probation corresponds to the remainder of the sentence

Table 16.1 continues overleaf

Table 16.1 continued

Country	Legislative basis	Decision-making body	Range of determinate prison sentences	Period before release	Absolute minimum period before release	Prognosis/ automatic release	Additional grounds for early release (good time, etc.)	Conditions and period of community supervision
Lithuania	ss. 157 ff. Law for the Execution of Punishments, in force since 1 May 2003	Lower court in the district where the prison is situated	3 months–20 years (exceptionally 25 years)	1/3 or 1/2; according to different groups; 2/3–3/4 or no release for particularly dangerous recidivists or after a recall of probation terms	–	Prisoner must have proved his ability to improve by good behaviour and/ or good working results	–	Supervision is obligatory Period of supervision is equivalent to the suspended remainder of the sentence
Nether-lands	ss. 15–15l Criminal Code[11]	Public prosecutor	1 day–20 years (exceptionally: 30 years)	Prison sentence of up to 1 year: no early release; sentence of > 1 year up to 2 years: 1 year + 1/3 of the remainder of the sentence; sentence > 2 years: 2/3 (Art. 15)	1 year	Early release is postponed or denied if an explicit negative prognosis is given; also if the patient of a psychiatric clinic needs further treatment or if he has shown serious negative behaviour in prison, has tried to escape or has escaped from prison (Art. 15d)	–	Supervision if it contributes to prevention of recidivism (Art. 15b);[12] Participation in treatment programmes and electronic monitoring can be ordered (see Art. 15a) Period of probation is equivalent to the remainder of the sentence, min. 1 year (Art. 15c)

Poland	ss. 77 ff. Penal Code, Art. 159 ff. Law on the Execution of Sentences	Court of the execution of sentences at the District Court	1 month–15 years (in exceptional cases 25 years)	½; for recidivist offenders, ⅔ or ¾, 15 years with regards to the 25-year penalty	6 months; for recidivist offenders, 1 year	Positive prognosis (conditions may be tightened when imposing the original sentence)	–	Supervision obligatory for the intentional crimes of recidivist offenders and for juveniles Period of probation is equivalent to the remainder of the sentence, min. 2 years, max. 5 years (after former reoffending, min. 3 years)
Romania	Art. 59 ff. Criminal Code	Court on the application of the prisoner or of the release committee of the prison	15 days–25 years (exceptionally 30 years)	Intentional crimes: prison sentence max. 10 years: ⅔; more than 10 years: ¾ ½ for negligent offences and sentences of up to 10 years, otherwise: ⅔	–	Conditions: hard and disciplined working, rehabilitative improvements during the stay in prison; prior convictions are especially considered	–	– Period of probation is equivalent to the remainder of the sentence
Russia	Art. 79 ff. Criminal Code	Court, decision prepared by a release commission of the prison	6 months–20 years (exceptionally 30 years)	½–⅔, according to specific crimes	6 months	Prognosis that the offender is able to rehabilitate	For less serious crimes after ⅓ a substitution by other non-custodial sentences is possible	Supervision is obligatory (police) Period of probation is equivalent to the remainder of the sentence

Table 16.1 continues overleaf

Table 16.1 continued

Country	Legislative basis	Decision-making body	Range of determinate prison sentences	Period before release	Absolute minimum period before release	Prognosis/ automatic release	Additional grounds for early release (good time, etc.)	Conditions and period of community supervision
Scotland	Prisoners and Criminal Proceedings (Scotland) Act 1993	Parole Board, if not automatic release	5 days–30 years	Prison sentence < 4 years: ½. Prison sentence min. 4 years: ½; otherwise: $2/3$ [13]	If sentence is less than four months – ½ the sentence	Release must be granted on the expiry of $2/3$ custodial part of the sentence; earlier release may be granted only where offender is considered to present an acceptable risk	Where prisoner is considered by Ministers to present an acceptable risk and sentence is not for a sexual offence, they may serve up to ¼ of the sentence or 166 days on home detention curfew	For conviction on indictment for non-sexual offence where sentence is less than 3 years – directives and supervision possible; max. term: 1 year. Where the court imposes extended sentences for sexual or violent offences where the sentence is over 4 years, period on licence in the community may be up to 10 years in addition to sentence imposed by court
Slovenia	ss. 88, 89 Criminal Code; ss. 105 ff. Prison Act	Release Commission (3 members: 1 Supreme Judge, 1 Supreme Prosecutor, 1 representative of justice)	15 days–30 years (exceptionally life imprisonment)	½; prison sentences of more than 15 years: ¾; exceptionally after $1/3$ if special circumstance concerning the	–	Good prognosis ('justified' expectation that no further crimes will be committed)	Release by Prison Governor: max. 1 month before end of sentence after having served ¾ of the sentence	Supervision of the centre for social work possible since 2008; directives not obligatory

Spain	ss. 36 ff; 90 ff. Criminal Code ss. 72 General Penitentiary Law Title VIII ss. 191 ff Penitentiary Rules	Judge for the execution of sentences	6 months–20 years; exceptionally up to 40 years	¾; exceptionally after ⅔ or ½[14]	personality of the offenders are given	Mainly, prison behaviour, home leaves granted and period spent in an open prison are taken into account	Electronic monitoring for preparation of (early) release is possible	Probation period is equivalent to the remainder of the sentence not obligatory	Probation period is equivalent to the remainder of the sentence
Sweden	Ch. 26, ss. 6 ff. Criminal Code[15]	A postponement of release is decided by the head of the prison department	14 days–10 years (exceptionally: 14 years)	⅔	1 month	Regular (automatic) release, if not special grounds to object to such a release (for example recidivist offenders who have previously been sentenced to a probation sentence according to ch. 28, s. 3 Criminal Code) Postponement of max. 6 months is exceptionally possible because of disciplinary sanctions during the prison term.	–	Not obligatory	Min. 1 year, max. remainder of the sentence

Table 16.1 continues overleaf

417

Table 16.1 continued

Country	Legislative basis	Decision-making body	Range of determinate prison sentences	Period before release	Absolute minimum period before release	Prognosis/automatic release	Additional grounds for early release (good time, etc.)	Conditions and period of community supervision
Switzerland[16]	Art. 86 Criminal Code	Prison Administration; regularly the prison department of the canton; partly special release commissions	Regularly 6 months–20 years	$2/3$, exceptionally $1/2$ if special circumstances of the offender are given	3 months	Good behaviour, no indices for recidivism	–	Regular supervision by the Probation Service, directives (Art. 87) Probation period is equivalent to the remainder of the sentence, min. 1 year, max. 5 years

Notes:

1. This includes all forms of early release in terms of which the prisoner ceases to serve the originally imposed sentence fully in prison; that is, both conditional and unconditional forms of early release, including those that happen automatically and those that depend on the exercise of some form of discretion. It does not include life imprisonment and other indeterminate sentences, as typically they have their own, often complex, rules for release.
2. Of multidisciplinary composition: a judge, an expert in social reintegration and an expert in prison matters.
3. Differentiated for sentences of up to 1 year: under 5 months, possible after 15 days; between 4 and 7 months, possible after 1 month; between 7 and 8 months, possible after 2 months; between 8 and 12 months, possible after 3 months.
4. There is no general statutory absolute minimum. In practice, less serious crimes are not punished with imprisonment of less than 3 months. For other offences the relevant statutory provision sets a minimum period (at least 6 months).
5. The Act on the Execution of sentences of 31 May 2000, in force since 1 July 2001, and related legal changes have had an impact on the implementation of prison sentences and the rights of prisoners: detention (a less strict form of imprisonment of from 7 days to 6 months) has been abolished and the release of persons sentenced to life imprisonment is now also governed by statute.
6. Since 2006 the work of the Parole Board is restricted to indeterminate sentences and those recalled from licence for more than 28 days.
7. A further reduction of 3 months per year or 7 days per month (réduction de peine supplémentaire) can be obtained if the offender successfully participates in rehabilitative programmes (e.g. training, work, schooling programmes, but also makes efforts to compensate the victim).
8. The exclusion for repetitive recidivists was abolished from 1 March 2003.
9. Composed of lawyers and experts/professionals from other disciplines (psychologists, etc.), in a similar way to the Belgian Sentence Implementation Courts.

10. Early release and sentencing to a period under house arrest are possible when the remainder is more than 2 years and if regular parole (*affidamento in prova*) cannot be granted. Also for pregnant women or parents with sentences of up to 4 years if they have to take care of children under 10 years of age, and for seriously ill persons over 60 and young offenders under 21 with a corresponding remainder of up to 4 years.

11. On 1 July 2008 a new law came into force which reflected the continuing criticisms of the system of automatic early release without the possibility of imposing supervision and directives (see ss. 15–151 Criminal Code). The new law requires individual prognoses in cases of sentences of more than 1 year. Early release from sentences of less than 1 year (after having served at least 6 months) was abolished. However, this form of early release, as well as the automatic scheme, is applicable in the transitional period up to 1 July 2013 in cases dealt with by the courts before 1 July 2008.

12. The earlier system in force until 2008, which provided for a postponement or denial of early release only in exceptional cases, consisted of an automatic and unconditional release (i.e. neither directives nor a probation term and supervision by the Probation Service could be ordered).

13. The Crime and Disorder Act 1998 introduced the extended sentence for sexual offences and violent offences attracting a sentence of over 4 years. This sentence comprises two parts, a custodial term, of which a minimum of one half and a maximum of two thirds must be served in custody, with early release being at the discretion of the Parole Board, and an extension period of a maximum of 10 years. The offender remains on licence, under local authority supervision and liable to recall to prison, from the date of release until the expiry of the entire calendar period of the sentence.

14. If the prisoner has worked or participated continuously in rehabilitative programmes, or if he is over 70 years old and seriously ill, he may be released (early) at any time.

15. In force since 1 January 1999. For prisoners in detention before that date the old law applies, which does not provide an obligatory date for release. This was possibly more favourable for detainees as a release even after half of the sentence had been served.

16. On 1 January 2007 a total reform of the General Part of the Swiss Criminal Code came into force.

period and usually does set a period to be served.[10] In Scotland, the judge must set a 'punishment part', which must be served in full before release on parole can be considered. In England and Wales for a small number of very serious cases no minimum is set. In these cases, as for all the cases of life imprisonment in Lithuania, the Netherlands and Sweden early release is an act of grace and therefore no regulations containing legal criteria exist. In Ireland the minimum sentence to be served in cases of aggravated murder may be 40 years; in cases of attempted aggravated murder, 20 years. But the prisoner regularly receives remission of one quarter (related to the minimum term) and further remission and parole can be awarded. Therefore the time spent may be between 12 and 20 years (see Chapter 10).

Only Croatia, Norway, Portugal and Spain have no provision for life sentences. However the range of determinate sentences in Spain is up to 20, in exceptional cases up to 40 years; in Croatia for certain (recidivist) offenders and serious crimes, also up to 40 years, which results probably in about the same periods actually being served compared with those served by prisoners sentenced to life imprisonment in countries that provide for this penalty.

3.2.2 *Preconditions for release: requirements for the prognosis*
The fundamental distinctions that are drawn in the requirements for prognoses underpin the wide penal policy implications of early release. In Europe there are two fundamental types of early release, *viz.* the discretionary release system and the mandatory or automatic release system. Both are explicitly recognized by the 2003 Recommendation concerning Conditional Release of the Committee of Ministers of the Council of Europe. Discretionary release based on a positive individual prognosis is found in particular in Austria, Croatia, Estonia, Hungary, Poland, Russia, Slovenia, Spain and the Czech Republic. More or less automatic release dispenses to a great extent with individual prognoses. These forms of release are gaining increasing importance in Europe. Thus England and Wales, Finland, Greece, Sweden and Turkey (where good conduct in prison is required) have introduced a generally mandatory form of early release. In England and Wales there is, in addition to automatic release in the case of determinate sentences, the 'classical' release decision-making process on the basis of prognostic evaluation by the Parole Board in the case of indeterminate sentences (life imprisonment and so-called

[10]For the sentence of imprisonment for public protection which is a life sentence in all but name, the sentencing judge sets the minimum period, which may be very short.

extended sentences). The position in Scotland is similar, with early release (that is, at the two-thirds point) of all prisoners serving four years or more, and of all life prisoners, being based wholly upon assessment of risk by the Parole Board.

Some countries do not dispense with prognostic evaluations entirely but, in the face of practical problems with such evaluations, reduce the requirement in cases of uncertainty to the absence of a negative prognosis. This means that in the normal case early release takes place, and only in an exceptional case, where there is an obvious negative prognosis, is there no such early release. This form of regulation is found, for example, in Belgium, Denmark and Switzerland (as well as in the Netherlands for cases dealt with under the old law until 2013). In Sweden early release follows routinely after two thirds of the sentence, unless particular grounds militate against it. Since 1 January 2007 these grounds include the breach of a conditional sentence that results in it being revoked.

French criminal procedure has some noteworthy characteristics (see Art. 729 ff. CPP). The reforms of 2000 expanded the grounds on which early release can be granted. Instead of a prisoner having to produce strong evidence of his resocialization, he now has only to produce evidence that he has attempted to reform, which appears more realistic. Conditional release is – as we have mentioned – possible after half the sentence, or in the case of recidivists after two thirds of the sentence. A significant expansion is also contained in the rule that a parent who has a child of younger than 10 years, who was living with him or her before the sentence, is given extra consideration for release. This is designed to strengthen family relationships and reduce the negative effects of imprisonment. In such cases the minimum period that otherwise should be served falls away so that it is possible for someone to be released after a very short period. However, this form of early release appears to be used very rarely in practice. A similar family-oriented regulation is provided in Italy.

3.2.3 Further possibilities for reducing the time spent in prison

There is a long tradition of reducing the time spent in prison by what in the Anglo-American world is sometimes known as 'good time'. In this approach, reduction of the time spent in prison is guaranteed to prisoners who work, or in some cases simply behave well. In Greece one day worked counts as 1.5 days of imprisonment, which in the case of working prisoners means a reduction of the prison sentence by one third. (If the prisoner also performs well in other areas, further reductions are possible in exceptional cases.) If one adds to this that prisoners are normally released from prison after having served two fifths of their sentences, the actual time served could in some cases be as low as one fifth of the original sentence.

In France as well, wide-reaching reductions for good behaviour are possible: up to seven days per month or three months per year (see Table 16.1). Also in Ireland regular remission amounts to 25 per cent of the sentence. In contrast the German provisions of a reduction for working prisoners of six days per year seem extraordinarily modest. The German Federal Constitutional Court in its judgment in 1998 on the then current system of payment for prison labour could have given a clearer signal about the significance of the so-called non-monetary component of rewarding prison labour. Similarly, in 2001 it focused primarily on monetary compensation and held a moderate increase in the wages of prisoners from 5 to 9 per cent of the average national wage to be sufficient, although it did indicate that further increases in compensation would be required in the future. In the light of budgetary restrictions these increases in compensation may be made up largely of non-monetary components. However, the new legislation of the Federal states concerning youth imprisonment has left possible remission unchanged (with the exception of Berlin with an increase from 6 to 12 days per year).

In Spain, in contrast, a reduction of a sentence for good behaviour or labour was abolished in the 1990s, while in Italy the so-called *liberazione anticipata* that had been introduced in 1975 has remained in force. Here, the supervisory court can guarantee that a prisoner will be given a reduction of imprisonment of 45 days per 6 months, if the prisoner shows that he has participated in resocialization programmes.

What is problematic about good-time regulations linked to prison work is that, in the light of the high rate of unemployment in prison (particularly in Central and Eastern European countries; see van Zyl Smit and Dünkel 1999; 2001), equality of opportunity cannot be guaranteed. The problem can be exacerbated when prisoners are moved regularly between prisons for administrative rather than rehabilitative purposes. The prison system should provide for full employment of prisoners (a duty which the German *Länder* have in any event) so that the opportunity to reduce their sentences can be given to all prisoners. If the system fails to do so, prisoners who want to work but cannot should be compensated in other ways, which may be linked to early release.

3.2.4 Types of conditions

Some countries allow unconditional release or a form of remission, usually unconditional (although, illogically, even remission may sometimes include a condition not to reoffend). More often early release is conditional but the conditions very limited. Fundamental is the condition not to reoffend. But other conditions are often important.

What further conditions do we identify in this book? Prisoners may be released subject to a condition to report to and to maintain contact with a supervisor; they may have a residence requirement, or an obligation to undertake psychiatric/psychological/medical treatment; they may be required to have regular testing for illegal drugs; they may be required not only to live somewhere specific, but also be required not to go to certain places; they may be compelled not to take work with children or vulnerable adults; they may be subjected to a curfew, with or without electronic monitoring.[11] In Germany, there is a distinction between directives (*Weisungen*), which are oriented to future behaviour, and obligations (*Auflagen*), which are to compensate (*Genugtuungsfunktion*), for example, by paying a fine or by making different forms of reparation to the victim. But conditions may be disproportionately or unnecessarily burdensome. And the more conditions which are imposed, the more likely a prisoner is to be in breach of these conditions. Conditions may be imposed which are either incompatible or unenforceable. An offender overburdened with either incompatible or unenforceable conditions is less likely to respect the conditions as a whole. This is a conclusion of the English Inspector of Probation investigating high-profile supervision failures, where those on conditional release have been convicted of murder (Her Majesty's Inspectorate of Probation 2006a; 2006b). Future research should explore the use (and enforcement or enforceability) of release conditions in different countries.

3.2.5 Mechanisms to support early release

Most European countries have mechanisms that support offenders while they are serving part of their sentences in the community. In this regard the requirements that are set for such persons in Germany are common in other countries too, although without the doctrinal distinction between directives and obligations that German law draws in this regard. In some countries, such as Estonia, they

---

[11]See the chapter on England and Wales for a further list, which includes a copy of a possible licence containing standard conditions for a prisoner released conditionally in England.

are compulsory, while in others, such as Demark, France and Switzerland, they are used routinely. It is interesting that in some countries probationary supervision is compulsory, for example, in Belgium for sentences of more than three years imprisonment, Lithuania, Poland (for specific classes of recidivists) and Russia. It is not yet clear whether the supervision in Eastern European countries will be full-scale supervision by probation officers as we know it in the West or simply a form of reporting regularly to the authorities. However, there are signs that a system of parole comparable with that in Western Europe is beginning to emerge in countries such as the Czech Republic, Estonia, Poland and Slovenia (see van Kalmthout and Durnescu 2008).

The Netherlands until recently was an exception in this regard, as early release was not followed by probation supervision or the imposition of any directives or obligations. The reform of 2008 brought new opportunities to impose probationary supervision and directives to participate at training and treatment programmes.

In some countries early release is combined with electronic monitoring, for example, in the Netherlands, England and Wales, France, Spain, Sweden and Switzerland. Insofar as electronically monitored house arrest is not a community sanction imposed directly as an alternative to imprisonment it may be used to reduce the term of imprisonment by a maximum of 2 months (Sweden), 4½ months (England and Wales), 6 months (Finland, the Netherlands and Switzerland) or even 12 months (France). In Germany this strategy has not been promoted as a policy option, as most prisoners who would qualify for it are sufficiently supported by regular parole (the Probation Service). The reason is also that it does not have the potential for reducing the prison population significantly. However, in one Federal state (Baden-Württemberg), electronic monitoring will possibly be introduced as a preparatory measure for early release.

The period of conditional release is usually the remainder of the sentence. However, often, as in Germany, there are also absolute minimum and maximum periods that may extend supervision beyond the end of the prison term initially imposed. In Finland the maximum period is three years, and minimum terms have been abolished. In other countries (Austria, Hungary, Sweden, Switzerland and the Czech Republic) the minimum period is shorter (one year) than in Germany or in Poland (two years). This is important in the case of short periods of conditional release in particular, as otherwise this could lead to a disproportionate widening of the net of social control. An extreme example is Belgium where minimum periods of two, five or even ten years may be a reason for the growing tendency for prisoners simply to refuse conditional release. Assistance and supervision in the first year after release are usually sufficient as most recidivism occurs then.

3.2.6 Who should take the release decision?

Different decision-making bodies are responsible for early release in various European countries. It is not universally obvious that, as required by the German Constitution (Art. 104(2) GG), an independent court must decide about early release. In Belgium the Prison Administration makes the decision in all cases of imprisonment of up to three years; in other cases the decision is taken by Sentence Implementation Courts composed of three persons: a judge, an expert in social reintegration and an expert in prison matters. Also in Denmark, England and Wales, Finland, Sweden and Switzerland some decisions are taken by the Prison Administration or by a section of the Ministry of Justice. In England and Wales, the Parole Board, which decides cases of life and other indeterminate sentences, has an interdisciplinary composition like the Belgian Sentence Implementation Courts, and the Italian Commissions. Elsewhere, the idea of a specialized judge or tribunal with experience of the implementation of sentences has been accepted (for example, Croatia, France, Germany, Hungary, Italy, Poland, Slovenia and Spain). Only in a few countries is the court of first instance, which is not a specialist in this regard, also responsible for this decision (the Czech Republic, Estonia, Greece and Lithuania). A rather exceptional case is presented by the Netherlands, where the Public Prosecutor is responsible (see Table 16.1).

One should not be blinded by legal formalism, however. In some European countries conditional release is still sometimes decided directly by the prison authorities. This is true in Belgium for sentences of less than three years and in England and Wales when early release that goes beyond the statutory automatic period is considered. However, even where *de jure* this is not the case, the *de facto* influence of the prison authorities may be very significant. For example, temporary release may be used, as in Ireland, as a more permanent form of conditional release. Temporary release elsewhere is normally, but not necessarily, a preparation for conditional release. There is an important interplay between temporary and more permanent forms of early release (however categorized). Temporary release may in some jurisdictions be granted by the Prison Administration, and whether or not this can be achieved may have an important impact on subsequent decisions by parole boards or judges. The interaction of administrative, judicial and quasi-judicial bodies is clearly an area for further research. The vital decisions on conditional release may not in reality be taken by the formal body charged with the final decisions. In England and Wales, where this has always been recognized by the courts, the practice is also of fundamental importance. For example, where the English Parole Board formally makes the all-important decision on the release of lifers, the reality is that if the prison authorities have not moved the lifer to an 'open' prison and if the Probation Service has not completed a satisfactory release plan, the Parole Board is highly unlikely to recommend release (Padfield and Liebling 2000; Padfield 2002). Thus the true gatekeepers are not only the formal Parole Board but also the administrative players who supervise the progress of the prisoner through the 'system'. Yet the prisoner's rights (for example, to legal advice and to full disclosure of documentation) may be significantly less for these so-called administrative decisions.

Significant in this regard is also whether the decision-making body is automatically involved or whether it makes a decision only when called upon to do so. While in Germany the chamber responsible for the implementation of punishment may be called upon to make a decision by the prisoner when he is about to complete two thirds of his sentence, in many other countries the Prison Administration[12] or the prosecuting authority[13] may also make applications. There are also examples of other persons or institutions having the right to make applications (see Tubex and Tournier 2003: 18 ff.).

Prisoners' procedural rights in respect of these applications are fairly similar. In most countries (Cyprus and Luxembourg are exceptions) the prisoner is heard, and mostly he takes part in the proceedings (a hearing or an oral procedure). The right of access to documentation (in some cases via a lawyer) is recognized in most countries; however not in Bulgaria, Croatia, Cyprus, Latvia, Lithuania, Malta, Poland, Portugal, Slovakia and Turkey. Practically without exception prisoners are told of the outcome (Tubex and Tournier 2003: 19 ff.), although the question naturally remains in what form. The setting of a period within which another application cannot be brought is possible

[12]For example, Bulgaria, Croatia, Denmark, Greece, Iceland, Ireland, Italy, Latvia, Poland, Slovakia, Spain and Turkey.
[13]For example, Bulgaria, the Czech Republic, France, Slovakia and Turkey.

everywhere except in Sweden. However, the maximum period of one year in Belgium, Portugal, Romania, Scotland, Slovakia or the Czech Republic is clearly above the usual maximum of one, two, three or six months in the majority of European countries.

A scientific risk assessment in respect of the risk of offenders committing further crimes in the future takes place in only a few countries (for example, Denmark, in part in England and Wales, Italy, Norway, Poland and Scotland) and certainly not in those countries where there is quasi-automatic release. Often such risk assessment is used only for particular classes of prisoners who are regarded as dangerous or those who are serving life sentences.

3.2.7 Presenting conditional release

It is important too, to focus on the way the original sentence is presented. In England the period of 'conditional release' is often publically perceived as coming 'after' the prison sentence, rather than being part of the sentence as whole. There is no reason why this should be: the judge says when sentencing, for example, that the offender will go to prison for four years, explaining that the person will come out after two years, or even sooner on home detention curfew. The media misunderstand the fact that the second half of the sentence is 'real': real supervision and a very real likelihood of recall to prison, and not only for reoffending. An even bigger misperception in England comes with indeterminate sentences where the Judge specifies a 'minimum term': the media consistently report this is as the term the prisoner will serve, with no recognition that most lifers are likely to spend many more years in prison than the minimum term. In practice, unless the lifer has progressed through the system to an open prison, and has a well-supported release plan, he will not be released. As for fixed-term prisoners in Spain, for life-sentence prisoners, time in an open prison in England and Wales can be seen as a pre-release mechanism.

Another advantage of re-enforcing the message that the time served on conditional release is part of the sentence might be that conditional release could be more effectively used to shorten custodial terms. One may even need to go further where, as in Spain, the levels of classification for convicted prisoners are carefully distinguished in ways that range from strict imprisonment to full release. In Spain the classification is: first level – closed or maximum security prison; second level – ordinary prison; third level – open prison (which is only semi-detention, and those subject to a home detention curfew fall into this category, too); and fourth level – parole. Similar classifications exist elsewhere, but courts do not always pay attention to what level prisoners should be sent or how they should progress from one level to another In England both prisoners and prisons are classified, but the appropriate justifications for the classifications are not rigidly adhered to: many prisoners are held in prisons of a higher security classification than appropriate due to allocation and overcrowding challenges. In several countries, France, Spain and Germany among others, the judiciary is involved in overseeing the process of the prisoner through the system. This has clear advantages from the point of view of the rule of law. In jurisdictions where this is not the case attention should be paid to establishing safeguards to ensure that the progression system is properly followed, as well as to publicizing what steps are being taken at various stages, for early release is often part of a longer process which is not fully understood or subject to appropriate supervision.

3.3 Fundamental criminological questions about predicting future criminal conduct

3.3.1 Basic problems in predicting recidivism

Research on future criminal conduct, which had stagnated in the 1970s and 1980s, experienced an unexpected revival in the 1990s. There was a significant improvement in the quality of such research, not least as a result of new clinical, statistical studies that allowed some cautious optimism about progress in difficult cases of violent and sex crimes (Dahle 2006: 1 ff.; Nedopil 2007: 286 ff.). We can only sketch these developments here. More comprehensive accounts can be found in the extensive German and international literature on the subject (see Dünkel 2009 with further references). Notwithstanding the optimism expressed in some of these studies, the prediction of human conduct remains fundamentally problematic.

Predictions are statements of probability and thus always carry a risk of error. This inescapable truth must be emphasized in the context of the most recent German legislation. Section 454(2) sentence 1 of the German Criminal Procedure Act requires that before conditional release can be granted to offenders sentenced to life imprisonment or to sex offenders with a determinate sentence of more than two years, an expert assessor must make a positive finding that 'in respect of the offender there is no risk any more that the dangerous conduct demonstrated by the offence still exists'. In other words, the expert must definitely exclude any further dangerous behaviour, which, from the point of view of the empirical sciences, will never be possible. Prognoses are risk predictions and therefore can only explore probabilities and not give 100 per cent guarantees.[14]

The prognosis that is required at release in terms of s. 57 of the German Criminal Code faces similar problems to those experienced by long-term weather forecasts: the longer the forecast period, the greater the uncertainty. While in the case of temporary release the period for which a prediction must be made is relatively short, in the case of conditional release a period of a number of years is involved. That means situational factors that may influence recidivism become much more important, but these factors are very hard to predict.

The reliability of predictions depends on the following factors:

1. The basic rate – that is the number of recidivist, 'dangerous' offenders in a given population.

2. The selection quota – that is, the number of those who are predicted to be recidivists or 'dangerous'.

3. The efficacy of the prediction instruments, that is, the precision with which they allow the delineation of the two groups (Endres 2000: 69).

In reality there are only true or false prognoses. This means that one can put all possible true and false predictions into four fields. In the literature this is often illustrated by a simple tabulation (Table 16.2) (see, for example, Endres 2000: 69; similarly Dahle 2006: 14).

Table 16.2 True and false predictions

		Outcome	
		Recidivism	No recidivism
Prediction	Recidivism	True positives	False positives
	No recidivism	False negatives	True negatives

The terms 'false positive' and 'false negative', relate to the criterion that is to be predicted. If recidivism is to be predicted, the 'direct hit' (the recidivist) is the true positive; the person who, contrary to the prediction, is not a recidivist is the false positive. In terms of prognoses for release these two groups do not present a problem

[14]For criticism of the German legislation, which unfortunately was ignored in the legislative process, see Dahle (2006: 2 ff.); Nedopil (2007).

because, if there is a doubt, they may remain in prison and are therefore not recognized. The true negatives are also not a problem, as they are released with a good prognosis and in fact do not become recidivists. It is the false negatives that lead to a public outcry if, in spite of good prognoses, they commit further (serious) offences and are recognized as recidivists.

Penal policy generally aims to minimize the risk of false negatives. However, this does not take into account that by doing this the number of false positives is increased. This means that some prisoners, who would not commit further offences if they were to be released, in fact remain in prison. The number of false positives increases if crime policy tries to lower the likelihood of recidivism for groups of offenders with an *a priori* low base rate of recidivism in order to avoid false negatives (see the example in section 3.3.2 below). As an important legal right is involved, namely the freedom of the citizen, this source of errors should be highlighted more strongly.

3.3.2 The 'dangerousness' of predicting dangerousness
A fundamental problem of prediction is that there are always two possible errors: either someone who is wrongly regarded as not being dangerous is released, or someone is wrongly diagnosed as dangerous and remains in prison. The issue of false positives and false negatives is illustrated by Table 16.3.

This table can be illustrated further: assuming that, in spite of being given treatment, of 100 prisoners 10 per cent remain dangerous and the error quotient remains 10 per cent (a low estimate as prognoses in reality are more likely to have higher error rates), then one would identify nine of the ten are dangerous offenders and one would not be identified. Of the 90 who are not dangerous one would identify 90 per cent; i.e. 81; but 10 per cent, i.e. 9 would be wrongly identified as dangerous (false positives in terms of the criteria). In spite of an overall success rate of 90 per cent, this would mean that of the 18 identified as dangerous, 9, that is 50 per cent, objectively would not be dangerous. Of the 82 identified as not dangerous but who would include one objectively dangerous offender (false negative) the error quotient would amount to only 1.2 per cent. In penal policy debates, and particularly in the portrayal in the mass media, only the problem of the false negatives is emphasized and not the false positives who remain wrongly imprisoned. Current research indicates that in the case of violent offenders as many as 80 per cent may be wrongly regarded as dangerous.

Table 16.3 Errors in predictions of dangerousness

	Dangerous	Not dangerous
Objective of the evaluation	10 9 + 9	90 1 + 81
Error quotient	True *vs.* false positives: 9 : 9 = 50%	False *vs.* true negatives: *1* : 81 = 1.2%

Source: Derived from Kunz (2004: s. 35 notes 25–27).

If society enshrines the strategy of 'when in doubt keep offenders in prison' in legislation (see, for example, s. 67d(2) of the German Criminal Code and s. 454(2) of the German Criminal Procedure Act), then this sacrifice that the offenders who may be false positives are compelled to make should be compensated by giving them humane conditions of imprisonment which are strongly oriented towards meeting the highest standards of normalization – that is, which are as much like conditions on the outside as possible.[15] Furthermore, all possible steps should be taken to improve the predictions and to reduce the need to compensate for possible unjustified negative prognoses.

Were the proportion of truly dangerous offenders in the diagram above to be 20 per cent, one would have 31 per cent false positives (8 of 26; that is almost a third would be unjustly imprisoned) and 3 per cent false negatives (2 of 74). That would mean that the proportion of prisoners who would be wrongly detained would still exceed tenfold the proportion of wrongly released as not dangerous!

3.3.3 The reliability of predictions with different basic rates of recidivism

A further fundamental statistical problem that arises in this context is the difficulty of predicting human conduct in cases where the basic rate of recidivism is low. This can be observed in particular with sex and violent offences (see below). If the basic rate is lower than the rate of 'direct hits', the predictive methods give no additional knowledge. With a hit rate of 75 per cent and a low basic rate of 20 per cent of recidivism (which is realistic, for example, for sex offenders), one would reach a statistically better result by releasing all prisoners; with a high basic rate of 80 per cent it would statistically be better to regard all prisoners as positives and release none of them.

[15]On the principle of normalization, see Rule 5 of the European Prison Rules and s. 3(1) of the German Prison Act; see also Walker (1996).

Consider the example of a hit rate of 75 per cent combined with a basic recidivism rate of 20 per cent: 60 of 80 non-recidivists would, in terms of the criterion of expected recidivism, be predicted correctly (true negatives); 20 are false positives, that is, they are predicted to be recidivists but do not reoffend. Of the 20 whose recidivism is predicted 15 prognoses are correct ('true negative'); and 5 are falsely predicted not to reoffend (false negatives). The errors total 25 out of a 100 cases. If one had released all 100 prisoners without trying to predict their behaviour, there would statistically have been 20 errors (the basic rate of recidivism of 20 per cent), that is, $n = 5$ or 20 per cent fewer errors. At the same time, this example of how prediction works shows that four times as many would remain wrongly imprisoned ($n = 20$) as compared with those who would be wrongly released ($n = 5$).

This ratio is reversed when the basic rate is very high. If the basic rate is 80 per cent and the hit rate is constant, 20 would be wrongly released and 5 would wrongly remain in prison. This statistical relationship also requires normative evaluation, as is required, for example, by s. 57(1) sentence 1 of the German Criminal Code. Where the offences concerned are relatively minor, a 20 per cent proportion of false negatives (that is, recidivists) is acceptable, but where serious offences may be expected it surely is not acceptable (see also Frisch 1983: 144). In other words: what risks may be accepted is a policy question, but it can and should be decided on the empirical basis of what kind of further offences may reasonably be expected.

From these examples it is clear that empirically-determined basic rates of recidivism are critical for deciding whether it makes sense to make predictions about the future conduct of individuals. If statistically-sound probability predictions do not result in hit rates better than if it were simply left to chance, individual prognoses make no sense. To this extent normative solutions should be sought, for example, in the form of rules to which there are exceptions. An exception could be made if in an individual case particular circumstances indicated a higher risk of recidivism in respect of a serious offence. The rule in favour of early release should be applied in every case where the basic probability is a general one, or the risk of the commission of a further serious offence is low.

There is some indication that these policy decisions are being made by setting different 'hurdles' for different categories of prisoners within a jurisdiction. Many countries have different rules for recidivist offenders from those imposed on first offenders. (This of course leads to further definitional challenges: when is a first offender a first offender?) Both in England and Wales and in Scotland, the test for the release of lifers is different from that for determinate sentence prisoners. And in Scotland, the test for life prisoners is in effect 'no release until the Board is satisfied it is no longer necessary for the protection of the public that they continue to be detained'. The test for extended sentence prisoners is 'no release unless the Board is satisfied that it is no longer necessary for the protection of the public from serious harm that they continue to be detained'. Thus, the Board must be confident here that the risk is of serious harm to justify further detention. This illustrates the different standards that can be applied.

3.3.4   Unreliable or neutral midrange predictions

A constant theme in the literature on prediction is the so-called midrange in which predictions are unreliable or neutral. This refers to the fact that the majority of offenders at the stage when predictions are made about their future behaviour fall into a range where the likelihood of recidivism of around 50 per cent is precisely what the probability would be if it were simply left to chance. A classical study of the midrange is that of Meyer (1965; see in detail Dünkel 2009). He studied releases from young offender institutions in the 1960s and developed the prediction table that bears his name. In addition to the other problems of the so-called weak points procedures (*Schlechtpunkteverfahren*) it became clear that half of those released showed three to six negative factors and a recidivism rate of 56 per cent. A further 33 per cent had 0–2 negative factors and a recidivism rate of 20 per cent. For the 17 per cent with more than six such factors the recidivism rate was 100 per cent ($n = 30$) (see also Streng 2002: 320 ff.). In half the cases therefore, the hits achieved by the prediction process were the same as if one had simply thrown dice. This is again an argument for a normative solution, which would reduce the use made of individual prognoses, by using them only in cases where there is significant evidence in favour or against release. In contrast, the majority of cases, the midrange cases, should be released without any individual prognosis.

3.3.5   Likelihood of recidivism for various groups of offenders

The importance for predictions of future behaviour and for the number of errors of different basic rates of recidivism for different offences has been emphasized above. Other than previous convictions and age, differing basic rates are the strongest differentiating factors.

A literature survey by Groß and Nedopil (2005: 65 ff.; see also Dahle 2006: 16 ff.; Nedopil 2007: 291) reveals the following basic rates of recidivism:

- Recidivism rates of more than 50 per cent: traffic offences, drug offences and sexual offences related to homosexual paedophilia.
- Recidivism rate of 25–50 per cent: assault, property offences, exhibitionism and sexual offences in the context of paedophilia.
- Recidivism rates of 10–25 per cent: robbery, arson, rape and sexual assault.
- Recidivism rates of 3–10 per cent: incest and violent offences in the context of paedophilia.
- Recidivism rate of 0-3 per cent: murder and manslaughter.

These figures can be regarded only as rough guides. However, they are similar to the general findings of prison research that prisoners who had been sentenced for crimes of violence have significantly lower recidivism rates than those convicted of property and economic crimes, who in the prison context one should put in the group whose recidivism rates are above 50 per cent.

The recidivism statistics that were published in Germany in 2003 confirm these tendencies (Jehle *et al.* 2003). This study, which covers all offenders sentenced or released in 1994 over a four-year period (almost 950,000 cases), shows an overall recidivism rate (i.e. not only for the same offences) of 41 per cent for rape/sexual assault, 27 per cent for homicide, 59 per cent for aggravated theft and for robbery, 35 per cent for fraud and 22–24 per cent for drunk-driving and traffic offences. There is also a clear interaction effect with the type of sanction. Of those convicted of theft and sentenced to a fine, only 37 per cent were reconvicted, while for those released from youth imprisonment following a conviction for the same offence the rate was 82 per cent (Jehle *et al.* 2003: 129).

In general, when recidivism is related to reconviction for the same type of offence, rates are much lower than described above. This is particularly true for crimes of violence. However, it must be borne in mind that most of these studies do not consider the dark figure of unreported crimes.

It is worth emphasizing that, in addition to those convicted of crimes of violence, the recidivism rates of sex offenders at around 20–30 per cent are relatively low. This is true both in the German case and internationally (see in summary Dünkel 2009). Indeed, an international meta-evaluation comes to the conclusion that recidivism rates might be as low as 13 per cent. However, if very long periods of more than 5 years are used for the assessment of whether offenders remain at risk, the rates increase to 35–45 per cent (see Hanson 2001; also the differentiated account of Endres 2000: 73 ff.; Hood *et al.* 2002).

3.4 Conditional release and recidivism: criminological aspects

Empirical findings on the question of recidivism in Germany are mostly based on investigations in the 1970s and 1980s, as in the 1990s there was less interest from research institutes in the topic. However, there are empirical findings that underline the positive potential of early release (for an early example from Austria, see Pilgram 1975; subsequently from France, see Kensey 2004; 2007: 213 ff.)

Methodologically the problem is that those prisoners who are released early, in contrast to those who serve their full sentences, are a positively selected group and there is no immediate comparator. However, a point of comparison can be found in regional and temporal variations in approach. Thus, in some Federal states or local districts prisoners are released whereas in neighbouring states or districts similar prisoners are not be released, but, because of the application of more restrictive standards or traditions, they have to serve their terms in full. Also, over a period of time the criteria for release may change, so that one can – insofar as other conditions remain constant – make comparisons.

If one compares, on the basis of the German Federal Central Register for 1984–90, the recidivism rates of prisoners who were released conditionally with those who served their whole sentences, one finds a recidivism rate of 40 per cent compared with a rate of 71 per cent for those who were released conditionally and then recalled, or 72 per cent for those who served their whole sentences (see the summary in Dünkel 2009).[16] As only around a third to 50 per cent of prisoners released early are normally recalled, these figures indicate that, generally, conditionally released prisoners are clearly less likely to become recidivists than those who serve their whole sentences in prison. In the Federal State of North Rhine-Westphalia the recidivism rate for conditionally released prisoners was as high as 63 per cent but that for those serving their whole sentences in prison it was 75 per cent. The current Federal recidivism statistics for juveniles show a rate of 40 per cent for those released conditionally compared with 50 per cent for those serving their whole sentences. The current figures

[16]Of the recidivists, four out of five cases relate to renewed imprisonment.

for adults were comparable: 22 per cent as opposed to 33 per cent, respectively (Jehle *et al.* 2003).

These statistics are confirmed by investigations in countries other than Germany (for example, France; see below). However, one must always bear in mind the normatively loaded, prognostic evaluations that underlie early release. To this extent, studies in which there are control groups of some kind are more significant. The investigation by Dünkel in Berlin-Tegel examined for the first time the legal and social biographical characteristics (previous convictions, type of offence, and age) of offenders in order to identify comparable groups, which in one case were released early and in the other served their full prison terms. The study showed that the former had a 13 per cent lower recidivism rate in the sense of a further sentence of imprisonment (see, in summary, Dünkel 2009). Some further findings of this study are also noteworthy: for some types of offenders the recidivism rates were strikingly different. For robbers, sex offenders and traffic offenders the rates were 17, 21 and 18 per cent less, respectively, while the rates for thieves and fraudsters were only 11 or 9 per cent different, respectively. Offenders convicted of assault showed no difference at all. In none of the cases was early release demonstrated to be disadvantageous. It is noteworthy that the advantages of early release also applied at the special social therapeutic unit of Berlin-Tegel, which is a training prison, although the overall recidivism rate there was already 18–20 per cent lower than in 'ordinary' prison departments and the early release rates twice as high. (The judges, who ordered early release were therefore in a sense taking a greater risk: see in this regard the study by Dünkel and Geng (1993) of so-called career criminals after a ten-year risk period.) Additional, albeit minor, differences were also apparent, depending on whether the released offenders were placed under the supervision of a probation officer or not. This research is confirmed by other German sample-based studies.

The German studies, notwithstanding their methodological short-comings, are confirmed by research findings in other European countries that show the advantages of conditional release in terms of special prevention, on the one hand, while not finding, on the other hand, any identifiable loss of security to the public as a result of extensive early release practices.

Kensey and Tournier in France showed lower rates of recidivism among those released conditionally compared with those who served their whole sentence in prison (Kensey and Tournier 2005). This applies in particular to first offenders imprisoned for the first time, of whom 44 per cent, as compared with 77 per cent in the case of those serving their full sentences, were reconvicted (for similar results in Austria, see Chapter 3 this volume).

Kensey (2004) studied 1,157 prisoners released in 1982. Of those who were released conditionally, 23 per cent were sentenced to an unsuspended term of imprisonment again, while of those who served their whole sentences in prison, the proportion was 40 per cent (a difference of 17 per cent). If the factors of age, type of offence and previous convictions were kept constant that revealed a difference of 8 per cent in favour the conditionally released (see also Kensey 2007: 213 ff., 218). If further differentiation was made in terms of type offence the ratios in favour of early release were as follows: 11 per cent for theft (64:75 per cent for those who served their whole sentences in prison); 25 per cent for robbery (39:64 per cent); 26 per cent for assault (35:61 per cent); and 22 per cent for rape (25:47 per cent). Overall the studies conducted by Kensey, like the study by Dünkel mentioned above, make it clear that the likelihood that those who are conditionally released will remain within the law is to some extent an effect of selection. Nevertheless, it remains the case that conditional release combined with subsequent assistance for and control of the offender by the Probation Service has a noteworthy net effect. The secondary Anglo-American meta–analyses confirm this trend (Goldblatt and Lewis 1998; Mackenzie in Sherman *et al.* 1998; Harper and Chitty 2004).

Finally it is worth noting that criminological research has made us aware that early release may in practice be refused on grounds which are not necessarily justified by 'objective' risk assessments. Thus, for example, foreign prisoners may be refused early release not because of the risk they pose but because their early release is considered impracticable. Within the EU this may eventually be resolved to some extent by the new Framework Decision on mutual recognition in relation to 'judgments and probation decisions with a view to the supervision of probation measures and alternative sanctions',[17] which should allow conditional release begun in one country to be continued in another. However, this Decision will address only a small part of the problems faced by foreigners in European prison systems. As the chapter of Belgium makes clear, foreign prisoners also often face additional procedural hurdles and

---

[17]Council Framework Decision 2008/947/JHA of 27 November 2008. The problems relating to the enforcement of this Framework Decision are discussed in Chapter 2.

exclusion from certain reintegration activities, as well as language or cultural problems when preparing for release. The same issues arise in several other European countries too (see, in general, van Kalmthout *et al.* 2008). Also, ethnic minorities, even when they are not foreign citizens, may face similar issues. The detailed European provisions on non-discrimination, which are specifically applied to all aspects of imprisonment by the European Prison Rules,[18] should be followed strictly in respect of early release and the process leading up to it, to ensure that shortcomings are avoided.

4. Possible solutions: extend the use of early release to reduce overcrowding, increase security and increase the reintegration of offenders

The common problem of prison overcrowding that is found in many countries compels the consideration of penal policy initiatives to limit or reduce rates of imprisonment. Such initiatives can adopt either 'front door' or 'back door' strategies, in that either the number of sentenced prisoners is reduced (by increasing the use of alternatives such as fines, community service or probation or, in terms of continental European systems, suspended sentences) or the number of early releases is increased (see Dünkel 2010: s. 38 side note 66 for further references). In respect of early release one could recommend, in the light of both international practice and empirical criminological research that, on the one hand, release after half the sentence should be extended and that, on the other hand, 'neutral' prognoses should be reduced by making release the rule and not releasing the prisoner an exception requiring justification (Frisch 1983; 1990; Schüler-Springorum 1991: 269 ff.; Streng 1995: 118). Nevertheless, in cases of very serious offences against life or limb or sexual autonomy one would, even where the recidivism rate was *a priori* relatively low, require an individual prognosis – notwithstanding its relative unreliability. This reflects the fundamental German legal position, which requires special expert opinions only in cases of serious violent or sexual offences.

[18]See Rule 13 of the European Prison Rules which follows the wording of Art. 14 of the European Convention on Human Rights in outlawing discrimination on grounds 'such as sex, race, colour, language, religion, political or other opinion, national or social origin, association with a national minority, property, birth or other status'.

A practice which allows more or less automatic release after half or two thirds of the sentence seems to be more appropriate and has been followed in several countries. As we have argued, it is precisely where there are very low basic recidivism rates, as is paradoxically the case with offenders who commit violent or sex crimes, that the proportion of errors is greater with individual prognoses than if one simply were to release all offenders early. This dilemma cannot be resolved scientifically; one can only do so normatively. For the rest, step-by-step strategies should be tried, as they systematically introduce relaxations of the prison regime (such as open prisons and temporary release) which make correct prognoses more likely and create a social space into which the offender is more likely to be received and integrated successfully (Nedopil 2007: 293 ff.).

Restrictions on purely general preventive grounds, such as those provided for by the Austrian Criminal Code (although since 2008 this has applied only to the decision to release after an offender has served half but not two thirds of his prison term; see s. 46 of the Austrian Criminal Code), are not justified by international comparisons. As far as we know, nowhere else are such criteria laid down. Criteria for conditional release (in so far as the system does not operate automatically in favour of the prisoner) should be determined solely on grounds of special prevention.

In summary, it can be concluded that in the light of the current state of empirical research on the effectiveness of sentences and of the prognoses of future behaviour it would be appropriate to extend the use that is made in Europe of conditional release in those countries which rely on individual prognoses instead of automatic, or almost automatic, early release. Such release has the additional advantage that the supportive measures taken by the Probation Service and the positive obligation placed on the offender can create a special preventive framework that is conducive to reintegration. In this way the pressure of overcrowding that is found in so many countries can be seen as an opportunity for a rational and humane penal policy.

Will this happen? National chapters shed light on the often-conflicting pressures for and against the increased use of early release in individual countries. However there is a specifically European dimension that might move aspects of release policy beyond exclusively national debates. We started the book with a chapter on 'Europe' and looked at the subject from the different perspectives of 'Brussels' and of 'Strasbourg'. We do not go so far as to suggest that at this time in history a standardized European rule is possible or even to be encouraged. But we would encourage further thought into whether a European 'model', perhaps with release at half time for those sentenced to determinate lengths of time in prison, subject to supervision, would be helpful. This is certainly not the direction in which current policy appears to be travelling: this book has highlighted many interesting contrasts. Thus, while the Netherlands is currently moving away from almost automatic early release after two thirds to something rather more discretionary, England and Wales seem to be going in another direction with many fewer cases being considered by the Parole Board.

The different roles of the Council of Europe and the European Union were noted in Chapter 2. It might be fair to summarize that the approach of the Council of Europe has been much more rehabilitative, with a Council of Ministers advised by penological experts, whereas the more recent interest of the EU in criminal justice matters has been led by a politicized fear of crime, and a more populist and punitive agenda. At the level of the EU the latest Council Framework Decision of 27 November 2008 'on the application of the principle of mutual recognition to judgments in criminal matters imposing custodial sentences or measures involving deprivation of liberty for the purpose of their enforcement in the European Union' has the potential to make significant changes in this area. Prisoners may be sent home to serve their sentence, whether or not they agree. This raises the vital, but as yet not fully resolved, question as to whether release mechanisms will be simply those of the receiving country (the executing state). By Art. 29 of the Framework Decision, Member States are obliged to implement this Framework Decision by 5 December 2011. Member States, when enacting implementing legislation, may 'provide that any decision on early or conditional release may take account of those provisions of national law, indicated by the [sending] State, under which the person is entitled to early or conditional release at a specified point in time'; and that, if the sending state wants to make sure that the prisoner does not get out of prison more quickly as a result of the transfer, it can ask the executing state to warn it of an impending early release, so that it can then cancel the transfer and bring the prisoner back again. This seems a deeply unfair system: we would urge that states adopt a scheme which does not penalize transferred prisoners. A prisoner should not lose a more favourable regime simply by being transferred. As van Zyl Smit and Spencer point out in Chapter 2, this Framework Decision is distinctly authoritarian. Significantly, it does not deal with the other side of problem: the prisoner who, as a result of the transfer, will end up spending significantly longer in prison than he would have served if the transfer had not taken place – a situation which could arise, and cause significant unfairness. In the light of the wider political uncertainties surrounding the governance of the EU – it is particularly difficult to assess the potential impact of this Framework Decision until we know more about the developments in the constitutional structures of the Union.

Can we expect a flood of cases before the Court of Justice of the European Union to match the rising tide of cases relating to release, that we have already seen in the European Court of Human Rights? We simply do not know. Equally unclear is whether the ECtHR will develop further the rather hesitant supervision it has exercised over early release in national states. Promising in this regard is the dictum of several judges who argued strongly in the Grand Chamber of the Court that all prisoners including those sentenced to life imprisonment should have at least the prospect of release:

> Once it is accepted that the 'legitimate requirements of the sentence' entail reintegration, questions may be asked as to whether a term of imprisonment that jeopardises that aim [by not providing for the possibility of release] is not in itself capable of constituting inhuman and degrading treatment.[19]

This emphasis on reintegration as an element of European human rights law may stimulate further forms of release that are designed better to achieve this goal.

What is clear is that the European dimension of the decision to release is likely to become increasingly important, not only for the individual prisoners who may be sent 'home' to serve their sentences but also because European states inevitably will be examining the early release policies of their neighbours more closely. In their 2003 Recommendation concerning conditional release, the Committee of Ministers of the Council of Europe provided in some detail not only for better statistics on conditional release but also for wider research designed to 'obtain more knowledge about the appropriateness of existing conditional release systems and their further development' (s. 40). If this book has clarified more fully what is being done in respect of early release in Europe that would go some way towards

---

[19]Joint partly dissenting opinion of Judges Tulkens, Cabral Barreto, Fura-Sandström and Spielmann: *Kafkaris* v. *Cyprus* (12 February 2008 s. 5). The majority of the Court too accepted that there should be the *de jure* and *de facto* possibility of release for all prisoners sentenced to life imprisonment.

meeting the objectives of the Committee of Ministers. If the more critical analyses in several of the chapters of current national practices inform more enlightened policy-making on early release across Europe, we would have achieved our wider objective.

References

Aebi, M., Aubusoson de Cavarlay, B. and Stadnic, N. (2007) 'Prison entries and length of detention. The diversity of the correctional systems. Situation in Europe', *Penal Issues*: 7–10.

Boone, M. (2000) *Recht voor commuun gestraften*. Deventer: Gouda Quint.

Cavadino, M. and Dignan, J. (2008) *Penal Systems: A Comparative Approach*. London: Sage.

Dahle, K.-P. (2006) 'Grundlagen und Methoden der Kriminalprognose', in H.-L. Kröber, D. Dölling, N. Leygraf and H. Saß (eds) *Handbuch der Forensischen Psychiatrie. Vol. 3*. Darmstadt: Steinkopff.

Delmas-Marty, M. (2002) *Towards a Truly Common Law: Europe as a Laboratory for Legal Pluralism*. Cambridge: Cambridge University Press.

Delmas-Marty, M. (2003) *L'Harmonisation des sanctions penales en europe*. Paris: Société de législation comparée.

Dünkel, F. (2010) 'Kommentierung § 57 StGB', in U. Kindhäuser, U. Neumann and H. Paeffgen (eds) *Nomos Kommentar zum Strafgesetzbuch. Vol. 1* (3rd edn). Baden-Baden: Nomos Verlag.

Dünkel, F. and Geng, B. (1993) 'Zur Rückfälligkeit von Karrieretätern nach unterschiedlichen Strafvollzugs- und Entlassungsformen', in G. Kaiser and H. Kury (eds) *Kriminologische Forschung in den 90er Jahren*. Freiburg: Max-Planck-Institut für ausländisches und internationales Strafrecht.

Dünkel, F. and Vagg, J. (eds) (1994) *Waiting for Trial. International Perspectives on the Use of Pre-trial Detention and the Rights and Living Conditions of Prisoners Waiting for Trial*. Freiburg: Max-Planck-Institut für ausländisches und internationales Strafrecht.

Endres, J. (2000) 'Die Kriminalprognose im Strafvollzug. Grundlagen, Methoden und Probleme der Vorhersage von Straftaten', *Zeitschrift für Strafvollzug und Straffälligenhilfe*, 49: 67–83.

Frisch, W. (1983) *Prognoseentscheidungen im Strafrecht*. Heidelberg: Kriminalistik Verlag.

Frisch, W. (1990) 'Dogmatische Grundfragen der bedingten Entlassung und der Lockerungen des Vollzugs von Strafen und Maßregeln', *Zeitschrift für die gesamte Strafrechtswissenschaft*, 102: 707–92.

Goldblatt, P. and Lewis, C. (eds) (1998) *Reducing Offending: An Assessment of Research Evidence on Ways of Dealing with Offending Behaviour*. London: Home Office.

Groß, G. and Nedopil, N. (2005) 'Basisraten für kriminelle Rückfälle – Ergebnisse einer Literaturübersicht', in N. Nedopil (ed.) *Prognosen in der Forensischen Psychiatrie – Ein Handbuch für die Praxis*. Lengerich: Pabst Science Publisher.

Hanson, R.K. (2001) 'Sex offender risk assessment', in C.R. Hollin (ed.) *Handbook of Offender Assessment and Treatment*. Chichester: Wiley.

Harper, G. and Chitty, C. (2004) *The Impact of Corrections on Re-offending: A Review of 'What Works'* (HORS 291). London: Home Office.

Her Majesty's Inspectorate of Probation (2006a) *An Independent Review of a Serious Further Offence Case: Damien Hanson and Elliot White*. London: Home Office.

Her Majesty's Inspectorate of Probation (2006b) *An Independent Review of a Serious Further Offence Case: Anthony Rice*. London: HMIP (available online at http://www.inspectorates.homeoffice.gov.uk).

Hood, R., Shute, S., Feilzer, M. and Wilcox, A. (2002) 'Sex offenders emerging from long-term imprisonment', *British Journal of Criminology*, 42: 371–94.

Jehle, J.-M., Heinz, W. and Sutterer, P. (2003) *Legalbewährung nach strafrechtlichen Sanktionen: Eine kommentierte Rückfallstatistik*. Berlin: Bundesministerium der Justiz.

Kensey, A. (2004) 'Conditional release and the prevention of re-offending', in Council of Europe (ed.) *Crime and Crime Policy in Europe*. Strasbourg: Council of Europe.

Kensey, A. (2007) *Prison et récidive*. Paris: Armand Collin.

Kensey, A. and Tournier P.V. (2000) *Placement à l'extérieur, semi-liberté, libération conditionnelle... Des aménagements d'exception*. Paris: Ministère de la Justice.

Kensey, A. and Tournier, P.V. (2005) *Prisonniers du passé? Cohorte des personnes condamnées, libérées en 1996–1997: examen de leur casier judiciaire 5 ans après la levée d'écrou (échantillon national aléatoire stratifié selon l'infraction)* (direction de l'administration pénitentiaire, Coll. Travaux & Documents, n. 68). Paris: Ministère de la Justice.

Kunz, K.-L. (2004) *Kriminologie* (4th edn). Berne, Stuttgart and Vienna: Haupt.

Lévy, R. (2008) 'Pardons and amnesties in France', in M. Tonry (ed.) *Crime, Punishment, and Politics in Comparative Perspective. Crime and Justice. Vol. 36*. Chicago and London: University of Chicago Press.

Meyer, F. (1965) 'Der gegenwärtige Stand der Prognoseforschung in Deutschland', *Monatsschrift für Kriminologie und Strafrechtsreform*, 48: 225–46.

Mucchielli, L. (2008) *La frenesie securitaire: retour a l'ordre et nouveaau controle social*. Paris: Editions La Decouverte.

Nedopil, N. (2007) *Forensische Psychiatrie* (3rd edn). Stuttgart and New York: Thieme.

Nelken, D. (2009) 'Comparative criminal justice: beyond ethnocentrism and relativism', *European Journal of Criminology*, 6: 291–312.

Padfield, N. (2002) *Beyond the Tariff: Human Rights and the Release of Life Sentence Prisoners*. Cullompton: Willan Publishing.

Padfield, N. and Liebling, A. with Arnold, H. (2000) *An Exploration of Decision-making at Discretionary Lifer Panels. Home Office Research Study 213*. London: Home Office.

Padfield, N. and Roberts, J. (forthcoming) 'Victim submissions at parole in England and Wales and Canada: probative or prejudicial?', in A.E. Bottoms and J. Roberts (eds) *Victims in Contemporary Society*. Cullompton: Willan Publishing.

Pilgram, A. (1975) 'Bedingte Entlassung und Rückfall', *Österreichische Juristenzeitung*: 387–91.

Proband, S.C. (2008) 'Prison populations stable', *Newsletter of the European Society of Criminology*, 7: 1, 11–14.

Reitz, K.R. (2004) 'Questioning the conventional wisdom of parole release authority', in M. Tonry (ed.) *The Future of Imprisonment*. New York: Oxford University Press.

Schüler-Springorum, H. (1991) *Kriminalpolitik für Menschen*. Frankfurt/M.: Suhrkamp.

Sherman, L.W., Gottfredson, D.C., MacKenzie, D.L., Eck, J., Reuter, P. and Bushway, S.D. (1998) *Preventing crime, What works, What Doesn't, What's Promising?* Washington, DC: US Department of Justice, Office of Justice Programs, National Institute of Justice.

Streng, F. (1995) 'Strafrechtliche Folgenorientierung und Kriminalprognose', in D. Dolling (ed.) *Die Täter-Individualprognose*. Heidelberg: Kriminalistik Verlag.

Streng, F. (2002) *Strafrechtliche Sanktionen. Die Strafzumessung und ihre Grundlagen* (2nd edn). Stuttgart: Kohlhammer.

Tournier, P. (2004) 'Recommendation (rec(2003)22) of 24 September 2003 – pleading the case for conditional release,' Paper presented at the *ad hoc* conference of Directors of Prison Administration and Probation Services, Rome, 25–27 November.

Tubex, H. and Tournier, P.V. (2003) *Study of Conditional Release (Parole) in the Member States, Analysis of Replies to the General Questionnaire* (Council for Penological Co-operation, PC-CP (2000) 24 Rev 4 [restricted]).

Tulkens, H.J.J. (1988) *Graden van Vrijheid Over hervormingsmogelijkheden van de vrijheidsstraf*. Arnhem: Gouda Quint.

van Kalmthout, A.M. and Durnescu, I. (2008) *Probation in Europe*. Nijmegen: Wolf Legal Publishers.

van Kalmthout, A.M., Hofstee-van der Meulen, F. and Dünkel, F. (eds) (2008) *Foreigners in European Prisons. Vols. 1 and 2*. Nijmwegen: Wolf Legal Publishers.

van Zyl Smit, D. (1994) 'Degrees of freedom', *Criminal Justice Ethics*, 13: 31–8.

van Zyl Smit, D. (2008) 'Lange vrijheidsbeneming in binnen- en buiteland', *Sancties*, 6: 317–27.

van Zyl Smit, D. and Dünkel, F. (eds) (1999) *Prison Labour: Salvation or Slavery?* Aldershot: Dartmouth.

van Zyl Smit, D. and Dünkel, F. (eds) (2001) *Imprisonment Today and Tomorrow – International Perspectives on Prisoners' Rights and Prison Conditions* (2nd edn). Deventer and Boston: Kluwer.

Walker, N. (1996) 'Ethical and other problems', in N. Walker (ed.) *Dangerous People*. London: Blackstone Press.

Index